The sort of sight that prompted a young man to decide that a career with steam engines was the only job worth pursuing. Castle 4-6-0 7007 'Great Western' stands in ex-works condition at Leamington with an up express in July 1948.

At one level this is a narrative about moving through the various steam links at Tyseley and how the author rose through the ranks in the footplate grades on the Great Western's northern main line. At another – since there is more to a railway than the sides of an engine's cab – it is a detailed description of the Birmingham district with considerable emphasis being placed on the trains, passenger and goods, as well the travails of the footplate. Motive Power and Traffic were inseparable in real life and there seems nothing to be gained by breaking the tradition here.

At first glance the Great Western and Birmingham seemed an ill assorted pair. The Great Western – and no one should be under any misapprehension that the title disappeared at the end of 1947 – was popularly associated with Western holiday resorts and the Shire Counties; locations reflected in the appearance of its trains and engines. Such romantic perceptions – none of which were challenged by the company – tended to overlook the industries of Bristol and the South Wales coalfield although, it has to be admitted, the Great Western seemed to move its goods traffic with far less fuss than some other railways.

Whilst the Great Western may have seemed out of place in Birmingham, the system owed much of its shape to the area which had a far greater historical significance for the railway than is generally realised.

With its ambitions turning towards the black country and, in particular, Merseyside, the early Great Western embarked upon an expensive war with the London & North Western, the result being through running to Birkenhead at a price which left the company weak and in disorder. More significant was the fact that having absorbed a number of minor companies which made up the route north of Oxford, the Great Western was no longer wholly broad gauge and the consequent mix of gauges advanced considerably the question of standardisation.

The Broad gauge clung on for a further forty years but at the end of the day the standard gauge won and it is arguable that had it not been for the Birmingham, Wolverhampton, et al, the resolution of the gauge question might have taken a very different direction.

Once established the Great Western gave the conurbation quite a different railway from the pair it was used to. The Midland and LNWR infected themselves with the worst atmospheric features of the area whilst the Great Western lent a breath of Shire County ambience, ensuring that Snow Hill could never be mistaken for anything but a relation of Paddington. The Great Western also put Birmingham and Wolverhampton on a trunk line which is more than the LNWR managed to do, its services, impressive though they were in many respects, vying for place with the west coast trains with which they mingled south of Rugby.

Euston services tended to be on the light side, powered by nothing bigger than a 5XP 4-6-0 whilst the Paddington expresses loaded to fourteen or more vehicles and were accorded the accolade of an 8P King 4-6-0; the largest on the system. The weight of Great Western trains was not the only reason for large engines since, in contrast to the level route of the LNWR, the line via Banbury and Bicester was hilly and required both good engines and energetic crews.

The LNWR was not Paddington's only competitor since the Great Western had to compete with the Midland for the through traffic to the west of England and to do so, constructed a new route to Chel-

Acknowledgement and thanks for assistance with text and illustrations is due to:
C. Bentley, P.Webb, N. Lester, M. Bentley, J.T.S. Cat, R. White, W. S. Becket, D. Potts, B. Dangerfield, R. Carpenter, M. Mensing, B. Gould, P. Kingston, B. Ashworth, Patrick Kingston, G. Coltas and T. Bradshaw
Copyright : L.C. Jacks. 1999

tenham via Stratford on Avon. Whilst not as mountainous as the Midland line, the North Warwickshire line was no sinecure and, although well used by goods traffic, it never really established itself as a popular alternative to the Midland and for most of its existence its prestige passenger traffic was limited – except on summer Saturdays - to a single through service between Wolverhampton and Penzance.

Supporting the main line workings was an adequate service of local trains based on Birmingham, Wolverhampton, Stratford and Leamington; the only large-scale suburban service the Great Western operated outside London.

Although Birmingham Snow Hill was the focal point of the northern mainline's commercial activities, it suffered from a number of operational weaknesses. Unlike New Street which had a wealth of facilities, Snow Hill had no south facing bay platforms to accommodate arrivals from the London direction and consequently terminating trains from the south had to occupy and clear one of the two through platforms without delaying following services. Some amelioration was given by Moor Street suburban station but this was not commercially ideal since many passengers used the local trains to connect into main line services and were not impressed at having to walk the distance between the two stations.

The lack of platforms similarly inhibited the number of London trains that could be worked from Snow Hill. Empty stock was based at Tyseley, south of Birmingham, and had to run through Snow Hill to run-round and reverse at Handsworth in order to be able to reach an up platform. The number of movements involved was a liability in a busy area and for operational convenience most London services started back at Wolverhampton.

Wolverhampton had its saturation point and during the height of the summer season many of the additional trains had to start from Birmingham. A number ran the gauntlet of local movements by reversing in Handsworth but a considerable proportion had to be based on Moor Street. A detailed explanation of how the Birmingham district dealt with this large volume of traffic is given in the book by the author.

Adding to the difficulties of Snow Hill was the 1 in 45 gradient on the approach from the south which, being hidden in a tunnel, caught more than one driver unawares and saw one of the Snow Hill pilots having to drag trains into the station and onto level track. To exacerbate many northbound goods trains were obliged by the trackwork to start the gradient at no more than a walking pace and the author gives several graphic descriptions of how – and how not – to work trains through Snow Hill tunnel.

Whilst Tyseley shed had no shortage of long distance goods work, envious eyes were cast at the two-hour London trains which were the province of Stafford Road and Old Oak sheds. Eventually, as recounted in the following pages, Tyseley was able to persuade the authorities to give them to take a share of the expresses where it was quickly discovered that the technique needed to work a Hall 4-6-0 on a fast freight to Banbury was very different to that needed by a King on the heavy 18.10 Birkenhead express.

One of the most attractive aspects of Tyseley shed – from the perspective of a railwayman who was also an enthusiast – lay in the variety of motive power that could be experienced and how quickly one had to adapt from one class to another. The standard engine for

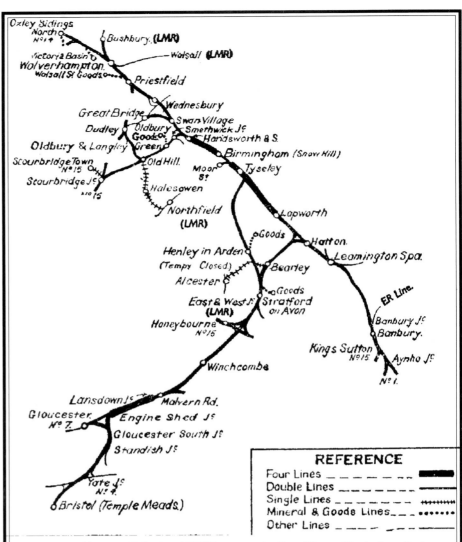

Unlike the neighbouring Midland and LNWR systems, the Great Western Birmingham district was a relatively neat package of lines consisting of the main Paddington - Birkenhead route, the Birmingham - Cheltenham cross-country line and the secondary line to Worcester via Stourbridge Junction. The busiest section of line was the stretch between Birmingham and Banbury where the volume of traffic was so heavy that many through goods services had to be routed via Stratford, Honeybourne and Oxford. The map above shows the system as depicted by the Great Western in its operating publications but does not cover anything like the extent of mileage worked by Tyseley crews whose duties extended from Paddington to Chester and Birmingham to Bristol and Aberystwyth. One Hall 4-6-0 duty involved a run from Snow Hill to Moor Street via Stratford, Cheltenham, Gloucester, Stroud, Swindon, Didcot, Oxford, Honeybourne and Stratford; a working that could be performed with out leaving the engine at any intermediate point.

most Birmingham main line workings was the Hall 4-6-0 but many of the duties involved engines from foreign sheds, ranging from County 4-6-0's to Austerity 2-8-0's and from Kings to Panniers. The author describes the working of each and how he did his best to get the best from each; especially on engines such as the Counties which were not generally held in the highest esteem.

Regarding the book itself, it has been produced as an offering for those who want a detailed insight into how part of the railway operated and not as a work of art. Many of the photographs were taken by the author and his colleagues whilst on duty and no pretensions have been made as to artistry. To ignore them and select illustrations on the basis of graphic quality alone would deprive readers of the subject matter and we believe that would be the worst of two evils.

There are a number of novel features in the book. One is a series of hourly line diagrams showing where trains were and the type of en-

gines booked to them on a normal 1954 day (not that matters changed greatly during the decade). The intention has been to give a clear picture of the traffic volume and to help the reader's imagination take him back to days spent on the lineside; being able to see the trains that were approaching and those that had passed. One can also become an armchair controller since diagrams of a similar type were used by the district controllers to give regulating instructions to signalboxes and stations. (To have shown every single piece of track would have rendered the diagrams unintelligible, and the lines shown have been limited to the principal running lines).

Another novelty is a series of tables which show not just the locomotive allocations for the principal sheds, but every engine that moved in or out of the district during the decade. The intention has been to recreate some of the atmosphere of the Northern main line during the 1950s and we trust the reader will find the result useful.

2

SMALL HEATH

Birmingham-style suburban. Although the 51xx 2-6-2T's were widely used by the Great Western, the heaviest concentrations were to be found in the Birmingham division where nearly seventy of the class were distributed between Tyseley, Stourbridge, Leamington and Wolverhampton sheds. In 1952 an abortive attempt was made to replacesome of the Tyseley allocation with BR 3MT 2-6-2T's but by the end of the following year the 51xx's were back in control with the newcomers being sent away to South Wales. 5139 pulls away from Knowle & Dorridge with a Snow Hill stopping train.

Brought up in a house with a yard which backed onto Bordesley North signalbox, I was a Great Western aspirant from birth, spending for the most part an idyllic existence during the 1930's where the panoply of the Great Western was spread before me at no greater cost than having to walk out of the kitchen. The present was represented by the continuous stream of trains that passed only a few feet away whilst my future was embodied in the occasional sight of a relative who was a fireman with the company and who on one occasion appeared at the back of the house on the footplate of Saint 4-6-0 2988 'Rob Roy'.

Glued to the backyard, it took no ordinary train of events to dislodged me from my perch and it took Hitler, his henchmen and their war to prise me away when I was evacuated to Ullenhall, a village not far from Henley in Arden on the Bordesley – Stratford line.

For all their faults the Third Reich succeeded in promoting me from watcher to passenger and the early days of the war found me, with several hundred others, waiting on Bordesley platform for one of the many trains that had been arranged for evacuees. Just about every class of engine that could turn a wheel seemed to be in service and my greatest anxiety revolved around the type my train would have. The evils of war were brought home to me in no uncertain manner when my service turned up behind an everyday 51xx 2-6-2T – the standard Birmingham

suburban engine – whilst friends disappeared to their destinations behind six-coupled tender engines. All Adolf's fault, of course.

Rural life has its charms but the absence of marshalling yards and motive power depots from the pastoral element cut very little ice with me and civilisation as I understood the term centred on occasional visits to Danzey station where on one occasion I was lucky enough to be present when an S160 (USA) 2-8-0 in light grey livery ran through with a goods working.

Victory celebrations came in the form of a ride from Wood End – where I had been relocated in 1944 - to Small Heath, Bordesley, in a three-coach service hauled by Duke 4-4-0 3284 'Isle of Jersey'.

Isolated from detailed railway activity for the duration, once back home I made up for lost time by reinforcing my backyard vigils with excursions to points of interest in the locality, spending days at places such as Small Heath and Snow Hill where, amongst other sights, I was able to catch the Duke 4-4-0's and Aberdare 2-6-0's working out the last months of their lives. There were few signs of change – and few to come over the coming decade – but I recall seeing 2-6-2T 4100 newly overhauled with 'BRITISH RAILWAYS' freshly painted on its tanks. I also managed to catch sight of 5108 which, being allocated to Newton Abbot, was reckoned to be the rarest 51xx in the book. It had come down to Birmingham for a works visit

but my sighting did not insulate me from accusations of 'fudging' by my fellow locospotters: the most heinous crime known to man.

The stars of the line were of course the London expresses, many of which were in the hands of King class 4-6-0's although Castles and Stars took a respectable share of the workings: two of the regulars on the London trains being 4018 'Knight of the Grand Cross' and 4021 'British Monarch'; both being Wolverhampton (Stafford Road) engines. We were also greatly impressed by the sight of one of the new County 4-6-0's with their high boiler pressure and rather old-fashioned splasher arrangement. The topic of the day was the extent to which they might replace the Castles on express workings.

I made several formal attempts to get round Tyseley loco but none were successful and as an alternative we used to go down a passage-way off Roma Road where at least one could see what engines were waiting to go into the workshops. Although partly hidden by wagons, I could usually manage to get a 'cop' in spite of the fact that G.W.R. number plates were not always the easiest to read from a distance. As a rule, the exercise was worthwhile even if after a couple of minutes we were chased off by some of the residents.

My education broadened with the acquisition of a one and sixpeny 'ref', which listed the locomotives of the Great Western, and the discovery of the LMS; a colleague introducing

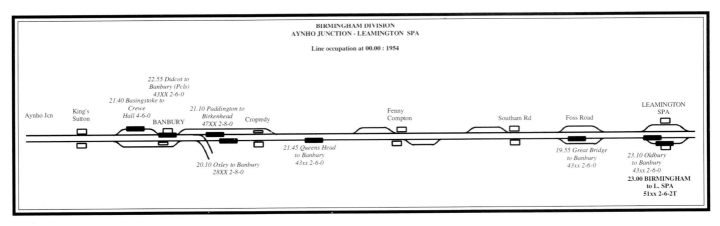

me to the delights of Landor Street where the Midland and LNW main lines could be seen from a common vantage point.

After a few days of watching activity in the Lardor Street triangle – and it was a rare moment when at least one engine was not in sight – we decided to explore further and, having an idea that Saltley MPD was somewhere in the area, set out to find it. It was not an easy task and even for someone used to the geometry of Birmingham it took some time before we found ourselves outside the foreman's office where we stood and rehearsed our plea for admittance to the shed.

Experience had shown that such interviews tended to be short and sharp -

"Can we look round the shed, Mister?"

"Clear off before I call the police…"

- and therefore skills in the art of diplomatic exchange had to be honed to a nicety. In the event we were saved by a passing railwayman who, guessing our purpose, indicated a point from which we could watch the shed's activities without the formality of the running foreman's permission.

It was a paradise with trains passing and engines coming on and off shed without interuption. Much of what we saw was made up of 3F and 4F 0-6-0's but the surprise of the day came when a 2-6-6-2 Garratt, my first sighting of one, came onto the shed for coal and water.

Idyllic as our Saltley grandstand was, it lacked shelter and, in an age where a soaking could lead to a painful reception back at home, rain was not a welcome development. Predictably an hour after our arrival the heavens opened but the activity unfolding before our eyes made retreat unthinkable. Looking around we noticed that the area in which we were standing was a parking lot for LMS Scammel three-wheel road vehicles and, finding them unlocked, we continued our vigil in the comfort of an enclosed cab. (They were probably left unlocked and unguarded since they were so conspicuous, no sane thief would think of stealing one).

Up to then I had always regarded Bordesley as being Great Western territory but a bit of exploration during my newspaper round revealed a Midland Railway intrusion into the area in the shape of the Camp Hill section of the Derby – Bristol main line. The Camp Hill shunting engine, 0-6-0T No. 1777, delighted me with its great antiquity as did its occasional substitute, 1879.

In the weeks following I recorded many interesting sights at Camp Hill. 0-6-0 tender engine 22630 (later renumbered 58110) would come by on a fairly regular basis and made a stark contrast with the 2-6-6-2 Garratts which also made frequent appearances. Another loco I remember seeing – probably en route to Derby for an overhaul - was Somerset & Dorset 2-8-0 13800. Other curiosities included 0-8-0's 9672 and 9674 which although shedded temporarily at Saltley were soon to join the rest of the class on the Lancashire & Yorkshire. (It was a time when some of the wartime exchanges had yet to be undone and I even saw a couple of Southern Railway locomotives go by. In later years as a fireman I would listen sympathetically to horror stories concerning borrowed LNER J25s 0-6-0's, some of which I saw waiting to enter Tyseley works). Not everything on the Midland was an antique and on one of my stints at Landor Street I caught a fleeting glimpse of Diesel-electric 10000 which was not normally a regular performer in the Birmingham area.

Most summer evenings would find me in the Camp Hill locality, fascinated at the banking operations which involved LMS 2-6-4 tanks and Midland 3F 0-6-0's. One developed a certain sympathy with the crews of the latter since the return leg involved running tender first, with no protection from rain, from Kings Heath. The train I would look out for with particular interest was the 20.00 Ashchurch – Birmingham New Street which ran via Redditch and the Camp Hill line and was booked for one of the new Ivatt 43xxx 2-6-0's.

Eventually I discovered the pleasures of New Street station and although I had not forsaken my first love, the Great Western, the fact that a visit to Snow Hill required the purchase of a platform ticket whereas New Street was free, was something to be considered. There was always plenty to see from my favourite spot at the north end of Platform 1, opposite Number 5 signal box and it was dur-

LOCO	CLASS	IN	OUT	LOCO	CLASS	IN	OUT
3837	8F : 28xx 2-8-0 (1938)			5346	4MT : 43xx 2-6-0 (1911)		
2848	8F : 28xx 2-8-0 (1903)			5369	4MT : 43xx 2-6-0 (1911)		
2849	8F : 28xx 2-8-0 (1903)			5370	4MT : 43xx 2-6-0 (1911)		
2867	8F : 28xx 2-8-0 (1903)			6336	4MT : 43xx 2-6-0 (1911)		
3016	7F : R.O.D. 2-8-0 (1917)			7317	4MT : 43xx 2-6-0 (1911)		
6971	5MT : MOD-HALL 4-6-0 (1944)			3101	4MT : 31xx 2-6-2T (1938)		
7912	5MT : MOD-HALL 4-6-0 (1944)			3151	4MT : 3150 2-6-2T (1906)		
7913	5MT : MOD-HALL 4-6-0 (1944)			3180	4MT : 3150 2-6-2T (1906)		
7918	5MT : MOD-HALL 4-6-0 (1944)			8410	4F : 94XX 0-6-0T (1949)		
7929	5MT : MOD-HALL 4-6-0 (1944)	New 12/50		8415	4F : 94XX 0-6-0T (1949)		
7800	5MT : MANOR 4-6-0 (1938) -		To Banbury 12/50	8452	4F : 94XX 0-6-0T (1949)		
4924	5MT : HALL 4-6-0 (1928)			9432	4F : 94XX 0-6-0T (1949)	New 12/50	
4959	5MT : HALL 4-6-0 (1928)			2203	3MT : 2251 0-6-0 (1930)		
4964	5MT : HALL 4-6-0 (1928)			2206	3MT : 2251 0-6-0 (1930)	Ex Machynlleth 12/50	
4980	5MT : HALL 4-6-0 (1928)		To Banbury 12/50	2238	3MT : 2251 0-6-0 (1930)		
5907	5MT : HALL 4-6-0 (1928)			2257	3MT : 2251 0-6-0 (1930)		
5909	5MT : HALL 4-6-0 (1928)			2292	3MT : 2251 0-6-0 (1930)	Ex Machynlleth 12/50	
5916	5MT : HALL 4-6-0 (1928)			2296	3MT : 2251 0-6-0 (1930)		
5927	5MT : HALL 4-6-0 (1928)			3624	3F : 57xx 0-6-0T (1933)		
5950	5MT : HALL 4-6-0 (1928)			3625	3F : 57xx 0-6-0T (1933)		
5993	5MT : HALL 4-6-0 (1928)			3650	3F : 57xx 0-6-0T (1933)		
5997	5MT : HALL 4-6-0 (1928)			3653	3F : 57xx 0-6-0T (1933)		
6904	5MT : HALL 4-6-0 (1928)			3657	3F : 57xx 0-6-0T (1933)		
6942	5MT : HALL 4-6-0 (1928)		To Stafford Rd 11/50	3658	3F : 57xx 0-6-0T (1933)		
6843	5MT : GRANGE 4-6-0 (1936)			3660	3F : 57xx 0-6-0T (1933)		
6847	5MT : GRANGE 4-6-0 (1936)			3664	3F : 57xx 0-6-0T (1933)		
6853	5MT : GRANGE 4-6-0 (1936)			3673	3F : 57xx 0-6-0T (1933)		
6858	5MT : GRANGE 4-6-0 (1936)			3689	3F : 57xx 0-6-0T (1933)		
6866	5MT : GRANGE 4-6-0 (1936)			3693	3F : 57xx 0-6-0T (1933)		
6611	5MT : 56xx 0-6-2T (1927)			3743	3F : 57xx 0-6-0T (1933)		
6630	5MT : 56xx 0-6-2T (1927)			3751	3F : 57xx 0-6-0T (1933)		
2932	4MT : SAINT 4-6-0 (1902)			3769	3F : 57xx 0-6-0T (1933)		
8108	4MT : 81xx 2-6-2T (1938)			4605	3F : 57xx 0-6-0T (1933)		
4101	4MT : 51xx 2-6-2T (1928)			4648	3F : 57xx 0-6-0T (1933)		
4106	4MT : 51xx 2-6-2T (1928)			4683	3F : 57xx 0-6-0T (1933)		
4107	4MT : 51xx 2-6-2T (1928)			8784	3F : 57xx 0-6-0T (1933)		To Neath 12/50
4110	4MT : 51xx 2-6-2T (1928)			9608	3F : 57xx 0-6-0T (1933)		
4111	4MT : 51xx 2-6-2T (1928)			9610	3F : 57xx 0-6-0T (1933)		
4116	4MT : 51xx 2-6-2T (1928)			9614	3F : 57xx 0-6-0T (1933)		
4147	4MT : 51xx 2-6-2T (1928)			9635	3F : 57xx 0-6-0T (1933)		
4157	4MT : 51xx 2-6-2T (1928)			9680	3F : 57xx 0-6-0T (1933)		
4159	4MT : 51xx 2-6-2T (1928)			9682	3F : 57xx 0-6-0T (1933)		
4165	4MT : 51xx 2-6-2T (1928)			9724	3F : 57xx 0-6-0T (1933)		
4166	4MT : 51xx 2-6-2T (1928)			9733	3F : 57xx 0-6-0T (1933)		
4170	4MT : 51xx 2-6-2T (1928)			9748	3F : 57xx 0-6-0T (1933)		
4172	4MT : 51xx 2-6-2T (1928)			9753	3F : 57xx 0-6-0T (1933)		
5102	4MT : 51xx 2-6-2T (1928)			9793	3F : 57xx 0-6-0T (1933)		
5106	4MT : 51xx 2-6-2T (1928)			9798	3F : 57xx 0-6-0T (1933)		
5152	4MT : 51xx 2-6-2T (1928)			5700	3F : 57xx 0-6-0T (1929)		
5156	4MT : 51xx 2-6-2T (1928)			5712	3F : 57xx 0-6-0T (1929)		
5164	4MT : 51xx 2-6-2T (1928)			5736	3F : 57xx 0-6-0T (1929)		
5166	4MT : 51xx 2-6-2T (1928)			5738	3F : 57xx 0-6-0T (1929)		
5171	4MT : 51xx 2-6-2T (1928)			5745	3F : 57xx 0-6-0T (1929)		
5175	4MT : 51xx 2-6-2T (1928)			5790	3F : 57xx 0-6-0T (1929)		
5177	4MT : 51xx 2-6-2T (1928)			7713	3F : 57xx 0-6-0T (1929)		
5182	4MT : 51xx 2-6-2T (1928)			7735	3F : 57xx 0-6-0T (1929)		
5187	4MT : 51xx 2-6-2T (1928)			7758	3F : 57xx 0-6-0T (1929)		
5188	4MT : 51xx 2-6-2T (1928)			8700	3F : 57xx 0-6-0T (1929)		
5190	4MT : 51xx 2-6-2T (1928)			9008	2P : 90xx 4-4-0 (1936)		
5198	4MT : 51xx 2-6-2T (1928)			9010	2P : 90xx 4-4-0 (1936)		
4337	4MT : 43xx 2-6-0 (1911)	Ex Stafford Rd 12/50		7438	2P : 74xx 0-6-0T (1936)		
5333	4MT : 43xx 2-6-0 (1911)						

No one could accuse the Midland side of Birmingham of elegance and whether trains were worked by a 3F 0-6-0 or a Garratt, there was the same industrial utilitarianism which the Great Western strove hard to avoid. Garratt 2-6-6-2 47978 pounds past Brickyard Crossing on the climb to Camp Hill with a train from Toton to Bristol in August 1953

ing these visits that I saw the last of the L.N.W.R. big guns: the final Caughton and Prince of Wales engines. I also caught one of the last Precursor 4-4-0s, 25297 'Sirocco'.

Another familiar sight at New Street was Webb Coal Tank 58928, which was shedded at Monument Lane and worked the south end pilot. This was unofficially named 'Chipper' after a dog featured in a cartoon strip in a local newspaper and had its name chalked on the leading splasher. The resting place of 'Chipper' was on the middle road between Platforms 3 and 4 but every now and again it would be called out for a shunting movement. Coughing and wheezing its way about the station it completed whatever task was required of it but there was no disguising the relief of its crew when it got back, in one piece, to its resting place.

Absorbing though my spotting career was, I was conscious of being on the extreme periphery of the science and only the jump from amateur to professional was going to make me privy

to the secrets of what made the railway tick. Coincidentally the time when I should have to earn a living was fast approaching and after a little family resistance – the Post Office was the recommended choice of career – it was accepted that I had a vocation and, after an interview at Snow Hill, was appointed as a Vanguard whose duties included assisting the driver of horse-drawn delivery vehicles. It was not, of course, the post I aspired to but being only 16 I was a year too young to be considered for footplate work. I was however a railwayman.

Conscious that even in 1948 horses were something of an anachronism – Snow Hill parcels department must have been the most conservative element of a thoroughly conservative railway – and that my interest lay with the iron variety, I nevertheless decided that my best chances of promotion lay in doing a good job and I determined that my driver, a charming lady Edith Weston (who looked after me like a mother), should have no cause for complaint.

In the league of Vanguards, I was going to be in the top link.

My job was to look after the goods in the cart and to sort and deliver them as we proceeded on our rounds, leaving Edith to concentrate on navigation and the horse.

I quickly learnt that the road to hell is indeed paved with good intentions. Guarding (with my life should it be necessary) a consignment of deliveries on my first day, I drew from the pile of packages in the van a box of sausages for our first port of call and placed it on the tailboard, ready for the most efficient of deliveries. Alas, I did not sign the road and was unprepared for the hill up Bath Row which required a smart gallop from our horse, Dolly.

To give Dolly credit, she produced a fair turn of speed and had the van bucking all over the road, a sensation I was quite happy with until a passing car drew my attention to the sausages which had been shaken off the tail-

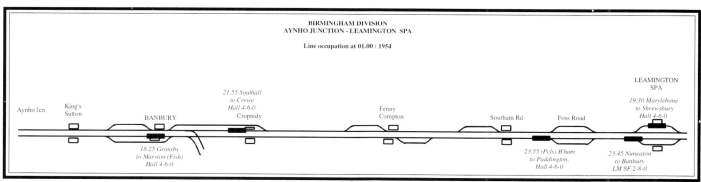

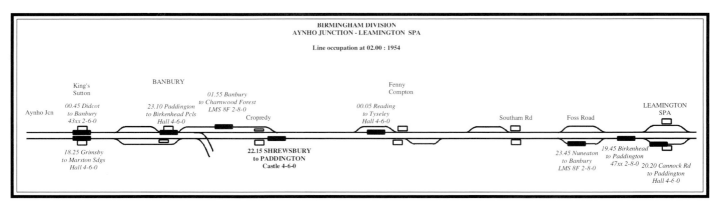

board and were lying in the middle of the road with a large and deep tyremark through them.

Edith stopped the cart telling me to go back and retrieve the box, which had become a gooey mess of meat, rubber and dirt, and no more was said until we reached the shop the sausages were intended for. I had no idea how Edith was going to get around the problem and was by no means happy when she told me to go and deliver them as though nothing had happened. Sheepishly I took them in and the manager could only stare at the package and then at me. No words were spoken, no tip was given, he just signed for it 'damaged'. It would have been more appropriate to have signed for them as 'destroyed'

When I came out Edith left me in no doubt that I had better learn from the experience.

In addition to taking care (or not) of consignments, the Vanguard was also responsible for walking the horse to and from its stable which was situated under the north end of Snow Hill station.

I dislike horses and I suspect Dolly knew and acted upon it. Whilst her stable mates would be casually led from their stalls and coupled without difficulty to their carts, dolly would wait for me to come alongside and then lean on me so that I was pinned powerless to the wall. When, after a considerable struggle, I wriggled out from under half a ton of horseflesh and reached for her collar, her neck would suddenly straighten way out of reach. Eventually I discovered that she had a weakness for cabbage and I was able through bribery to make the task a little easier.

Getting her collar on was only part of the job since I then had to run her 'light' to the van and couple her up. I would, with great difficulty and many cabbages, line her up with the cart only to find that when I went back to drop the shafts over her, she would move forward and I would have to start all over again. It almost became a routine variety act with the staff lining up to watch the performance whilst I cajoled, cursed and tried to manoeuvre the wretched beast into position.

For all her cussedness she has to take credit for teaching me something about grammatical construction following an incident when she managed to take a bite out of someone's motor car.

One day Edith decided to deliver a parcel and left me holding Dolly's reins to prevent her from charging off into the line of traffic which was inching past us. I supposed a more experienced hand would have held her with a firmer grip but I was taken off guard when she suddenly lowered her head and took a bite at the boot of an adjacent car. Suddenly I had Edith on one side of me and the car's owner on the other, all three of us looking daggers at each other

whilst Dolly, now good as gold, peered innocently into the curb. Eventually names and addresses were exchanged and, when we got back to Snow Hill, I had to make a report out which I submitted to the chief clerk.

"..regret that my horse," he read out in a voice that made everyone look in our direction, "made a scratch on an Austin car three inches long."

"That's it." I confirmed.

"I did not know until this minute," he announced to the assembled scribes, "that Austin made cars as small as that...."

After a months service I received my railway identity card which entitled me to quarter fare privilege tickets and enabled me to widen the scope of my locospotting outings. My first 'priv' was used from Tyseley to Wolverhampton on a Sunday on May 1948 when I went with a 'civilian' enthusiast to 'do' Stafford Road, Oxley and Bushbury sheds plus the works at Wolverhampton.

Feeling somewhat superior at having only paid a fraction of what my colleague had had to stump up, we travelled down to Wolverhampton and walked the short distance to Stafford Road shed. As we walked it was agreed that as the 'professional' I should take charge of the negotiations to gain us access.

By no means certain of my authority, I nevertheless went up to the timekeeper, flashed my identity card and asked if we could go round the shed. He turned round to the foreman, muttered something and, returning my card, nodded towards the shed. It had worked. What a whole new world my 'priv' had opened up! A magic pass into any loco shed, or so I thought.

Being Sunday afternoon the place was full of Kings, Castles, Stars, Counties plus the lesser types of the Great Western and we had a field day.

Leaving the shed we thanked the timekeeper and he nodded at me as though I was his equal with forty-odd years of service. We crossed the road outside and walked the short distance to the Works entrance. There were no gates or doors open and it seemed that there was no official way in. Eventually we gave up and, finding a gap in the fence, entered in the time-honoured manner.

So near yet so far. We were on the works premises but every door was locked and half an hours exploration failed to produce a means of access. Eventually a compromise was called for and, making a pile of spare bricks, we managed to make enough height to be able to peer through one of the work's windows. It was frustrating in the extreme since I could make out a Cambrian 0-6-0 and a Taff Vale 0-6-2T but could not see the numbers. Deciding that we would have to move our pile of bricks to an-

other window, we jumped down and landed face to face with a grim visaged watchman, pencil and notebook ready for our names. We recited our names and address and then I played my trump card.

"I'm a railwayman."

For a second I thought I had scored but he nodded at my colleague.

"What about him?"

My friend shook his head from side to side.

That scuppered any chances we might have had on being given a royal tour of the works but at least we were escorted back to the hole of the fence with the promise that no further action would be taken.

Undaunted we set off along the viaduct, canal and path that led to Oxley shed to be rewarded by yet another wonderful assortment of locos which we approached for closer inspection. Half way down the yard we were stopped by one of the shed men.

"Clear off…"

I took my magic 'priv' out of my pocket and waved it.

"I'm a railwayman. I've got an ID"

"I don't care if you've got a gold bloody pass, clear off."

Back on the main road we agreed that our luck was taking a turn for the worst and that trying our luck with Bushbury might be tempting providence a little too far. After all it was only an LMS shed and the prospect of spending a trolley bus fare with no guarantee of success did not appeal.

So after one victory, a draw and a defeat we returned home, determined to come back at a later date

My father, who had recently been demobbed from the army, had taken a job as a loader on the goods deck at Hockley and on one or two occasions I was sent there to get his wages which gave me an opportunity to stare at the open-cab 1701 0-6-0T pannier tanks shunting in the yard. Shortly afterwards he was transferred to Small Heath Empty Shed where his brother-in-law, a driver, worked.

I remember the first time I climbed aboard his 57xx 0-6-0PT. The smell of hot oil and the heat from the firebox was something to savour. Once having heard the ring of the shovel on the fire hole, the singing of the injectors and the strong beat of the engine when pulling a load, you never forget them.

Still too young to get into the footplate line of promotion, I applied for a transfer to the operating grades, hoping for a post as a train register lad, or booking lad as they were known. Eventually I was taken before the chief signalling inspector and given an examination which consisted of a short writing test and 'could I get up early?' At the end of the interview I was told to report to the station master at Small Heath station next Monday at nine o'clock.

I told Edith that I would soon be going into a signalbox to work and left the parcels department as I had entered it.

Dwelling on the intricate operating manoeuvres I would be masterminding a few days hence, I jumped aboard the cart, fished a huge tin of cream from the pile of parcels and absent-mindedly placed in on the tailboard, forgetting that we were fast approaching a mass of tram lines.

Doing a fair lick, Dolly hurled herself and the cart from one side of Loveday street to the other, the cart shuddering and banging as it crashed over the tram lines with the tin of cream arcing a beautiful parabola from the tailboard to the road where it split open and spread across the road. To make matters worse the cream was for industrial use, with the viscosity of oil, and by the time several cars had run through it, the road was like a skating rink with vehicles narrowly missing each other as they slid out of control. Eventually the fire brigade had to be called to hose the road down to get rid of the cream.

Edith remarked rather acidly that it was probably cheaper for the railway to have me locked up in a signalbox than to be let loose on the streets.

At nine o'clock on 9 November 1948 I presented myself to Mr. Beaufoys, the station master at Small Heath, who welcomed me by announcing that no one had told him about me or my appointment. All the same he took me out of his office to the running lines and over to Small Heath North signal box which I had spent a childhood looking at from my back yard.

Leaving me awe-struck by the row of seventy-eight levers and the mysterious looking block instruments, the station master conferred silently signalman. Eventually he nodded in my direction as he departed through the doorway.

"Let's have a look at you." The signalman said and grunted discouragingly. His trainee and the box lad also gave me a brief critical eye before returning to their respective tasks.

I quickly learnt that a signalbox is no place for idiots and that there is little scope for sloppy working in signalling where a simple misunderstanding can have serious consequences. Fortunately my lesson came early in my career and left its mark. Joe Cooper, who was learning the frame, was in the process of signalling an engine from the down main to the up sidings via the up main and anxious to be of use I stood poised to call out as soon as the engine was inside clear. Alas, I was too keen and shouted out "That's over" when the engine had crossed onto the up main with half the movement still to complete.

I realised my mistake as soon as the words were out but it was too late. Nothing was said but the looks directed towards me would have frozen the Medusa. Crestfallen I allowed myself to be shunted behind the booking desk out of harm's way and determined for the time being to speak only when spoken to.

Leaving the running of trains to the professionals, I took a good look at my new surroundings. The box was spotless, the windows were clean, the handles of the levers were all burnished, the frame was black-leaded, and the floor, which was covered by linoleum, was polished so much that it shone. I soon settled down, learning the booking of trains, where they started from and their destinations, and after a while I was able to recognise where some freight trains had started from at a glance. What with keeping the box clean, getting coal in, and running odd errands over to the office at Bordesley Junction, it was a full time job.

Small Heath North was a very busy box having no less than seven running lines: up and down main, up and down relief, up and down goods, and a through line in the up direction known as the New Departure line, with a pilot engine outside the box shunting almost continuously.

My first day on my own as booking lad – I had a couple of weeks training with my predecessor, Peter Bricknal - coincided with Mr. Cooper's first day in charge and a coating of fog which was, as they say on the railway, as thick as a bag. I arrived at 6.50 a.m and with more help from Mr. Cooper than I was strictly entitled to, managed to survive the shift.

Once the rudiments of the job became second nature I was able to combine it with my interest in locomotive matters and never missed an engine number. Naturally I became a valued source of information to my friends outside the industry and was able to pass on snippets of information that might otherwise have been lost to them. At the time Bagnalls of Stafford were building the 84xx 0-6-0PTs, and their movements were made known to all signal boxes which lay on their route to Swindon. They usually came up in pairs next to the train engine and in this way I saw a lot of this class before they entered revenue-earning service.

As the months went by Joe Cooper took me firmly under his wing. He sent my mother a note – which rather nonplussed her at first - saying that he didn't think it was hygienic to wrap my sandwiches up in newspaper and from that date my food started to be wrapped in paper bags. He took me home to meet his family, who lived near Dorridge, and I was invited up there regularly, always being treated to some fine country hospitality. Some years later I joined the clan by marrying his second daughter.

One of my duties was to watch all trains as they passed the box and naturally it was a task I revelled in. Some services were watched more closely than others and a particular favourite was the 11.45 Stourbridge Junction – Bordesley goods which was regularly booked to one of the last Aberdare 2-6-0's, 2655 of Stourbridge shed.

I also saw 2-6-2Ts Nos.4170-73 and No.4175, brand new, enter traffic on the local passenger services, all sporting black and lined livery and one of the first engines I saw outshopped from Stafford Road Works was No.4555 which has since been preserved. Occasionally rarities from distant parts turned up and I was surprised one morning to find 4-6-0 5926 'Grotrian Hall' standing outside the box. Usually representatives of the Hall class (the Great Western's Black 5) were as common as loose change but this particular one was from far-off Fishguard and not often seen east of Swansea. After some enquiries I discovered that it had been in Swindon work and been used on a filling-in turn to Birmingham before being returned to Wales. Another memorable sight was a train from Aberystwyth, running empty to Tyseley carriage sidings, headed by a 'Duke' and assisted by a 'Bulldog No.3377. One 4-4-

TYSELEY ALLOCATION : 1951

LOCO	CLASS	IN	OUT	LOCO	CLASS	IN	OUT
2848	8F : 28xx 2-8-0 (1938)			5370	4MT : 43xx 2-6-0 (1911)		
2849	8F : 28xx 2-8-0 (1938)			6336	4MT : 43xx 2-6-0 (1911)		
2867	8F : 28xx 2-8-0 (1938)			7317	4MT : 43xx 2-6-0 (1911)		
3837	8F : 28xx 2-8-0 (1938)			3101	4MT : 31xx 2-6-2T (1938)		
3016	7F : R.O.D. 2-8-0 (1917)			3151	4MT : 3150 2-6-2T (1906)		
6971	5MT : MOD-HALL 4-6-0 (1944)			3180	4MT : 3150 2-6-2T (1906)		
7912	5MT : MOD-HALL 4-6-0 (1944)			8410	4F : 94XX 0-6-0T (1949)		To Duffryn 8/51
7913	5MT : MOD-HALL 4-6-0 (1944)			8415	4F : 94XX 0-6-0T (1949)		
7918	5MT : MOD-HALL 4-6-0 (1944)			8452	4F : 94XX 0-6-0T (1949)		To Banbury 6/51
7922	5MT : MOD-HALL 4-6-0 (1944)	Ex Chester 3/51	To Chester 5/51	8463	4F : 94XX 0-6-0T (1949)	New 1/51	
7929	5MT : MOD-HALL 4-6-0 (1944)			8468	4F : 94XX 0-6-0T (1949)	New 3/51	
7800	5MT : MANOR 4-6-0 (1938)	Ex Banbury 7/51	To Banbury 10/51	9432	4F : 94XX 0-6-0T (1949)		
4924	5MT : HALL 4-6-0 (1928)			2203	3MT : 2251 0-6-0 (1930)		
4959	5MT : HALL 4-6-0 (1928)			2206	3MT : 2251 0-6-0 (1930)		To Shrewsbury 3/51
4964	5MT : HALL 4-6-0 (1928)			2238	3MT : 2251 0-6-0 (1930)		To Machynlleth 8/51
5907	5MT : HALL 4-6-0 (1928)			2238	3MT : 2251 0-6-0 (1930)	Ex Machynlleth 11/51	
5909	5MT : HALL 4-6-0 (1928)			2257	3MT : 2251 0-6-0 (1930)		
5916	5MT : HALL 4-6-0 (1928)			2292	3MT : 2251 0-6-0 (1930)		
5927	5MT : HALL 4-6-0 (1928)			2296	3MT : 2251 0-6-0 (1930)		
5950	5MT : HALL 4-6-0 (1928)			3624	3F : 57xx 0-6-0T (1933)		To Leamington 9/51
5972	5MT : HALL 4-6-0 (1928)	Ex Laira 10/51		3625	3F : 57xx 0-6-0T (1933)		
5993	5MT : HALL 4-6-0 (1928)		To Laira 1/51	3650	3F : 57xx 0-6-0T (1933)		
5993	5MT : HALL 4-6-0 (1928)	Ex Laira 10/51		3653	3F : 57xx 0-6-0T (1933)		
5997	5MT : HALL 4-6-0 (1928)			3657	3F : 57xx 0-6-0T (1933)		
6904	5MT : HALL 4-6-0 (1928)			3658	3F : 57xx 0-6-0T (1933)		To Stafford Rd 5/51
6843	5MT : GRANGE 4-6-0 (1936)			3660	3F : 57xx 0-6-0T (1933)		
6847	5MT : GRANGE 4-6-0 (1936)			3664	3F : 57xx 0-6-0T (1933)		To Stafford Rd 6/51
6853	5MT : GRANGE 4-6-0 (1936)			3673	3F : 57xx 0-6-0T (1933)		
6858	5MT : GRANGE 4-6-0 (1936)			3689	3F : 57xx 0-6-0T (1933)		
6866	5MT : GRANGE 4-6-0 (1936)			3693	3F : 57xx 0-6-0T (1933)		
6611	5MT : 56xx 0-6-2T (1927)		To Wrexham 6/51	3743	3F : 57xx 0-6-0T (1933)		To Stourbridge 6/51
6630	5MT : 56xx 0-6-2T (1927)			3751	3F : 57xx 0-6-0T (1933)		To Stourbridge 6/51
2932	4MT : SAINT 4-6-0 (1902)		w/d 6/51	3769	3F : 57xx 0-6-0T (1933)		
8108	4MT : 81xx 2-6-2T (1938)			4605	3F : 57xx 0-6-0T (1933)		To Stafford Rd 5/51
4101	4MT : 51xx 2-6-2T (1928)			4648	3F : 57xx 0-6-0T (1933)		
4106	4MT : 51xx 2-6-2T (1928)			4683	3F : 57xx 0-6-0T (1933)	To Croes Newydd 1/51	
4107	4MT : 51xx 2-6-2T (1928)			7713	3F : 57xx 0-6-0T (1933)		
4110	4MT : 51xx 2-6-2T (1928)			7735	3F : 57xx 0-6-0T (1933)		
4111	4MT : 51xx 2-6-2T (1928)			7758	3F : 57xx 0-6-0T (1933)		
4116	4MT : 51xx 2-6-2T (1928)			9608	3F : 57xx 0-6-0T (1933)		
4147	4MT : 51xx 2-6-2T (1928)			9610	3F : 57xx 0-6-0T (1933)		
4157	4MT : 51xx 2-6-2T (1928)			9614	3F : 57xx 0-6-0T (1933)		
4159	4MT : 51xx 2-6-2T (1928)			9635	3F : 57xx 0-6-0T (1933)		
4165	4MT : 51xx 2-6-2T (1928)			9680	3F : 57xx 0-6-0T (1933)		
4166	4MT : 51xx 2-6-2T (1928)			9682	3F : 57xx 0-6-0T (1933)		
4170	4MT : 51xx 2-6-2T (1928)			9724	3F : 57xx 0-6-0T (1933)		
4172	4MT : 51xx 2-6-2T (1928)		To Stourbridge 12/51	9733	3F : 57xx 0-6-0T (1933)		
5102	4MT : 51xx 2-6-2T (1928)			9748	3F : 57xx 0-6-0T (1933)		
5106	4MT : 51xx 2-6-2T (1928)			9753	3F : 57xx 0-6-0T (1933)		
5151	4MT : 51xx 2-6-2T (1928)	Ex Stafford Rd 4/51	To Stafford Rd 5/51	9793	3F : 57xx 0-6-0T (1933)		To Wrexham 6/51
5152	4MT : 51xx 2-6-2T (1928)			9798	3F : 57xx 0-6-0T (1933)		
5156	4MT : 51xx 2-6-2T (1928)			5700	3F : 57xx 0-6-0T (1929)		To Oswestry 9/51
5164	4MT : 51xx 2-6-2T (1928)			5712	3F : 57xx 0-6-0T (1929)		
5166	4MT : 51xx 2-6-2T (1928)			5736	3F : 57xx 0-6-0T (1929)		
5171	4MT : 51xx 2-6-2T (1928)			5738	3F : 57xx 0-6-0T (1929)		
5175	4MT : 51xx 2-6-2T (1928)			5745	3F : 57xx 0-6-0T (1929)		
5177	4MT : 51xx 2-6-2T (1928)			5790	3F : 57xx 0-6-0T (1929)		
5182	4MT : 51xx 2-6-2T (1928)			8700	3F : 57xx 0-6-0T (1929)		
5187	4MT : 51xx 2-6-2T (1928)			9008	2P : 90xx 4-4-0 (1936)		
5188	4MT : 51xx 2-6-2T (1928)			9010	2P : 90xx 4-4-0 (1936)		
5190	4MT : 51xx 2-6-2T (1928)			7438	2P : 74xx 0-6-0T (1936)		
5198	4MT : 51xx 2-6-2T (1928)			15101	0F : 350HP GW 0-6-0 (1948)	Ex Old Oak Common 6/51	
4337	4MT : 43xx 2-6-0 (1911)		w/d 11/51	15103	0F : 350HP GW 0-6-0 (1948)	Ex Old Oak Common 6/51	
5333	4MT : 43xx 2-6-0 (1911)			12070	0F : 350hp 0-6-0	New 4/51	
5346	4MT : 43xx 2-6-0 (1911)		w/d 5/51	12071	0F : 350hp 0-6-0	New 4/51	
5369	4MT : 43xx 2-6-0 (1911)		To Banbury 7/51	12072	0F : 350hp 0-6-0	New 4/51	
5369	4MT : 43xx 2-6-0 (1911)	Ex Banbury 11/51		12087	0F : 350hp 0-6-0	New 4/51	

Tyseley loco works in September 1948 with 2-6-2T 5162, 2-8-0 3033, 4-4-0 9025 and several others undergoing repairs.

0 was an uncommon sight on the Great Western: two together was almost unheard of.

One of the major perks of being a box lad was that you spoke to a wide variety of people and as a result came to be known. Some of these contacts were yard staff and drivers and this quite naturally led to free footplate trips – especially when my Uncle was on duty - on the engine which shunted the Caledonia yard opposite the box. Although youthful interest lay at the root of these journeys, the time spent was by no means wasted since the experience gave me an opportunity to gain a number of footplate tips which would later prove useful. I also spent some time in brake vans and picked up a certain amount of understanding of what went on at the rear of a goods train.

As a box lad I was not permitted to operate any of the signalling equipment but, like every other box lad in the country worth his salt, I did, partly as a means to gaining experience in signalling – if you could work Small Heath North you could work any box on the system – and partly to allow the signalman to have his supper in peace. (The reverse side of the coin was

LOCO	CLASS	IN	OUT	LOCO	CLASS	IN	OUT
3829	8F : 28xx 2-8-0 (1938)	Ex Chester 7/52		7317	4MT : 43xx 2-6-0 (1911)		
3837	8F : 28xx 2-8-0 (1938)			3101	4MT : 31xx 2-6-2T (1938)		To Gloucester 10/52
3839	8F : 28xx 2-8-0 (1938)	Ex Banbury 10/52		3101	4MT : 31xx 2-6-2T (1938)	Ex Gloucester 11/52	
2826	8F : 28xx 2-8-0 (1903)	Ex Canton 7/52		3151	4MT : 3150 2-6-2T (1906)		w/d 3/52
2848	8F : 28xx 2-8-0 (1903)			3180	4MT : 3150 2-6-2T (1906)		
2849	8F : 28xx 2-8-0 (1903)			8415	4F : 94XX 0-6-0T (1949)		
2856	8F : 28xx 2-8-0 (1903)	Ex Stourbridge 10/52		8463	4F : 94XX 0-6-0T (1949)		
2867	8F : 28xx 2-8-0 (1903)			8468	4F : 94XX 0-6-0T (1949)		
3016	7F : R.O.D. 2-8-0 (1917)		To Oxley 12/52	9432	4F : 94XX 0-6-0T (1949)		
6971	5MT : MOD-HALL 4-6-0 (1944)			82000	3MT 2-6-2 (1952)	Ex Swindon 9/52	
7912	5MT : MOD-HALL 4-6-0 (1944)			82001	3MT 2-6-2 (1952)	New 5/52	
7913	5MT : MOD-HALL 4-6-0 (1944)			82002	3MT 2-6-2 (1952)	New 5/52	
7918	5MT : MOD-HALL 4-6-0 (1944)			82003	3MT 2-6-2 (1952)	New 5/52	
7929	5MT : MOD-HALL 4-6-0 (1944)			82004	3MT 2-6-2 (1952)	New 5/52	
7800	5MT : MANOR 4-6-0 (1938)	Ex Banbury 6/52	To Chester 10/52	82005	3MT 2-6-2 (1952)	New 5/52	
4924	5MT : HALL 4-6-0 (1928)		To Oxley 11/52	82006	3MT 2-6-2 (1952)	New 6/52	
4959	5MT : HALL 4-6-0 (1928)		To Oxley 10/52	82007	3MT 2-6-2 (1952)	New 6/52	
4964	5MT : HALL 4-6-0 (1928)			82008	3MT 2-6-2 (1952)	New 6/52	
5907	5MT : HALL 4-6-0 (1928)			82009	3MT 2-6-2 (1952)	New 6/52	
5909	5MT : HALL 4-6-0 (1928)			2203	3MT 2251 0-6-0 (1930)		To Shrewsbury 1/52
5912	5MT : HALL 4-6-0 (1928)	Ex Wrexham 6/52		2203	3MT 2251 0-6-0 (1930)	Ex Shrewsbury 2/52	
5916	5MT : HALL 4-6-0 (1928)		To Canton 7/51	2238	3MT 2251 0-6-0 (1930)		
5927	5MT : HALL 4-6-0 (1928)			2257	3MT 2251 0-6-0 (1930)		To Wrexham 7/52
5950	5MT : HALL 4-6-0 (1928)		To Banbury 9/52	2257	3MT 2251 0-6-0 (1930)	Ex Wrexham 10/52	
5972	5MT : HALL 4-6-0 (1928)		To Oxley 10/52	2292	3MT 2251 0-6-0 (1930)		To Machynlleth 5/52
5993	5MT : HALL 4-6-0 (1928)		To Oxley 4/52	2292	3MT 2251 0-6-0 (1930)	Ex Machynlleth 9/52	To Oxford 11/52
5997	5MT : HALL 4-6-0 (1928)		To Oxley 4/52	2296	3MT 2251 0-6-0 (1930)		
6904	5MT : HALL 4-6-0 (1928)			3625	3F 57xx 0-6-0T (1933)		
6843	5MT : GRANGE 4-6-0 (1936)			3650	3F 57xx 0-6-0T (1933)		
6847	5MT : GRANGE 4-6-0 (1936)		To Ebbw Jcn 10/52	3653	3F 57xx 0-6-0T (1933)		
6853	5MT : GRANGE 4-6-0 (1936)			3657	3F 57xx 0-6-0T (1933)		
6858	5MT : GRANGE 4-6-0 (1936)			3660	3F 57xx 0-6-0T (1933)		
6866	5MT : GRANGE 4-6-0 (1936)			3673	3F 57xx 0-6-0T (1933)		
6630	5MT : 56xx 0-6-2T (1927)		To Stourbridge 10/52	3689	3F 57xx 0-6-0T (1933)		
8108	4MT : 81xx 2-6-2T (1938)			3693	3F 57xx 0-6-0T (1933)		
4101	4MT : 51xx 2-6-2T (1928)		To Duffryn 10/52	3769	3F 57xx 0-6-0T (1933)		
4106	4MT : 51xx 2-6-2T (1928)		To Landore 10/52	4648	3F 57xx 0-6-0T (1933)		
4107	4MT : 51xx 2-6-2T (1928)		To Landore 10/52	9608	3F 57xx 0-6-0T (1933)		
4110	4MT : 51xx 2-6-2T (1928)			9610	3F 57xx 0-6-0T (1933)		
4111	4MT : 51xx 2-6-2T (1928)			9614	3F 57xx 0-6-0T (1933)		
4116	4MT : 51xx 2-6-2T (1928)			9635	3F 57xx 0-6-0T (1933)		
4147	4MT : 51xx 2-6-2T (1928)		To Wolverhampton 10/52	9680	3F 57xx 0-6-0T (1933)		
4157	4MT : 51xx 2-6-2T (1928)		To Bristol 10/52	9682	3F 57xx 0-6-0T (1933)		
4159	4MT : 51xx 2-6-2T (1928)		To Bristol 10/52	9724	3F 57xx 0-6-0T (1933)		
4165	4MT : 51xx 2-6-2T (1928)		To Chester 10/52	9733	3F 57xx 0-6-0T (1933)		
4166	4MT : 51xx 2-6-2T (1928)		To Newton Abbot 7/52	9748	3F 57xx 0-6-0T (1933)		
4170	4MT : 51xx 2-6-2T (1928)			9753	3F 57xx 0-6-0T (1933)		
4172	4MT : 51xx 2-6-2T (1928)	Ex Stourbridge 2/52		9798	3F 57xx 0-6-0T (1933)		To Wolverhampton 7/52
5102	4MT : 51xx 2-6-2T (1928)		To Neath 10/52	9798	3F 57xx 0-6-0T (1933)	Ex Wolverhampton 11/52	
5106	4MT : 51xx 2-6-2T (1928)	To Wolverhampton 11/52		5712	3F 57xx 0-6-0T (1929)		
5152	4MT : 51xx 2-6-2T (1928)			5736	3F 57xx 0-6-0T (1929)		
5156	4MT : 51xx 2-6-2T (1928)			5738	3F 57xx 0-6-0T (1929)		To Wolverhampton 7/52
5164	4MT : 51xx 2-6-2T (1928)			5745	3F 57xx 0-6-0T (1929)		
5166	4MT : 51xx 2-6-2T (1928)			5790	3F 57xx 0-6-0T (1929)		
5171	4MT : 51xx 2-6-2T (1928)		To Carmarthen 10.52	7713	3F 57xx 0-6-0T (1929)		
5175	4MT : 51xx 2-6-2T (1928)		To Lara 10/52	7735	3F 57xx 0-6-0T (1929)		To Wolverhampton 7/52
5177	4MT : 51xx 2-6-2T (1928)	To Chester 11/52		7735	3F 57xx 0-6-0T (1929)	Ex Wolverhampton 11/52	
5182	4MT : 51xx 2-6-2T (1928)		To Bristol (SPM) 10/52	7758	3F 57xx 0-6-0T (1929)		
5187	4MT : 51xx 2-6-2T (1928)		To Wolverhampton 7/52	8700	3F 57xx 0-6-0T (1929)		
5188	4MT : 51xx 2-6-2T (1928)		To Wolverhampton 10/52	12070	350hp 0-6-0		
5190	4MT : 51xx 2-6-2T (1928)		To Wolverhampton 10/52	12071	350hp 0-6-0		
5198	4MT : 51xx 2-6-2T (1928)			12072	350hp 0-6-0		
5333	4MT : 43xx 2-6-0 (1911)			12087	350hp 0-6-0		
5369	4MT : 43xx 2-6-0 (1911)			13000	350hp 0-6-0	New 12/52	
5370	4MT : 43xx 2-6-0 (1911)			15101	350hp 0-6-0		
5386	4MT : 43xx 2-6-0 (1911)	Ex Oxley 10/52		15103	350hp 0-6-0		
5391	4MT : 43xx 2-6-0 (1911)	Ex Banbury 9/52	To Oxley 11/52	9008	2P : 90xx 4-4-0 (1936)		To Oswestry 5/52
6321	4MT : 43xx 2-6-0 (1911)	Ex Wolverhampton 10/52		9010	2P : 90xx 4-4-0 (1936)		To Oswestry 5/52
6336	4MT : 43xx 2-6-0 (1911)			7438	2P : 74xx 0-6-0T (1936)		

(1) When it is necessary for a train to pass at Danger a defective stop signal, or subsidiary signal, in rear of the box, before the Handsignalman takes up his duties, the Signalman must, where circumstances permit, proceed to the defective signal and explain to the Driver why it cannot be lowered. If, however, the Signalman is unable to leave his box and there are no facing points or switch diamonds over which the train has to run, he must, after the train has come to a stand, and there is no risk of another Driver mistaking a hand signal, exhibit to the Driver a green hand signal, held steadily, which must be regarded by the Driver as an intimation to pass the signal at Danger, and to proceed as far as the signal box for instructions.

If there are facing points or switch diamonds the Signalman must, before authorising the Driver to pass the defective signal, satisfy himself that they are set in position for the line over which the train has to run.

Where the defective stop signal, or subsidiary signal, is in advance of the signal box, the Signalman must, until the Handsignalman takes up his duties, stop each train at his box in accordance with Rule 40, and explain the circumstances to the Driver.

If a train has passed the signal box before the defect is observed, the Signalman must verbally explain to the Driver why the signal cannot be lowered, leaving his box if necessary and circumstances permit, or take the most expeditious means to inform the Driver.

In every case until a Handsignalman is appointed, the Driver, before passing over any facing points or switch diamonds, must satisfy himself that they are in the proper position for his train.

The small print of Rule 81. No minor responsibility for someone just out of school.

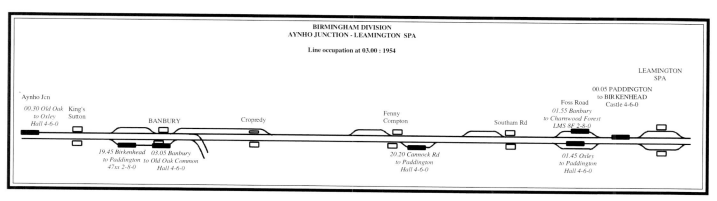

that whilst you were clambering up and down the frame and banging away on block bells, you also had to do your own job at the same time. No one could say that the railway did not get value for money from its box lads....)

On top of all this it was the lad's duty to make the tea and do the washing up, which entailed emptying the teapot. Not unnaturally this was done in the quickest (and most obvious way) by pouring the contents out of the window to be lectured by the lineman now and again on the damage that tea leaves could do to the cranks and compensators of the point rodding which lay below. Of course we took not the slightest bit of notice.

One day I emptied the kettle in the usual way and invoked a string of words from below that could only be described as the most basic of English. The outpouring was closely followed by Fred Cox, the lineman, hurling himself up the steps and into the cabin. With his head and shoulders covered in tea leaves – "How many times do I have to tell you bloody lads" – he advanced towards me intent either on murder or giving my backside a pretty good bruising. The signalman mentally tossed a coin and decided to come to my defence, placating poor old Fred by giving him a cup of tea and assuring him that stupidity would never be eradicated from society so long as a single box lad lived and breathed. Afterwards, as Fred's shadow diminished, he suggested that in future I should empty the pot over the ashes in the coal bunker outside the box.

Occasionally I found myself in a different kind of firing line as happened one afternoon when our down main home signal failed and became stuck in the on position. Word was sent out for the lineman to attend and in the meantime I was nominated to stand by the defective signal with a green flag and carry out the provisions of rule 81(1) which involved communicating with the signalman to ensure the road was clear and, if it was, to authorise drivers to pass the signal at danger. I flagged the 08.56 Ramsgate – Birkenhead and 10.33 Weymouth – Wolverhampton without incident and was then told that the next down was the prestige 14.10 Paddington – Birkenhead.

All trains were important but some were more important than others and into this latter bracket fell the two-hour Paddington workings which you delayed at your peril. Their drivers took the same view and as soon as he saw our distant against him, his whistle began to shriek as though we were stopping him for the sheer fun of it. Still whistling the King 4-6-0 rolled slowly down the platform, the racket only ceasing when the driver caught sight of me and my flag. Proudly I stood to attention and gave him a green to which the driver responded with a brief toot. Then he opened up with a roar that must have rattled windows for quite a distance.

On other regions, the larger the engine the quieter the exhaust but not on the Great Western. The King – its lever probably somewhere near the trailing driving wheel – started forward like a gun turret on a battleship, each exhaust going off like a cannon with smoke and steam erupting everywhere as it plunged under the bridge. It struck me as a sobering fact that only a short time ago I had been sitting in a school classroom yet here I was signalling the most important trains in the world.

During the summer the number of excursions that ran during the late afternoons and early evening to and from the holiday resorts was unbelievable. The goods service all but disappeared in order to provide engines and men for the addition passenger workings, all of which were filled to capacity.

The procession usually started with the return Bournemouth's and Margate's followed by the West of England's with, in between, the regular London expresses for which we somehow squeezed a passage into Snow Hill. To me the returning 'Wests' were always the most thrilling to watch, usually hauled by a 68xx or 'Castle from a shed west of Bristol: 'all cops'. Most of them had nigh-on empty tenders, blowers screwed out and crews looking more than a little dusty.

Needless to say still being a trainspotter I didn't miss many numbers but if I did I would phone the signalman either side and ask them what it was. They were all very kind doing this little chore for me and probably regarded my passion for numbers as an amusing idiosyncrasy.

Much of our stock in trade consisted of light engines to or from Tyseley shed which had to be weaved between the dense main line traffic but now and again a special light engine movement would take place; something I took especial interest in since many of these involved new engines making their first run from Stafford Road works, Wolverhampton. The first warning was usually given by a box to box message – "light engine Banbury" when the pilot was returning after assisting a down express to Bir-

TYSELEY ALLOCATION : 1953

LOCO	CLASS	IN	OUT	LOCO	CLASS	IN	OUT
3829	8F : 28xx 2-8-0 (1938)			3101	4MT : 31xx 2-6-2T (1938)		
3837	8F : 28xx 2-8-0 (1938)		To Didcot 9/53	3180	4MT : 3150 2-6-2T (1906)		To Gloucester 3/53
3839	8F : 28xx 2-8-0 (1938)			8415	4F : 94XX 0-6-0T (1949)		
2826	8F : 28xx 2-8-0 (1903)			8462	4F : 94XX 0-6-0T (1949)	Ex Wolverhampton 9/53	To Wolverhampton 10/53
2848	8F : 28xx 2-8-0 (1903)			8463	4F : 94XX 0-6-0T (1949)		To Landore 9/53
2849	8F : 28xx 2-8-0 (1903)			8468	4F : 94XX 0-6-0T (1949)		
2856	8F : 28xx 2-8-0 (1903)			9432	4F : 94XX 0-6-0T (1949)		
2867	8F : 28xx 2-8-0 (1903)			82000	3MT 2-6-2 (1952)		To Barry 8/53
6971	5MT : MOD-HALL 4-6-0 (1944)			82001	3MT 2-6-2 (1952)		To Barry 9/53
7912	5MT : MOD-HALL 4-6-0 (1944)			82002	3MT 2-6-2 (1952)		To Barry 9/53
7913	5MT : MOD-HALL 4-6-0 (1944)			82003	3MT 2-6-2 (1952)		To Barry 9/53
7918	5MT : MOD-HALL 4-6-0 (1944)			82004	3MT 2-6-2 (1952)		To Barry 9/53
7929	5MT : MOD-HALL 4-6-0 (1944)			82005	3MT 2-6-2 (1952)		To Barry 9/53
7818	5MT : MANOR 4-6-0 (1938)	Ex Oxley 3/53		82006	3MT 2-6-2 (1952)		To Barry 9/53
7821	5MT : MANOR 4-6-0 (1938)	Ex Shrewsbury 12/53		82007	3MT 2-6-2 (1952)		To Barry 9/53
4934	5MT : HALL 4-6-0 (1928)	Ex Oxley 6/53	To Gloucester 11/53	82008	3MT 2-6-2 (1952)		To Barry 9/53
4964	5MT : HALL 4-6-0 (1928)			82009	3MT 2-6-2 (1952)		To Barry 9/53
5900	5MT : HALL 4-6-0 (1928)	Ex Westbury 3/53		2203	3MT : 2251 0-6-0 (1930)		To Bristol (BR) 4/53
5907	5MT : HALL 4-6-0 (1928)		To Gloucester 11/53	2238	3MT : 2251 0-6-0 (1930)		
5909	5MT : HALL 4-6-0 (1928)			2257	3MT : 2251 0-6-0 (1930)		
5912	5MT : HALL 4-6-0 (1928)			2296	3MT : 2251 0-6-0 (1930)		
5927	5MT : HALL 4-6-0 (1928)			3625	3F : 57xx 0-6-0T (1933)		
6904	5MT : HALL 4-6-0 (1928)			3650	3F : 57xx 0-6-0T (1933)		To Bristol (BR) 10/53
6938	5MT : HALL 4-6-0 (1928)	Ex Worcester 1/53	To Gloucester 11/53	3653	3F : 57xx 0-6-0T (1933)		To Didcot 9/53
6843	5MT : GRANGE 4-6-0 (1936)			3657	3F : 57xx 0-6-0T (1933)		To Neyland 9/53
6853	5MT : GRANGE 4-6-0 (1936)			3660	3F : 57xx 0-6-0T (1933)		
6858	5MT : GRANGE 4-6-0 (1936)			3673	3F : 57xx 0-6-0T (1933)		
6866	5MT : GRANGE 4-6-0 (1936)			3689	3F : 57xx 0-6-0T (1933)		
6614	5MT : 56xx 0-6-2T (1927)	Ex Barry 9/53		3693	3F : 57xx 0-6-0T (1933)		
6620	5MT : 56xx 0-6-2T (1927)	Ex Barry 9/53		3694	3F : 57xx 0-6-0T (1933)	Ex Banbury 9/53	To Banbury 11/53
6646	5MT : 56xx 0-6-2T (1927)	Ex Stourbridge 10/53	Stourbridge 11/53	3769	3F : 57xx 0-6-0T (1933)		
6668	5MT : 56xx 0-6-2T (1927)	Ex Barry 9/53		4648	3F : 57xx 0-6-0T (1933)		To Wellington 2/53
6669	5MT : 56xx 0-6-2T (1927)	Ex Barry 9/53		5712	3F : 57xx 0-6-0T (1933)		
6105	4MT : 61xx 2-6-2T (1931)	Ex Reading 9/53		5724	3F : 57xx 0-6-0T (1933)	Ex Banbury 9/53	To Banbury 11/53
6116	4MT : 61xx 2-6-2T (1931)	Ex Didcot 10/53		5736	3F : 57xx 0-6-0T (1933)		
6118	4MT : 61xx 2-6-2T (1931)	Ex Didcot 9/53		5738	3F : 57xx 0-6-0T (1933)	Ex Wolverhampton 3/53	
6121	4MT : 61xx 2-6-2T (1931)	Ex Old Oak Common 9/53	To Old Oak Common 10/53	5745	3F : 57xx 0-6-0T (1933)		To Wellington 7/53
6134	4MT : 61xx 2-6-2T (1931)	Ex Didcot 9/53		5790	3F : 57xx 0-6-0T (1933)		
6139	4MT : 61xx 2-6-2T (1931)	Ex Southall 9/53		9608	3F : 57xx 0-6-0T (1933)		
6166	4MT : 61xx 2-6-2T (1931)	Ex Didcot 9/53		9610	3F : 57xx 0-6-0T (1933)		To Bristol (BR) 10/53
9303	4MT : 43xx 2-6-0 (1932)	Ex Reading 11/53		9614	3F : 57xx 0-6-0T (1933)		
9319	4MT : 43xx 2-6-0 (1932)	Ex Reading 11/53		9635	3F : 57xx 0-6-0T (1933)		
8108	4MT : 81xx 2-6-2T (1938)			9680	3F : 57xx 0-6-0T (1933)		
4103	4MT : 51xx 2-6-2T (1928)	Ex Wolverhampton 10/53	To Wolverhampton 11/53	9682	3F : 57xx 0-6-0T (1933)		
4110	4MT : 51xx 2-6-2T (1928)			9724	3F : 57xx 0-6-0T (1933)		
4111	4MT : 51xx 2-6-2T (1928)			9733	3F : 57xx 0-6-0T (1933)		
4116	4MT : 51xx 2-6-2T (1928)			9748	3F : 57xx 0-6-0T (1933)		To Penzance 9/53
4170	4MT : 51xx 2-6-2T (1928)			9753	3F : 57xx 0-6-0T (1933)		
4172	4MT : 51xx 2-6-2T (1928)			9798	3F : 57xx 0-6-0T (1933)		
5112	4MT : 51xx 2-6-2T (1928)	Ex Shrewsbury 2/53	To Wolverhampton 8/53	7713	3F : 57xx 0-6-0T (1929)		
5152	4MT : 51xx 2-6-2T (1928)			7735	3F : 57xx 0-6-0T (1929)		
5156	4MT : 51xx 2-6-2T (1928)			7758	3F : 57xx 0-6-0T (1929)		
5163	4MT : 51xx 2-6-2T (1928)	Ex Leamington 2/53		8700	3F : 57xx 0-6-0T (1929)		
5164	4MT : 51xx 2-6-2T (1928)			7438	2F : 74xx 0-6-0T (1936)		
5166	4MT : 51xx 2-6-2T (1928)			12070	0F : 350hp 0-6-0		
5181	4MT : 51xx 2-6-2T (1928)	Ex Chester 9/53		12071	0F : 350hp 0-6-0		
5195	4MT : 51xx 2-6-2T (1928)	Ex Barry 9/53	To Merthyr 10/53	12072	0F : 350hp 0-6-0		
5198	4MT : 51xx 2-6-2T (1928)			12087	0F : 350hp 0-6-0		
5322	4MT : 43xx 2-6-0 (1911)	Ex Oxford 5/53		13000	0F : 350hp 0-6-0		To Bristol (SPM) 12/53
5333	4MT : 43xx 2-6-0 (1911)			13001	0F : 350hp 0-6-0	new 1/53	To Bristol (SPM) 12/53
5369	4MT : 43xx 2-6-0 (1911)			13002	0F : 350hp 0-6-0	new 1/53	To Bristol (SPM) 12/53
5370	4MT : 43xx 2-6-0 (1911)			13003	0F : 350hp 0-6-0	new 1/53	To Bristol (SPM) 12/53
5386	4MT : 43xx 2-6-0 (1911)			13004	0F : 350hp 0-6-0	new 1/53	
6307	4MT : 43xx 2-6-0 (1911)	Ex Swindon 3/53		13025	0F : 350hp 0-6-0	New 12/53	
6321	4MT : 43xx 2-6-0 (1911)			13026	0F : 350hp 0-6-0	New 12/53	
6336	4MT : 43xx 2-6-0 (1911)			13027	0F : 350hp 0-6-0	New 12/53	
6342	4MT : 43xx 2-6-0 (1911)	Ex Banbury 9/53		13028	0F : 350hp 0-6-0	New 12/53	
6394	4MT : 43xx 2-6-0 (1911)	Ex Taunton 11/53		13029	0F : 350hp 0-6-0	New 12/53	
7309	4MT : 43xx 2-6-0 (1911)	Ex Westbury 3/53	To Wolverhampton 6/53	15101	0F : 350hp 0-6-0		To Old Oak Common 1/53
7317	4MT : 43xx 2-6-0 (1911)			15103	0F : 350hp 0-6-0		To Old Oak Common 11/53

The last of the old order. 4-4-0's had a far shorter reign on the Great Western than with any other company although a handful of examples remained in traffic until the late 1950's. Bulldog 4-4-0 3454 'Skylark' of Reading stands on Tyseley shed on 17th June 1951, five months before withdrawal.

mingham for example – and one day Bordesley called out "light engine Old Oak Common": an usual distance for a light engine to travel.

Guessing that it was a loco returning home from Stafford Road works I kept a weather eye open and was surprised to see an 0-6-0 pannier tank bowling along, running like a sewing machine with new paint on its front shining in the afternoon sun. Its number was 8763 but what made the difference was that Stafford Road had adorned the black livery with a highly attractive red, cream and grey lining.

The 0-6-0 scurried by and I wondered if it was going to set a new trend in liveries – there was quite a degree of experimenting going on at the time - but as it happened 8763 was the only pannier I saw in this livery although I believe one or two others were similarly treated.

8763 spent most of its time at Old Oak Common, working empty stock to and from Paddington, and I came across it years later at Swindon when it was working out its last days as works shunter. The thickness of grime covering most of the engine had taken some years to build up but some enterprising soul at Swindon had noticed that underneath the filth it had a slightly different livery from its class-mates and had rubbed clean a small patch on the side of one of the tanks. It surprised me that Wolverhampton's efforts had survived something

like a decade and a half although it was a pity the cleaning effort had not embraced the entire locomotive.

Although I worked with a regular signalman (and got to know his ways) occasionally his place would be filled by a relief man who would often be a total stranger to me, the box and the area. One of these occasionals was an old boy who liked his beer and when on the late turn would send me down to the Marlborough to refill the quart bottle which he always travelled with. "Go and wind the clock up" he would say handing me the empty bottle.

I once had this particular individual for a week whilst my signalman was on leave and every evening, just after opening time, I would do his bidding and disappear to wind the clock up. He was normally glad to see me and his bottle return in one piece but one evening when I approached the box I found him standing with his back in the doorway frantically waving a duster behind his back. Had I been a little more streetwise I might have suspected that he was sending me some sort of warning signal but in my innocence I bounded up the steps, handed him his bottle and found the district inspector sitting comfortable in the seat with an enquiring expression on his face. How the bottle was explained away, I do not know, but it did not

deter him from sending me to wind the clock up the following day.

Satisfying though my job was, I was still keen to pursue my original aim of a career on the footplate and as my birthday approached I made an application for a departmental move and was sent to Park House, Swindon, to sit a medical and eyesight test.

My time at Small Heath had been so busy that the opportunity to use my privilege tickets on a wide scale had not arisen and my journey to Swindon was the first long distance trip I had ever made. It was therefore with a sense of both business and pleasure that I caught the 07.40 from Small Heath to Knowle & Dorridge (51xx 2-6-2T) to connect with the 06.45 Wolverhampton – Paddington which I used as far as Banbury. The latter ran majestically into Knowle behind a King resplendent in blue livery. I got in, made myself comfortable and tried to be at ease for the ride to Banbury although it was further than I had ever been before and I kept a sharp look out for station names to be well prepared for my change of trains. Leaving Leamington I was very pleased to get my first look at its shed, noting the numbers of a couple of 51xxs waiting their next call of duty. More important was a really old double framed pannier tank standing at the coal-stage with a

The difficulties of the Snow Hill bottleneck where four lines converged into two at the south end of the station were made worse by the 1/45 gradient through the tunnel. Even though the maximum loads for down goods workings was reduced from 100 to 68 wagons for the gradient, not all trains managed to reach the summit. A 28xx 2-8-0 has to be rescued by 2-6-2T 5105 after stalling on the gradient and holding up northbound traffic for miles around.

frustratingly indiscernible number. It took some considerable research in the days that followed to discover that it was 1287 and was being used as a stationary boiler for washing out purposes.

I managed to catch sight of Fosse Road signalbox and give it Joe Cooper's silent regards – he had once worked there - as we sped by but the loop was clear of trains and the journey devoid of interest until the brakes went on for Banbury and I stood in the corridor, amazed at the enormity of the yards either side of the line.

I got out at Banbury and joined my train that was standing in the up bay platform headed by a 4-6-0 of some description. The blue King stormed out of Banbury and within a few minutes we were on our way. As we left the station it was my good fortune to be sitting on the Banbury loco shed side which was crammed with more 28xx 2-8-0's than I was capable of noting as we gathered speed.

Our local train stopped at all stations, most of which I had never heard of although they would become very familiar in the coming years. The next loco shed sighting was Oxford which was also packed with engines of all sorts shapes and sizes but due to wagons being in front of most of them I was unable to make out any of the numbers.

As the journey progressed, the ride seemed to get lonelier and the butterflies in my stomach increased. We left Oxford and after stopping at a few more stations we slowed down for what I guessed was Didcot, my final change of trains. I looked eagerly for the shed and it would have helped if I had known in which direction to look. Fortunately it was a busy location and whichever side of the train one was, there was invariably something of interest to see. In my case, as we went round the long curve towards the station, I noticed a pannier tank of considerable vintage with a queer sort of chimney (a

spark arresting type) and an equally strange three-digit number, 907. I made sure that I would remember the number and transfer it to my 'ref' when I got back home.

After getting out of the train and making my way over to number one platform to catch the train to Swindon, the second of my Didcot memories occured. It was an absolute thrill to see two Castle hauled expresses, one either way, come thundering through the station at what seemed breakneck speed. Noting the station announcer's warning ' to stand well back as the next train does not call here' one could fail to be highly impressed by the spectacle and I wondered if the future would see me firing on such jobs. (I also wondered if my seven stone would in any way disbar me).

My train ran in and I secured a seat by the window and took a keen interest in the ride to Swindon but like most of the journey the station names meant little to me. I did catch sight

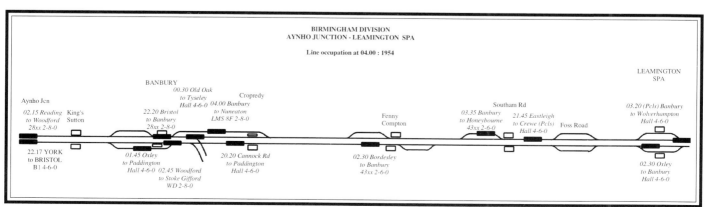

Although the R.O.D. 2-8-0's were widely scattered over the system, the preferred mineral engine at Tyseley was the 28xx 2-8-0 and very few of the former were allocated to the shed during the 1950's. After nearly two years without a single representative of the type, 3012 and 3023 arrived from Oxford in October 1955. A third, 3017, arrived from Bristol in September 1955 as a replacement for 3023 which was taken out of traffic a month later. 3023 stands on Tyseley shed during its last month of activity.

of a brand new tender loco in what I later identified as Marston Sidings and as we slowed down for the approach to Swindon I kept a sharp look out for some rare numbers that would grace the pages of my 'ref'

Ignoring the temptation to linger on the station, I reported to the clerk at Park House and he directed me to a waiting room where several young men bent on the same quest were waiting their turn. It seemed that they were all from South Wales and whilst talking to them I found out which sheds they were from. To me they were only names that I knew only from my trusty 'ref'

Whilst waiting to be seen, I learnt that there was a tradition in which every prospective fireman wrote his name and shed on the wall and I duly added mine to the long list of hopefuls who dated back to the early days of the company.

Unfortunately my actions turned out to be a little premature for when the doctor finished his examination he promptly failed me, saying that if I was still interested in pursuing a career in the locomotive department I should return in six months time.

I sat on the platform bench thinking how cruel the world could be and felt even more depressed when a freshly overhauled Castle came slowly through the station with its crew evidently proud to be working on such a fine machine.

My ride home was a misery and failure hung hard upon me. I thought for a while of giving up the railway and going to sea until Joe Cooper brought me back on course. The months passed and with them hope returned and December saw me retracing my steps by making the same journey, catching the same trains and changing at the same stations. I even saw old No. 907 again which bred in me an uncomfortable feeling that history was beginning to repeat itself.

Back in the waiting room I was again invited to write my name on the wall but I pointed out that it was already on there and explained the reason for my second visit; an explanation that brought a certain amount of silence from the usually talkative lads concerned.

This time I passed with flying colours, and it appeared that last time I was slightly underweight. I was overjoyed and went down to the clerk so as he could enter my particulars in his book. I then had to contribute five shillings to join the Great Western Railway Mutual Aid Society, which provided sickness benefit and a pension scheme for enginemen and was a condition of service. I was then taken by an elderly gentleman to collect my overalls, two sets plus one of those splendid Great Western enginemans caps. It was that piece of the uniform that thrilled me most when donning it for the first time.

The trip home was in complete contrast to the last time. I was elated and though the journey was in darkness I enjoyed every minute of it. All that remained was for a replacement booking lad to be found to take my place and once he was trained in the arts of the job I would be released from this department and be able to put my foot on the first rung of the ladder that would eventually allow me to climb to achieve my boyhood ambition, that of being an 'engine driver'

BORDESLEY DAYS

The 72xx 2-8-2 tanks were generally associated with mineral traffic in the South Wales area although a small number could be found at Oxley and Oxford. 7241 however had become unbalanced in the West Midlands and was used on a Bordesley - Banbury working whilst arrangements were made to return it to its home shed, Barry. Although they were very powerful machines, they were not well suited to the Great Western line south of Birmingham which had no water columns between Leamington and Banbury. More than once a driver finding himself with a 72xx had, because of delays in loops, to uncouple and run light to Leamington to refill the tanks. 7241 is seen standing at Fenny Compton on August 1959.

With almost eighteen months signalling experience under my belt, in April 1950 I set off on what I had always regarded as my real vocation and presented myself to Mr Chamberlain, the Foreman Cleaner at Tyseley loco who looked me up and down, told me a few tales about his own time on the main line and set me to work with a gang of other lads of my age and ambitions.

Tyseley loco was a typical Great Western standard shed, with two large roundhouses having something like thirty roads radiating from their manually operated turntables. One of the sheds was reserved for the larger engines and the 51xx suburban 2-6-2 tanks whilst the other tended to be used for shunting engines and boiler washouts.

In addition the shed had its own workshops where quite a variety of jobs such as motion repairs, valves and pistons, re-tubing boilers, hot axleboxes, and slight collision damage were carried out. Some of the work was quite ambitious and I can remember a Grange 4-6-0 having a new smokebox fitted. I also saw a 3lxx 2-6-2T shorn of its tanks, cab and boiler lagging having a steam test.

It was all too good to be true and before I had been at Tyseley for more than a couple of days I sneaked into the works during a lunch-break to have take a look round. Being rather a new boy I was a little more than uncertain as to my authority for being there but no one stopped

me and by the time I had bagged a couple of 47xx 2-8-0's I ceased worrying. I was, after all, a bona-fide locoman. Delving more deeply I found a pair of 51xx 2-6-2 tanks, 4-4-0 No. 9010 (one of a pair allocated to the shed) and, at the far end, King 4-6-0 6022 'King Edward 111'.

From that day on I made frequent visits, not only deriving great pleasure from what I saw but learning a great deal too. The two strangest locos I saw in there under repair included a 'Super D' 0-8-0 from Shrewsbury, and Fowler 2-6-4T 43243 of Stockport; both receiving attention for hot axleboxes.

Cleaning on the Great Western was not so much a chore as a philosophy but two engines, 5907 'Marble Hall', and 0-6-0PT 9733, were picked out for special attention. The 4-6-0 worked one of Snow Hill's principal evening rush-hour jobs and it was therefore not unreasonable to give it an extra shine but why 9733 should have been similarly honoured was a question that went unanswered except that Mr Chamberlain had his reasons.

5907 stayed at Tyseley until November 1953 when it was transferred to Gloucester in exchange for 5900 'Hinderton Hall' which came to us from Westbury. Until then it was the regular engine on the shed's top turn, the 16.53 Snow Hill – Leamington and the 20.30 return; the local trains being a prelude to main part of the diagram, the 21.50 Snow Hill – Swindon parcels via Stratford and Gloucester and the

01.50 return to Moor Street which was routed via Oxford, Honeybourne and Stratford.

At the other end of the scale were a pair of Austerity 8F 2-8-0's - 'Japanese Compounds' as an LMS controller once christened them - and a couple of Dukedog 4-4-0's, 9008 and 9010. Quite why the 4-4-0's were on the books at Tyseley was a minor mystery since I cannot recall them working anything other than the 'Target' which involved relieving engines on down goods trains at Small Heath South so that they could be turned, coaled and watered without suffering the delay incurred by working into Bordesley Yard. In May 1952 someone twigged that the 4-4-0's could be used to better advantage elsewhere on the system and both were reallocated to Oswestry for working over the Cambrian.

It was on 9010 that I discovered how dextrous I could be when the occasion demanded. I was cleaning the inside motion one afternoon and had stuck fast, wishing that when designing engines Swindon would take account of the proportions of engine cleaners, in an awkward position behind the big ends.

"Give me a hand." I called out to anyone who might be around and saw a colleagues' face peering through the frames.

"What's up?"

"I'm stuck."

"Keep still, Colin, I'll move her forward to give you a bit more room…"

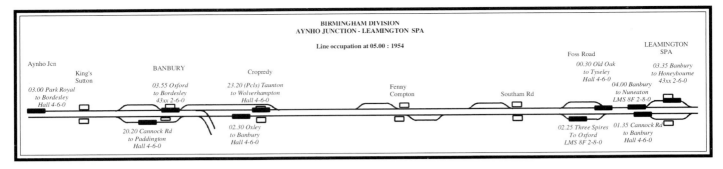

BIRMINGHAM DIVISION
AYNHO JUNCTION - LEAMINGTON SPA

Line occupation at 05.00 : 1954

Aynho Jcn — King's Sutton — BANBURY — Cropredy — Fenny Compton — Southam Rd — Foss Road — LEAMINGTON SPA

03.00 Park Royal to Bordesley Hall 4-6-0
03.55 Oxford to Bordesley 43xx 2-6-0
23.20 (Pcls) Taunton to Wolverhampton Hall 4-6-0
20.20 Cannock Rd to Paddington Hall 4-6-0
02.30 Oxley to Banbury Hall 4-6-0
00.30 Old Oak to Tyseley Hall 4-6-0
03.35 Banbury to Honeybourne 43xx 2-6-0
04.00 Banbury to Nuneaton LMS 8F 2-8-0
02.25 Three Spires To Oxford LMS 8F 2-8-0
01.35 Cannock Rd to Banbury Hall 4-6-0

Before he could take a step I was out.

I like to think he would not actually have carried his threat out and in fact many lasting friendships had their roots in our days as cleaners. Some of my colleagues possessed talents beyond the call of duty and included one – Dick Potts – who was not only a gifted artist in the conventional sense but could imitate almost anything on wheels: stopping you in your tracks with his impression of a double-header coming down Washwood Heath Road. Another colleague – Dennis Herbert – was a gifted engineer and when not working with engines, built them in miniature.

One of the things the railway took an especial pride in was the Royal Train and during my short time as a cleaner I took part in the preparations for the visit by Princess Elizabeth to Stratford-upon-Avon in April 1950.

Two of our engines Hall 4-6-0's 4980 'Wrottesley Hall' and 5997 'Sparkford Hall were selected for the duty and we cleaned each of them for a week prior to the great day. The curious thing was that neither of our Hall's was booked to haul a royal body – the Princess and her entourage were taken from Paddington to Stratford by a pair of Old Oak Castles – but

instead worked the empty stock from Stratford to Tyseley and back again.

Having seen our Halls off to Stratford we then had to stand by for the arrival of the two Old Oak engines, 5000 'Launceston Castle' and 7001 'Sir James Milne', and give them a good clean before they ran back light to Stratford for the return journey. As it happened Old Oak had done such a good job on them – to describe them as highly polished would be an understatement – that all we had to do with give them a rub over.

For some days afterwards we expected someone to come up with some sort of complaint but if anyone had been trying to find something wrong with our handiwork they failed and no adverse comments came back to the shed. We all felt satisfied at our 'Royal' days work.

Most of our normal work was of a (slightly) less exacting nature although on at least one occasion it stimulated me into a course of action that might not otherwise have been followed. I was on duty in the passenger shed one morning when 9000 itself drifted in, having been in Stafford Road works. Being a rarity, I took a good look at it and was intrigued at its shedcode, 'PMDC'. This started a train of thought which culminated in a desire to do a bit of exploring

and, after persuading a fellow cleaner to join me, decided to take a trip to discover the source of the Cambrian.

This meant applying for one of the three free passes we received annually which in turn involved a degree of sparring with Bill Cox, the staff clerk. The issuing of a pass was accompanied by an unbelievable amount of clerical work for the clerk which, although balanced by a slight increase in salary, made applicants – especially young ones - decidedly unpopular. After the routine delaying tactics ("come back when my relief is on duty…") we eventually received passes for Aberystwyth and left Snow Hill at an absurd hour the following Sunday behind a 43xx 2-6-0.

It cannot be said that my first visit to Wales encouraged me to return. The route was almost entirely single lined – quite beneath the dignity of a 'main line' enthusiast to take an interest in – whilst the station names were just an alphabet stew. At one stage in the journey our 2-6-0 came to a halt outside a totally unpronounceable signalbox with the track ahead completely submerged in water. Eventually we reached our destination and made a bee-line for the shed which was really our only reason for making the journey.

No sooner had we crossed the threshold than we were confronted by the rudest individual imaginable who not only refused to listen to what we had to say but abruptly expelled us from the premises.

By unanimous decision North Wales was immediately declared to be unworthy of our presence and we resolved that our next trip would be to Mecca or, as we spelt it, Swindon. Mindful, however, that we lived in an authoritarian age – half the people who had any sort of petty rank seemed unable to drop the habit of looking for German spies – I took the precaution of writing a letter of request and forwarding it to the works in advance of our journey. It worked like a charm although the wording of the reply – This is to permit Mr C. Jacks and his cleaner friends to visit Swindon works – caused quite a ripple of amusement: shades of three inch Austins.

Such excursions – the successful ones at any rate – were no more than busmen's holidays and the pleasure derived was really no greater than that obtained on duty at Tyseley where I had the dual pleasures of working amongst steam engines and not having to worry about being ejected (as had happened several times in earlier years) by the running foreman.

For all my extra-mural activities and trips to Aberystwyth and Swindon, I was far being the only idiosyncratic at Tyseley and it was not long before I detected the symptoms in my employer, Mr Chamberlain. His weakness had nothing to do with engine chasing but concerned the amount of oil he doled out for the cleaning of locomotives. In war or peace a clean engine was the hallmark of the Great Western yet the

TYSELEY ALLOCATION : 1954							
LOCO	CLASS	IN	OUT	LOCO	CLASS	IN	OUT
3829	8F : 28xx 2-8-0 (1938)		To Banbury 9/54	9303	4MT :43xx 2-6-0 (1932)		
3839	8F : 28xx 2-8-0 (1938)			9319	4MT :43xx 2-6-0 (1932)		
2826	8F : 28xx 2-8-0 (1903)		To Shrewsbury 9/54	5322	4MT : 43xx 2-6-0 (1911)		To Oxford 10/54
2848	8F : 28xx 2-8-0 (1903)			5333	4MT : 43xx 2-6-0 (1911)		
2849	8F : 28xx 2-8-0 (1903)			5369	4MT : 43xx 2-6-0 (1911)		
2856	8F : 28xx 2-8-0 (1903)			5370	4MT : 43xx 2-6-0 (1911)		
2867	8F : 28xx 2-8-0 (1903)		To Banbury 9/54	5386	4MT : 43xx 2-6-0 (1911)		
3012	7F : R.O.D. 2-8-0 (1917)	Ex Oxford 10/54		6307	4MT : 43xx 2-6-0 (1911)		
3023	7F : R.O.D. 2-8-0 (1917)	Ex Oxford 10/54		6321	4MT : 43xx 2-6-0 (1911)		
6614	5MTT : 56xx 0-6-2T (1927)			6327	4MT : 43xx 2-6-0 (1911)	Ex Stourbridge 1/54	
6620	5MTT : 56xx 0-6-2T (1927)			6336	4MT : 43xx 2-6-0 (1911)		To Oxford 10/54
6668	5MTT : 56xx 0-6-2T (1927)			6342	4MT : 43xx 2-6-0 (1911)		
6669	5MTT : 56xx 0-6-2T (1927)			6394	4MT : 43xx 2-6-0 (1911)		
6971	5MT : MOD-HALL 4-6-0 (1944)			7317	4MT : 43xx 2-6-0 (1911)		
7912	5MT : MOD-HALL 4-6-0 (1944)			8415	4FT : 94XX 0-6-0T (1949)		
7913	5MT : MOD-HALL 4-6-0 (1944)			8468	4FT : 94XX 0-6-0T (1949)		
7918	5MT : MOD-HALL 4-6-0 (1944)			9432	4FT : 94XX 0-6-0T (1949)		
7929	5MT : MOD-HALL 4-6-0 (1944)			2238	3MTT : 2251 0-6-0 (1930)		
7818	5MT : MANOR 4-6-0 (1938)			2257	3MTT : 2251 0-6-0 (1930)		
7821	5MT : MANOR 4-6-0 (1938)			2279	3MTT : 2251 0-6-0 (1930)	Ex Stourbridge 1/54	
4904	5MT : HALL 4-6-0 (1928)	Ex Shrewsbury 9/54		2296	3MTT : 2251 0-6-0 (1930)		
4964	5MT : HALL 4-6-0 (1928)			3625	3FT : 57xx 0-6-0T (1933)		
5900	5MT : HALL 4-6-0 (1928)			3660	3FT : 57xx 0-6-0T (1933)		
5909	5MT : HALL 4-6-0 (1928)		To Laira 12/54	3673	3FT : 57xx 0-6-0T (1933)		
5912	5MT : HALL 4-6-0 (1928)			3689	3FT : 57xx 0-6-0T (1933)		
5927	5MT : HALL 4-6-0 (1928)			3693	3FT : 57xx 0-6-0T (1933)		
6904	5MT : HALL 4-6-0 (1928)			3769	3FT : 57xx 0-6-0T (1933)		
6843	5MT : GRANGE 4-6-0 (1936)			4648	3FT : 57xx 0-6-0T (1933)		
6853	5MT : GRANGE 4-6-0 (1936)			9608	3FT : 57xx 0-6-0T (1933)		
6858	5MT : GRANGE 4-6-0 (1936)		To Shrewsbury 9/54	9614	3FT : 57xx 0-6-0T (1933)		
6866	5MT : GRANGE 4-6-0 (1936)			9635	3FT : 57xx 0-6-0T (1933)		
6105	4MTT 61xx 2-6-2T (1931)			9680	3FT : 57xx 0-6-0T (1933)		
6116	4MTT 61xx 2-6-2T (1931)			9682	3FT : 57xx 0-6-0T (1933)		
6118	4MTT 61xx 2-6-2T (1931)			9724	3FT : 57xx 0-6-0T (1933)		
6134	4MTT 61xx 2-6-2T (1931)			9733	3FT : 57xx 0-6-0T (1933)		
6139	4MTT 61xx 2-6-2T (1931)			9753	3FT : 57xx 0-6-0T (1933)		
6166	4MTT 61xx 2-6-2T (1931)			9798	3FT : 57xx 0-6-0T (1933)		
8108	4MT : 81xx 2-6-2T (1938)			5736	3FT : 57xx 0-6-0T (1929)		
4110	4MTT : 51xx 2-6-2T (1928)			5738	3FT : 57xx 0-6-0T (1929)		
4111	4MTT : 51xx 2-6-2T (1928)			5790	3FT : 57xx 0-6-0T (1929)		
4116	4MTT : 51xx 2-6-2T (1928)			7713	3FT : 57xx 0-6-0T (1929)		
4170	4MTT : 51xx 2-6-2T (1928)			7735	3FT : 57xx 0-6-0T (1929)		
4171	4MTT : 51xx 2-6-2T (1928)	Ex Leamington 5/54	To Leamington 9/54	7758	3FT : 57xx 0-6-0T (1929)		
4172	4MTT : 51xx 2-6-2T (1928)			8700	3FT : 57xx 0-6-0T (1929)		
4178	4MTT : 51xx 2-6-2T (1928)	Ex Wellington 12/54		7438	2PT : 74xx 0-6-0T (1936)		
5152	4MTT : 51xx 2-6-2T (1928)			12070	0F: 350hp 0-6-0		
5156	4MTT : 51xx 2-6-2T (1928)			12071	0F: 350hp 0-6-0		
5163	4MTT : 51xx 2-6-2T (1928)			12072	0F: 350hp 0-6-0		
5164	4MTT : 51xx 2-6-2T (1928)			12087	0F: 350hp 0-6-0		
5166	4MTT : 51xx 2-6-2T (1928)			13004	0F: 350hp 0-6-0		
5181	4MTT : 51xx 2-6-2T (1928)			13025	0F: 350hp 0-6-0		
5192	4MTT : 51xx 2-6-2T (1928)	Ex Carmarthen 9/54		13026	0F: 350hp 0-6-0		
5198	4MTT : 51xx 2-6-2T (1928)			13027	0F: 350hp 0-6-0		
3101	4MTT : 31xx 2-6-2T (1938)			13028	0F: 350hp 0-6-0		
				13029	0F: 350hp 0-6-0		

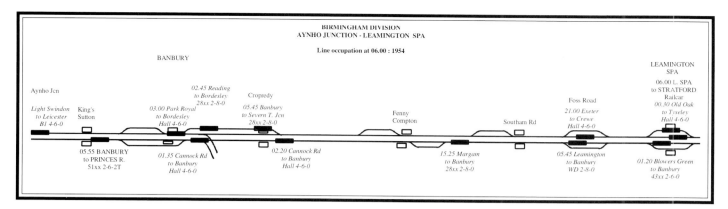

amount of oil given us to maintain this reputation was laughable: half a pint for any engine up to a 51xx 2-6-2T with another half for any engine that had a tender. Mr Chamberlain was just that little bit too senior to pick an argument with and, presuming that he either had to pay for it himself or was on some sort of a bonus system, we found it was necessary to resort to all sorts of subterfuge if our engines were to go out in a proper condition. One way was to try the fireman's toolboxes which – if someone had been idiotic enough to leave one unlocked – usually produced enough oil to supplement the Chamberlain quota. Another source was the old shedman – Yorkie – part of whose duties was to syringe the water from loco axleboxes and refill them with oil. The trick was to wait until he was about to reach for the oil and then create a diversion during which time a considerable quantity of his oil would be siphoned off. It probably set a record for criminal activities: robbing the Great Western to give to the Great Western. What Robin Hood would have made

of it, I didn't know but then, he had been a Midland man…

With engines coming on and off shed and moving up and down the yard, it would have been too much to expect us not to go for the occasional footplate ride between the shed and the water column, even though it was strictly forbidden. Most of the drivers turned a blind eye but the foreman was unlikely to and we therefore had to make sure we scrabbled onto the engine on the goods shed side which was out of the Foreman's line of vision. To mount the engine from the passenger shed side was courting trouble although the greatest risk was the possibility of running into the chargehand cleaner on the walk back from the column.

Naturally we all wanted – more than anything - to do some firing but the prohibition on footplate rides put this aim out of reach and under the pretext of getting a little practice should we suddenly be called upon to work a two-hour Paddington (!), we would simulate operations using the stationary boiler which provided hot water for washing out operations in the shed.

They were not actually very easy to fire. The fireboxes were at ground level with the firehole rather high up and it called for considerable skill to get an even bed of fire over the grate. After having a go I reflected that had I been on the main line I should not have got very far and the old boy who was in charge took the shovel from me before some irate boiler washer turned up demanding to why the supply of steam and water had ceased.

The boiler was also used by wash-out staff for cleaning themselves up when leaving duty, water being supplied through a perforated pipe and collected in a rather rude trough below. The heat of the water was regulated by a pair of steam and cold water valves which, with a little practised manipulation, could give you water sufficiently warm for washing with. Enemies from within were swiftly despatched by waiting until they had had covered their faces with soap and, eyes shut, were feeling for the water supply. A stealthy hand would quietly ease the cold water valve back a little leaving a blast of near superheated water whilst the recipient of our summary justice floundered wildly, frantically trying to locate the cold water valve before the soap set hard.

One thing you rarely had to bother about on the loco was promotion since everything was controlled by a golden number: one's Date entered Service (DES). If a monkey had come to Tyseley a day before Einstein, the physicist would be cleaning whilst the ape was driving and one day my number came up – it was all dead men's shoes – and I found myself a member of the No.1 cleaning link, whose job it was to look after the larger engines.

Cleaning fell into two parts, the inner motion of an engine and the boiler, and selection was usually determined by a toss of a coin. Personally I was less than happy crawling around the innards since there was always the nagging possibility that some idiot might move the engine whilst you were suspended, unseen, amongst the motion. There was of our a 'Not to be moved' board affixed to the engine but nonetheless one was mindful of stories, apocryphal or otherwise, that circulated around the shed…..

When cleaning an engine we usually had a good idea of the duty it was booked to although once we were given a Hall 4-6-0 with the comment that it was booked for some sort of special, hush-hush, job. With no further idea of what the engine was going to do – or who might see it – we became enthusiast conspirators, cleaned it to perfection and presented the fruits of our handiwork for inspection. Mr Chamberlain simply grunted and told us that the boiler barrel had to be coated in petroleum jelly. No reason was given but when he returned with our allocation of jelly he solemnly apportioned just

LOCO	CLASS	IN	OUT	LOCO	CLASS	IN	OUT
3839	8F : 28xx 2-8-0 (1938)			3101	4MTT : 31xx 2-6-2T (1938)		
2848	8F : 28xx 2-8-0 (1903)			9303	4MT :43xx 2-6-0 (1932)		
2849	8F : 28xx 2-8-0 (1903)			9319	4MT :43xx 2-6-0 (1932)		
2856	8F : 28xx 2-8-0 (1903)			5333	4MT :43xx 2-6-0 (1911)		
2857	8F : 28xx 2-8-0 (1903)	Ex Banbury 7/55		5369	4MT :43xx 2-6-0 (1911)		
3012	7F : R.O.D. 2-8-0 (1917)			5370	4MT :43xx 2-6-0 (1911)		
3017	7F : R.O.D. 2-8-0 (1917)	Ex Bristol (SPM) 9/55		5386	4MT :43xx 2-6-0 (1911)		
3023	7F : R.O.D. 2-8-0 (1917)		w/d 10/55	6307	4MT :43xx 2-6-0 (1911)		
6614	5MTT : 56xx 0-6-2T (1927)			6321	4MT :43xx 2-6-0 (1911)		
6620	5MTT : 56xx 0-6-2T (1927)			6327	4MT :43xx 2-6-0 (1911)		To Bristol (SPM) 1/55
6644	5MTT : 56xx 0-6-2T (1927)	Ex Neyland 8/55		6342	4MT :43xx 2-6-0 (1911)		
6668	5MTT : 56xx 0-6-2T (1927)			6394	4MT :43xx 2-6-0 (1911)		To Reading 2/55
6669	5MTT : 56xx 0-6-2T (1927)			7317	4MT :43xx 2-6-0 (1911)		
6971	5MT : MOD-HALL 4-6-0 (1944)			8407	4FT : 94XX 0-6-0T (1949)	Ex Banbury 5/55	To Duffryn 8/55
6980	5MT : MOD-HALL 4-6-0 (1944)	Ex Shrewsbury 5/55	To Shrewsbury 7/55	8415	4FT : 94XX 0-6-0T (1949)		
7908	5MT : MOD-HALL 4-6-0 (1944)	Ex Shrewsbury 9/55		8468	4FT : 94XX 0-6-0T (1949)		
7912	5MT : MOD-HALL 4-6-0 (1944)		To Shrewsbury 5/55	9426	4FT : 94XX 0-6-0T (1949)	Ex Banbury 5/55	To Cathays 8/55
7912	5MT : MOD-HALL 4-6-0 (1944)	Ex Shrewsbury 7/55		9432	4FT : 94XX 0-6-0T (1949)		
7913	5MT : MOD-HALL 4-6-0 (1944)		To Shrewsbury 5/55	9498	4FT : 94XX 0-6-0T (1949)	New 3/55	
7913	5MT : MOD-HALL 4-6-0 (1944)	Ex Shrewsbury 7/55		2238	3MT : 2251 0-6-0 (1930)		
7918	5MT : MOD-HALL 4-6-0 (1944)			2257	3MT : 2251 0-6-0 (1930)		
7929	5MT : MOD-HALL 4-6-0 (1944)		To Bristol (SPM) 7/55	2279	3MT : 2251 0-6-0 (1930)		
7818	5MT : MANOR 4-6-0 (1938)			2296	3MT : 2251 0-6-0 (1930)		
7821	5MT : MANOR 4-6-0 (1938)			3625	3FT : 57xx 0-6-0T (1933)		
4904	5MT : HALL 4-6-0 (1928)			3660	3FT : 57xx 0-6-0T (1933)		
4915	5MT : HALL 4-6-0 (1928)	Ex Shrewsbury 5/55	To Shrewsbury 7/55	3673	3FT : 57xx 0-6-0T (1933)		
4964	5MT : HALL 4-6-0 (1928)		To Canton 11/55	3689	3FT : 57xx 0-6-0T (1933)		
4988	5MT : HALL 4-6-0 (1928)	Ex Exeter 9/55		3693	3FT : 57xx 0-6-0T (1933)		
5900	5MT : HALL 4-6-0 (1928)		To Oxley 11/55	3769	3FT : 57xx 0-6-0T (1933)		
5912	5MT : HALL 4-6-0 (1928)			4648	3FT : 57xx 0-6-0T (1933)		
5927	5MT : HALL 4-6-0 (1928)			9608	3FT : 57xx 0-6-0T (1933)		
5986	5MT : HALL 4-6-0 (1928)	Ex Shrewsbury 7/55	To Shrewsbury 9/55	9614	3FT : 57xx 0-6-0T (1933)		
6904	5MT : HALL 4-6-0 (1928)			9635	3FT : 57xx 0-6-0T (1933)		
6843	5MT : GRANGE 4-6-0 (1936)		To Carmarthen 7/55	9680	3FT : 57xx 0-6-0T (1933)		
6853	5MT : GRANGE 4-6-0 (1936)			9682	3FT : 57xx 0-6-0T (1933)		
6861	5MT : GRANGE 4-6-0 (1936)	Ex Oxley 11/55		9724	3FT : 57xx 0-6-0T (1933)		
6866	5MT : GRANGE 4-6-0 (1936)			9733	3FT : 57xx 0-6-0T (1933)		
6105	4MTT 61xx 2-6-2T (1931)		To Neyland 4/55	9753	3FT : 57xx 0-6-0T (1933)		
6105	4MTT 61xx 2-6-2T (1931)	Ex Neyland 5/55		9798	3FT : 57xx 0-6-0T (1933)		
6116	4MTT 61xx 2-6-2T (1931)			5736	3FT : 57xx 0-6-0T (1929)		
6118	4MTT 61xx 2-6-2T (1931)			5738	3FT : 57xx 0-6-0T (1929)		
6134	4MTT 61xx 2-6-2T (1931)			5790	3FT : 57xx 0-6-0T (1929)		
6139	4MTT 61xx 2-6-2T (1931)			7713	3FT : 57xx 0-6-0T (1929)		
6166	4MTT 61xx 2-6-2T (1931)			7735	3FT : 57xx 0-6-0T (1929)		
8108	4MTT : 81xx 2-6-2T (1938)			7758	3FT : 57xx 0-6-0T (1929)		
4110	4MTT : 51xx 2-6-2T (1928)			7763	3FT : 57xx 0-6-0T (1929)	Ex Banbury 10/55	
4111	4MTT : 51xx 2-6-2T (1928)			8700	3FT : 57xx 0-6-0T (1929)		
4116	4MTT : 51xx 2-6-2T (1928)			7438	2PT : 74xx 0-6-0T (1936)		
4155	4MTT : 51xx 2-6-2T (1928)	Ex Wellington 5/55		12070	0F : 350hp 0-6-0		
4170	4MTT : 51xx 2-6-2T (1928)			12071	0F : 350hp 0-6-0		
4172	4MTT : 51xx 2-6-2T (1928)			12072	0F : 350hp 0-6-0		
4178	4MTT : 51xx 2-6-2T (1928)		To Wellington 2/55	12087	0F : 350hp 0-6-0		
5152	4MTT : 51xx 2-6-2T (1928)		To Banbury 9/55	13004	0F : 350hp 0-6-0		
5156	4MTT : 51xx 2-6-2T (1928)			13025	0F : 350hp 0-6-0		
5163	4MTT : 51xx 2-6-2T (1928)			13026	0F : 350hp 0-6-0		
5164	4MTT : 51xx 2-6-2T (1928)		To Wellington 5/55	13027	0F : 350hp 0-6-0		
5166	4MTT : 51xx 2-6-2T (1928)			13028	0F : 350hp 0-6-0		
5181	4MTT : 51xx 2-6-2T (1928)			13029	0F : 350hp 0-6-0		
5192	4MTT : 51xx 2-6-2T (1928)			13192	0F : 350hp 0-6-0		New 11/55
5198	4MTT : 51xx 2-6-2T (1928)						

TYSELEY ALLOCATION : 1955

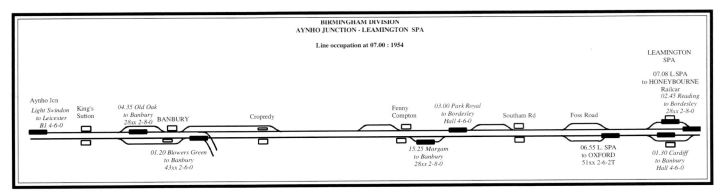

BIRMINGHAM DIVISION
AYNHO JUNCTION - LEAMINGTON SPA

Line occupation at 07.00 : 1954

LEAMINGTON
SPA

07.08 L.SPA
to HONEYBOURNE
Railcar
02.45 Reading
to Bordesley
28xx 2-8-0

Aynho Jcn
*Light Swindon
to Leicester
B1 4-6-0*

King's
Sutton

04.35 Old Oak
to Banbury
28xx 2-8-0

BANBURY

Cropredy

Fenny
Compton

03.00 Park Royal
to Bordesley
Hall 4-6-0

Southam Rd

Foss Road

*01.20 Blowers Green
to Banbury
43xx 2-6-0*

*15.25 Margam
to Banbury
28xx 2-8-0*

06.55 L. SPA
to OXFORD
51xx 2-6-2T

*01.30 Cardiff
to Banbury
Hall 4-6-0*

about enough to cover a small burn. How we extended it to the entire boiler surface is something I have forgotten.

As the summer approached with footplatemen taking an annual leave and hundreds of special trains being arranged, several of my colleagues with DES dates in advance of mine found themselves marked out of spare firing turns. Given the rigidity of the seniority system it brought home to me the fact that a few more dead men's shoes would see me on the footplate as well and I scoured the duty sheets until, on 8 June 1950, I saw my name pencilled in as a Fireman at Bordesley Junction.

The day dawned and I booked on at 1.00pm. with a Driver Davies to travel to Bordesley and relieve No. 6 shunting engine, known as the Field engine. I of course was elated but my driver took a rather more sanguine view of things and announced, as soon as we reached Bordesley, that he would go over to the club to finish his 'dinner'. I had better things to do and pulled myself on the engine, 0-6-0 5701, and took stock of my new responsibility.

The cab was nice and clean but the Great Western had ingrained its passion for cleanliness to such an extent that I thought another rub over the pipework with a patch of cotton waste wouldn't come amiss. I looked at the fire, low and saucer-shaped, checked we had a full boiler of water and noted about 140 pounds of steam on the pressure gauge.

As I was on my own, I decided to go through the preparation stages. As cleaners we had talked expertly about preparation although very few of us had actually done it. Now my chance had arrived.

I worked the sand levers in the cab and got off the engine to confirm that the sanders were actually working. There was no need to check the smokebox but I couldn't resist opening it to ensure that there were no leaking tubes and that the arrester plate was properly secure. I gave it my seal of approval and then found I couldn't get the wretched smoke box door to close. There is, as I discovered later, a knack to the business but it eluded me and when my driver returned I

was still trying to secure the thing. He put a casual hand out and deftly achieve what I had been trying to do for half an hour.

"Not to worry, Bach, at least you did try,' he said not unkindly.

Drivers, I was to discover, came in two sizes. There were those who left you to get on with the job and those – the majority – who would not let you scratch your backside without being permission. I was lucky, on my first day at least, and allowed to gain confidence by being given complete freedom with the shovel.

Davies was tolerant of my inexperience and took considerable pains to help me without actually interfering. Even on a humble 0-6-0 pilot there was a great to understand, not the least of which was the business of standing and firing whilst shunting was taking place. I also learnt a great deal about managing the injectors so that the boiler level could be kept at the proper level without wasting water.

It was a pleasant afternoon and 21.00, when the shunters released us from our duties, came too soon. We had to take the engine back to Tyseley shed and it was evident I had more fire in the box than was desirable for disposal. Fortunately there was a queue of engine waiting to be dealt with and by time the firedroppers got to 5701 most of it would have burned through. Driver Davies gave me his benediction, saying that the fire should always be run down before taking an engine on shed and that I should always leave an engine as I would wish to find it.

I went home feeling on top of the world, having 'made the grade', and went home to deliver a profound address – at length - to my parents on the subject of locomotive management.

My time as a passed cleaner was very short and I was very soon promoted to full fireman being based, as all new entrants were, at Bordesley Junction where we had six engines manned around the clock, one engine being changed by rote on a weekly basis so that none stayed in the yards for more than a week without being returned to Tyseley for servicing.

It is surprising how many railway books dealing with the Birmingham area barely give Bordesley a mention since in many respects it was the focal point of the district where the level of continuous activity made that at even the larger passenger stations pale by comparison. Much of the traffic came in on trips from the Midland Railway, approximately one train per hour coming in from Washwood Heath with loaded coal from the East Midlands coalfields, the 3F 0-6-0's and 8F 2-8-0's involved – and which, incidentally, were amongst the filthiest looking engines to be seen – being crossed over to the down side for their return trips.

In passing, not all the LMS trains changed engines at Bordesley and the exception was the 18.50 Washwood Heath to Oxford which ran via Stratford and Kingham, the 8F 2-8-0 working as far as Long Marston where it changed places with a 47xx 2-8-0 on the 15.00 Slough – Washwood Heath. Both engines turned on the Honeybourne angle.

I started firing on Number Nine engine on the afternoon turn, our engine being 5733, and all the shift long we pulled and pushed the coal trains that were brought up from Washwood Heath by the dirtiest-looking 4F's and 8F's that it was possible to see.

The mileage worked by the 57xx's at Bordesley was impossible to calculate – an rule of thumb estimate was made for clerical purposes – but it must have been considerable. A Midland train would run into the yard and, after the 4F had been released, we would take its place whilst the shunters ran down the train, looking at each wagon label and cutting the train accordingly. After a few minutes there would be a shout followed by a hand signal and we would pull away with a handful of wagons which would then be propelled into an adjacent road. We would return to the train and with half a dozen or more similar shunts, redistribute it in sections to be collected by the 57xx's in the Baltic and Baulks yards to be further broken down and made up into onward workings. Occasionally a train would run in from Washwood Heath with its entire load for a single destina-

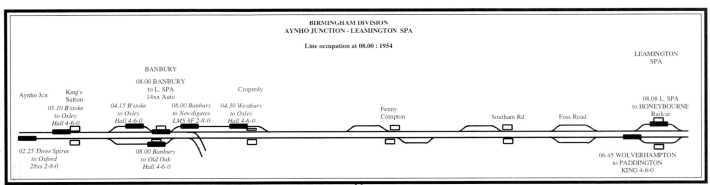

BIRMINGHAM DIVISION
AYNHO JUNCTION - LEAMINGTON SPA

Line occupation at 08.00 : 1954

LEAMINGTON
SPA

BANBURY

08.00 BANBURY
to L.SPA
14xx Auto

Cropredy

08.08 L. SPA
to HONEYBOURNE
Railcar

Aynho Jcn

King's
Sutton

*05.10 B'stoke
to Oxley
Hall 4-6-0*

*04.15 B'stoke
to Oxley
Hall 4-6-0*

08.00 Banbury
to Newdigates
LMS 8F 2-8-0

04.30 Westbury
to Oxley
Hall 4-6-0

Fenny
Compton

Southam Rd

Foss Road

*02.25 Three Spires
to Oxford
28xx 2-8-0*

08.00 Banbury
to Old Oak
Hall 4-6-0

06.45 WOLVERHAMPTON
to PADDINGTON
KING 4-6-0

A week's cleaning went into the preparation of Hall 4-6-0's 4980 'Wrottesley Hall' and 5997 'Sparkford Hall' in April 1950 when Princess Elizabeth travelled from Paddington to Stratford-upon-Avon. The Tyseley Hall's did not actually haul the royal party but worked the empty stock from Stratford to Tyseley and back again. The engines still had to be in the pink of condition.

tion but it was more usual for a thirty wagon train to have wagons on for ten or a dozen different destinations. (On the few occasions that a full load did run in from the Midland, the district control would know in advance and would arrange for an engine to be sent out from Tyseley to work it forward as a special. All we would do would be to make up the load to the maximum while the train was waiting to go forward).

In the pauses between waltzing up and down the yards at Bordesley my driver, Walter Austin, introduced me rather bluntly to the topic of railway politics by demanding to know which of the two unions I belonged to. Although it was not a subject which interested very many people of my age – I had no first hand experience of the difficult prewar years – I had routinely joined ASLEF and told him so. Unfortunately Walter was one of the minority who belonged to the National Union of Railwaymen and made no bones about the fact that I was in the wrong body. There were times when relations between the two unions made a middle east jihad seem like an amiable disagreement and matters went from cold to freezing when he found out that I was related to the local ASLEF representative. In Walter's eye's I was some sort of a spy in the camp and during my first

few days he made a point of telling anyone who came near the engine that I was there as a agent provocateur.

When it eventually dawned on him that I was not at Bordesley as some sort of agent provocateur, he thawed out and regaled me – several times a shift – with his early days on the Welshpool & Llanfair Light Railway and how each night would clean one of the company's two engines; 'The Earl' and 'Countess'. When in the mood he would wax almost poetic, punctuating his address with photographs of the Abermule disaster, about how he worked the Salop Mail and of pounding up Talerddig with Cambrian 0-6-0's. He produced pictures of horses being used to do the shunting at somewhere like Welshpool as though it was a practice that died in the dark ages and I had to prevent myself from telling him that there were still parts of the country where it was still commonplace.

Walter was not all hot air and he went to considerable lengths to teach me things that were likely to be important in the years ahead. Working over single lines was a speciality of his and we spent hours leaning over the cabside of our 57xx collecting and surrendering unseen tokens from imaginary signalmen and posts. What the

shunters, watching from a distance, thought we were up to, I cannot imagine.

"My drivers," he would boast, "never slowed down to let me collect a staff. And I never missed one."

As an instructor, there was a lot to be said for Walter but as a driver I could sometimes have hit him. He gave no margin for initiative and had a set of instructions for everything that had to be done.

"Fire three up the sides, two in the back corners, put the injector on, knock it off, sweep up and sit down." was his creed and litany and after a few weeks I was beginning to feel more like a robot than a fireman. It was more than galling to know that other drivers gave their firemen a completely free hand whilst I had drawn one with all the inflexibility of a council clerk. I was on the point of doing something – exactly what I was not certain – about it when my father advised me to ride it out and not to let things get out of proportion.

In the event it was as well I quashed my spirit of rebellion since on my first night turn I allowed the unthinkable to happen. Our part of the yard was quiet, Walter had disappeared to the canteen for a quick game of darts whilst I was eating my heart out at not being able to manage the engine as I thought it ought to be

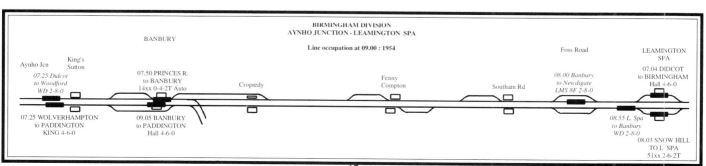

The 1950 Royal train was worked by Castle 4-6-0's 7001 'Sir James Milne' and 5000 'Launceston Castle', both from Old Oak Common but running light from Stratford to Tyseley for cleaning before taking the royal party back to Paddington in the evening. The pride taken in the working of 'the Grove' is reflected in Driver Hobbs' face as he poses with 7001 during servicing at Tyseley.

done. Leaving a small fire on the engine – keeping them blowing off got you a bad name – I disappeared into the shunters cabin, had my supper and dozed off.

The next thing I knew Walter had returned and was dancing around like a man possessed. Dragging me out of the cabin and onto the engine he open the firebox doors and pointed to where the fire ought to have been. In its place was a mass of black and very lifeless ash.

Ducking a broadside of abuse that would have raised quite a few eyebrows in the Cambrian chapels, I tried to make amends by scouring the yard for odd for odd and ends of sleepers which I lit and threw into the firebox. For once Walter refrained from giving me detailed instructions – presumably he had never been in such a position before and in any case was too involved in piling abuse on my head – and, thanks be to God, the wood kindled sufficiently for us to get on the move without too much delay.

What the penalty was for such neglect I never found out because I did have a hold over Walter that he was loath to relinquish. Cigarettes, which Walter lived on, were still rationed

and my being a non-smoker meant that he could double his supply by using my quota. It was a valuable card to hold and not only did it save my bacon after the business of the fire but eventually persuaded Walter to let me drive the engine – much to the envy of my contemporaries – when he was approaching the last of his fags. (Only much later did it occur to me that these driving privileges were only proffered when it was raining on the drivers side of the cab....).

For as long as anyone could remember 57xx 0-6-0T's had been the usual type of engine on the Bordesley shunts but by 1950 the new 94xx tanks had arrived at Tyseley and Walter and I were given one for a weeks shunting. I don't think poor old Walter noticed the difference between one engine and another but I knew that the 94xx's needed a different firing technique because they had a sloping firebox unlike the engines we usually worked. Walter saw no reason to change his instructions and by the end of the first shift, following his orders to the letter, we had a fire that could have taken us to Salop and back. All my fault, of course.

After an apprenticeship of thirty-eight weeks at Bordesley I was moved back to Tyseley and started to get some main line work, my first trip coming on February 1951 when, on a very wet Sunday morning, I relieved the 05.05 Penzance (Marazion) – Oxley class D vacuum goods for the last leg of its journey.

Although it was a Sunday, the Marazion ran through Birmingham at a busy time of the day and we had quite an interesting path. Our train followed the 04.30 Westbury – Oxley – also a class D – block and block to Bordesley where the order was reversed, our train leaving three minutes ahead. We however trickled down the relief line to wait the departure of the 10.00 Snow Hill to Great Malvern whilst the Westbury overtook us on the main line and had a clear run to Birmingham in the wake of the 08.30 Leamington – Birkenhead semi-fast.

Once the Westbury was ahead we ran main line through Snow Hill and overtook the Malvern stopping train as it called at Soho & Winson Green.

Our engine was Hall 4-6-0 6937 'Conyngham Hall' which was in good nick al-

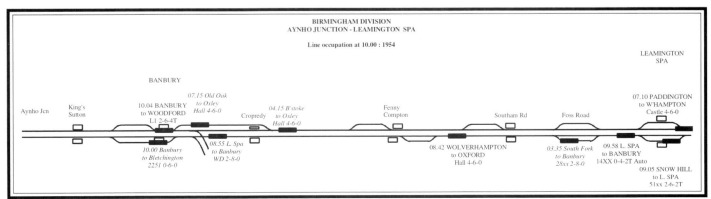

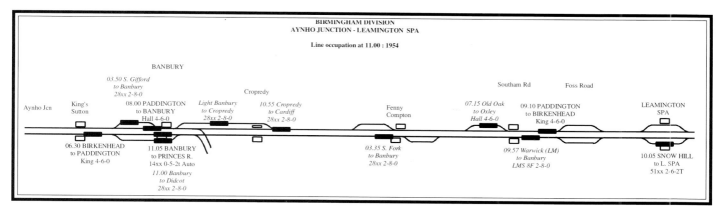

though steam pressure fluctuated more than usual. The load a light one and creeping down to Bordesley with a longish wait at the South box for the other trains to clear, we had more than enough steam. The slog through the tunnel with its 1/45 climb and some good running after Snow Hill brought the pressure down quite considerably but with Oxley only a few miles away there was no need for concern and I enjoyed myself tremendously.

After slipping through Wolverhampton Low Level station, down past Stafford Road loco, up the short steep bank, we came to a stand at the top, opposite Stafford Road Factory. I looked across at all the engines in the small yard, some looking very smart after their overhaul and making quite a contrast with the appearance of those waiting to go into the works. The board cleared and we moved slowly across the viaduct into the large yard at Oxley, where we were hooked off, and took our engine onto Oxley loco. While my mate was booking the engine on the shed and seeing if there were any orders for return working, I nipped round the shed to do a bit of spotting. The place was full and I had a field day. Recalling the difficulties I had had on a previous Sunday visit, I mentioned to my driver that I had never been round Stafford Road works and he promptly walked me over, keeping the watchman engaged in conversation whilst I made a note of everything there was to be seen.

The next day I was formally placed in the No. 9 link with Driver George Print to work on the trip and shunting workings, similar to those at Bordesley but at a variety of locations which often entailed getting there by working a train first. Perhaps the best of these duties was the Swan Village shunt – the farthest extent of shunting for Tyseley engines - which involved a fair amount of main line running, starting off with the 06.10 goods from Bordesley and returning with the 19.40 goods back to Bordesley. Business was so brisk at Swan Village that a second shunt was needed which worked a trip down from Bordesley at 10.15, shunted three hours and went back with the 14.55 to Bordesley. The arrangement fitted well with crewing requirements and the men involved changed footplates at 14.30.

The Wolverhampton district took a share in the Swan Village traffic and ran trains at 04.00 from Cannock Road and 07.00 from Oxley, both of which had to reverse on the main line to the south of Swan Village station in order to get access to the sidings, most of which were located on the branch to Great Bridge. The first of these workings – 33 bank train – was a impressive sight to watch as it hammered up the 1/60 through the station with a 57xx 0-6-0 on each end of the train even though the load was limited to twenty vehicles. A more placid but only slightly less interesting sight to be seen at Swan Village was the local passenger service to Dudley which was worked almost entirely by GWR railcars.

Whether shunting at Swan Village, Moor Street, Hockley or Handsworth – all of which were covered by the link – life was enjoyable to a degree. There was no night work or engine preparation and the element of main line work gave me considerable experience of duties on the main line even though our engines were nothing larger than 57xx and 84xx 0-6-0T's.

It goes without saying that I saw my fill of main line engines whilst keeping a look-out from the footplate during my shunting expeditions yet two of the rarest engines actually came into Tyseley loco to have their motion taken down before being towed to Crewe or Derby for overhaul. The engines concerned were survivors of the 2021 (A class) 0-6-0 Dean panniers and were 2182 from St Blazey and 2134 of Danygraig. Why they were sent to the LMS for overhaul no-one seemed to know although members of the class were favoured by the LM on the joint line at Birkenhead. Before being returned they were worked as the loco yard shunter at Tyseley for a week or so.

Suddenly a cloud started to obscure the sunshine of my idyllic life. Although the railway had been a reserved occupation during the war, the post-war national service did not seem to recognise the distinction and in April 1951 I was sent for an army medical examination which I passed as A1. Older colleagues shook their heads and said as a railway firemen I was exempt and that the medical was due to some sort of clerical mix up. Less reassuring was a conversation at the medical with an army Sergeant who assured me that I would be drafted into the Railway Operating Division.

Weeks rolled by with no more being said and just as I had been lulled into a sense of security, a buff coloured envelope arrived in the post instructing me to report to Catterick Camp for national service training. Clearly my occupation wasn't quite as reserved as some people liked to think and I consoled myself with the thought that a spell in the Railway Operating Division would be little different from an ordinary temporary transfer within the GW.

TYSELEY ALLOCATION : 1956

LOCO CLASS	IN	OUT	LOCO CLASS	IN	OUT
2897 8F : 28xx 2-8-0 (1938)	Ex Banbury 11/56		9308 4MT :43xx 2-6-0 (1932)		
2898 8F : 28xx 2-8-0 (1938)	Ex Bristol (SPM) 6/56		9319 4MT :43xx 2-6-0 (1932)	Ex Reading 8/56	To Shrewsbury 10/56
3839 8F : 28xx 2-8-0 (1938)			5317 4MT : 43xx 2-6-0 (1911)		To Oxley 7/56
2848 8F : 28xx 2-8-0 (1903)		To Chester 12/56	5325 4MT : 43xx 2-6-0 (1911)	Ex Banbury 4/56	w/d 11/56
2849 8F : 28xx 2-8-0 (1903)			5333 4MT : 43xx 2-6-0 (1911)	Ex Oxley 7/56	
2851 8F : 28xx 2-8-0 (1903)	Ex Ebbw Jcn 6/56		5369 4MT : 43xx 2-6-0 (1911)		
2856 8F : 28xx 2-8-0 (1903)			5370 4MT : 43xx 2-6-0 (1911)		
2857 8F : 28xx 2-8-0 (1903)			5386 4MT : 43xx 2-6-0 (1911)		
3012 7F : R.O.D. 2-8-0 (1917)		w/d 5/56	6307 4MT : 43xx 2-6-0 (1911)		
3017 7F : R.O.D. 2-8-0 (1917)		w/d 10/56	6321 4MT : 43xx 2-6-0 (1911)		w/d 3/56
3044 7F : R.O.D. 2-8-0 (1917)	Ex Pontypool Rd 6/56	w/d 10/56	6342 4MT : 43xx 2-6-0 (1911)		
6614 5MTT : 56xx 0-6-2T (1927)		To Canton 6/56	7317 4MT : 43xx 2-6-0 (1911)		
6620 5MTT : 56xx 0-6-2T (1927)		To Shrewsbury 1/56	8415 4FT : 94XX 0-6-0T (1949)		
6620 5MTT : 56xx 0-6-2T (1927)	Ex Neyland 8/56	To Duffryn 9/56	8468 4FT : 94XX 0-6-0T (1949)		
6644 5MTT : 56xx 0-6-2T (1927)		To Canton 2/56	9432 4FT : 94XX 0-6-0T (1949)		
6668 5MTT : 56xx 0-6-2T (1927)			9498 4FT : 94XX 0-6-0T (1949)		
6669 5MTT : 56xx 0-6-2T (1927)		To Gloucester 6/56	2238 3MT : 2251 0-6-0 (1930)		
73036 5MT 4-6-0 (1951)	Ex Shrewsbury 10/56		2257 3MT : 2251 0-6-0 (1930)		
73037 5MT 4-6-0 (1951)	Ex Shrewsbury 10/56		2279 3MT : 2251 0-6-0 (1930)		
6971 5MT : MOD-HALL 4-6-0 (1944)			2296 3MT : 2251 0-6-0 (1930)		To Wrexham 6/56
7908 5MT : MOD-HALL 4-6-0 (1944)			3625 3FT : 57xx 0-6-0T (1933)		
7912 5MT : MOD-HALL 4-6-0 (1944)			3660 3FT : 57xx 0-6-0T (1933)		
7913 5MT : MOD-HALL 4-6-0 (1944)			3673 3FT : 57xx 0-6-0T (1933)		
7918 5MT : MOD-HALL 4-6-0 (1944)			3689 3FT : 57xx 0-6-0T (1933)		
7812 5MT : MANOR 4-6-0 (1938)	Ex Newton Abbot 6/56	To Newton Abbot 7/56	3693 3FT : 57xx 0-6-0T (1933)		
7813 5MT : MANOR 4-6-0 (1938)	Ex Newton Abbot 6/56	To Newton Abbot 7/56	3769 3FT : 57xx 0-6-0T (1933)		To Wolverhampton 2/56
7818 5MT : MANOR 4-6-0 (1938)			4648 3FT : 57xx 0-6-0T (1933)		
7821 5MT : MANOR 4-6-0 (1938)			9608 3FT : 57xx 0-6-0T (1933)		
4904 5MT : HALL 4-6-0 (1928)			9614 3FT : 57xx 0-6-0T (1933)		
4988 5MT : HALL 4-6-0 (1928)			9635 3FT : 57xx 0-6-0T (1933)		
5912 5MT : HALL 4-6-0 (1928)			9680 3FT : 57xx 0-6-0T (1933)		
5927 5MT : HALL 4-6-0 (1928)			9682 3FT : 57xx 0-6-0T (1933)		
6904 5MT : HALL 4-6-0 (1928)			9724 3FT : 57xx 0-6-0T (1933)		
6853 5MT : GRANGE 4-6-0 (1936)			9733 3FT : 57xx 0-6-0T (1933)		
6861 5MT : GRANGE 4-6-0 (1936)			9753 3FT : 57xx 0-6-0T (1933)		
6866 5MT : GRANGE 4-6-0 (1936)			9798 3FT : 57xx 0-6-0T (1933)		
6105 4MTT 61xx 2-6-2T (1931)			5736 3FT : 57xx 0-6-0T (1929)		To Newport (Pill) 2/56
6116 4MTT 61xx 2-6-2T (1931)			5738 3FT : 57xx 0-6-0T (1929)		
6118 4MTT 61xx 2-6-2T (1931)			5790 3FT : 57xx 0-6-0T (1929)		
6134 4MTT 61xx 2-6-2T (1931)			7713 3FT : 57xx 0-6-0T (1929)		
6139 4MTT 61xx 2-6-2T (1931)			7735 3FT : 57xx 0-6-0T (1929)		
6166 4MTT 61xx 2-6-2T (1931)			7758 3FT : 57xx 0-6-0T (1929)		
8108 4MTT : 81xx 2-6-2T (1938)			7763 3FT : 57xx 0-6-0T (1929)		
4110 4MTT : 51xx 2-6-2T (1928)		To Wellington 12/56	8700 3FT : 57xx 0-6-0T (1929)		
4111 4MTT : 51xx 2-6-2T (1928)			8713 3FT : 57xx 0-6-0T (1929)	Ex Oxley 2/53	
4116 4MTT : 51xx 2-6-2T (1928)			7438 2PT : 74xx 0-6-0T (1936)		
4155 4MTT : 51xx 2-6-2T (1928)			12070 0F : 350hp 0-6-0		
4170 4MTT : 51xx 2-6-2T (1928)			12071 0F : 350hp 0-6-0		
4172 4MTT : 51xx 2-6-2T (1928)			12072 0F : 350hp 0-6-0		
5156 4MTT : 51xx 2-6-2T (1928)			12087 0F : 350hp 0-6-0		
5163 4MTT : 51xx 2-6-2T (1928)			13004 0F : 350hp 0-6-0		
5166 4MTT : 51xx 2-6-2T (1928)			13025 0F : 350hp 0-6-0		
5181 4MTT : 51xx 2-6-2T (1928)			13026 0F : 350hp 0-6-0		
5192 4MTT : 51xx 2-6-2T (1928)			13027 0F : 350hp 0-6-0		
5198 4MTT : 51xx 2-6-2T (1928)			13028 0F : 350hp 0-6-0		
3101 4MTT : 31xx 2-6-2T (1928)			13029 0F : 350hp 0-6-0		
9303 4MT :43xx 2-6-0 (1932)		To Banbury 9/56	13192 0F : 350hp 0-6-0		

THE OTHER HALF

Great Central R.O.D 9757 of the Egyptian State Railways passes Fanara with a northbound goods in February 1953. Ostensibly a 2-8-0 and little different in appearance from those based at Tyseley, careful inspection reveals the coupling rod missing between the first and second driving wheels. Whether or not the engines were designated as 2-2-6-0's was never ascertained.

Two staff officers sat in the bowels of the war office. One of them picked a piece of paper from a vast pile and looked at it.

"I say sir, " he said to his colleague, "there shouldn't be a problem matching this chap up."

"Oh." murmured the other looking up.

"Well. According to this he's a railwayman – a fireman apparently. Just the thing for the R.O.D. don't you think. I mean they're running pretty short of railway chaps just now."

"Where's he from?"

The younger man read through the form.

"Here it is. Place called Birmingham, which is – er – somewhere the other side of Potters Bar…..."

He read on.

"I've got it. He's a fireman at somewhere called Tyseley – Great Western. Well just the job. I'll have him send down to Longmoor right away."

"Hold on a minute. Great Western did you say? No good for the R.O.D."

"But he knows all about these engine things, sir. Be jolly useful there, wouldn't you say."

"Absolutely not. Always trouble with these Great Western wallahs – can't get on with the other chaps. They want to go round putting copper caps on chimneys and all that sort of caper. Colonel won't like it. Remember that last one we had? Told the adjutant's wife that the second coming was going to happen in Swindon and that all the world's natural meridians met in Bristol."

"Bless my soul!"

"Exactly. What would Monty think. Send him to the signals section – fellah can spend his time sending morse code. Railways have signals so he should feel quite at home…."

Thus, and as a result of the above machinations or something very much like them, The R.O.D. and I were spared each others company and I spent the greater part of 1952 sending morse code from various parts of North Africa, a sojourn which included several interesting long distance railway journeys in the Sudan and Eritrea. Towards the end of the year I found myself in Egypt, billeted almost of top of the 47th milepost (from Port Said) of the Egyptian State Railways where I spent a great deal of time confounding the Queen's enemies by observing the highly interesting movements on the main line.

To insert into a narrative on the Great Western a few paragraphs concerning an overseas railway may appear to border on the unforgivable but in the first place I had been taken away from my vocation at Tyseley and in the second I discovered a link with the GWR which, though tenuous, may act as mitigation for the diversion.

I quickly learnt that the Egyptian State Railways were not one of the ramshackle affairs that are popularly supposed to pass for railways anywhere east of Rome and in fact the system was quite sophisticated and very heavily used. Looking through a pre-war timetable I discovered that not only had it been possible to cover the 148 miles between Cairo and Port Said in less than three and a half hours – good going by any reckoning – but many of the services had been equipped with Pullman cars. What a shame it was that wars and the development of the aeroplane stifled the Cape to Cairo proposal.

In 1953 the passenger service did not appear to have been restored to its pre-war position and most of the trains I saw were goods services although there were a good deal of them.

My first view of the line was not encouraging since there was nothing to see except an up and a down line passing through the desert, the four-foot being entirely covered – like most things in Egypt – by sand. In the distance and coming towards me was a plume of black oily smoke belching high into the still warm air accompanied by an exhaust beat that was vaguely familiar.

As the train got nearer I thought that I was dreaming since at the head of the train was none other than an ex Great Central R.O.D. 2-8-0, of which of course we had a number on the Great Western. As soon as it and its train had lumbered by, another goods train passed in the opposite direction, doing a good lick downhill behind a Stanier 2-8-0. Apart from the sand and flies it was almost like being at Banbury.

Apart from their conversion to oil burning both engines were quite recognisable except that, for some reason, the Great Central engines had had the coupling rod removed from the leading drivers turning them into 4-6-0's (or perhaps 2-2-6-0's). I could not find out why this had been done - presumably there was a good reason for it – although none of the Stanier engines had been modified in the same way.

Standing in a desert and seeing two home-made products, I was wondering what the local variety was like when a third train came by, hauled by a small-wheeled (about 4' 6") 2-6-0 of very English appearance but not of a design I recognised.

Goods trains formed by far and away the greater proportion of services and the only passenger train I observed ran north in the very early morning to return in the afternoon. It was however worth turning out for since the working, which consisted of six white bogie coaches, was worked by an Atlantic 4-4-2 of curious appearance; the front part having echoes of Belgian design, the centre French and the rear

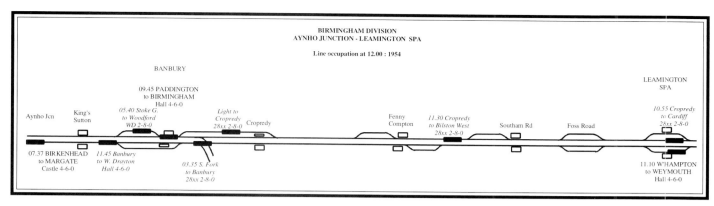

BIRMINGHAM DIVISION
AYNHO JUNCTION - LEAMINGTON SPA

Line occupation at 12.00 : 1954

like nothing I'd seen before. For all their short-falls in terms of appearance, they seemed to run well and certainly streaked past my milepost.

Although the Atlantics and 2-8-0's made a curious contrast with each other, there was not a great deal of variety on the ESR – or at least the part of it I saw – and the fleet seemed to consist only of both types of 2-8-0, the Atlantics and two types of Mogul, a small version for goods work and a larger for passenger traffic.

After nine months at milepost 47 the time came for me to return to England and in June 1953 I resumed my duties at Tyseley, none the worst for having done my bit to put the world to rights.

Having hardly set foot on an engine since leaving England there was nothing I would have liked better than to have taken a King up to Paddington on a two-hour express but the chief clerk cooled my impatience by telling me that the railway assumed that a period of acclimatisation would be needed and that I would do a spell of shunting in the cripple link before resuming my proper position in the links.

The cripple link got its name from the fact that its drivers were men who had come off main line workings because of some infirmity (usually old age) or other and my driver – Archie Sanders – was no exception. With retirement fast approaching he hardly had the strength to haul himself onto the engine and had long since redesigned his own set of duties to make sure that his firemen did rather more than they were paid for. Charlie didn't see why he should oil the inside motion or compile the engineman's record (and a dozen other tasks) whilst a youngster blooming with health and youth was available and as result most firemen finding they were booked with Archie would move heaven and earth to get another job. For me though it was just what the doctor ordered and I was only too happy to throw myself back into railway life by doing anything that needed doing.

Our duties involved the shunting at Hockley goods, a mile or so north of Snow Hill, where no less than three engines were employed for the greater part of the day. On such jobs we rarely ran in one direction for more than a few yards and we would run back and forward, back and forward all day, poor old Archie cursing the

fitters each time he struggled to altered the reversing lever. I knew without him having to say a word that another job was about to be added to the fireman's quota so before he could open his mouth I suggested that life might be easier if I moved the lever every time we changed direction.

We must have looked a proper set of comics to the shunters who would handsignal to two men on the driver's side, one of whom would operate the reverser whilst the other would open the regulator. Every time we changed direction Charlie would mutter:

"I'll ask them fitters to look at that lever."

But he never did.

I spent three months in the cripple link before picking up my place in No. 9 link where I was paired with Driver Arthur Gould – a pretty decent sort of a chap – working early morning goods trips from Bordesley to locations in the Birmingham area and shunting the yards. One week was very much like another except that we had a couple of star turns in the link, one preparing a Hall 4-6-0 for the 08.00 Birmingham to Hereford and running it light to Snow Hill and the other the 12.40 semi-fast from Snow

A Stanier LMS 8F masquerades as Egyptian State Railways 878 and runs north through Fanara in March 1953. The LMS cabs were a blessing in the temperate English climate but in the desert conditions on the footplate must have come close to being unbearable.

The Egyptian Atlantics which looked like something out of a Franco-Belgian O-gauge train set. In spite of appearances they seemed to run very well and usually powered the daily Suez - Port Said express. The sand which permeated everything must have been a thorn in the side of the Egyptian valve-setters.

Hill to Lapworth on Saturdays. The first of these duties enable one to work an engine that did not have pannier tanks whilst the other actually got me onto a passenger train on the main line.

Alas, I did not cover myself with glory on my first trip with the 12.40. Standing ready to leave in Snow Hill and desperately anxious not to show myself up by running short of steam, I ladled a good proportion of 4116's bunker into the firebox and nearly killed it. We got to Acocks Green, our first stop, in the booked time so far as I could tell but came to a stand with a black

The 12.40 Snow Hill to Lapworth may not seemed much in the timetable but to a fireman on his first passenger trip it was quite a challenge especially as the Saturday version was a heavily used season ticket train. Timing was critical since the 12.45 Birmingham to Leamington was right behind and any delay to the 12.40 would be transmitted to the following train. Unlike most local trains the 12.40 ran non-stop through Bordesley, Small Heath and Tyseley.

fire and the needle falling like a brick. We pulled away with only 100lbs on the clock and Arthur had to nurse the 2-6-2T pretty gently between the remaining stations.

It took until Lapworth, where we turned and worked the 13.36 all stations back to Birmingham, before the fire began to show and we went from one extreme to the other with the engine blowing off all the way to Snow Hill without my having to touch the shovel. It was no way to fire an engine though and I revised my ideas pretty quickly.

Arthur could have torn a strip off me but he didn't and by way of thanking him providence later presented me with a challenge which balanced the books.

We had been given an additional Sunday duty, working a 22xx 0-6-0 on a fully loaded special goods from Bordesley to Oxley sidings. Next to the engine was an open goods wagon followed by about half a dozen empty petrol tanks.

Getting the road, we pulled out of the down yard onto the down relief road which was not the easiest of routes since we had to negotiate the Moor Street crossover at the foot of the 1/45 bank to Snow Hill at 25 mph.

We entered the tunnel with the train trickling over the relief to main crossover and as soon as Arthur judged the points to be clear he opened up the 0-6-0, giving it the works in order to avoid stalling on the bank. It worked too well since the exhaust of the engine contained a fair percentage of my fire and as we came out of the tunnel and passed the south end of Snow Hill, everyone on the platform seemed to be dancing up and down and pointing furiously at our train. I looked back and saw the wagon next to the engine well ablaze with its flames waving dangerously close to the tankers.

I shouted to Arthur who shut off and brought to train to a pretty smart stop at the north end of the station. The signalman gesticulated in the direction of the water column and, getting the message, I told Arthur to ease the engine forward as far as the column as soon as I gave him the word. Nipping off the engine I uncoupled the burning wagon, yelled to Arthur and ran like a scalded cat to the column wheel.

With water cascading all over the place it did not take long to get the fire out and I presumed our next job would be to shunt the wagon, which had extensive damage to the sides and floor, somewhere out of the way before returning to our train. A rather phlegmatic carriage and wagon examiner had different ideas and after kicking the smouldering vehicle a couple of times declared it fit to continue its journey. Arthur and I raised our eyebrows a little but, as he was the expert, we backed up to the train and carried on to Oxley as though nothing had happened.

Leaning out of the cab at Oxley, waiting for the road with our return working and hailing myself as the hero of the moment by saving Birmingham and its suburbs from certain immolation from exploding oil tankers, I was brought back to earth by our guard who turned to me after giving Arthur details of the load.

"Fireman, when you hook off in Snow Hill like you did earlier, be sure to secure the rear portion of the train, as I had a very difficult job in holding it with my brake."

I bit my lip and decided to let Birmingham burn the next time.

Soon afterwards I was promoted to No.8 link – the down local link – which ran goods train from Bordesley to either Oxley, Stourbridge or Banbury together with a good deal of inter-

Literally motionless. 2021 class 0-6-0PT 2134 of Swansea (Danygraig) stands at Tyseley after being hauled from Derby where it had been given a general overhaul in April 1950. The visit to Tyseley was to allow the motion and siderods to be refitted after which the engine worked the coal stage shunt before being sent back to South Wales. 2134 operated on the Swansea docks network and had a warning bell fitted in front of the cab.

mediate shunting. My driver was Bob Hunt, a easygoing partner who asked little more of me than avoiding smoke when passing Acocks Green since he lived there and had to answer to Mrs Hunt for any smuts that besmirched her washing.

HALSOWEN SERVICES : 1954			
Train	Arr	Co,	Dep Destination
21.10 Bordesley	00.11	GW	
		GW	01.40 Bordesley
00.30 Washwood Heath	02.13	LM	
01.45 Stourbridge Jcn	02.15	GW	02.25 Longbridge
		MR	02.50 Longbridge
03.25 Longbridge	04.05	GW	
03.50 Longbridge	04.40	MR	
		MR	05.00 Longbridge
04.15 Stourbridge Jcn	05.35	GW	
04.15 Bordesley	05.45	GW	06.16 Longbridge
Light ex Stourbridge Jcn	06.05	GW	
06.50 Old Hill pass	06.55	GW	06.55 Longbridge
07.15 Old Hill pass	07.20	GW	07.21 Longbridge
07.25 ECS Longbridge	07.54	GW	
07.50 ECS Longbridge	08.10	GW	
08.10 Longbridge	08.30	GW	
		GW	08.40 Tyseley ECS
08.20 Longbridge	09.12	MR	
		MR	09.45 Longbridge
10.52 Longbridge	11.20	MR	
		MR	11.50 Longbridge
12.55 Longbridge	13.20	MR	
		MR	13.50 Washwood Heath
13.20 Stourbridge Jcn	14.10	GW	
		GW	15.05 EBV Blowers End
ECS Tyseley	15.22	GW	
Light ex Stourbridge Jcn	16.11	GW	
15.45 Longbridge	16.15	MR	
		GW	16.30 ECS Longbridge
		GW	16.45 ECS Longbridge
17.09 pass Longbridge	17.27	GW	17.28 Old Hill
17.40 pass Longbridge	17.58	GW	17.59 Old Hill
		GW	18.07 EBV Longbridge
2 light engines Old Hill	18.40	GW	
		MR	18.31 Longbridge
		GW	19.10 Oldbury
18.55 Longbridge	19.20	GW	
		GW	19.40 Light Old Hill
Light ex Old Hill	20.10	GW	
		GW	20.25 Longbridge
		MR	20.42 Longbridge
		GW	21.00 Queens Head
		GW	22.00 Oldbury
21.50 Longbridge	22.15	GW	
22.10 Longbridge	22.35	MR	
		MR	22.50 EBV Washwood Heath
		GW	22.50 Dudley
		GW	23.50 Lye

My first trip to Banbury took place in the late summer of 1953 and was interesting in that it introduced me to some of the changes that were in the air. We worked up uneventfully on 0-6-0 2202 with a special Sunday goods and were given a brand new BR standard, 4MT 4-6-0 75045, to take back light to Tyseley. Unfortunately we did not have an opportunity to really test 75045 but I reflected that to be only the second fireman to work on a new engine might be something to bore any future grandchildren with. The interesting thing was that the 4-6-0 had just been built at Swindon yet was destined for the London Midland. Times were a-changing and 75045 was in fact en route to Accrington.

Amongst the attractions of No.8 link was the work done on the Halsowen branch, a fiercely graded nine-mile single line connecting the Snow Hill – Hereford route with the Midland main line from New Street to Bristol. Although skirting the fringes of west Birmingham the passenger service, other than a handful of workmen's trains, had disappeared in 1927 partly because Halsowen and Longbridge, the principal points on the line, were close enough to the main lines to be served by Old Hill and Northfield respectively and also because the goods service was difficult enough to work without having to run the gauntlet of local passenger trains.

Most of the Great Western turns on the line were based at Stourbridge Junction but we had a couple of workings, one being the 04.15 goods from Bordesley, the other being one of the afternoon workmen's trains from Longbridge to Old Hill. 74xx 0-6-0T Panniers were used for both diagrams and it was a distinct pleasure to work the goods, early though it was, on a summer morning when it was clear daylight as we pulled away from Bordesley.

Worked by electric staff, it was one of the few lines on which I had to remember to collect and exchange tokens, something I never really mastered. We would come off the main line at Old Hill, collect a token for the section to Halesowen and hand it in when we arrived. Since we spent half at hour at Halsowen I was spared what I regarded as the difficult contortions required when delivering and collecting on the move but if we were late away to Longbridge we would cross one of the empty workmen's trains at Rubery where the signalman would be hanging out of one of the carriage compartments. Slogging up the 1 in 50 bank I generally considered I had enough to cope with without lugging around the very heavy tokens that were used on the line and with speed rising as we topped the summit and started falling down the 1 in 60 to Rubery, the signalman and his token seemed to approach at an unbelievable speed. Somehow I managed each time to surrender and collect tokens without crashing them together in mid flight and getting one (or both) under the train.

Being both busy and isolated the branch was a reliable source of overtime especially as Great Western trains came under Midland dominion once they entered the joint section at Halesowen. One old boy – Joe Taylor – once became stuck in a snowdrift miles from anywhere on the most remote stretch of the line and sat contentedly on his 74xx mentally calculating the overtime as it mounted up. He probably assumed, if he thought about it at all, that since he was on the joint section, his overtime would deplete the exchequer at Derby and he was therefore doing his own company a great favour. Eventually the guard struggled through the snow up to the engine.

"I think we're going to be here some time."

"Aye."

"I'll walk up to the box and let them know."

The same engine, 2134, seven years later en route from Birkenhead to Swindon for scrapping. The engine was transferred from Danygraig to Birkenhead in October 1951 and remained in Merseyside dock service until being withdrawn in June 1957 having run an estimated total of just under a million miles: equivalent to about fifty miles for every day in service.

"O'roight."

"Shall I tell control to send out relief?"

Joe jumped up as though he'd had an electric shock.

"No." he roared. "Tell them to send out sandwiches…."

Not all our duties were in the sticks and one of the advantages of being in a link whose drivers worked up and down the main line was that we were the first port of call for any express work that could not be covered by the normal crews and thus it was I had my first taste of class 1 firing.

The duplication of booked trains in the 1950s was extraordinary and on a ordinary weekday from April until October it was by no means unusual to have most of the morning departures from Birkenhead – especially those to the south of England – running in two if not three parts. The twelve coach 07.35 Birkenhead to Ramsgate would usually run with an eight coach relief from Snow Hill whilst the 08.55 Paddington would be duplicated by an eight coach train from Wrexham. The most expansive of the lot was the 09.20 Birkenhead – Bournemouth which was routinely enlarged to three trains conveying a total of twenty-nine coaches: ten starting at Wolverhampton for Bournemouth and preceding the booked eleven coach service by a short margin. The through Birkenhead – Cardiff coach that was normally detached at Shrewsbury was itself developed into a full train of eight coaches. Some of the summer workings struck a rather bizarre note and one of my favourites concerned a regular entrant in the special traffic notices: "08.15 Bristol Temple Meads to Pontypool Road to be extended to Manchester."

Even this largess sometimes failed to satisfy demand and a fourth Bournemouth relief train would have to be laid on from Snow Hill which is how I came to cut my teeth on express working, the usual supply of enginemen having been exhausted by the demands of the special traffic notice.

Our train was the 12.40 Birmingham to Bournemouth West which were booked to work as far as Oxford where a Southern man would take over.

Being a newcomer to main line work – and still mindful of my narrow escape with the 12.40 local not long before – I was fortunate enough to be paired with a very understanding driver, Fred Moxey, and a good engine: Hall 4-6-0 5938 'Stanley Hall'. (To add to the pleasure of the occasion 5938 was no ordinary local engine but a stranger from far-off Carmarthen which had come down on a special goods and had enough time in its turn-round to be used on a return trip

TYSELEY ALLOCATION : 1957						
LOCO	CLASS	IN	OUT	LOCO	CLASS	IN	OUT
2897	8F : 28xx 2-8-0 (1938)			5333	4MT : 43xx 2-6-0 (1911)		
2898	8F : 28xx 2-8-0 (1938)			5341	4MT : 43xx 2-6-0 (1911)	Ex Oxley 9/57	
3839	8F : 28xx 2-8-0 (1938)			5369	4MT : 43xx 2-6-0 (1911)		
2809	8F : 28xx 2-8-0 (1903)	Ex Oxley 12/57		5370	4MT : 43xx 2-6-0 (1911)		
2841	8F : 28xx 2-8-0 (1903)	Ex Oxley 1/57	To Worcester 3/57	5378	4MT : 43xx 2-6-0 (1911)	Ex St Blazey 7/57	
2849	8F : 28xx 2-8-0 (1903)			5386	4MT : 43xx 2-6-0 (1911)		To Didcot 12/57
2851	8F : 28xx 2-8-0 (1903)			5391	4MT : 43xx 2-6-0 (1911)	Ex Reading 1/57	w/d 3/57
2856	8F : 28xx 2-8-0 (1903)			6307	4MT : 43xx 2-6-0 (1911)		
2857	8F : 28xx 2-8-0 (1903)			6342	4MT : 43xx 2-6-0 (1911)		To Stourbridge 12/57
6631	5MTT : 56xx 0-6-2T (1927)	Ex Gloucester 4/57		7317	4MT : 43xx 2-6-0 (1911)		
6668	5MTT : 56xx 0-6-2T (1927)			8415	4FT : 94XX 0-6-0T (1949)		
5651	5MTT : 56xx 0-6-2T (1924)	Ex Stourbridge 9/57		8468	4FT : 94XX 0-6-0T (1949)		
73036	5MT 4-6-0 (1951)			9432	4FT : 94XX 0-6-0T (1949)		
73037	5MT 4-6-0 (1951)			9498	4FT : 94XX 0-6-0T (1949)		To Shrewsbury 11/57
6971	5MT : MOD-HALL 4-6-0 (1944)			2238	3MT : 2251 0-6-0 (1930)		
7908	5MT : MOD-HALL 4-6-0 (1944)			2257	3MT : 2251 0-6-0 (1930)		
7912	5MT : MOD-HALL 4-6-0 (1944)			2279	3MT : 2251 0-6-0 (1930)		
7913	5MT : MOD-HALL 4-6-0 (1944)			3605	3FT : 57xx 0-6-0T (1933)	Ex Aberdare 3/57	To Worcester 4/57
7918	5MT : MOD-HALL 4-6-0 (1944)			3625	3FT : 57xx 0-6-0T (1933)		
7818	5MT : MANOR 4-6-0 (1938)			3660	3FT : 57xx 0-6-0T (1933)		
7821	5MT : MANOR 4-6-0 (1938)			3673	3FT : 57xx 0-6-0T (1933)		
4904	5MT : HALL 4-6-0 (1928)		To Shrewsbury 6/57	3689	3FT : 57xx 0-6-0T (1933)		
4943	5MT : HALL 4-6-0 (1928)	Ex Reading 2/57		3693	3FT : 57xx 0-6-0T (1933)		
4988	5MT : HALL 4-6-0 (1928)			4648	3FT : 57xx 0-6-0T (1933)		
5912	5MT : HALL 4-6-0 (1928)			9608	3FT : 57xx 0-6-0T (1933)		To Taunton 10/57
5927	5MT : HALL 4-6-0 (1928)			9614	3FT : 57xx 0-6-0T (1933)		
5984	5MT : HALL 4-6-0 (1928)	Ex Worcester 2/57	To Worcester 9/57	9635	3FT : 57xx 0-6-0T (1933)		
6904	5MT : HALL 4-6-0 (1928)			9680	3FT : 57xx 0-6-0T (1933)		
6853	5MT : GRANGE 4-6-0 (1936)			9682	3FT : 57xx 0-6-0T (1933)		
6861	5MT : GRANGE 4-6-0 (1936)			9724	3FT : 57xx 0-6-0T (1933)		
6866	5MT : GRANGE 4-6-0 (1936)			9733	3FT : 57xx 0-6-0T (1933)		
6105	4MTT 61xx 2-6-2T (1931)			9753	3FT : 57xx 0-6-0T (1933)		
6116	4MTT 61xx 2-6-2T (1931)			9798	3FT : 57xx 0-6-0T (1933)		
6118	4MTT 61xx 2-6-2T (1931)			5738	3FT : 57xx 0-6-0T (1929)		To Duffryn 4/57
6134	4MTT 61xx 2-6-2T (1931)		To Leamington 11/57	5790	3FT : 57xx 0-6-0T (1929)		To Aberbeeg 10/57
6139	4MTT 61xx 2-6-2T (1931)			7713	3FT : 57xx 0-6-0T (1929)		
6160	4MTT 61xx 2-6-2T (1931)	Ex Slough 6/57	To Slough 8/57	7735	3FT : 57xx 0-6-0T (1929)		
6166	4MTT 61xx 2-6-2T (1931)		To Severn T Jcn 10/57	7758	3FT : 57xx 0-6-0T (1929)		To Duffryn 4/58
8108	4MTT : 81xx 2-6-2T (1938)			7763	3FT : 57xx 0-6-0T (1929)		
4111	4MTT : 51xx 2-6-2T (1928)			8700	3FT : 57xx 0-6-0T (1929)		
4116	4MTT : 51xx 2-6-2T (1928)			8713	3FT : 57xx 0-6-0T (1929)		
4125	4MTT : 51xx 2-6-2T (1928)	Ex Birkenhead 3/57	To Severn. T. Jcn 10.57	7438	2PT : 74xx 0-6-0T (1936)		
4127	4MTT : 51xx 2-6-2T (1928)	Ex Birkenhead 3/57	To Severn T. Jcn 10.57	12070	0F : 350hp 0-6-0		
4146	4MTT : 51xx 2-6-2T (1928)	Ex Stourbridge 1/57	To Stourbridge 4/57	12071	0F : 350hp 0-6-0		
4155	4MTT : 51xx 2-6-2T (1928)			12072	0F : 350hp 0-6-0		
4170	4MTT : 51xx 2-6-2T (1928)			12087	0F : 350hp 0-6-0		
4172	4MTT : 51xx 2-6-2T (1928)			13004	0F : 350hp 0-6-0		
5156	4MTT : 51xx 2-6-2T (1928)		To Hereford 10/57	13026	0F : 350hp 0-6-0		
5163	4MTT : 51xx 2-6-2T (1928)			13027	0F : 350hp 0-6-0		
5166	4MTT : 51xx 2-6-2T (1928)		To Severn T. Jcn 10.57	13028	0F : 350hp 0-6-0		
5181	4MTT : 51xx 2-6-2T (1928)		To Severn T. Jcn 10.57	13029	0F : 350hp 0-6-0		
5192	4MTT : 51xx 2-6-2T (1928)			13037	0F : 350hp 0-6-0	Ex Oxley 3/57	To Oxley 4/57
5198	4MTT : 51xx 2-6-2T (1928)		To Leamington 10/57	13192	0F : 350hp 0-6-0		
3101	4MT : 31xx 2-6-2T (1938)		w/d 9/57				
5325	4MT : 43xx 2-6-0 (1911)		w/d 8/57				

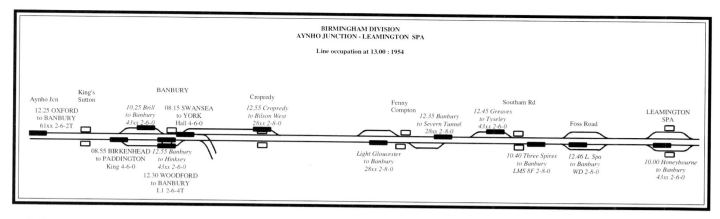

to Oxford). I was also fortunate in not being thrown completely into the deep end since we were booked to take our engine light to Queens Head carriage sidings, Handsworth, which gave me six miles of light engine running to orientate myself and generally get ready for the seventy mile trip to Oxford.

Coupling up to the stock at Handsworth, my greatest concerns were whether I should be able to keep a good head of steam with a clean fire and whether I should make a mess of things with the scoop on Rowington troughs. Tales of woe related by other firemen sprung to mind and for a horrible moment I could see myself standing short of steam on a downhill section with an empty tender whilst the remains of our scoop littered the sixfoot at Hatton. I had also done a calculation that even if the engine was in good order I should probably have to move a ton and a half of coal in each direction whilst noting that our train did not have the benefit of the usual Banbury stop.

Back on the footplate Fred put my mind at rest by showing me how to get a good fire going and just as 5938 was getting good and hot we got the signal to pull out for Snow Hill.

Once we were on the move my fears evaporated as I became too busy to bother with imaginary doubts. 5938 steamed beautifully and although I had to keep feeding it, at no time was I short of steam in any degree. The scoop was dropped accurately at Rowington and the pick up was quite successful although I held my breath until I had the scoop up and locked. We called at Leamington and carried on, right away Oxford, without any problems at all although it seemed an age before Fred sung out that the dreaming spires were in sight and shut the regulator.

As soon as we came to a stand I jumped off and uncoupled, not wishing to delay the engine change although I was amused to see that the Southern had sent a full blown 7P Pacific to take over from a modest Hall 4-6-0. Our back working was to be a similar working to the one

we had brought up and after turning the engine and having a quick bite to eat I returned to 5938 to build the fire up whilst Fred went round with the oil.

With our Hall looking rather small against the ugly bulk of the Spam which brought our train in, we backed onto the stock, hooked up and pulled away. 5938 was sizzling away nicely to begin with but by the time we had passed Kidlington we seemed to be heading for trouble with pressure falling although there appeared to be nothing amiss with the fire. I wondered helplessly what on earth was the matter with the thing.

"Give it a good lift up." Called Fred looking in the firebox and the penny dropped. It was something I should have done at Oxford and quick as a flash I turned put the jet on, pulled down the pricker and gave the fire a good lift to get some air under it. It did the trick and from Aynho onwards the whole trip was a piece of cake. It was a lesson I never forgot and many a time afterwards I was able to transform a poorly steaming engine through the simple expedient of lifting the fire.

Some years later on this same job I had a completely different experience. Our engine was Hall 5912 'Queen's Hall' and I was firing to Driver Owen Williams. We had come down Hatton bank at a fair pace, over the canal bridge when, just before we passed under the next road bridge, I saw a young lad lift up his arm and throw something at us. Instinctively I moved in from my side of the footplate and next thing there was an almighty crash as the front cab window at my side shattered into a thousand pieces. There seemed to be glass everywhere and it was amazing that so much glass could come from such a small pane.

Such incidents happened but they were mercifully rare, at least until a week or so before my run on 5912. The BBC in one of their new television drama's had a plot which revolved around a lout who slung a brick at an engine and

blinded the driver. Now half the teenagers in the country seemed to be at it, having been giving lessons on how to stone trains by some stupid producer.

We ran into Leamington, where Owen reported the matter. I knocked out what bits of glass remained in the frame, swept it all up, and deposited it in the firebox. We thought of asking for a fresh engine but knowing the rubbish they kept at Leamington decided to press on and get the window fixed whilst we were at Oxford.

I usually enjoyed the run but, quite apart from my shaking, the day was chilly and the wind that howled through the open gap was not only freezing cold but was carrying lubrication oil – most of which ended up over me - which 5912 seemed to be losing from its front end.

The express work was great fun but the real value of being in the link came from learning how to handle heavy unbraked goods trains with 57xx 0-6-0T's, 31xx and 51xx 2-6-2T's and 56xx 0-6-2T's. With only half the wheels of a tender engine, keeping mineral trains under control with a tank engine was more of an art than a science and I was fortunate that I worked with drivers who were willing to let me take over the regulator and handbrake - about all the stopping power we had – to learn how it was done.

Earning a little more than I had as a cleaner and still unable to distinguish between business and pleasure, my 'ref', which accompanied me on all firing expeditions, gave second place to a new camera. In 1953 there was no reason to believe that steam would not go on forever but I was conscious that the work I did contained very much more interest than most jobs and it seemed sensible to record it on film as I went along. Drivers seeing me snap away at some commonplace Castle or Hall thought I was mad – and generally said so – until I turned the camera towards them when they would immediately adopt a style of pose that would not have disgraced Hollywood.

LEARNING LOOSE COUPLED

Although the 43xx 2-6-0's dated from 1911 and had been superseded by large numbers of 4-6-0's, over two hundred and thirty remained at work during the early 1950's. Their size belied their usefulness since their goods haulage capacity was identical to that of a Hall 4-6-0. 5368 of Gloucester passes Toddington circa 1953 with the 13.10 Bordesley to Stoke Gifford goods, a fifty-eight wagon working which did not reach its destination until 19.03. 5368 was a well travelled engine, moving from Neyland to Gloucester in October 1952 and to Reading in September 1953 after a brief stay at Plymouth, Laira, in May 1953. It was withdrawn after a working life of thirty-nine years in September 1958.

One thing you had to learn about quickly at Birmingham was how to get a goods train up and down steep banks in one piece. One of the reasons we looked down our noses at the LNWR at New Street was because they came and went from the flatlands in the east which was as level as a putting green. We on the other hand had the fearful Hatton bank with its two miles at 1/182 to Budbrook and two and a quarter miles at 1/122, with short stretches at almost 1/100, to Hatton. In spite of its name the climbing did not finish at Hatton but continued, after a slight fall to Rowington, for seven miles as far as Solihull. To make things more difficult, the hard work involved northbound trains whose firemen had already been working for a considerable distance and it was not until passing Solihull that one could ease up.

The operators, not always the most considerate of people, regarded Hatton with some respect and took it into account when preparing the timings of trains. Normally an express from Paddington via Bicester was allowed 455 tons (500 if it was booked to a King) unless it was running to a two-hour timing in which case the load was reduced by three coaches to ensure that a decent rate could be maintained up Hatton. (Interestingly a 43xx 2-6-0 or a 51xx 2-6-2T could be booked for a two hour express provided the load did not exceed eight coaches. It would have made a fascinating proposition had it ever been put to the test.)

Goods trains were given a concession in the shape of an 81xx 2-6-2T (and on occasions a 22xx 0-6-0 when a 2-6-2T was not available)

81xx 2-6-2T WARWICK BANKER			
Arr	Point	Dep	Train
	Warwick	06.23	00.30 Old Oak - Tyseley
06.37	Hatton	Light	
Light	Warwick	07.02	05.45 Banbury - Severn T. Jcn
07.27	Hatton	Light	
Light	Warwick	12.10	10.55 Banbury - Cardiff
12.42	Hatton	Light	
Light	Warwick	13.35	12.35 Banbury - Severn T. Jcn
13.51	Hatton	Light	
Light	Warwick	15.27	13.30 Banbury - Margam
15.46	Hatton	Light	
Light	Warwick	17.21	15.00 Banbury - Cardiff
17.40	Hatton	Light	
Light	Warwick	19.50	18.50 Cropredy - Pengam
20.12	Hatton	Light	
Light	Warwick	21.00	13.50 Reading - Bordesley
21.14	Hatton	Light	
Light	Warwick	22.07	20.35 Banbury - Margam
22.26	Hatton	Light	
Light	Warwick	22.59	22.00 Banbury - Severn T. Jcn
23.19	Hatton	Light	
Light	Warwick	23.20	22.30 Cropredy - Cardiff
23.48	Hatton	Light	
Light	Warwick		

The Warwick Pilot existed mainly for the iron ore trains that started in the Banbury area although it was available for any service that had doubts about Hatton Bank. A second engine had to assist with the banking on the night shift since the 21.10 Cropredy - Croes Newydd left Warwick at the time time as the 22.00 Severn Tunnel Junction.

which assisted in rear from Warwick to Hatton, a move which prevented loads from being reduced because of the incline.

Working down trains up the climb from Warwick to Hatton and Solihull could be a worrying (and back-breaking) business but was nothing like the southbound descent where the danger of running away was always present. At Widney Manor the driver would start holding the train back with the engine brake and as we passed under the three-arch bridge at Hatton station I would screw the tender handbrake hard on in order to provide a little more braking power and to get the wagons buffered up to the tender. Budbrook box, two miles down the bank from Hatton, generally provided an element of nail-biting since every trip downhill raised doubts as to the ability to stop there should the signals be on. Fortunately the block section at Warwick North provided a buffer between Budbrook and Warwick station and I never recollect seeing Budbrook's distant in the on position.

The Warwick station distant was the real worrier since a caution indication suggested that we were being routed into the up station loop which, because of the low speed required through the entrance points, meant slowing down to a crawl as soon as the signal was sighted. If braking was left even a fraction too late, stopping at the far end of the loop was next to impossible and more than one normally conscientious soul found himself the wrong side of the home signal – and on the wrong line – when he eventually

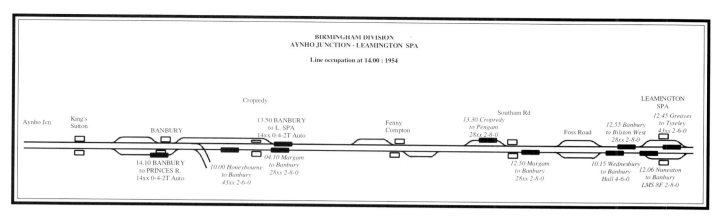

came to a stand. Since the reason for being put inside on the loop was to allow a faster train to overtake on the adjacent main line, reversals back inside the loop were undertaken pretty hastily. Fortunately the signalmen at Warwick seemed to be an unusually sympathetic bunch and such run-throughs were generally hushed up; a level of co-operation that was as welcome as it was unusual. It only needed a bit of brass around, the station master or an inspector, for Form One's to be scattered about like confetti.

The guards of such trains were not usually as understanding. Having braked their train nicely to a halt, they would just be sliding into their seat when with an almighty jolt the brakevan would be sent backwards propelling the unsuspecting occupant from one end of the van to the other. It was not unknown for the guard to be hurled out of his van into the four foot.

If on the other hand Warwick's distant was off one had to be prepared for the danger of the train becoming divided as it climbed over the 'cut bridge' when the line rose for a short distance before dropping again through the station. The usual method of avoiding a severe rug was to ease the tender brake off to get the train buffered-up on both sides of the hump.

It may be that a combination of experience and the right type of engine provided the key to getting from Hatton to Leamington in one piece. One Tyseley crew who took a coal train from Bordesley to Banbury in June 1962 – the time when the railways were just starting to fall apart – found themselves with LMS Royal Scot 46123 'Royal Irish Fusilier' which had somehow come across from its home shed at Saltley and with its 6'9" drivers should never have been used on a loose coupled train.

What sort of speed they were doing down the bank was not recorded – the driver had things other than speedometer needles on his mind – but the Budbrook signalman noticed nothing amiss and did not therefore say anything to Warwick who decided to stick the train in the up loop. It was an unfortunate decision and the Scot all but ended on top of the up platform surface after ploughing through the exit points and through the stops.

The train was rerailed, hauled back towards Budbrook and taken on to Banbury by another engine later in the day but 46123 remained isolated for some time before it was dragged back onto the loop and returned to the London Midland who took it out of traffic a few months later.

Trying though it could be, the London line was like a billiard table compared to the North Warwick route where the gradients between Stratford on Avon and Birmingham were like the side of a house. Leaving Stratford for Birmingham trains were almost immediately faced

with a mile and a half at 1 in 75 which acted as a prelude to Danzey bank where trains had to pound up a ten mile slog at 1 in 150 to Earlswood Lakes. To make matters even more difficult, most of the engines that had to be flogged up the banks had already been steaming continuously for some distance and were not always in the peak of condition.

With a respectable local service to Snow Hill and Leamington few goods train ever got a clear run through Stratford - they had to stop for water in any event - and to get them moving again a Tyseley-based 22xx 0-6-0 would buffer up to the brake van and give banking assistance up the 1 in 75 to Wilmcote. If however assistance was needed through to Earlswood, the 0-6-0 was allowed to continue beyond Wilmcote but had to be coupled to the brakevan and it was therefore necessary to make it clear at Stratford precisely what sort of assistance was required and it fell to the fireman of the train engine to walk back and ensure that the banking crew and signalmen knew what was wanted.

Requests for assistance through to Earlswood usually met with some resistance at Stratford, partly because the Inspector disliked losing one of his bankers for so long but more especially because the banking crew disliked the sixteen-mile tender-first return journey. Need-

less to say it was generally raining when banking to Earlswood was requested.

Two bankers were held at Stratford for most of the day, one banking goods trains whilst the other attended to passenger trains, shunting and the odd goods trip to S & M Junction.

Passenger banking was limited to a push in rear as far as the East signalbox after which train engines were supposed to fend for themselves. On at least one occasion things worked in reverse as happened when one of the then new County 4-6-0's ran in with the ten-coach 10.35 Penzance – Wolverhampton 'Cornishman'. At that time Tyseley was sending a pair of its 90xx 'Dukedog' 4-4-0's to Stratford and 9010 ran up to the rear coach, ready to push.

After station work had been completed the right away was given to the banker who whistled up, giving the County authority to blow the brakes off. The banker driver opened up his 4-4-0 which went into an immediate slip whilst the big 4-6-0, making an exhaust like a cannon, romped out of the station leaving 9010 skidding wildly and barely managing a walking pace as the Cornishman roared its way towards Bearley. Eventually, with the tail lamp of the express disappearing ahead, the banking driver gave up any pretence at being useful and limped back to his siding, wilting under the amused laughter of

TYSELEY ALLOCATION : 1958							
LOCO CLASS	IN	OUT		LOCO CLASS	IN	OUT	
2885 8F : 28xx 2-8-0 (1938)	Ex Stourbridge 6/58			5333 4MT : 43xx 2-6-0 (1911)			
2886 8F : 28xx 2-8-0 (1938)	Ex Banbury 4/58			5341 4MT : 43xx 2-6-0 (1911)			
2897 8F : 28xx 2-8-0 (1938)				5345 4MT : 43xx 2-6-0 (1911)	Ex Bristol (SPM) 7/58	To Bristol (SPM) 8/58	
2898 8F : 28xx 2-8-0 (1938)		To Ebbw Jcn 1/58		5369 4MT : 43xx 2-6-0 (1911)			
3831 8F : 28xx 2-8-0 (1938)	Ex Banbury 4/58			5370 4MT : 43xx 2-6-0 (1911)			
3839 8F : 28xx 2-8-0 (1938)				5378 4MT : 43xx 2-6-0 (1911)			
2809 8F : 28xx 2-8-0 (1903)		To Newton Abbot 6/58		6305 4MT : 43xx 2-6-0 (1911)	Ex St Blazey 7/58	To Carmarthen 8/58	
2812 8F : 28xx 2-8-0 (1903)	Ex Banbury 8/58	To Stourbridge 12/58		6307 4MT : 43xx 2-6-0 (1911)			
2849 8F : 28xx 2-8-0 (1903)				6337 4MT : 43xx 2-6-0 (1911)	Ex Taunton 7/58	To Taunton 10/58	
2851 8F : 28xx 2-8-0 (1903)				6357 4MT : 43xx 2-6-0 (1911)	Ex Shrewsbury 4/58		
2856 8F : 28xx 2-8-0 (1903)				6360 4MT : 43xx 2-6-0 (1911)	Ex Bristol (SPM) 7/58	To Bristol (SPM) 8/58	
2857 8F : 28xx 2-8-0 (1903)		To Pontypool Rd 6/58		6367 4MT : 43xx 2-6-0 (1911)	Ex Worcester 4/58	To Kidderminster 8/58	
2882 8F : 28xx 2-8-0 (1903)	Ex Banbury 8/58			6377 4MT : 43xx 2-6-0 (1911)	Ex Taunton 7/58	To Carmarthen 9/58	
6631 5MTT : 56xx 0-6-2T (1927)				6391 4MT : 43xx 2-6-0 (1911)	Ex Bristol (SPM) 7/58	To Bristol (SPM) 8/58	
6668 5MTT : 56xx 0-6-2T (1927)				6399 4MT : 43xx 2-6-0 (1911)	Ex Westbury 12/58		
5606 5MTT : 56xx 0-6-2T (1924)	Ex Stourbridge 9/58			7317 4MT : 43xx 2-6-0 (1911)			
5651 5MTT : 56xx 0-6-2T (1924)		To Shrewsbury 10/58		8415 4FT : 94XX 0-6-0T (1949)			
5658 5MTT : 56xx 0-6-2T (1924)	Ex Stourbridge 9/58			8468 4FT : 94XX 0-6-0T (1949)			
73036 5MT 4-6-0 (1951)		To Shrewsbury 1/58		9432 4FT : 94XX 0-6-0T (1949)			
73037 5MT 4-6-0 (1951)		To Shrewsbury 1/58		2238 3MT : 2251 0-6-0 (1930)			
6971 5MT : MOD-HALL 4-6-0 (1944)				2257 3MT : 2251 0-6-0 (1930)			
7908 5MT : MOD-HALL 4-6-0 (1944)				2279 3MT : 2251 0-6-0 (1930)			
7912 5MT : MOD-HALL 4-6-0 (1944)				3625 3FT : 57xx 0-6-0T (1933)			
7913 5MT : MOD-HALL 4-6-0 (1944)		To Bristol (SPM) 4/58		3660 3FT : 57xx 0-6-0T (1933)			
7918 5MT : MOD-HALL 4-6-0 (1944)				3673 3FT : 57xx 0-6-0T (1933)			
7818 5MT : MANOR 4-6-0 (1938)				3689 3FT : 57xx 0-6-0T (1933)			
7821 5MT : MANOR 4-6-0 (1938)		To Hereford 2/58		3693 3FT : 57xx 0-6-0T (1933)			
4943 5MT : HALL 4-6-0 (1928)				4648 3FT : 57xx 0-6-0T (1933)			
4974 5MT : HALL 4-6-0 (1928)	Ex Pontypool Rd 11/58			9614 3FT : 57xx 0-6-0T (1933)			
4982 5MT : HALL 4-6-0 (1928)	Ex Cardiff (C) 11/58			9635 3FT : 57xx 0-6-0T (1933)			
4988 5MT : HALL 4-6-0 (1928)		To Bristol (SPM) 4/58		9680 3FT : 57xx 0-6-0T (1933)			
5912 5MT : HALL 4-6-0 (1928)				9682 3FT : 57xx 0-6-0T (1933)			
5927 5MT : HALL 4-6-0 (1928)				9724 3FT : 57xx 0-6-0T (1933)			
6904 5MT : HALL 4-6-0 (1928)				9733 3FT : 57xx 0-6-0T (1933)			
6853 5MT : GRANGE 4-6-0 (1936)				9753 3FT : 57xx 0-6-0T (1933)			
6861 5MT : GRANGE 4-6-0 (1936)				9798 3FT : 57xx 0-6-0T (1933)			
6866 5MT : GRANGE 4-6-0 (1936)				7713 3FT : 57xx 0-6-0T (1929)			
6105 4MTT : 61xx 2-6-2T (1931)				7735 3FT : 57xx 0-6-0T (1929)			
6116 4MTT : 61xx 2-6-2T (1931)				7763 3FT : 57xx 0-6-0T (1929)			
6118 4MTT : 61xx 2-6-2T (1931)		To Severn T. Jcn 7/58		8700 3FT : 57xx 0-6-0T (1929)			
6139 4MTT : 61xx 2-6-2T (1931)				8713 3FT : 57xx 0-6-0T (1929)			
8108 4MT : 81xx 2-6-2T (1938)				7438 2PT : 74xx 0-6-0T (1936)			
4111 4MTT : 51xx 2-6-2T (1928)				12070 0F : 350hp 0-6-0			
4116 4MTT : 51xx 2-6-2T (1928)		To Gloucester 8/58		12071 0F : 350hp 0-6-0			
4125 4MTT : 51xx 2-6-2T (1928)	Ex Oxford 6/58	To Oxford 7/58		12072 0F : 350hp 0-6-0			
4126 4MTT : 51xx 2-6-2T (1928)	Ex Radyr 12/58			12087 0F : 350hp 0-6-0			
4155 4MTT : 51xx 2-6-2T (1928)				13004 0F : 350hp 0-6-0			
4161 4MTT : 51xx 2-6-2T (1928)	Ex Merthyr 4/58	To Wolverhampton 10/58		13025 0F : 350hp 0-6-0			
4162 4MTT : 51xx 2-6-2T (1928)	Ex Merthyr 4/58	To Leamington 10/58		13026 0F : 350hp 0-6-0			
4170 4MTT : 51xx 2-6-2T (1928)				13027 0F : 350hp 0-6-0			
4172 4MTT : 51xx 2-6-2T (1928)				13028 0F : 350hp 0-6-0			
5163 4MTT : 51xx 2-6-2T (1928)				13029 0F : 350hp 0-6-0			
5192 4MTT : 51xx 2-6-2T (1928)		To Didcot 9/58		13192 0F : 350hp 0-6-0			
9305 4MT : 43xx 2-6-0 (1932)	Ex Southall 7/58	To Didcot 9/58					

As described in the text, coming down Warwick bank with an unfitted mineral train was a difficult enough proposition with a familiar engine and when a foreign express passenger locomotive was substituted, trouble followed. The engine concerned was Rebuilt Royal Scot 4-6-0 46123 'Royal Irish Fusilier' which failed to hold its train on the fall towards Warwick and almost ended up on the platform. The incident occurred in June 1962 yet the engine still displays a BR emblem which had been out of date for six years.

The Great Western was very keen on moving its engines from one shed to another and changed shed allocations far more quickly than was the case on other regions. Hall 4-6-0 6968 'Woodcock Hall', seen arriving in Warwick up loop with a Bordesley - Banbury coal train in May 1959, managed against the odds to survive the 1950's at one decade, being based at Reading (81D) until May 1960 when it was transferred to Westbury.

the congregated trainspotters. It was not much of an advertisement for the 4-4-0's –22xx 0-6-0's replaced them on banking duties shortly afterwards – but it gave food for thought as regards the Counties which at the time were new and taken to be the shape of things to come.

Banking being an instance of two trains in the same block section at the same time was strictly regulated and on the odd occasion when a passenger train needed more help than the shove the length of the platform provided, the banker would act as pilot and double head as far as Earlswood. It was not, however, simply a matter of banging the pilot ahead of the train engine and letting rip out of the station as was the case almost anywhere else in the country and placing the assisting engine ahead of the train engine could only be done from Stratford if the pilot was in the same class or larger than the train engine.

Since most services were worked by Hall or Castle 4-6-0's whilst the pilot was a 22xx 0-6-0, the latter had to be placed between the 4-6-0

and the first coach; a time consuming business which probably cost as much time as the incline itself.

An interesting exception to the rule, and one that was never taken up by the diagramming authorities, was that a 2-6-2 tank with driving wheels greater than 5' 7" could assist on the front of the train engine. Alas there was never a spare 51xx available at Stratford when one was needed.

Why the Great Western should have been so particular about double-heading is something long forgotten although questions should have been asked to the time. On numerous occasions I arrived in Stratford with a heavy load and poorly steaming Hall, only to have to mess around to let a 22xx 0-6-0 between my engine and the train. Once on the move the 0-6-0 always seemed to be exhausted by the time we had got to Wilmcote and on the rest of the grind to Earlswood we not only had to haul the train but had to handle the dead weight of the pilot as well.

Strictly speaking we were supposed to release the pilot at Earlswood but in practice, and provided the driver signed the road, we would continue double-headed to Snow Hill which saved time at Earlswood and allowed the 0-6-0 to turn and go back to Stratford chimney first.

The main line from Birmingham to Wolverhampton was generally level although there was a short but not insignificant hump at Handsworth Junction, two miles at 1 in 100 for down trains and three miles which varied from 1/58 and 1/147 in the opposite direction. Banking assistance was not authorised in either direction, the presumption being that northbound services had sufficient time in Snow Hill to blow up for the climb whilst the majority of up trains were re-engined at Wolverhampton and were therefore in good nick.

The Stourbridge route, very much a main line, presented quite a challenge since the gradients coming into Birmingham were such as to restrict even Castle-hauled services to a mere nine vehicles whilst the Hall 4-6-0's, which

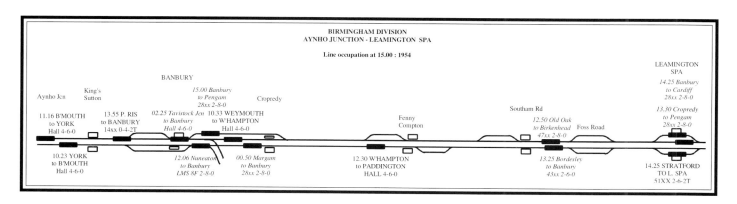

BIRMINGHAM DIVISION
AYNHO JUNCTION - LEAMINGTON SPA

Line occupation at 15.00 : 1954

The penalty for running early. 28xx 2-8-0 2856 and the 09.25 Bordesley to Swindon via Gloucester is shunted onto the goods branch at Henley to clear the down main line for the 09.35 Snow Hill - Stratford passenger. The 09.25 was booked to stand at Tyseley for half an hour but if it left Bordesley in good time it was usual to give it a run in the hope that it would get to Stratford ahead of the passenger. As can be seen above, the ploy was not always successful.

worked the majority of trains, were limited to seven coaches non-stop or six if an intermediate stop was made.

The worst of the climbing was from Lye, a mile and a quarter out of Stourbridge Junction, to Rowley Regis with gradients of around 1 in 50 for much of the way. Needless to say almost all trains were given assistance, goods services being banked in the rear whilst passenger workings often took a pilot as far as Rowley. Most of the goods banking was done by the dozen-odd 56xx 0-6-2T's – a class more normally associated with South Wales - based at Stourbridge Junction whilst 51xx 2-6-2T's were used to pilot the passenger trains.

The branch from Old Hill to Dudley – the Bumble 'ole - was no easier to work than the main line to Stourbridge especially as the crossing gates at Cox's Lane always seemed to be set in favour of road traffic. Level Crossings were not regarded as an obstruction for signalling purposes and it was quite in order for a signalman to accept a train whilst cars and lorries were crossing, closing the gates and pulling off when he judged it was appropriate. Unfortu-

nately Cox's Lane never seemed to acquire the judgement necessary and it was by no means unusual to find a handsignalman regulating the road traffic whilst a mangled set of gates lay by the lineside.

I once fired to Driver Billy Williams on an oil train from the LMS to Rowley Regis, our engine being a Stanier 8F 2-8-0 which worked through. We stopped at Blowers Lane for the guard to pin down wagon brakes to hold us back on the bank down to Cox's but Billy for some reason was impatient to get on the move and whistled up, rather early I thought, to tell the guard to return to his van.

Half a train length later Bill realised that he had been a little peremptory and told me to hop off the engine at Windmill Lane Halt and jump on the leading brake van – the Rowley Regis workings always had a van at each end – and screw the handbrake down.

It was easier said than done and as we approached the wooden platform I crouched between the engine and tender, ready to spring off. Alas, the train was doing a fair speed, I hit the platform rather hard and by the time I had

picked myself up half the train had streaked by, travelling far too fast for me to catch the trailing brake let alone the leading van. Muttering all sorts of unrepeatable descriptions at drivers generally and Bill Williams in particular I set off in pursuit on foot, expecting the skyline at any moment to be lit up as the train hit Old Hill and exploded.

It was with something approaching disappointment that I got to Cox's Lane and found that they had managed to stop normally after all. I told the guard I felt cheated by their survival.

The regular passenger service over the Bumble 'ole was operated by a GW railcar which shuttled between Dudley and Old Hill with occasional extensions to Snow Hill. In the autumn an excursion would be run from Snow Hill to Blackpool via Dudley, picking up at Old Hill (High Street), Darby End, Windmill End and Baptist End. I fell for one of these turns once and was amazed at the difficulty we had in getting away from the stops in spite of having a 51xx 2-6-2T as pilot to our 68xx Grange 4-6-0. All the same I felt I had the easier part of the job

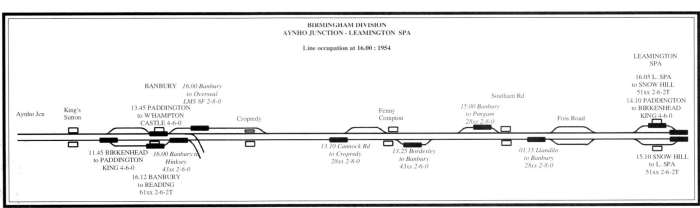

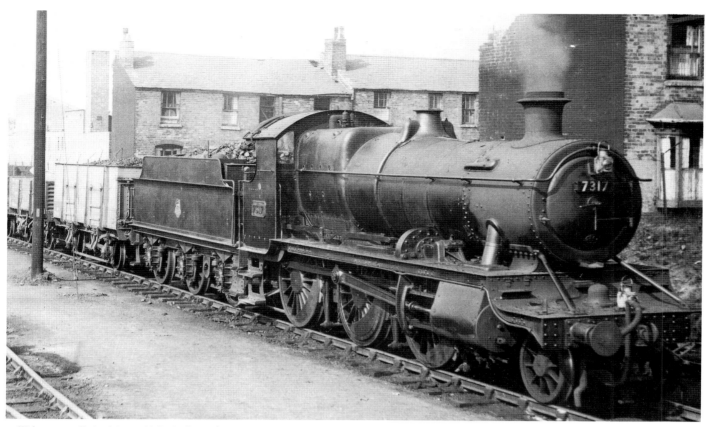

With a wagon limit of sixty vehicles in the up direction from Bordesley to Banbury and having a capacity to work loads of fifty-one minerals, the 43xx 2-6-0's were only marginally inferior to the 28xx 2-8-0's. 7317 of Tyseley wait for the right away with the 11.30 Bordesley - Banbury in March 1953.

and didn't envy my opposite number who had to return with the train in the dark, feeling his way for the dimly lit halts at which he had to draw up several times.

Snow Hill, Birmingham, could be an awkward place since it sat on the peak of two rather stiff inclines, the one from the north rising at 1/47 albeit only for about a hundred yards whilst the rise from the south consisted of about five hundred yards in tunnel at 1 in 45. Originally the latter had been in a cutting but as the city expanded it was covered over giving train crews the psychological benefit of not being able to see the track rise ahead of them. On the other had it was not a feature of the line to forget about and on a number of occasions drivers, many probably on their first trip, would shut off too early thinking they could cruise the last half mile to Birmingham, only to find themselves stuck in the tunnel and having to walk for assistance.

For most passenger trains the Moor Street incline did not present too much of a problem since express services, provided they had a clear road, usually had sufficient momentum to sweep through the tunnel and into the station without difficulty whilst the light loads of local trains lay well within the capacity of the 2-6-2 tanks.

Through goods services coughed a little but provided they were given a clear run usually got to Snow Hill without difficulty. The troubles usually came from goods workings that had started from Bordesley with an engine that was a little cool because the injector had been applied to keep things quiet waiting the right away. The Great Western wasn't keen on engines that blew off continuously in the LMS style and we had been brought up to keep them quiet even though a full boiler tended to cause priming when starting off.

As a result drivers would take things very easily whilst their firemen got everything into shape on the move, the problem being that even with a clear run there was no question of charging the bank and you would slog slowly through the tunnel echoing the engine's exhaust: "Will it….Won't it, Will it….Won't it…..".

We usually won the day but every now and again a stiff wagon or greasy rail would bring a train to a noisy halt in the tunnel which meant the fireman having to walk up to the box to arrange for the pilot to back on and give a pull into Snow Hill.

Where we did bless the surefootedness of Great Western engines was on the handful of goods working which called at Moor Street to

detach before backing out onto the down relief to continue forward. There was no question of getting a run at the bank but at least the engine was hot and usually we got to Snow Hill in one piece even though we rattled a few windows in the process.

Amongst the heaviest workings we handled were the iron ore trains which started from the iron ore sidings between Banbury and Cropredy and which came into Bordesley where Tyseley engine and men would take them over. A good engine was essential on these workings especially where Snow Hill Tunnel was concerned. The favourite was a 28xx 2-8-0 which would walk away with the load although few crews complained if they were given a Great Central ROD 2-8-0 as a substitute. The latter had no speed and waddled about the countryside like a duck but they were strong and reliable. Foreign engines, on the other hand, were a curse since they could not keep their feet and there were some long faces and loud expressions if an Austerity or LMS 8F was substituted. (Midland men swore by the latter yet we could never quite get used to them and given the same treatment as a 28xx, they would simply lose all adhesion and slip to a halt. The fault, however, may have had its roots in the fact that we saw

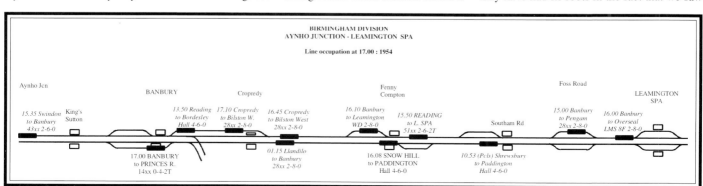

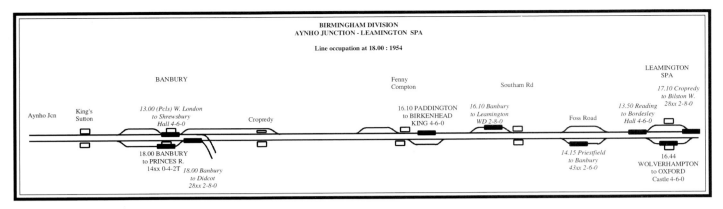

BIRMINGHAM DIVISION
AYNHO JUNCTION - LEAMINGTON SPA

Line occupation at 18.00 : 1954

very few of the class and therefore lacked the opportunity to get used to them. As for the Austerities, the less said the better….).

Now and again we would relieve a train on the main line to prevent it having to come into Bordesley and usually we would travel out to Solihull where the 'Stonies' went in to reduce their loads for the Birmingham section. We almost came to grief on one occasion when the guard, it was his first trip, asked the driver what the load was for a 28xx.

"44 equal 88" my driver replied, rather surprised that he should have to be asked.

A little later we got the right away and pulled away from Solihull, the engine working rather harder than usual. I leant back and exchanged signals with the guard.

"The brake sidelights seem a long way back." I remarked and he took a look backwards himself.

"Bordesley!" he roared at the signalman as we struggled by.

The line falls at 1 in 475 from Solihull to Olton and we needed every inch of it to get on the move whilst easing off and coming down to a walking pace to go inside at Bordesley was even more difficult since the train was pushing

us far more than usual. I doubt if we received any help from the brake since the guard was unaware that we were going into Bordesley but by leaning hard on the tender brake – God knows what the driver was doing with the reverser – we manage to come to a stand in the reception yard where I swung off the engine and walked back, counting wagons. The guard met me half way down.

"What have we come in here for?"

"Never mind that. What's our load?"

"Sixty of course."

I looked at him as though he was a lunatic, which he may have been.

"Sixty?" I echoed.

He started to look a little unsure of himself and walked back to his brake. I followed him noticing a quizzical shunter at the engine, probably asking the driver which train we were.

Inside the van the guard fumbled through his loading table trying to recall the formula he used to marshal the train at Solihull. Eventually he gave up.

"Your mate told me eighty-eight of mineral but the length limit is sixty so that's what I've made up."

I grabbed the book from him and found our section of line in it.

"My mate told you nothing of the sort. Look here. Maximum load Bordesley to West Brom' – that's us – eighty-eight goods equal to forty-four mineral with a length limit of sixty".

He didn't argue and just stared at the page I pushed under his nose.

"You'd better get up to the shunter and get us reduced before someone starts asking questions…."

We drew forward, knocked sixteen wagons onto an adjacent road, backed up to our brake and continued forward. My driver smiled as he knocked his pipe on the cab side.

"I thought we were a bit heavy. We'd have sat in Snow Hill tunnel all day with that lot."

He would have but I would have been charging all over the place. Sticking on the bank meant the guard going back to protect the train whilst the fireman went to the South box to sort out wrong line order forms; a procedure that few could remember in the heat of action. The forms were different colours, one being for the failed train, another for the assisting engine and others for the signalman and you would sit with the bobby whilst he filled them in and discussed who got which colour. He would then get the 'Big Pilot', a Hall or Grange 4-6-0, to back up to the box whilst the fireman waited to show him (what he hoped was the correct) wrong line order form. Eventually the fireman would have to guide the pilot back into the murk of the tunnel and try and remember exactly where his train had failed. Once the engines had been coupled up there then remained the job of locating the guard who was supposed to walk back to Moor Street to protect the train. With both engines coupled and the guard back in his van, the fireman would get back on his footplate and sort his fire out whilst the two drivers tried to get the train moving. Whistles would be exchanged and after a round of slipping both engines would come pounding out of the station to the satisfaction of the inevitable audience of passengers who stood on the station watching events.

The group on the down side were, unless their train had been delayed, usually just interested spectators whilst those on the up platform looked openly hostile as they hung out of the windows of their train which was not allowed to depart until we had cleared the tunnel. Which ever way you looked it was highly embarrassing.

It was instinctive to ask for an assisting engine when you stuck in the tunnel although I once saw an engine rescue itself without assistance. I was sitting in the 12.10 local from Snow Hill, on my way to Tyseley, keeping an eye on the down side since the 10.10 'Cambrian Coast'

LOCO	CLASS	IN	OUT	LOCO	CLASS	IN	OUT
			TYSELEY ALLOCATION : 1959				
48402	LMS 8F 2-8-0 (1935)	Ex Chester 5/59		75024	4MT 4-6-0 (1951)	Ex Swindon 8/59	
48412	LMS 8F 2-8-0 (1935)	Ex Chester 5/59	To Bristol (SPM) 6/59	75026	4MT 4-6-0 (1951)	Ex Chester 3/59	To Machynlleth 6/59
48415	LMS 8F 2-8-0 (1935)	Ex Chester 5/59		5318	4MT : 43xx 2-6-0 (1911)	Ex Pontypool Rd 6/59	To Pontypool Rd 9/59
48417	LMS 8F 2-8-0 (1935)	Ex Chester 5/59		5322	4MT : 43xx 2-6-0 (1911)	Ex Reading 6/59	To Swindon 8/59
48418	LMS 8F 2-8-0 (1935)	Ex Chester 5/59		5333	4MT : 43xx 2-6-0 (1911)		To Hereford 1/59
48424	LMS 8F 2-8-0 (1935)	Ex Chester 5/59		5341	4MT : 43xx 2-6-0 (1911)		To Llanelly 1/59
48430	LMS 8F 2-8-0 (1935)	Ex Chester 5/59		5369	4MT : 43xx 2-6-0 (1911)		
48444	LMS 8F 2-8-0 (1935)	Ex Chester 5/59		5370	4MT : 43xx 2-6-0 (1911)		To Llanelly 8/59
48471	LMS 8F 2-8-0 (1935)	Ex Chester 5/59		5378	4MT : 43xx 2-6-0 (1911)		To Croes Newydd 3/59
48475	LMS 8F 2-8-0 (1935)	Ex Bristol (SPM) 6/59		6307	4MT : 43xx 2-6-0 (1911)		To Croes Newydd 3/59
2885	8F : 28xx 2-8-0 (1938)		To Stourbridge 3/59	6357	4MT : 43xx 2-6-0 (1911)		To Croes Newydd 3/59
2886	8F : 28xx 2-8-0 (1938)		To Stourbridge 3/59	6399	4MT : 43xx 2-6-0 (1911)		w/d 11/59
2897	8F : 28xx 2-8-0 (1938)		To Stourbridge 3/59	7317	4MT : 43xx 2-6-0 (1911)		
3831	8F : 28xx 2-8-0 (1938)		To Stourbridge 3/59	8415	4FT : 94XX 0-6-0T (1949)		
3839	8F : 28xx 2-8-0 (1938)		To Stourbridge 3/59	8468	4FT : 94XX 0-6-0T (1949)		
2849	8F : 28xx 2-8-0 (1903)		To Didcot 11/59	9432	4FT : 94XX 0-6-0T (1949)		w/d 12/59
2851	8F : 28xx 2-8-0 (1903)		To Taunton 3/59	2211	3MT : 2251 0-6-0 (1930)	Ex Banbury 6/59	
2856	8F : 28xx 2-8-0 (1903)		To Stourbridge 3/59	2238	3MT : 2251 0-6-0 (1930)		
2882	8F : 28xx 2-8-0 (1903)		To Taunton 3/59	2257	3MT : 2251 0-6-0 (1930)		
6631	5MTT : 56xx 0-6-2T (1927)			2267	3MT : 2251 0-6-0 (1930)	Ex Worcester 2/59	
6668	5MTT : 56xx 0-6-2T (1927)			2279	3MT : 2251 0-6-0 (1930)		w/d 1/59
5606	5MTT : 56xx 0-6-2T (1924)		To Wrexham (GC) 1/59	3625	3FT : 57xx 0-6-0T (1933)		
5658	5MTT : 56xx 0-6-2T (1924)			3660	3FT : 57xx 0-6-0T (1933)		
6971	5MT : MOD-HALL 4-6-0 (1944)			3673	3FT : 57xx 0-6-0T (1933)		
7908	5MT : MOD-HALL 4-6-0 (1944)			3689	3FT : 57xx 0-6-0T (1933)		To Croes Newydd 1/59
7912	5MT : MOD-HALL 4-6-0 (1944)			3693	3FT : 57xx 0-6-0T (1933)		
7918	5MT : MOD-HALL 4-6-0 (1944)			4648	3FT : 57xx 0-6-0T (1933)		
7818	5MT : MANOR 4-6-0 (1938)		To Newton Abbot 6/59	9614	3FT : 57xx 0-6-0T (1933)		To Leamington 12/59
7821	5MT : MANOR 4-6-0 (1938)		To Newton Abbot 6/59	9635	3FT : 57xx 0-6-0T (1933)		
7824	5MT : MANOR 4-6-0 (1938)	Ex Newton Abbot 8/59		9680	3FT : 57xx 0-6-0T (1933)		
4902	5MT : HALL 4-6-0 (1928)	Ex Oxford 12/59		9682	3FT : 57xx 0-6-0T (1933)		
4974	5MT : HALL 4-6-0 (1928)			9724	3FT : 57xx 0-6-0T (1933)		To Leamington 12/59
4982	5MT : HALL 4-6-0 (1928)			9733	3FT : 57xx 0-6-0T (1933)		
5912	5MT : HALL 4-6-0 (1928)			9753	3FT : 57xx 0-6-0T (1933)		
5927	5MT : HALL 4-6-0 (1928)			9798	3FT : 57xx 0-6-0T (1933)		
5930	5MT : HALL 4-6-0 (1928)	Ex Banbury 11/59		7713	3FT : 57xx 0-6-0T (1929)		To Taunton 8/59
5959	5MT : HALL 4-6-0 (1928)	Ex Exeter 9/59		7735	3FT : 57xx 0-6-0T (1929)		w/d 5/59
6904	5MT : HALL 4-6-0 (1928)		To Newton Abbot 8/59	7763	3FT : 57xx 0-6-0T (1929)		w/d 11/59
6853	5MT : GRANGE 4-6-0 (1936)			8700	3FT : 57xx 0-6-0T (1929)		
6861	5MT : GRANGE 4-6-0 (1936)			8713	3FT : 57xx 0-6-0T (1929)		To St Blazey 9/59
6866	5MT : GRANGE 4-6-0 (1936)			8713	3FT : 57xx 0-6-0T (1929)	Ex St Blazey 11/59	
6871	5MT : GRANGE 4-6-0 (1936)	Ex Laira 11/59		8737	3FT : 57xx 0-6-0T (1929)	Ex Bristol (SPM) 6/59	To St Blazey 9/59
6105	4MTT : 61xx 2-6-2T (1931)		To Didcot 11/59	7420	2PT : 74xx 0-6-0T (1936)	Ex Stourbridge 3/59	w/d 7/59
6116	4MTT : 61xx 2-6-2T (1931)			7424	2PT : 74xx 0-6-0T (1936)	Ex Swindon 7/59	
6139	4MTT : 61xx 2-6-2T (1931)		To Oxford 11/59	7438	2PT : 74xx 0-6-0T (1936)		w/d 2/59
8108	4MTT : 81xx 2-6-2T (1938)			12070	0F : 350hp 0-6-0		
4111	4MTT : 51xx 2-6-2T (1928)			12071	0F : 350hp 0-6-0		
4126	4MTT : 51xx 2-6-2T (1928)			12072	0F : 350hp 0-6-0		
4155	4MTT : 51xx 2-6-2T (1928)			12087	0F : 350hp 0-6-0		
4170	4MTT : 51xx 2-6-2T (1928)			13004	0F : 350hp 0-6-0		
4172	4MTT : 51xx 2-6-2T (1928)			13025	0F : 350hp 0-6-0		
5163	4MTT : 51xx 2-6-2T (1928)		w/d 11/59	13026	0F : 350hp 0-6-0		
5192	4MTT : 51xx 2-6-2T (1928)			13027	0F : 350hp 0-6-0		
75004	4MT 4-6-0 (1951)	Ex Swindon 8/59		13028	0F : 350hp 0-6-0		
75005	4MT 4-6-0 (1951)	Ex Chester 3/59		13029	0F : 350hp 0-6-0		
75006	4MT 4-6-0 (1951)	Ex Chester 3/59		13192	0F : 350hp 0-6-0		
75020	4MT 4-6-0 (1951)	Ex Chester 3/59	To Machynlleth 6/59				

Paddington to Aberystwyth and Barmouth was due. Its fascination lay partly in the fact it was a heavy two-hour express from London and partly because it connected two of the largest conurbations in the country with the most remote stations imaginable. I was musing on the novelty of being able to travel from Banbury to Borth when my attention was drawn to the unmistakable sound on a train sticking in the tunnel.

It was unusual for any express to stall on the approach to Snow Hill but the Cambrian was clearly in trouble. There was a tremendous burst of slipping from the tunnel followed by silence and a further roar of slipping after which nothing could be heard except for the sound of an injector being put on. The signalman and his lad stood peering towards the south, doubtless expecting an angry fireman to make an appearance and ask for assistance.

From the tunnel came the sound of an engine blowing off and, which surprised me, the roar of the large ejector. He was blowing the brakes off and trying a restart. I shook my head at the foolishness of it as the engine whistled up from inside the tunnel.

The first exhaust beat was like a gun going off and so was the second and third but, incredibly, instead of floundering into another bout of slipping, 6026 'King John' blasted out of the tunnel and thundered down the platform. The Old Oak driver caught sight of me and the Tyseley men I was with and casually breathed onto his finger nails, polishing them on his lapel. Clearly neither the tunnel or the gradient held any fears for the Cockneys.

Unfortunately we didn't have King Class 4-6-0's on the iron ore workings but in 1959 someone decided that banking through Snow Hill tunnel might have some benefits and ar-

ranged for a 53xx 2-6-0 to do some trials. The Moor Street area was far too congested to have a banking engine messing about and so the ore trains were assisted in rear from Bordesley to Snow Hill, the engine running to Moor Street on light steam sufficient to keep buffered up to the train. At Moor Street the 53xx opened up and, although getting up the bank as though it was level, somehow managed to give each train a violent snatch on the sharpest part of the climb in the tunnel.

Several different methods of working the 53xx were tried in an attempt to avoid the rug which was probably due to half the train getting onto the level at Snow Hill whilst the rear half was still on the gradient. Traffic and loco inspectors scratched their heads and exchanged theories but at the end of the second day we reverted to the normal method of working and the banking initiative was quietly forgotten.

All in all the Birmingham district was an interesting area in which to work and all of its routes called for considerable skill on the part of its enginemen. One thing you didn't come across very often even though it was authorised between Leamington and Claydon Crossing, Banbury, was the coupling of trains on the main line; a device used in extremis to reduce line occupation on the approach to the yards at Banbury. It was not a unique measure – the Midland used it for goods trains on the outskirts on London – but it was uncommon in the countryside, even on lines where it was permitted.

My experience of coupling had been limited to overhearing a couple of drivers talking about it whilst the small print was so well hidden in the mass of the Sectional Appendix that I was scarcely aware of it.

It was not unusual for traffic at Bordesley to outstrip the capacity of booked trains and when congestion loomed a special weekend working would be arranged with an hourly service of Sunday trains operating between Bordesley and Banbury. On one of these weekends I found myself paired with Driver Bob Hunt working 2-8-0 2830 at the time when I had just rejoined the service after returning from Egypt and was still finding my feet.

Forty miles to the south, Banbury seemed to lie on a different planet and although we had an allowance of ninety-nine minutes for the trip, an average of 25 mph for a heavy unfitted coal train was no sinecure especially as I was by no means certain as to my main line ability.

Fortunately 2830 was in peak condition and the trip as far as Leamington, including the troughs at Rowington, was covered in textbook style. At Leamington South, however, we were pulled up at the starter after being told by the signalman that we were to attach another goods train on our brake and to proceed coupled to Banbury.

The reason for invoking this unusual procedure was that the freight office clerks did not time the trains in the normal way but listed an hourly set of departures from Bordesley, each being allowed the standard ninety-nine minutes without any regard being made for passenger trains. Signalmen naturally threaded them between higher class trains with the result that every inch of slow or relief track was occupied by goods trains; a situation not helped by the fact that a number of smaller boxes were unmanned on Sundays. Eventually the district controller would have to step in to ease the deadlock and one of the solutions was to couple trains together at Leamington.

After a short wait another 28xx and its train coupled up to our brakevan and, when the starter came off, our hundred-wagon train with engines operating in the American style pulled away. Looking back along the two trains as we traversed some of the sweeping curves, it made a fine not to mention unusual sight from our cab.

With such an unorthodox way of operating coal trains I expected that the movement would be accompanied by inspectors or station masters but in fact it was treated by the operators as an everyday event. The two drivers did not seem unduly concerned and drove their engines, in spite of the distance between them, in the usual way and we climbed the 1 in 330 vank to Fenny Compton without any difficulties, the easier gradient beyond allowing us to lose momentum nicely so that we were able to draw up at the Claydon home signal without the slightest difficulty.

We parted company at Claydon and ran the last five miles on our own, the second train running up alongside us shortly after we had come to a halt in Banbury yard. I was glad to have taken part in an unusual procedure – it was all experience under the belt – and relieved that nothing had gone wrong.

LOCO	CLASS	IN	OUT	LOCO	CLASS	IN	OUT
			TYSELEY ALLOCATION : 1960				
48402	LMS 8F 2-8-0 (1935)			2257	3MT : 2251 0-6-0 (1930)		
48415	LMS 8F 2-8-0 (1935)			2267	3MT : 2251 0-6-0 (1930)		
48417	LMS 8F 2-8-0 (1935)			3625	3FT : 57xx 0-6-0T (1933)		
48418	LMS 8F 2-8-0 (1935)			3660	3FT : 57xx 0-6-0T (1933)		
48424	LMS 8F 2-8-0 (1935)			3673	3FT : 57xx 0-6-0T (1933)		
48430	LMS 8F 2-8-0 (1935)			3693	3FT : 57xx 0-6-0T (1933)		To Swansea (E. Dk) 5/60
48444	LMS 8F 2-8-0 (1935)		To Bristol (SPM) 8/60	4648	3FT : 57xx 0-6-0T (1933)		
48460	LMS 8F 2-8-0 (1935)	Ex Canton 2/60		9614	3FT : 57xx 0-6-0T (1933)	Ex Leamington 1/60	
48471	LMS 8F 2-8-0 (1935)		To Bristol (SPM) 8/60	9635	3FT : 57xx 0-6-0T (1933)		
48475	LMS 8F 2-8-0 (1935)		To Bristol (SPM) 8/60	9680	3FT : 57xx 0-6-0T (1933)		To St Blazey 7/60
2886	8F : 28xx 2-8-0 (1938)		To Aberdare 4/60	9682	3FT : 57xx 0-6-0T (1933)		To Aberbeg 7/60
6631	5MTT : 56xx 0-6-2T (1927)			9724	3FT : 57xx 0-6-0T (1933)		
6668	5MTT : 56xx 0-6-2T (1927)			9733	3FT : 57xx 0-6-0T (1933)	Ex Leamington 1/60	
5658	5MTT : 56xx 0-6-2T (1924)			9753	3FT : 57xx 0-6-0T (1933)		
6971	5MT : MOD-HALL 4-6-0 (1944)			9798	3FT : 57xx 0-6-0T (1933)		
7908	5MT : MOD-HALL 4-6-0 (1944)			8700	3FT : 57xx 0-6-0T (1929)		
7912	5MT : MOD-HALL 4-6-0 (1944)			8713	3FT : 57xx 0-6-0T (1929)		
7918	5MT : MOD-HALL 4-6-0 (1944)			7424	2PT : 74xx 0-6-0T (1936)		
7806	5MT : MANOR 4-6-0 (1938)	Ex St Blazey 9/60		12070	0F : 350hp 0-6-0		
7816	5MT : MANOR 4-6-0 (1938)	Ex St Blazey 9/60		12071	0F : 350hp 0-6-0		
7824	5MT : MANOR 4-6-0 (1938)			12072	0F : 350hp 0-6-0		
4902	5MT : HALL 4-6-0 (1928)		To Didcot 2/60	12087	0F : 350hp 0-6-0		
4910	5MT : HALL 4-6-0 (1928)	Ex Banbury 7/60	To Banbury 9/60	13004	0F : 350hp 0-6-0		To Stourbridge 8/60
4974	5MT : HALL 4-6-0 (1928)		To Stourbridge 4/60	13025	0F : 350hp 0-6-0		To Stourbridge 7/60
4982	5MT : HALL 4-6-0 (1928)			13026	0F : 350hp 0-6-0		To Oxley 7/60
5912	5MT : HALL 4-6-0 (1928)		To Stourbridge 4/60	13027	0F : 350hp 0-6-0		To Oxley 7/60
5921	5MT : HALL 4-6-0 (1928)	Ex Banbury 6/60	To Westbury 9/60	13028	0F : 350hp 0-6-0		To Oxley 7/60
5927	5MT : HALL 4-6-0 (1928)			13029	0F : 350hp 0-6-0		To Stourbridge 7/60
5930	5MT : HALL 4-6-0 (1928)		To Stourbridge 4/60	13192	0F : 350hp 0-6-0		To Stourbridge 8/60
5959	5MT : HALL 4-6-0 (1928)			D3518	0F : 350hp 0-6-0	Ex Exeter 2/60	
6853	5MT : GRANGE 4-6-0 (1936)			D3748	0F : 350hp 0-6-0	Ex Ebbw Jcn 6/60	To Shrewsbury 7/60
6855	5MT : GRANGE 4-6-0 (1936)	Ex Stourbridge 4/60		D3950	0F : 350hp 0-6-0	Ex Old Oak C. 6/60	
6861	5MT : GRANGE 4-6-0 (1936)			D3951	0F : 350hp 0-6-0	Ex Old Oak C. 6/60	
6866	5MT : GRANGE 4-6-0 (1936)			D3952	0F : 350hp 0-6-0	Ex Old Oak C. 6/60	
6871	5MT : GRANGE 4-6-0 (1936)		To Taunton 1/60	D3956	0F : 350hp 0-6-0	New 6/60	
6879	5MT : GRANGE 4-6-0 (1936)	Ex Stourbridge 4/60		D3957	0F : 350hp 0-6-0	Ex Old Oak C. 6/60	
6116	4MTT 61xx 2-6-2T (1931)			D3958	0F : 350hp 0-6-0	New 6/60	
8108	4MTT : 81xx 2-6-2T (1938)			D3965	0F : 350hp 0-6-0	Ex Old Oak C. 7/60	
4105	4MTT : 51xx 2-6-2T (1928)	Ex Exeter 9/60		D3966	0F : 350hp 0-6-0	Ex Old Oak C. 6/60	
4111	4MTT : 51xx 2-6-2T (1928)			D3968	0F : 350hp 0-6-0	Ex St Blazey 7/60	
4120	4MTT : 51xx 2-6-2T (1928)	Ex Wellington 7/60		D3969	0F : 350hp 0-6-0	Ex St Blazey 7/60	
4126	4MTT : 51xx 2-6-2T (1928)			D3973	0F : 350hp 0-6-0	New 7/60	
4155	4MTT : 51xx 2-6-2T (1928)			D3974	0F : 350hp 0-6-0	New 7/60	
4170	4MTT : 51xx 2-6-2T (1928)		w/d 8/60	D3975	0F : 350hp 0-6-0	Ex Ebbw Jcn 7/60	
4172	4MTT : 51xx 2-6-2T (1928)			D3981	0F : 350hp 0-6-0	New 7/60	To Stourbridge 8/60
5167	4MTT : 51xx 2-6-2T (1928)	Ex Shrewsbury 1/60	To Banbury 4/60	D3982	0F : 350hp 0-6-0	New 7/60	To Stourbridge 8/60
5174	4MTT : 51xx 2-6-2T (1928)	Ex Exeter 9/60		D3983	0F : 350hp 0-6-0	New 7/60	
5192	4MTT : 51xx 2-6-2T (1928)			D3984	0F : 350hp 0-6-0	New 7/60	
75000	4MT 4-6-0 (1951)			D3985	0F : 350hp 0-6-0	New 7/60	
75003	4MT 4-6-0 (1951)	Ex Worcester 7/60		D3986	0F : 350hp 0-6-0	New 8/60	To Gloucester 9/60
75005	4MT 4-6-0 (1951)		To Worcester 7/60	D3987	0F : 350hp 0-6-0	New 8/60	To Bromsgrove 9/60
75006	4MT 4-6-0 (1951)			D3988	0F : 350hp 0-6-0	New 8/60	To Stourbridge 9/60
75024	4MT 4-6-0 (1951)			D3989	0F : 350hp 0-6-0	New 8/60	To Stourbridge 9/60
5369	4MT : 43xx 2-6-0 (1911)			D3990	0F : 350hp 0-6-0	New 8/60	
6364	4MT : 43xx 2-6-0 (1911)	Ex Banbury 1/60		D3991	0F : 350hp 0-6-0	New 8/60	To Stourbridge 9/60
7317	4MT : 43xx 2-6-0 (1911)			D3994	0F : 350hp 0-6-0	New 9/60	
8415	4FT : 94XX 0-6-0T (1949)		To Worcester 7/60	D3995	0F : 350hp 0-6-0	New 9/60	
8468	4FT : 94XX 0-6-0T (1949)		w/d 5/60	D3996	0F : 350hp 0-6-0	New 9/60	
2211	3MT : 2251 0-6-0 (1930)			D3997	0F : 350hp 0-6-0	New 9/60	

GOODS AND PASSENGER

Great Western standardisation had been so effective that from a distance one engine looked very much like another. In the gloom of Snow Hill the above service was initially thought to be just another relief train with an everyday 2-6-0 or 4-6-0 at its head but a closer inspection revealed a 28xx 2-8-0 about to work a passenger service - not a common sight by any reckoning. 2-8-0 2851 waits in 1 and 2 platforms with a northbound special in the summer of 1957.

I liked to think my experience with loose coupled trains was responsible for getting me into No.7 'the London' link but, of course, promotion was purely a matter of dead men's shoes. The experience however was nonetheless useful since the majority of work performed in the link – in spite of its name it was years since anyone had been to London – involved loose coupled workings to either Oxley or Banbury.

My driver was 'Gentleman Jim' Rudge whose sobriquet was derived partly from his well mannered behaviour but mainly from the style of dress he effected which included a silver-knobbed black cane. His speech was grammatically impeccable and I never heard him utter an expletive – indeed he could freeze errant firemen so successfully with a sideways glance that he had no need for strong language. As was right and proper, I gave him every assistance I

LOCO	CLASS	LEAMINGTON ALLOCATION : 1950		
			IN	OUT
90685	8F : WD 2-8-0 (1943)			To Chester 12/50
7208	8F : 72xx 2-8-2T (1934)			
7218	8F : 72xx 2-8-2T (1934)			
7237	8F : 72xx 2-8-2T (1934)			
6625	5MT : 56xx 0-6-2T (1927)			
6632	5MT : 56xx 0-6-2T (1927)			
6657	5MT : 56xx 0-6-2T (1927)			
6697	5MT : 56xx 0-6-2T (1927)			
5634	5MT : 56xx 0-6-2T (1924)			
7810	5MT : MANOR 4-6-0 (1938)			To Shrewsbury 12/50
5954	5MT : HALL 4-6-0 (1928)			
6833	5MT : GRANGE 4-6-0 (1936)			
6924	5MT : HALL 4-6-0 (1928)		Ex Wolverhampton 12/50	
8100	4MTT : 81xx 2-6-2T (1938)			
8109	4MTT : 81xx 2-6-2T (1938)			
4102	4MTT : 51xx 2-6-2T (1928)			
4112	4MTT : 51xx 2-6-2T (1928)			
4171	4MTT : 51xx 2-6-2T (1928)			
5104	4MTT : 51xx 2-6-2T (1928)			
5144	4MTT : 51xx 2-6-2T (1928)			
5161	4MTT : 51xx 2-6-2T (1928)			
5163	4MTT : 51xx 2-6-2T (1928)			
5185	4MTT : 51xx 2-6-2T (1928)			
5192	4MTT : 51xx 2-6-2T (1928)			
5194	4MTT : 51xx 2-6-2T (1928)			
2933	4MT : SAINT 4-6-0 (1902)			
8454	4FT : 94XX 0-6-0T (1949)			
3631	3FT : 57xx 0-6-0T (1933)			
9740	3FT : 57xx 0-6-0T (1933)			
7702	3FT : 57xx 0-6-0T (1929)			
26	1P : RAILCAR			To Stourbridge 11/50
29	1P : RAILCAR			
29	1P : RAILCAR		Ex Stourbridge 12/50	

could – as I did to all my drivers – and in recognition Jim would mark each Christmas by presenting me, with proper solemnity, a pound note.

The hours in the shift tended to detract from the pleasure of the thing and most turns either commenced in the very early morning or very late at night: the time, of course, when goods activity was at its height. There were compensations however, one being the return home from Banbury if we arrived with a train at about seven in the morning and had no back working.

"Home passenger on the eight o'clock." The foreman would shout and I would race across to the station to catch the Leamington Auto with its 14xx 0-4-2T and single coach which made a considerable change from the usual 4-6-0 and nine corridors. The auto saloon was a luxurious reminded of Edwardian times with its well pad-

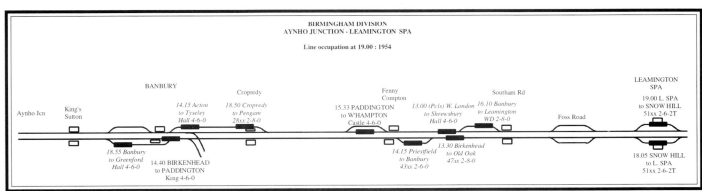

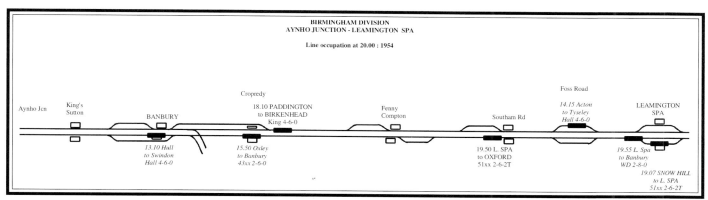

BIRMINGHAM DIVISION
AYNHO JUNCTION - LEAMINGTON SPA

Line occupation at 20.00 : 1954

Aynho Jcn | King's Sutton | BANBURY | Cropredy — 18.10 PADDINGTON to BIRKENHEAD King 4-6-0 | Fenny Compton | Southam Rd | Foss Road — 14.15 Acton to Tyseley Hall 4-6-0 | LEAMINGTON SPA

13.10 Hull to Swindon Hall 4-6-0 | 15.50 Oxley to Banbury 43xx 2-6-0 | 19.50 L. SPA to OXFORD 51xx 2-6-2T | 19.55 L. Spa to Banbury WD 2-8-0 | 19.07 SNOW HILL to L. SPA 51xx 2-6-2T

ded seats and wide windows although at one time the trip became even more memorable when the 0-4-2T was transferred away and the train – still an auto coach – had to be worked by a Banbury Hall 4-6-0.

Alas Jim and I invariably had most of the train to ourselves and although it called at Cropredy, Fenny Compton and Southam Road, very few passengers joined and it was obvious the intermediate stations were not going to grace the timetable for very many years ahead.

I thought at first that the dearth of passengers might simply have been because the auto ran at an inconvenient time but later when working the 17.20 Snow Hill to Oxford and the 18.55 Leamington – Banbury, I could lean from the cab at the intermediate stations and count the number of passengers on the fingers of one hand. The stations however were beautifully kept, especially Southam Road which had an array of sweet peas that should have won prizes. The signalbox at Southam Road was similarly spotless and locomen, who trailed a train of coal dust, were not encouraged to linger after signing the register:

"Aye up bobby, we're clear inside. How long are you going to keep us here?"

"Mind that bloody floor, I've spent the last hour washing it."

"My driver wants to know if we'll be following the London?"

"Keep your hands off that desk, you'll have dust all over the place…."

The rule book required fireman to wait in the box and check that all levers were guarded by collars but in practice you were frozen out by the signalmen to spent the delay on the footplate which was no great hardship since it allowed me to watch, uninterrupted, the procession of trains that roared through, one after another. Our Banbury jobs did not have the highest of priorities but the sight of King class 4-6-0's sweeping through at 75 mph more than compensated for the wait.

I was always happy to be regulated into the loop at Fenny Compton where if I was lucky I might catch sight of something on the Stratford & Midland Joint with its 4F 0-6-0's and Austerity 2-8-0's. It was not a line I ever worked

over but occasionally I would bump into a driver who had and would be held spellbound with tales of Iron Ore trains worked by 4F 0-6-0's and the difficulties of holding heavy loads back on Ettington bank.

The SMJ's value to the Great Western was overlooked for years and it was not until the late 1950's that it dawned on someone at Paddington that the distance from Banbury to Stratford via Kineton was eleven miles less than our route via Leamington. Eventually, in 1960, a link was laid between the two systems bringing a new lease of life to the SMJ. Prior to that

LEAMINGTON ALLOCATION : 1951			
LOCO	CLASS	IN	OUT
90010	8F : WD 2-8-0 (1943)	Ex Oxley 11/51	
90685	8F : WD 2-8-0 (1943)	Ex Chester 1/51	To Ebbw Jcn 6/51
7208	8F : 72xx 2-8-2T (1934)		
7218	8F : 72xx 2-8-2T (1934)		
7237	8F : 72xx 2-8-2T (1934)		
6625	5MTT : 56xx 0-6-2T (1927)		
6632	5MTT : 56xx 0-6-2T (1927)		
6657	5MTT : 56xx 0-6-2T (1927)		
6697	5MTT : 56xx 0-6-2T (1927)		
5634	5MTT : 56xx 0-6-2T (1924)		
4987	5MT : HALL 4-6-0 (1928)	Ex Chester 7/51	
5923	5MT : HALL 4-6-0 (1928)	Ex Chester 1/51	To Severn T. Jcn 5/51
5954	5MT : HALL 4-6-0 (1928)		
5966	5MT : HALL 4-6-0 (1928)	Ex Chester 1/51	
6924	5MT : HALL 4-6-0 (1928)		
6833	5MT : GRANGE 4-6-0 (1936)		
6835	5MT : GRANGE 4-6-0 (1936)	Ex Banbury 5/51	To Banbury 6/51
8100	4MTT : 81xx 2-6-2T (1938)		
8109	4MTT : 81xx 2-6-2T (1938)		
4102	4MTT : 51xx 2-6-2T (1928)		
4112	4MTT : 51xx 2-6-2T (1928)		
4171	4MTT : 51xx 2-6-2T (1928)		
5104	4MTT : 51xx 2-6-2T (1928)		
5144	4MTT : 51xx 2-6-2T (1928)		
5161	4MTT : 51xx 2-6-2T (1928)		
5163	4MTT : 51xx 2-6-2T (1928)		
5185	4MTT : 51xx 2-6-2T (1928)		
5192	4MTT : 51xx 2-6-2T (1928)		
5194	4MTT : 51xx 2-6-2T (1928)		
2933	4MT : SAINT 4-6-0 (1902)		To Duffryn 8/51
8454	4FT : 94XX 0-6-0T (1949)		
3619	3FT : 57xx 0-6-0T (1933)	Ex Chester 9/51	
3624	3FT : 57xx 0-6-0T (1933)	Ex Tyseley 9/51	
3631	3FT : 57xx 0-6-0T (1933)		
9740	3FT : 57xx 0-6-0T (1933)		
7702	3FT : 57xx 0-6-0T (1929)		
26	1P : RAILCAR		
29	1P : RAILCAR		

there had been no direct connection between the two routes which did not involve shunting in the station yard.

The signalbox was particularly interesting since it had two frames, one for the Midland and the other for the Great Western.

There cannot have been many railwaymen – or anyone else – who cared much for taking duty at 03.17 (not, note, three-twenty or a quarter past) but I was the exception since the duty involved relieving the 22.55 Paddington goods and working it to Oxley with one of the gigantic

47xx 2-8-0's. They were huge engines and could master anything – if only we had had more of them – and it is only a matter of regret that their being restricted to the Wolverhampton and Plymouth roads acted as a limit on their numbers.

The 22.55 Paddington was a class D partially fitted goods which ran via Bicester and one of the most important workings on the line. To give a measure of how it was run, it passed Leamington four minutes after the departure of the 23.10 Paddington – Birkenhead Parcels and maintained the same margin throughout, running past Tyseley just as the Parcels was rolling into Snow Hill. With sixty wagons of goods behind the tender, no ordinary engine was deemed fit for the job: hence the 47xx.

Our leg of the run was not quite so dramatic since we were allowed almost three and a half hours to run from Bordesley to Wolverhampton; part of the time being occupied by detaching traffic at Bordesley and Hockley and the rest because we were booked to dawdle for the best part of two hours at Bilston until the night traffic at Oxley had thinned sufficiently for us to be accepted. It seemed a curious contrast to the way the train had thundered through Oxfordshire but as often as not we would get a clear run when the sheer power of the 47xx was enough to make one stand up and cheer.

The class was as smooth to ride on as a passenger coach and if I had to find a fault with them, it would be with the design of the cab which made it difficult to avoid banging ones head when standing up after a bout of firing. It was a small price to pay though for being able to work on such a superb machine.

Once in a blue moon I would get a 47xx on one of our workday trips to Banbury and I recall firing to Fred Salmon, an artist of an engineman, on 4705. We had a full load of sixty-two minerals which 4705 simply played with. The banks at Fosse Road and Harbury might just as well have not existed and the engine simply gobbled the miles, getting to Banbury almost before I was aware of it.

Unfortunately not all workings ran as smoothly – although they might have done had there been a few more 47xx's to play with – and it was with Gentleman Jim that I had my first

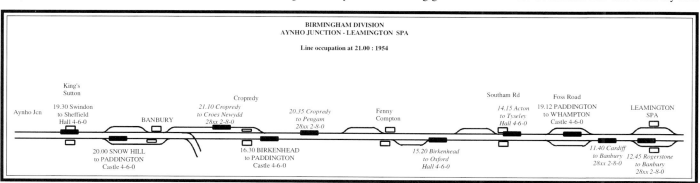

BIRMINGHAM DIVISION
AYNHO JUNCTION - LEAMINGTON SPA

Line occupation at 21.00 : 1954

King's Sutton | 19.30 Swindon to Sheffield Hall 4-6-0 | Aynho Jcn | BANBURY | Cropredy — 21.10 Cropredy to Croes Newydd 28xx 2-8-0 | 20.35 Cropredy to Pengam 28xx 2-8-0 | Fenny Compton | Southam Rd | Foss Road — 14.15 Acton to Tyseley Hall 4-6-0 | 19.12 PADDINGTON to W'HAMPTON Castle 4-6-0 | LEAMINGTON SPA

20.00 SNOW HILL to PADDINGTON Castle 4-6-0 | 16.30 BIRKENHEAD to PADDINGTON Castle 4-6-0 | 15.20 Birkenhead to Oxford Hall 4-6-0 | 11.40 Cardiff to Banbury 28xx 2-8-0 | 12.45 Rogerstone to Banbury 28xx 2-8-0

Apart from the cab which was designed to bruise firemen of even moderate dimensions, the 47xx's were one of the best engines to run on the Great Western and it is a pity that their route restrictions limited the class to only nine engines. Used not infrequently on West of England expresses from Paddington, their availability on passenger workings over the Wolverhampton line was limited by their being restricted to local services not exceeding 60 mph. 4702 stands at Old Oak Common in 1952.

(but not last) experience of stopping the job by sticking on the bank in Snow Hill tunnel.

Preparing 2-6-0 6355 for the 11.55 Bordesley – Oxley goods, I noticed when testing the gauge that the water returning to the glass after I had blown it through was distinctly dark brown in colour, an indication that the engine was well overdue for a boiler washout. Jim looked rather glum at being given the news but said nothing beyond reminding me not to get the boiler too full.

We took 6355 off shed but even running light engine to the yard, water was pumping out of the chimney; a warning I ought to have taken more note of.

We backed on to our train at Bordesley, the guard gave Jim the loading, the signal was lowered and we had the tip off the shunter to pull away to join the queue of trains on the down departure, each waiting its turn to get through Snow Hill.

I had a good fire in No.6355's firebox, well built up under the doors. I favoured this method rather than side firing although I never really mastered the 2-6-0s. The engine blew off two or three times and each time I put a drop more water in the boiler to keep it quiet. It proved to be my undoing although the Great Western attitude against letting an engine blow off was so thoroughly ingrained that it was difficult to do anything else. How very different each region – or company since it took thirty years for nationalisation to make itself known – was in this respect. The Midland could hardly turn a wheel without an engine blowing off furiously and the LNER would like to have done the same except that their management forbade it. The Southern

had a fleet of engines which couldn't be kept quiet because they lacked dampers whilst wasting steam on the Great Western was viewed like going into mixed company with your flies undone. I could no more have kept my hand off

LEAMINGTON ALLOCATION : 1952			
LOCO	CLASS	IN	OUT
90010	8F : WD 2-8-0 (1943)		
7208	8F : 72xx 2-8-2T (1934)		To Oxley 1/52
7218	8F : 72xx 2-8-2T (1934)		To Oxley 1/52
7237	8F : 72xx 2-8-2T (1934)		To Severn T. Jcn 8/52
6624	5MTT : 56xx 0-6-2T (1927)	Ex Shrewsbury 8/52	To Gloucester 10/52
6625	5MTT : 56xx 0-6-2T (1927)		To Banbury 3/52
6632	5MTT : 56xx 0-6-2T (1927)		To Croes Newydd 1/52
6657	5MTT : 56xx 0-6-2T (1927)		
6697	5MTT : 56xx 0-6-2T (1927)		
5634	5MTT : 56xx 0-6-2T (1924)		To Shrewsbury 3/52
4987	5MT : HALL 4-6-0 (1928)		To Banbury 10/52
5954	5MT : HALL 4-6-0 (1928)		To Banbury 1/52
5966	5MT : HALL 4-6-0 (1928)		To Oxley 10/52
6924	5MT : HALL 4-6-0 (1928)		
6833	5MT : GRANGE 4-6-0 (1936)		To Banbury 1/52
8100	4MTT : 81xx 2-6-2T (1938)		
8109	4MTT : 81xx 2-6-2T (1938)		
4102	4MTT : 51xx 2-6-2T (1928)		To Banbury 1/52
4102	4MTT : 51xx 2-6-2T (1928)	Ex Banbury 3/52	To Banbury 4/52
4112	4MTT : 51xx 2-6-2T (1928)		
4171	4MTT : 51xx 2-6-2T (1928)		
5104	4MTT : 51xx 2-6-2T (1928)		
5144	4MTT : 51xx 2-6-2T (1928)		w/d 1/52
5161	4MTT : 51xx 2-6-2T (1928)		
5163	4MTT : 51xx 2-6-2T (1928)		
5185	4MTT : 51xx 2-6-2T (1928)		
5192	4MTT : 51xx 2-6-2T (1928)		
5194	4MTT : 51xx 2-6-2T (1928)		
2933	4MT : SAINT 4-6-0 (1902)		
3619	3FT : 57xx 0-6-0T (1933)		
3624	3FT : 57xx 0-6-0T (1933)		
3631	3FT : 57xx 0-6-0T (1933)		
9740	3FT : 57xx 0-6-0T (1933)		To Shrewsbury 3/52
7702	3FT : 57xx 0-6-0T (1929)		
26	1P : RAILCAR		
29	1P : RAILCAR		

the injector than I could have gone to work in a bank.

We worked our way to the front of the queue and after a down passenger had passed, got the road. I blew the gauge glass again in the hope that it would clear but still there was nothing but dirty brown water.

6355 pounded through Bordesley station and, with the train over the hump, Jim opened the second valve for the dash over the viaduct

and up the bank. The 2-6-0 coughed and started to prime with dirty spots of unhealthy water appearing on the eye glasses.

With water entering the cylinders, Jim had no option but to open the drain cocks which not only added to our difficulties by reducing cylinder power just when we needed it most but also blew water onto the rail immediately ahead of us. 6355 slipped violently and Jim eased off the regulator causing further loss of power. On hearing the commotion we were making the signalman at Moor Street ran to his window and stood there, shaking his head. He had a pretty accurate idea of how far we were going to get on Moor Street bank.

We entered the tunnel and Jim, throwing caution out of the cab window, shut the drain cocks and gave 6355 second valve. For a few moments the engine became stable and I though we were going to pick up our train and get through to Snow Hill. Just as I was starting to cheer 6355 went into a furious, prolonged slip and we came to a stand.

Perversely 6355 started to blow off and, knowing that no further damage could be done, I put the injector on and opened the firebox doors to quieten it down and keep smoke down to a minimum. Jim didn't say a word but busied himself with trying to fill in a wrong line order form whilst I secured the engine by screwing down the tender handbrake.

He handed me the form and I dropped off the engine for the walk to Birmingham South box, noticing another omission as I passed the engine. Neither headlight was lit which was not only against regulations when working through Snow Hill tunnel but would make it very diffi-

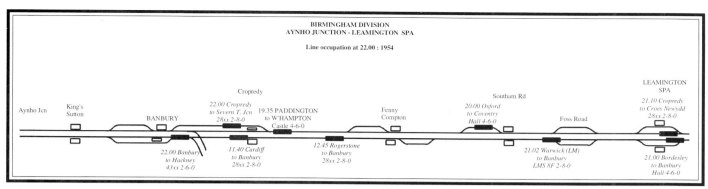

BIRMINGHAM DIVISION
AYNHO JUNCTION - LEAMINGTON SPA

Line occupation at 22.00 : 1954

cult for the driver of the assisting engine to know where we were as he backed down in the smoky darkness. Fumbling for matches I got one of them alight, conscious not only of the time which was passing but of the fuss we would be causing elsewhere. The line between Moor Street and Snow Hill would be blocked in both directions whilst the 10.10 Paddington – Aberystwyth express would by now be standing at somewhere like Moor Street. The district controller would be tearing his hair out and all because an engine had not had a boiler wash out. And, I reflected guiltily, the fireman might have used a bit more ingenuity. Some experience was hard won.

"Stuck in the tunnel?" asked the signalman unnecessarily, taking the form and shuffling it with the ones he'd made out himself. "The big pilot's just coming up from the north."

Half a minute later a Grange 68xx 4-6-0 backed up and I climbed aboard to guide them back to where 6355 and its train was standing.

"We ain't paid to work goods trains, y'know," said the driver pulling my leg as he eased opened the regulator. "We're top link men, we are…"

Coupling the two engines up in the smoky blackness was a filthy business made worse by having to pipe up the two engines in order to ensure that the braking power of both engines was available should the train run backwards and try to take the locomotives with it.

Eventually I climbed back onto the footplate of 6355 and nodded to Jim who exchanged whistles with the Grange before opening up. We started to move with both engines working flat out and very quickly blasted out of the tunnel to be greeted by an audience of passengers and staff who seemed to be either cheering us on or cursing us for delaying the down Cambrian: given the noise of the two engines it was difficult to be sure which.

We knocked the pilot off at the north end of Snow Hill and carried on, getting to Oxley with no further problems although I was careful to see that the water level was held at a lower level than normal. Blowing off was infinitely better than getting stuck and there were some tricky

sections of line between Birmingham and Wolverhampton.

If any correspondence was generated by the incident – and it is difficult to suppose there was none – Jim kept it to himself and said nothing to me about it.

As Tyseley was predominately a freight shed where traffic demands fluctuated considerable from one week to the next, we had quite a number of spare turns in the link where you could be used for any job that came up at short notice. A few weeks as a spare fireman was a

first class way of gaining experience since on a Monday you could be doing the shed shunt whilst Tuesday could see you on a class 1 express.

On one particular week's spare work, I spent from Monday to Wednesday turning engines on the turntable; a pushing and shoving job for which the most miserable colonial railway would have hired an elephant. It was not the most romantic of duties but I did it with as much enthusiasm as I could muster in the hope that the latter half of the week would bring something more interesting. I was not disappointed and was initially relieved to be booked to the 16.00 Snow Hill – Hereford (and 18.50 return) express. My elation dampened a little when I saw I was booked to work with driver Billy

Roles who had a reputation for being a rail-bending fireman-killer.

"How long've you been on the company" he asked as he came across me preparing our engine, Modified Hall 4-6-0 7913 'Little Wyrley Hall'.

"Six years."

"Well I've never heard of you."

I didn't tell him that I had heard of him because I got the impression from the look on his face and tone of voice that he had decided to dislike me before we had turned a wheel together. Matters did not improve when he found out that I had never fired over the Hereford road before.

"You get plenty of fire in its bowels" he said nodding towards 7913. "You're going to need it…"

We left the shed and made our way to the carriage sidings to pick up our train, a light six coach formation. It seemed to me that I had the worst and best of both worlds. On the one hand a driver who was in a filthy mood and had made up his mind to be awkward whilst on the other the train was a lightweight with the engine in tip-top condition. The main problem was my not knowing the road; something that was essential if only to know when to apply the injector. If I filled the boiler up at the foot of an incline, the engine might die on us with me, given the mood my driver seemed to be in, following shortly afterwards.

We got the road and trundled past Moor Street and through Snow Hill, to back into No.4 bay where I changed the headcode to open lights, a lamp above each buffer, and got the 4-6-0 good and hot for what I reckoned was going to be a difficult trip.

The train, being timed too early for the ordinary office worker, was designed for businessmen; a breed not unknown for their flair for making complaints. Billy made no attempt to disguise his intention of getting them to their destinations on time if not early and as soon as we had the right away, he had 7913 full open and shooting up the bank from Snow Hill like a shot out of a gun.

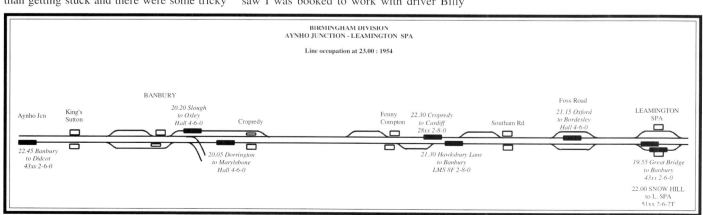

BIRMINGHAM DIVISION
AYNHO JUNCTION - LEAMINGTON SPA

Line occupation at 23.00 : 1954

The loading limit for a 22xx between Leamington and Wolverhampton was only eight coaches but that did not prevent the crew of 2296 from pulling the stops out when they had to take over the twelve-coach 09.10 Paddington - Birkenhead from a failed King 4-6-0 in March 1955. The 0-6-0 is seen haring through Tyseley station with less than three miles to go before giving way to a Hall 4-6-0, waiting to take over at Snow Hill.

It was not a bad train for learning the express passenger way of things since a stop was made at Smethwick Junction, only four miles and seven and a half minutes into the journey. I think he used the first leg to see what I was made of and I wasn't going to let him beat me. We drew up at Smethwick in a cloud of steam, hot oil and the screeching of carriage brakes.

"You all right on these expresses, then?"

"I'm okay."

He pulled up the regulator and we shot off again with the lever well down until the engine got up to 40 mph after which he held our speed on the brake to get us through Old Hill tunnel and the bank at Cradley Heath. This was a colliery area and the track seemed to be much too rough for express traffic but Billy took no notice, flogging 7913 until he had to shut off for Stourbridge Junction.

"You still all right?"

"I'm okay."

"Right then."

We stood in Stourbridge for a few minutes and then, after the right away, streaked off to-

wards Kidderminster. It's a bit uphill leaving Stourbridge, but you would not have thought so the way Bill went. What sort of speed we hit on the bank through Hagley I have no idea but it seemed no time at all before we were pulling up in Kidderminster platform. So far I

had managed to keep up with him but I had now reached the limit of my road knowledge whilst the darkness outside would prevent me from using my eyes.

"Still all right?"

"You know I don't know the road from here…"

Billy looked down his nose at me before turning away to lean out of the window.

"I think I shall be able to manage."

He said it in a tone of heavy sarcasm.

I did my best to gauge the road ahead but in the pitch black outside I couldn't see a thing and I had no idea whether we were climbing or falling. The best I could do was to keep an eye on the way Billy handled the regulator and make what assumptions I could as to the road ahead. The enthusiast in me reminded me that I was now handling an engine on a route used by London expresses since a number of Wolverhampton – Paddington services used the stretch of line we were now running over. We eased through Droitwich and Bill beckoned me to his side of the cab.

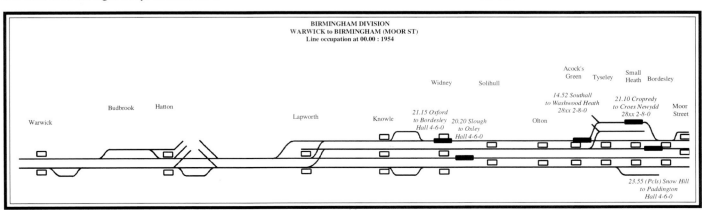

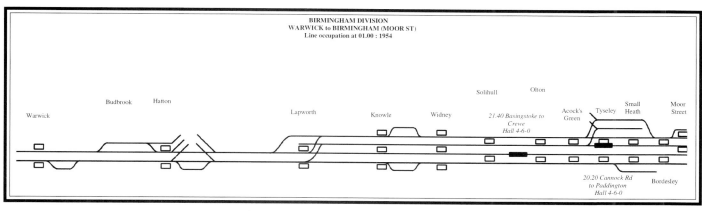

BIRMINGHAM DIVISION
WARWICK to BIRMINGHAM (MOOR ST)
Line occupation at 01.00 : 1954

"When we get to Foregate Street there'll be some tea for us."

I thought for a moment he had decided to take a liking to me and was giving me some sort of coded invitation.

"Jump off the engine when we pass the buffet and bring it over."

We were booked to stand in Worcester for seven minutes but, thanks to Billy's driving, we had a few minutes extra. I thought of asking him about the route between Foregate Street and Hereford but anticipating a discouraging reply, kept my silence.

We pulled away from Worcester and for the first time in the trip he started to mellow.

"Over there's the river and over there's the race track"

Surprised at his sudden descent to a conversational level I mumbled something about it being too dark for me to make them out. His tone changed abruptly.

"Well, you'll just have to take my word for it."

I fired in silence for a while and then he called my attention again. I looked across at him and he moved his hand from right to left finally pointing in the direction we were travelling. I deduced he was indicating that the route was level and a few minutes later he shouted and gave me another sign, his hand moving vertically.

This was the climb through the Malvern Hills where the seven and a half miles from Bransford Road climb as though they were going up the side of a house. Malvern Link and Great Malvern are both on a gradient of about 1/140 whilst the line steepens to 1 in 97 on the worst part of the climb to Malvern Wells and Colwall. It is without doubt one of the most attractive parts of England unless of course you happen to be a fireman trying not to gain an adverse reputation. To make things more difficult there was no question of rushing the bank since we called at all three Malvern stations

although I did my bit by keeping the engine hot and the needle on the red mark.

Perhaps the high point of the trip occurred when Billy pulled away from Great Malvern. With the regulator fully open and the cut-off as long as it could be without throwing the fire, 7913 simply bit into the track with a bark that was symphonic. We blasted up what appeared, from what little I could see, to be the side of a mountain and then without warning plunged into the single bore of Colwall tunnel, a suffocating

LEAMINGTON ALLOCATION : 1955			
LOCO	CLASS	IN	OUT
90010	8F : WD 2-8-0 (1943)		
90483	8F : WD 2-8-0 (1943)		
6624	5MTT : 56xx 0-6-2T (1927)		
6633	5MTT : 56xx 0-6-2T (1927)	Ex Shrewsbury 3/55	To Wrexham 7/55
6657	5MTT : 56xx 0-6-2T (1927)		
6697	5MTT : 56xx 0-6-2T (1927)		
8100	4MTT : 81xx 2-6-2T (1938)		
8109	4MTT : 81xx 2-6-2T (1938)		
4112	4MTT : 51xx 2-6-2T (1928)		
4118	4MTT : 51xx 2-6-2T (1928)		
4171	4MTT : 51xx 2-6-2T (1928)		
5104	4MTT : 51xx 2-6-2T (1928)		
5161	4MTT : 51xx 2-6-2T (1928)		
5184	4MTT : 51xx 2-6-2T (1928)		
5185	4MTT : 51xx 2-6-2T (1928)		
5194	4MTT : 51xx 2-6-2T (1928)		
3619	3FT : 57xx 0-6-0T (1933)		
3624	3FT : 57xx 0-6-0T (1933)		
3631	3FT : 57xx 0-6-0T (1933)		
7702	3FT : 57xx 0-6-0T (1929)		
17	1P : RAILCAR		
26	1P : RAILCAR		
29	1P : RAILCAR		

experience although Billy refused to ease the engine in the slightest.

We stormed out the tunnel and instantly exchanged the Mephistophelean blackness for the evening tranquillity of the Cotswolds, Billy shutting the regulator and giving me a downhill sign as we coasted through the pretty station at Colwall. I leaned out of the cab, taking in fresh air and what I could of the scenery.

"Shut the dampers and keep your head in."

He screwed the blower on and brought his own head in just as we entered Ledbury tunnel, the bore of which was only marginally wider

than the engine. I recollected someone telling me that if a train got stuck in Ledbury tunnel, you hadn't got enough room to open a carriage door and I could see what they meant.

During the stop at Ledbury I had a chance to look at the banker, one of a pair of 42xx 2-8-0T's based at Hereford, which I noticed was turned so as to be bunker first through the tunnels. What the footplate conditions would be like with two engines working through a pair of single bore tunnels was something that beggared the imagination although working bunker first would alleviate the worst of it.

The remaining fourteen miles were all downhill and gave me an opportunity to rally the engine whilst Billy concentrated on getting himself into the record books. I didn't think I had done too badly and although the engine had blown off more often than it should, we hadn't been short of steam. Musing thus we ran through the Junction with the joint line from Shrewsbury at Shelwick and came shortly afterwards to a stand in Barrs Court, Hereford. I started to look forward to having a look round Hereford loco.

"Hook off and don't forget to put a lamp on the tender."

"Are we turning on Hereford loco?"

"Be there all day. Turn on the angle."

It was a disappointment but couldn't be helped and obviously it was quicker to turn an engine on a triangle rather than queue up for a turntable. On the other hand it was rather a laborious procedure since I had to swap head and tail lamps every time the engine changed direction. We reversed at Barton & Brecon Curve Junction and ran down to Barrs Court Junction where I got off the engine to see to the lamps. Bill leaned out of the cab window as I was climbing down.

"Don't waste any time. There's a Northern about."

He made it sound more sinister than a flying bomb but anxious to please I tried to give an

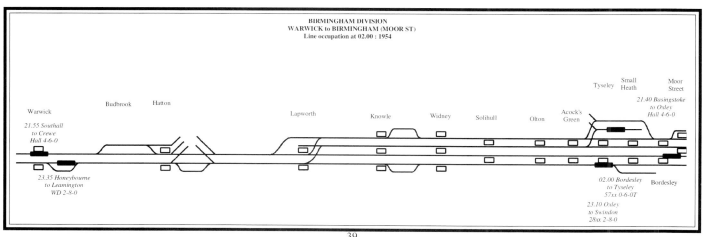

BIRMINGHAM DIVISION
WARWICK to BIRMINGHAM (MOOR ST)
Line occupation at 02.00 : 1954

Unlike the other regions, double heading on the Western was a complicated procedure where, generally, the more powerful of the two engines had to be placed in front. For this purpose 4-6-0 engines were regarded as superior to 2-8-0's thus Hall 4-6-0 5938 'Stanley Hall' pilots 28xx 2-8-0 3835 on a train of empty stock from Wolverhampton to the Southern Region. The ensemble is seen passing Leamington Spa in 1952.

impression of urgent co-operation by leaping from the engine down to the six foot. What Billy either did not know or chose not to tell me was that the S & T were in the middle of laying cables and had left a two-foot trench by the track side into which I fell. To make it worse it contained about eighteen inches of very muddy water and in the dark I had no idea what I had done. I shouted out and Billy stuck his head out of the cab.

"Have you changed those lamps yet?"

"Look at the bloody mess I'm in."

"The Northern'll be here any minute. Get a move on"

I muttered something fairly disrespectful about the Northern and told him to shine his torch in my direction. He directed a pretty disreputable beam of light towards me and eventually I managed to clamber out and change the lamps.

Back on the footplate I tried to scrape the mud off but most of it had to stay where it was. I was tempted to give Billy a piece of my mind for letting me fall into the trench but he was rather too senior to take any liberties with. Equally he obviously regarded me as being too junior to take much notice of.

"You'll soon dry out" he said as the Northern, the 15.00 Liverpool – Plymouth, ran by on the next track. I never did find out why he was so obsessed with it unless he was afraid I'd walk into it whilst I was changing the lamps although on reflection I didn't think he'd be that considerate.

We followed the Plymouth into the station and stood on the centre road whilst we snatched a bite to eat and got the engine ready for the back working. It seemed a long sixty-three miles back to Birmingham over a road that was against us for much of the way and I was begin-

ning to tire although once we were on the move, I found myself back in my element and happy in what I was doing.

Using the experience of the outward run, I worked back to Snow Hill in a far more confident state of mind and the only unusual element in the journey occurred at Ledbury, twenty minutes out of Hereford, as I was getting the engine ready for the 1 in 109 climb out of the station and through the single-bore tunnel. I had a good fire going and Billy nodded as he looked into the firebox.

"Leave it now and don't fire until we're out of the tunnel."

I put the shovel down as he started the train out of the station and was surprised to see him leave the regulator and lift the drop plate between the engine and tender.

"Put yer head down here." He ordered as he pushed open the regulator a little further and got down on his knees. For a moment I wondered if he belonged to one of those mysterious sects which face Mecca each evening but reason dawned as 7913 entered Ledbury tunnel and its

exhaust swirled into the cab, blanketing everything out and expelling all air except that which came up between the engine and tender. 7913 meanwhile pounded its way through the tunnel and up the bank on automatic pilot, sure-footed as ever. Eventually we came out and I could see for myself why such drastic action had been necessary – the handrails, tender brake and scoop handle were covered in a fine green slime all of which had been deposited during the few minutes we had been in the tunnel.

The rest of the trip was routine by comparison and by the time we left Kidderminster I was on familiar ground, making sure I had a fire good enough to get us up from Stourbridge to Rowley Regis with steam to spare. Running into Snow Hill I reflected that if I wasn't yet a main line fireman, I was well on the way to becoming one.

Sometime later I saw Bill's regular fireman, Harold Barnett, who told me how pleased Bill was with my performance on this first trip. "He did nothing but sweep the footplate up, water the coal, drink all the tea, and fall down holes half the night."

Coming from Billy Roles I took it as a three star commendation.

Shortly after my trip to Hereford I was moved into No 6 link which involved a great deal more passenger work although goods traffic, as was inevitable at a depot like Tyseley, continued to play a large part in my working life. Teamed with Driver Micky Mitchell our first job together was on the 09.25 class H (i.e. coal) Bordesley – Swindon which we worked for the sixty-odd miles to Gloucester. It was a long four hour working and we only worked one way, returning passenger to Birmingham; something that required skills in navigation since trains over the North Warwicks were few and

LEAMINGTON ALLOCATION : 1956			
LOCO	CLASS	IN	OUT
90010	8F : WD 2-8-0 (1943)		To Shrewsbury 7/56
90261	8F : WD 2-8-0 (1943)	Ex Shrewsbury 7/56	
90483	8F : WD 2-8-0 (1943)		
6624	5MTT : 56xx 0-6-2T (1927)		
6657	5MTT : 56xx 0-6-2T (1927)		
6697	5MTT : 56xx 0-6-2T (1927)		
8100	4MTT : 81xx 2-6-2T (1938)		
8109	4MTT : 81xx 2-6-2T (1938)		
4112	4MTT : 51xx 2-6-2T (1928)		
4118	4MTT : 51xx 2-6-2T (1928)		
4171	4MTT : 51xx 2-6-2T (1928)		
5104	4MTT : 51xx 2-6-2T (1928)		
5161	4MTT : 51xx 2-6-2T (1928)		To Penzance 6/56
5161	4MTT : 51xx 2-6-2T (1928)	Ex Penzance 7/56	
5184	4MTT : 51xx 2-6-2T (1928)		To Penzance 6/56
5184	4MTT : 51xx 2-6-2T (1928)	Ex Penzance 7/56	
5185	4MTT : 51xx 2-6-2T (1928)		
5194	4MTT : 51xx 2-6-2T (1928)		
3619	3FT : 57xx 0-6-0T (1933)		
3624	3FT : 57xx 0-6-0T (1933)		
3631	3FT : 57xx 0-6-0T (1933)		
7702	3FT : 57xx 0-6-0T (1929)		
17	1P : RAILCAR		
26	1P : RAILCAR		
29	1P : RAILCAR		

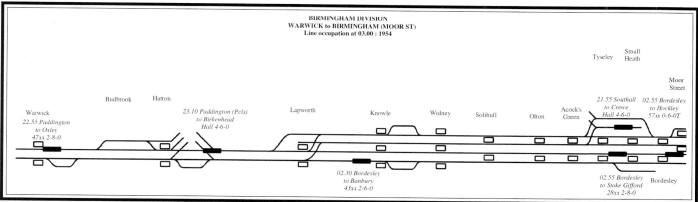

BIRMINGHAM DIVISION
WARWICK to BIRMINGHAM (MOOR ST)
Line occupation at 03.00 : 1954

far between and it was often quicker to travel back via Swindon and Banbury. The Midland route via Bromsgrove was the most direct although in 1955 we were a little vague as to whether we could use it although anyone sitting in a carriage wearing a driver's hat had, even if they didn't realise it, a free pass from anywhere to anywhere.

Our engine was a 28xx 2-8-0 and we took our load over Earlswood Lakes, through Stratford and Honeybourne without incident. I was estimating our time at Gloucester and trying to mentally calculate which train we would get back when Mick shut off steam and brought the train to a halt by Broadway box where the elderly signalman was exhibiting a red flag.

"What's up?" called Mick.

"Driver, there be cows on the line just past my up distant. See what you 'ee can do."

This then was the practical application of block regulation thirteen, a far cry from the sober and careful language used in writing. We took a walk down the line and sure enough, eating 'our' grass on the side of the line were two cows that had got through an open gate with numerous others enviously watching them from the far side of the fence.

A youth spent in urban Bordesley is not the best apprenticeship for shepherding cattle and Mick was no wiser than I was but after reviewing the scene we decided that I should go behind them, banging the rail with my shovel whilst Mick tried to direct them back through the gate.

Predictably it went horribly wrong and instead of the two cows returning back to their field, the other twenty animals came charging through the gate onto the line. Mick took one look at them as they approached and fled, blaming me for not driving the original pair in quickly enough, to the safety of the footplate.

Fortunately the district control, impatient as ever, were not prepared to have the line blocked by a pair of amateur cowboys and just as I was beginning to get desperate an engine arrived from the Gloucester direction with a

p.way man who jumped down and cleared them back into the field in no time at all.

During the course of my work I worked on most of the routine Great Western main line classes, Halls, 28xx's and 43xx's in particular, although the type that eluded me the most were the County 4-6-0's which in 1955 were still regarded as something of a novelty. They were not seen very much in the Birmingham district

LEAMINGTON ALLOCATION : 1957			
LOCO	CLASS	IN	OUT
90261	8F : WD 2-8-0 (1943)		
90483	8F : WD 2-8-0 (1943)		
6624	5MTT : 56xx 0-6-2T (1927)		To Cathays 10/57
6657	5MTT : 56xx 0-6-2T (1927)		
6697	5MTT : 56xx 0-6-2T (1927)		
8100	4MTT : 81xx 2-6-2T (1938)		
8109	4MTT : 81xx 2-6-2T (1938)		
6134	4MTT : 61xx 2-6-2T (1931)	Ex Tyseley 11/57	
4103	4MTT : 51xx 2-6-2T (1928)	Ex Wolverhampton 11/57	
4112	4MTT : 51xx 2-6-2T (1928)		
4118	4MTT : 51xx 2-6-2T (1928)		
4128	4MTT : 51xx 2-6-2T (1928)	Ex Chester 10/57	
4171	4MTT : 51xx 2-6-2T (1928)		
5101	4MTT : 51xx 2-6-2T (1928)	Ex Stourbridge 6/57	
5104	4MTT : 51xx 2-6-2T (1928)		
5161	4MTT : 51xx 2-6-2T (1928)		w/d 4/57
5184	4MTT : 51xx 2-6-2T (1928)		
5185	4MTT : 51xx 2-6-2T (1928)		
5194	4MTT : 51xx 2-6-2T (1928)		
5198	4MTT : 51xx 2-6-2T (1928)	Ex Tyseley 10/57	
3619	3FT : 57xx 0-6-0T (1933)		
3624	3FT : 57xx 0-6-0T (1933)		
3631	3FT : 57xx 0-6-0T (1933)		
7702	3FT : 57xx 0-6-0T (1929)		
17	1P : RAILCAR		
26	1P : RAILCAR		To Worcester 11/57
29	1P : RAILCAR		To Reading 11/57
5813	1P : 14xx 0-4-2T (1932)	Ex Bristol (BR) 4/57	w/d 11/57
5815	1P : 14xx 0-4-2T (1932)	Ex Worcester 4/57	

since the thirty engines were scattered amongst eight sheds, the nearest to us being four each at Shrewsbury and Chester for working the northern expresses beyond Wolverhampton.

But everything comes to he who waits and one Saturday in August 1955 I found myself booked with driver Jim Hill for an additional from Snow Hill to Chester. Most of the relief Birkenhead expresses ran through from London with Old Oak or Stafford Road men and I was curious to see what sort of engine we would be given for a working that commenced at Birmingham. I presumed that it would be one of the inevitable Halls which was all we had at Tyseley for express workings.

It was as well I didn't put money on it since Stafford Road had arranged for an engine to be transferred from Chester to Tyseley for the day,

the working being (theoretically) beyond the powers of a Hall 4-6-0.

"Have you ever fired a County class?" My driver asked me as I signed on and I shook my head.

"Well now's your chance to learn."

We walked over to our engine, 1024 'County of Pembroke', which had been prepared for us. The first thing I noticed was the livery which was not Brunswick green but lined black – although it still looked a picture – and recalled that the class, even though they had a greater tractive effort than a Castle, were technically mixed traffic engines. The second thing I noticed was the very high boiler pressure of 280lb which was a lot more than the 225lb of most Great Western engines. Jim saw me looking at the red mark.

"Just keep it round the 250 mark and we shall be okay."

That was encouraging but I had to tell him that I'd never been north of Oxley before.

"We shall be okay."

I had to admire his confidence.

We came off shed and ran over to the carriage sidings to pick our ten coach train up; the guard giving us the tonnage and other details:

"381 tons. Wolverhampton, Shrewsbury, Gobowen, Ruabon, Wrexham and Chester."

"Righto mate."

"Right away when you're ready."

Jim opened the regulator to get us onto the relief road and immediately I sensed that 1024 was a different kind of engine from the ones I was used to. The view from my cabside window of a very large boiler, bulging smokebox and massive steam pipes that conveyed an enormous feeling of power; a feeling that quickly became reality as 1024 started away.

We stood for a few minutes at Bordesley alongside the stock for the 11.05 Snow Hill – Pwllheli and Aberystwyth which had a 63xx 2-6-0 on it.

"Not so long ago," Jim volunteered, "they'd have had a Dukedog – and we'd have had their engine."

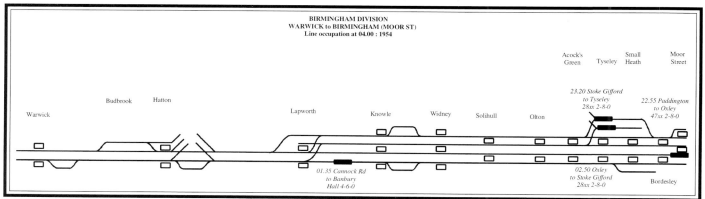

BIRMINGHAM DIVISION
WARWICK to BIRMINGHAM (MOOR ST)
Line occupation at 04.00 : 1954

I silently gave thanks that we lived in the enlightened times of 1955. I didn't care a great deal for the 2-6-0's and wouldn't have wanted one on a ten coach express to Chester.

Leaving Snow Hill, where the platform had been black with passengers, I very quickly learned that there is less to be afraid of with large engines than with small. 1024 was a beauty and not only did it ride and pull well hut I had no difficulty in keeping the needle just short of the 280lb mark. If anything I overdid things a little since, not knowing the road and therefore having no idea where Jim was going to shut off, the engine tended to blow off more than it should have. Jim winked at me.

"Better to have too much than not enough."

It was unusual for a Great Western driver to wink at wasted steam and no doubt had I been a little more experienced it would have earned me a lecture – and quite right too. But Jim's magnanimity and the way 1024 was going – it roared up Shifnal bank – made the duty something of a holiday as did Shrewsbury and Chester, neither of which I'd been to before.

Funnily enough the 85-mile trip from Birmingham to Chester had something of a doubtful reputation amongst the staff at Tyseley and one of my drivers, Harold Burton, in later days used to tell me: "It's a rough day's work, Chester and back (which it was, firing to him). On a sunny day the sun's on the fireman's back each way."

1024 levelled Coton Hill bank and in no time at all we were stopping to pick up a pilotman to take us into Chester General where we uncoupled to let the train reverse out behind a 2-6-0 to Birkenhead.

We turned 1024 on the angle and tied it down opposite the Great Western loco whilst we had lunch on a makeshift table of sleepers. It was too fine a day to go into the mess room and in any event my attention was focused on the LMS trains that passed by. It was astonishing to be paid for what I was doing.

Three quarters of an hour before our return working was due to leave, we started to get 1024 ready for the road by filling the tender and bringing the fire round. A good half of the coal had been used coming down and Jim and I spent some time moving the remainder forward, no easy task with the straight sided Hawksworth tenders which were very awkward to shovel in.

"D'you remember coming through Gresford on the way down?" asked Jim as we backed down to the station.

"No."

"Well you will going up."

Both he and the pilotman laughed, the latter telling me that it was the steepest bank in the district.

"One in eighty-two, it is. For more than four miles."

I banged a dozen in the front of the firebox and let 1024 heat up. Jim got the right away and we pulled out of Chester General with me sitting confidently, for the benefit of the trainspotters, as though I had done it twice a day for the last ten years. The pilotman dropped off at No.6 signalbox and Jim opened up, 1024 roaring away as we gained speed towards Saltney.

Nothing, I thought, could go wrong on a day like this and sensing, perhaps, my mood 1024 romped up Gresford bank on full regulator whilst I swung the shovel like a navvy to keep the needle as close to 280lb as I could. It was

great fun and hard work but I was glad to see the summit, not so much on account of my exertions but because the climb threatened to drain the boiler and the level was getting to the point where use of the injector would simply kill the engine by half filling it with cold water.

The stop in Wrexham General gave me a chance to put something back in the boiler without the needle falling too far and as we pulled away towards Ruabon I was desperately planning how I would get matters back to normal when Jim eased the regulator and muttered to himself. I looked out of the cab to see a distant signal against us and took the opportunity to fill the boiler a little more.

"It'll be block and block all the way from here?"

He went on to tell me how the railway had far more trains on summer Saturdays than it could cope with. He was right and we moved more or less from signal to signal which if it

LEAMINGTON ALLOCATION : 1958			
LOCO	CLASS	IN	OUT
90261	8F : WD 2-8-0 (1943)		
90483	8F : WD 2-8-0 (1943)		
6657	5MTT : 56xx 0-6-2T (1927)		
6697	5MTT : 56xx 0-6-2T (1927)		
4933	5MT : HALL 4-6-0 (1928)		To Westbury 8/58
42566	4MTT 2-6-4T (1935)	Ex Rugby 12/58	
8100	4MTT : 81xx 2-6-2T (1938)		
8109	4MTT : 81xx 2-6-2T (1938)		
6134	4MTT : 81xx 2-6-2T (1931)		To Severn T. Jcn 1/58
4103	4MTT : 51xx 2-6-2T (1928)		To Taunton 6/58
4112	4MTT : 51xx 2-6-2T (1928)		
4118	4MTT : 51xx 2-6-2T (1928)	Ex Worcester 1/58	To Westbury 8/58
4128	4MTT : 51xx 2-6-2T (1928)		
4162	4MTT : 51xx 2-6-2T (1928)		To Bristol (SPM) 2/58
4171	4MTT : 51xx 2-6-2T (1928)		To Taunton 6/58
5101	4MTT : 51xx 2-6-2T (1928)	Ex Taunton 9/58	
5104	4MTT : 51xx 2-6-2T (1928)		To Taunton 6/58
5184	4MTT : 51xx 2-6-2T (1928)		To Taunton 6/58
5184	4MTT : 51xx 2-6-2T (1928)		To Gloucester 7/58
5185	4MTT : 51xx 2-6-2T (1928)		To Banbury 2/58
5194	4MTT : 51xx 2-6-2T (1928)		
5198	4MTT : 51xx 2-6-2T (1928)		
82007	3MTT 2-6-2T (1952)		
3619	3FT : 57xx 0-6-0T (1933)		
3624	3FT : 57xx 0-6-0T (1933)		
3631	3FT : 57xx 0-6-0T (1933)		
7702	3FT : 57xx 0-6-0T (1929)		
41227	2MTT 2-6-2T (1946)	Ex Rugby 12/58	
41228	2MTT 2-6-2T (1946)	Ex Rugby 12/58	
41285	2MTT 2-6-2T (1946)	Ex Rugby 12/58	
17	1P : RAILCAR	Ex Shrewsbury 6/58	To Wellington 7/58
5815	1P : 14xx 2-4-2T (1932)	Ex Tyseley 10/58	

made a nonsense of the timetable at least resolved my boiler dilemma.

Matters improved after leaving Shrewsbury and we were able to give 1024 its head and regain some time although, as Jim pointed out, timekeeping on summer Saturdays was a secondary consideration. "The main thing is to get back to your starting point."

There was someone who had had a worse day than us and as we accelerated past Abbey Foregate Junction we passed our Tyseley colleagues who were waiting to follow us with their Cambrian train. There was no need to ask how they were doing since it was written all over their faces. Aberystwyth and back with a 63xx 2-6-0 is enough for a day's work for anyone.

"Another twenty minutes and we'll be home," announced Jim as we stood in Wolverhampton after a cracking run from Salop and I told him it was just as well since the tender was all but empty.

"I'll use that up for you." He cried as he cracked the regulator and sent 1024 barking out of the station and up the bank to Swan Village. I cleared out the tender, threw it in the firebox and sat down to enjoy the rest of the run to Snow Hill, musing on the fact that I had shifted something like seven tons of coal in one hundred and seventy miles, a consumption that seemed very high to me given that the LNER and LMS ran more than twice as far on only a ton more. 1024 had been running on something like ninety pounds of coal a mile – the ache in

my back could testify to the fact – which was about twice what it ought to have been. I thought it would be interesting to see how much a County would use on a long distance express without stops.

At Snow Hill I watched the crowds decant onto platform 7 from the coaches and tried to calculate the ratio between the cost of seven tons of coal and the price of a single ticket from Chester multiplied by ten carriages but gave it up, deciding instead that the railway had probably made a profit from the enterprise which, of course, was the object of the exercise. More importantly I had made my mark as an express passenger fireman.

I often looked back on the trip with 1024 as a happy experience but never more so than five months later when one bitterly cold evening Micky and I were sent passenger to Stratford to pick up 2-8-0 2807 of Worcester and run it light to Leamington loco. It promised to be a nice little job and Mick and I looked forward to a fairly quiet shift – it was too cold for heroics – as we boarded the 17.15 ex Snow Hill for the run to Stratford.

I thought it was curious that a Worcester engine should be wanted at a place like Leamington but, orders being orders, we got it ready for the road, not that much needed doing since it had only arrived a couple of hours earlier, and set off for the half-hour run. Hatton had his boards on and drew us up to the box.

"Tyseley loco." The bobby shouted from his window.

"Leamington." I called back.

"Naw. Control want you to Tyseley."

Fourteen miles tender first on the coldest night I could remember. They must have thought we were mad.

"Send us back to the west and we'll go round the north curve." I yelled to the box but he shook his head and said Hatton West had switched out. I turned to Mick and suggested we carry on to Leamington and turn before going on to Tyseley. He called across to the signalman as he wound the engine back.

"Pull off."

I couldn't believe it.

"You're not going tender-first all the way to Tyseley?"

"Ah well," he replied opening the regulator, "they might need the engine badly."

Caught unprepared I had not had an opportunity to water the coal in the tender and in addition to the biting wind, the cab started to fill with dust and small pieces of coal. Mick, deciding not to prolong the agony, opened up as hard as he could and probably set a world record for light engine speed: our speed rising as the temperature dropped. I waved my arms, jumped up and down and did all the gyrations I could think of to keep warm but it was no good and by the time we were halfway back, I was absolutely numb. How Mick managed to keep an eye on signals was a mystery since I couldn't see anything for coal dust and water although I marvelled at the way we got a clear run without a single signal check. All I wanted was a five minute stop so that I could get some heat from the firebox.

After an absolute nightmare of a trip we got back to Tyseley and I thought longingly of standing in brilliant sunshine on a County even if it meant shovelling two tender-loads of coal. 1024 seemed a long way away as I tried to thaw myself enough to screw 2807's tender handbrake on……

YOUR LIFE IN THEIR HANDS

The quiet beauty of the Cotswolds is appreciated more off the footplate than on where the crew are probably taking up the drop plate between the engine and tender to allow breathable air into the footplate while climbing through the single-bore Ledbury tunnel. Hall 4-6-0 5927 'Guild Hall' of Tyseley leaves Ledbury and heads for the tunnel with a Hereford - Worcester - Birmingham express in 1950.

Locomotive departments seemed to con-tained a greater proportion of characters than could be found elsewhere on the railway and Tyseley was no exception. No narrative of the place would be complete without trying to bring them back to life.

Driving, by and large, was a lonely occupa-tion since there wasn't much scope for conver-sation on the footplate of a moving steam en-gine and some drivers made up for it in a display of super-garrulity when the opportunity arose. Of these the star turn was Tommy Knight who was outbased at Bordesley Junction and who could talk the wheels of a twenty-eighter. It wouldn't have been so bad if his conversation had ever amounted to anything substantial but the unlucky recipient would receive a descrip-tion of the most commonplace events strung out like a Greek saga.

"My wife who I married in nineteen twelve because her father worked with my brother who was born....(and so on for twenty minutes)....made my tea when I got up this morning." All this to describe a numbingly rou-tine event which had taken place every morning for forty years.

A spell with him on a 57xx when things were quiet was not to be relished and every time the engine came to a stand you would get a prolonged account of how he paid his gas bill or the machinations involved in buying a newspa-per from a newsagent. One day he was watch-ing his fireman fill the tank of their pannier when the wind caught the tank filler lid and dropped it fair and square on Tom's head, an injury that

failed to stop the torrent of verbiage directed towards his fireman who had only filled the tank in the hope of escaping Tom's interminа-ble conversation for a few minutes. A group of concerned footplatemen rushed over to where Tom lay on the ground and helped him to his feet.

"What happened?"

"Well I was just standing here talking......."

And to the day he died he wondered why his audience suddenly fell about laughing.

Another old boy at Bordesley, trained at the same school as Tom but whose conversa-tion revolved around his hypochondria was dis-covered to be a useful mechanism for manage-ment purposes.

One of the trials of being a shedmaster was the time that drivers spent road learning or fa-

LEAMINGTON ALLOCATION : 1959		
LOCO CLASS	IN	OUT
90261 8F : WD 2-8-0 (1943)		To Banbury 8/59
90483 8F : WD 2-8-0 (1943)		To Banbury 9/59
6657 5MTT : 56xx 0-6-2T (1927)		
6697 5MTT : 56xx 0-6-2T (1927)		
42566 4MTT 2-6-4T (1935)		
8100 4MTT : 81xx 2-6-2T (1938)		
8109 4MTT : 81xx 2-6-2T (1938)		
4103 4MTT : 51xx 2-6-2T (1928)		To Oxford 8/59
4112 4MTT : 51xx 2-6-2T (1928)		
4118 4MTT : 51xx 2-6-2T (1928)		
4162 4MTT : 51xx 2-6-2T (1928)		
4171 4MTT : 51xx 2-6-2T (1928)		
5101 4MTT : 51xx 2-6-2T (1928)		
5184 4MTT : 51xx 2-6-2T (1928)		
5194 4MTT : 51xx 2-6-2T (1928)	Ex Worcester 12/59	
3619 3FT : 57xx 0-6-0T (1933)		
3624 3FT : 57xx 0-6-0T (1933)		
3631 3FT : 57xx 0-6-0T (1933)		
9614 3FT : 57xx 0-6-0T (1933)	Ex Tyseley 12/59	
9733 3FT : 57xx 0-6-0T (1933)	Ex Tyseley 12/59	
7702 3FT : 57xx 0-6-0T (1929)		
41227 2MTT 2-6-2T (1946)		To Rugby 9/59
41228 2MTT 2-6-2T (1946)		
41285 2MTT 2-6-2T (1946)		To Wrexham (SC) 9/59

miliarising themselves with diesel shunting en-gines. The first was the more serious problems since it was left to each individual driver to de-cide when he was ready to sign a particular road and drivers sent out road learning would disap-pear for days and sometimes weeks. Bordesley was no different and drivers would come into the yard to learn the sidings and it would be the last that was seen of them for some time.

One day an unusually alert shedmaster, or his assistant, came across the hypo and asked the fatal question:

"How are you?"

"Oh God, my feet have got (some technical medical term) and my right ankle has (another T.M.T.) and it's almost as bad as the left one. I went to the quack - the socks and shoes would be taken off for a close inspection - and he said he'd seen nothing like it so he called the con-sultant who had a look and he said he'd never seen anything like it in his career either, not even when he was in India and...."

So it went on from feet to scalp, omitting very little, and the shedmaster was lucky to escape in less than an hour. It did give him a gem of an idea and from that time it was decreed that the hypo would be the man nominated to do all road learning and diesel training. It was a stroke worthy of the Machiavelli himself and drivers were passing out in road and diesel knowledge in less than a shift. If only the Hypo could have been put on the main line......

Not all the Bordesley men were quite so bad, some were a pleasure to work with, and many a young fireman enjoyed a shifts enter-

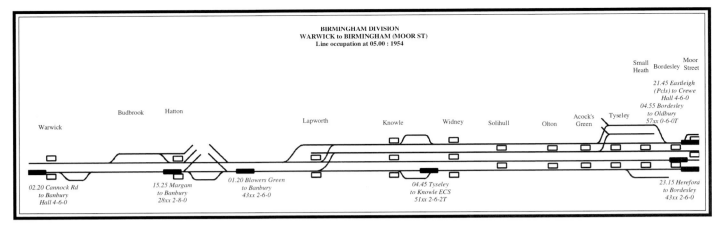

Small Heath Bordesley Moor Street

21.45 Eastleigh (Pcls) to Crewe
Hall 4-6-0
04.55 Bordesley to Oldbury
57xx 0-6-0T

Warwick   Budbrook   Hatton   Lapworth   Knowle   Widney   Solihull   Olton   Acock's Green   Tyseley

02.20 Cannock Rd to Banbury Hall 4-6-0   *15.25 Margam to Banbury 28xx 2-8-0*   *01.20 Blowers Green to Banbury 43xx 2-6-0*   *04.45 Tyseley to Knowle ECS 51xx 2-6-2T*   *23.15 Hereford to Bordesley 43xx 2-6-0*

tainment listening avidly as one of the old boys relived earlier glories and related tale after tale of what it was like to fire in Churchward's day.

Even though they had come off the main line for health reasons, there were still a few hard hitters at Bordesley who would blast up and down the yard as though they were taking 500 tons to Paddington. Of these, Bert Brown was one of the best known; not only for the speed of his engine but for his skill in being able to gauge precisely where a raft of wagons should stop. There was nothing that would infuriate yard shunters more than a driver who could not accurately propel wagons to a given spot on a siding but it was said that Bert Brown never had to come up for a second shove. Art is not an adjective commonly applied to marshalling yard work but to watch his 57xx 0-6-0T roar as it pushed half a dozen wagons and then to see them free-wheel to stop exactly where the shunter was standing was pretty impressive. Before they had come to a stand Bert would be pulling out another batch of wagons for the next shunt.

That is not to say that he did not occasionally come unstuck. The roads in Bordesley were not intended for high speeds and I can clearly remember seeing Bert's loco off the road all wheels with the smoke box at a ridiculous angle towards the sky. Not that derailments, even of engines, were a particular problem in marshalling yards. You simply packed the wheels with sleepers and whatever other material you could find in the vicinity and dragged the derailed engine back onto the track with another pilot. Sometimes they rerailed quite quickly, occasionally (as in the case of a 2000hp diesel at Ferme Park on the Great Northern) they had to be dragged the length of the yard, smashing chairs for as far as the eyes could see. Either way work was not held up for long and if you were lucky you could derail and rerail without anyone in authority being aware of the fact.

Even when 350hp diesels took over the job, the character of the drivers did not change and the only difference was that instead of talking to a fireman, they used to chat to themselves. With some pride they would claim to be the first fully trained diesel drivers on the system and it was with some disappointment that they learned that their experience did not qualify them

LEAMINGTON ALLOCATION : 1960			
LOCO	CLASS	IN	OUT
6657	5MTT : 56xx 0-6-2T (1927)		To Barry 3/60
6697	5MTT : 56xx 0-6-2T (1927)		To Barry 4/60
42566	4MTT 2-6-4T (1935)		
8100	4MTT : 81xx 2-6-2T (1938)		
8109	4MTT : 81xx 2-6-2T (1938)		
4112	4MTT : 51xx 2-6-2T (1928)		
4118	4MTT : 51xx 2-6-2T (1928)		
4162	4MTT : 51xx 2-6-2T (1928)		w/d 7/60
4171	4MTT : 51xx 2-6-2T (1928)		
5101	4MTT : 51xx 2-6-2T (1928)		
5177	4MTT : 51xx 2-6-2T (1928)	Ex Gloucester 3/60	
5184	4MTT : 51xx 2-6-2T (1928)		
5194	4MTT : 51xx 2-6-2T (1928)		
3619	3FT : 57xx 0-6-0T (1933)		
3624	3FT : 57xx 0-6-0T (1933)		To Neyland 9/60
3631	3FT : 57xx 0-6-0T (1933)		
9614	3FT : 57xx 0-6-0T (1933)		To Tyseley 1/60
9733	3FT : 57xx 0-6-0T (1933)		To Tyseley 1/60
7702	3FT : 57xx 0-6-0T (1929)		w/d 8/60
41228	2MT 2-6-2T (1946)		To Rugby 2/60
41285	2MT 2-6-2T (1946)		To Rugby 3/60
41285	2MT 2-6-2T (1946)	Ex Rugby 5/60	

to go back onto the main line to train steam drivers when the 2750hp diesel-electrics started to arrive in the early 1960's.

Idiosyncrasies were no less evident at Tyseley. One driver used to change his clothes after finishing duty, stowing his overalls and BR cap neatly in his locker. When asked why he replied – quite seriously – that they were company property and to take them off the premises was tantamount to theft.

Less scrupulous was a driver who was gifted in picking horses and had to be asked by the bookmaker on Warwick Road to minimise his bets since he was having trouble paying out the winnings. It was said the driver used to holiday in Bermuda two or three times a year.

Of another driver, Bernard P., it was said more happened to him in bringing an engine from the shed to the water column than happened in the entire careers of other drivers and not only did he revel in being supremely accident-prone but boasted about his problems as though they were in some way creditable. A typical example concerned a 56xx 0-6-2T which had been released from the factory after repairs to a hot axlebox. Bernard and his fireman had been delegated to prepare it and get it ready for some light goods duties before it returned to its shed in South Wales. Having oiled the engine he jumped up on the footplate to run forward to a water column. He opened up and the engine started away in reverse; the eccentrics having been improperly fitted. Normally the Royal train would have been coming up behind him but for once there was no damage and Bernard was delighted. He ran round the shed, waving his arms and describing his find with such aplomb that people initially thought he had won the pools.

Most of the Tyseley drivers were enthusiastic raconteurs and occasionally one wondered whether or not the stories had grown a bit in the telling for benefit of young wide-eyed firemen. One such was Frank Masefield who would hypnotise his audience by talking and coughing without the cigarette, which was permanently stuck to his upper lip, becoming dislodged. He was one of those smokers who got through thirty cigarettes a day but only one match. He was also the first person at the shed to hear of anything that was going to happen anywhere on the railway and his source was always the same.

"They're closing Old Oak Common and all the main line work is coming to Leamington."

"How do you know that, Frank?"

"Well, there was this chap from the top office riding with me and he told me…"

He once told a group of acolyte firemen about a trip he did on an ambulance special during the war.

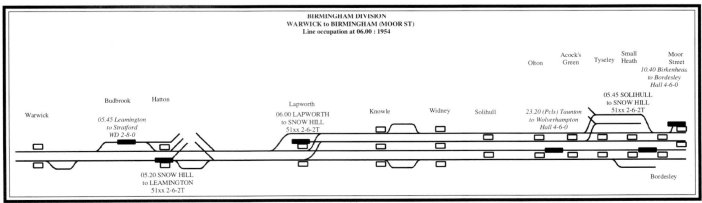

Olton Acock's Green Tyseley Small Heath Moor Street

10.40 Birkenhead to Bordesley Hall 4-6-0
05.45 SOLIHULL to SNOW HILL 51xx 2-6-2T

Warwick   Budbrook   Hatton   Lapworth   Knowle   Widney   Solihull

05.45 Leamington to Stratford WD 2-8-0   *06.00 LAPWORTH to SNOW HILL 51xx 2-6-2T*   *23.20 (Pcls) Taunton to Wolverhampton Hall 4-6-0*

05.20 SNOW HILL to LEAMINGTON 51xx 2-6-2T   Bordesley

Not all the venerable characters passing through the Birmingham district were Tyseley drivers and the passage of a Dean Goods on a Chester - Lambourne horsebox special in 1955 sparked off a few recollections by older members of the establishment. The appearance of 2513, seen at Lapworth, was all the more memorable since the engine was allocated to far-off Brecon.

"When we got to Banbury there was no relief so we went on to Oxford and there was no-one there and eventually we worked through to Southampton. The Southern made us work back to Birmingham as soon as it was unloaded and when we got back to Snow Hill they wanted another trip to Southampton, so since we now knew the road we did it. Birmingham to Southampton and back – twice in one day!"

He paused for effect only to be deflated by a shout from a disbelieving driver who was listening in the next room.

"They should have given you a bloody medal, Frank. One as big as your smokebox."

Located on the fringe of the Methodist belt, Tyseley had its spiritual element of which much was embodied in the person of Harold Burton who, for his sins, had me as his fireman and who believed that salvation was attainable only through continuous use of the shovel. Suffer little firemen and I certainly did, especially working to Chester which was where he originated. From the way he drove it was as though he couldn't wait to see the place going down and couldn't get away fast enough on the return. Strong language by his colleagues generally and his fireman in particular was frowned upon and when circumstances demanded an expletive, the expression 'Bless me' was used so frequently that it became his nickname.

If his language was less colourful than that of his contemporaries, he was an occasional master of the non-sequiteur.

"Have you got a wife?" he once asked me and I told him I was single.

"How old are you?"

"Twenty-eight."

His eyebrows went up.

"Bless me," he said, "by the time I was your age I had a piano and four children…"

For all his flogging of engines and firemen, Bless Me was at least honest which is more than can be said for the manifestation of Mammon which one saw in less scrupulous Drivers who would sell their families (and certainly their firemen) for a few pence overtime.

Running times were extended by an ingenious variety of dodges which included taking a minute more than booked on each section – not enough to earn a 'please explain' but sufficient to amount to a decent overtime payment on a long run – to arriving at turntables just as a queue of engines had formed. As a junior fireman one had no say or opinion but when you were leaving Banbury at the time you had an appointment to meet the (currently) most gorgeous woman in the world, you had to bite your lip. It was little wonder I was still single at twenty-eight.

The irony was that the overtime merchants spent so much time on the footplate that they never seemed to have the time to spend the money they made. I fired to Bert Watkins – who was as adept as any for making the odd penny's overtime - in No.5 link for a time and although I had little time to spend anything I was certainly the wealthiest fireman at Tyseley for a while. It was said of Bert that when he

BANBURY ALLOCATION : 1950							
LOCO	CLASS	IN	OUT	LOCO	CLASS	IN	OUT
2886	8F : 28xx 2-8-0 (1938)			6839	5MT : GRANGE 4-6-0 (1936)		
2897	8F : 28xx 2-8-0 (1938)			6854	5MT : GRANGE 4-6-0 (1936)		
2898	8F : 28xx 2-8-0 (1938)			6696	5MT : 56xx 0-6-2T (1927)		
2899	8F : 28xx 2-8-0 (1938)			2981	4MT : SAINT 4-6-0 (1902)		
3802	8F : 28xx 2-8-0 (1938)			4149	4MT : 51xx 2-6-2T (1928)		
3819	8F : 28xx 2-8-0 (1938)			5317	4MT : 43xx 2-6-0 (1911)		
3820	8F : 28xx 2-8-0 (1938)			5324	4MT : 43xx 2-6-0 (1911)		
3829	8F : 28xx 2-8-0 (1938)		To Chester 12/50	5332	4MT : 43xx 2-6-0 (1911)		
3831	8F : 28xx 2-8-0 (1938)			5361	4MT : 43xx 2-6-0 (1911)		
3849	8F : 28xx 2-8-0 (1938)			5391	4MT : 43xx 2-6-0 (1911)	Ex Newton A. 2/50	
3861	8F : 28xx 2-8-0 (1938)			6342	4MT : 43xx 2-6-0 (1911)		
3863	8F : 28xx 2-8-0 (1938)			6354	4MT : 43xx 2-6-0 (1911)	Ex Penzance 2/50	To Stourbridge 12/50
3865	8F : 28xx 2-8-0 (1938)			6390	4MT : 43xx 2-6-0 (1911)		
2805	8F : 28xx 2-8-0 (1903)			8400	4F : 94XX 0-6-0T (1949)		
2816	8F : 28xx 2-8-0 (1903)			8405	4F : 94XX 0-6-0T (1949)		
2847	8F : 28xx 2-8-0 (1903)			8407	4F : 94XX 0-6-0T (1949)		
2853	8F : 28xx 2-8-0 (1903)			8459	4F : 94XX 0-6-0T (1949)		
2863	8F : 28xx 2-8-0 (1903)			9426	4F : 94XX 0-6-0T (1949)	New 2/50	
2869	8F : 28xx 2-8-0 (1903)		To Chester 12/50	2256	3MT : 2251 0-6-0 (1930)		
2883	8F : 28xx 2-8-0 (1903)			2295	3MT : 2251 0-6-0 (1930)		
3020	7F : R.O.D. 2-8-0 (1917)			3216	3MT : 2251 0-6-0 (1930)		
3043	7F : R.O.D. 2-8-0 (1917)			3218	3MT : 2251 0-6-0 (1930)		
6979	5MT : MOD-HALL 4-6-0 (1944)			3630	3F : 57xx 0-6-0T (1933)		
7800	5MT : MANOR 4-6-0 (1938)	Ex Tyseley 12/50		3694	3F : 57xx 0-6-0T (1933)		
7805	5MT : MANOR 4-6-0 (1938)		To Yeovil 9/50	4631	3F : 57xx 0-6-0T (1933)		
7806	5MT : MANOR 4-6-0 (1938)		To Penzance 9/50	4646	3F : 57xx 0-6-0T (1933)		
7811	5MT : MANOR 4-6-0 (1938)			8787	3F : 57xx 0-6-0T (1933)		
4918	5MT : HALL 4-6-0 (1928)	Ex Chester 12/50		9782	3F : 57xx 0-6-0T (1933)		
4960	5MT : HALL 4-6-0 (1928)	Ex Wolverhampton 12/50		5724	3F : 57xx 0-6-0T (1929)		
4980	5MT : HALL 4-6-0 (1928)	Ex Tyseley 12/50		7763	3F : 57xx 0-6-0T (1929)		
5930	5MT : HALL 4-6-0 (1928)			8729	3F : 57xx 0-6-0T (1929)		
5967	5MT : HALL 4-6-0 (1928)			6418	2P : 64xx 0-6-0T (1932)		
5994	5MT : HALL 4-6-0 (1928)	Ex Old Oak C. 12/50		5404	1P : 54xx 0-6-0T (1931)		
6901	5MT : HALL 4-6-0 (1928)	Ex Wolverhampton 12/50		5407	1P : 54xx 0-6-0T (1931)		
6906	5MT : HALL 4-6-0 (1928)			5417	1P : 54xx 0-6-0T (1931)		
6929	5MT : HALL 4-6-0 (1928)			5424	1P : 54xx 0-6-0T (1931)		
6803	5MT : GRANGE 4-6-0 (1936)			1401	1P : 14xx 0-4-2T (1932)		
6816	5MT : GRANGE 4-6-0 (1936)			1411	1P : 14xx 0-4-2T (1932)		
6819	5MT : GRANGE 4-6-0 (1936)			1458	1P : 14xx 0-4-2T (1932)		To Stourbridge 12/50
6835	5MT : GRANGE 4-6-0 (1936)						

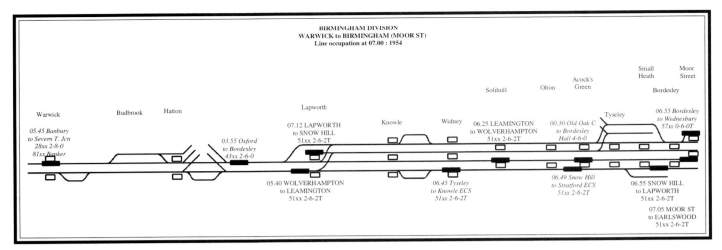

went off shed, he left his watch in his locker and relied on a calendar.

At the other end of the scale were the drivers who would spare nothing to get from one end of a run to the other in the minimum time possible and the devil take the fireman. One such was Fred 'Dr Woo' Delderfield who was a hard hitter especially when working the two-hour expresses between Paddington and Snow Hill. Saving a minute here and a minute there, by about Leamington he would exhort his fireman to keep his strength up and at the same time stuff a few pieces of barley sugar into his (the fireman's) mouth.

"What you need is glucose to keep your energy up." he would say as he wound the King forward and shot half the fire through the tubes.

"What I need," I would reply with a mouth full of his wretched sweets, "is a mechanical stoker…"

I never did get the benefit from them since my energies would only allow me to fire or eat but not both at the same time. As soon as his back was turned I would spit the rotten things over the side.

Frank 'Plum' Warner was another driver who liked to straighten out a few curves yet off-duty his passion was repairing the smallest and most delicate watches he could find. At home he would be lost in a reverie of minute mechanics, eye-glass in place and tweezers in hand whilst an hour later he would be hammering a 4-6-0 out of Snow Hill with all the subtlety of a crowbar. Had Hercules been a fireman, his eighth labour would have been trying to keep up with the Plum.

Hard-hitting was not confined to express services by any means and I remember coming light engine Gloucester to Tyseley with Stan 'Tiddley Dike' Sharp, whose name hinted at his Midland & South Western origins. At Stratford on Avon we were stopped by the signalman and asked to bank a train up to Wilmcote as the regular bankers were tied up. Stan nodded cheerfully to the bobby, buffered up to the rear of the waiting train and waited for the tip from the guard. It has to be said that Stratford men were not known for flogging their engines and usually banked a train with just enough assistance to get it over the top provided the train engine did its share of the work. Stan had no knowledge of Stratford customs and as soon as we had the right away, up came the regulator, down came the lever; the 2-6-0 pushing so well that the train engine, judging from the amount of steam I could see escaping from its safety-valves, got up the bank on a closed regulator. We heard a rumour later on that Stratford men seemed to have turned over a new leaf….

Stan was also known as 'old FHW' by virtue of his claim that in his early days on the M & SW Junction, one of his links alternated between passenger and goods work and that he kept a separate pair of boots for each. FHW may therefore have stood for Freeman, Hardy & Willis although it could equally have meant something like Flipping Hard Work, which it was for his firemen.

Some nicknames could be found at any main line shed and one of the most ubiquitous was 'Slasher', a name reserved for the worst of the hard-hitters when no other adjective could be found. The Tyseley Slasher was Ted Cartwright who would flog anything that had a fireman, as a friend of mine, John Harris, found out on his first turn at Tyseley after transferring from the LMS at Bournville.

It was a foggy – 'thick as a bag' – morning and they came off shed with 57xx 0-6-0T 3660 and made their way down to Bordesley Up Sidings where they were turned into what Slasher expected to be a through road. Peering through the spectacle glass and trying to look as though he knew where he was going, Slasher opened 3660 up as soon as they had passed the entry turnout, intending to run right down the road and then reverse into another to pick up his train.

Half a minute later the 0-6-0 hit the stops at the end of the road and ended up with its leading drivers sitting on a mess of wood and steel. Driver and fireman shook themselves and walked to the front to see the damage for themselves.

"How are we going to get out of this?" asked John with a sense of self-preservation but old Slasher couldn't have cared less.

"First thing, you can nip down to the shop and get me a morning paper. Second, you can make some tea."

John realised he was a long way from Bournville and the LMS where you only had to scratch your backside in a funny way to generate an official enquiry.

If John had reservations about Slasher's driving methods he had none about Slasher's daughter who he very soon started courting. Walking her home one night after an evening at the cinema, he remarked on the tantalising smell of bacon wafting out of the Cartwright family kitchen. John licked his lips, the femme Slasher got the message and five minutes later he had wrapped himself round two of the largest bacon sandwiches he could ever remember seeing.

An hour later he was signing on at the shed alongside a distinctly disconsolate looking driver. John, on the other hand, was on top of the world.

BANBURY ALLOCATION : 1951						
LOCO	CLASS	IN	OUT	LOCO	CLASS	IN	OUT
90192	8F : WD 2-8-0 (1943)	Ex Eastfield 12/51		6835	5MT : GRANGE 4-6-0 (1936)		To Leamington 5/51
90312	8F : WD 2-8-0 (1943)	Ex Swindon 5/51		6835	5MT : GRANGE 4-6-0 (1936)	Ex Leamington 6/51	
90313	8F : WD 2-8-0 (1943)	Ex Eastfield 12/51		6839	5MT : GRANGE 4-6-0 (1936)		
90579	8F : WD 2-8-0 (1943)	Ex Swindon 5/51		6854	5MT : GRANGE 4-6-0 (1936)		
2886	8F : 28xx 2-8-0 (1938)			6696	5MT : 56xx 0-6-2T (1927)		
2897	8F : 28xx 2-8-0 (1938)			2981	4MT : SAINT 4-6-0 (1902)		W/D 3/51
2898	8F : 28xx 2-8-0 (1938)			4149	4MT : 51xx 2-6-2T (1928)		
2899	8F : 28xx 2-8-0 (1938)			5137	4MT : 51xx 2-6-2T (1928)	Ex Wellington 6/51	w/d 10/51
3802	8F : 28xx 2-8-0 (1938)			5141	4MT : 51xx 2-6-2T (1928)	Ex Chester 8/51	
3819	8F : 28xx 2-8-0 (1938)			5317	4MT : 43xx 2-6-0 (1911)		
3820	8F : 28xx 2-8-0 (1938)			5324	4MT : 43xx 2-6-0 (1911)		
3831	8F : 28xx 2-8-0 (1938)			5332	4MT : 43xx 2-6-0 (1911)		
3849	8F : 28xx 2-8-0 (1938)		To Severn T. Jcn 5/51	5361	4MT : 43xx 2-6-0 (1911)		
3861	8F : 28xx 2-8-0 (1938)			5369	4MT : 43xx 2-6-0 (1911)	Ex Tyseley 7/51	To Tyseley 11/51
3863	8F : 28xx 2-8-0 (1938)			5391	4MT : 43xx 2-6-0 (1911)		
3865	8F : 28xx 2-8-0 (1938)		To Swindon 5/51	6332	4MT : 43xx 2-6-0 (1911)	Ex Stourbridge 7/51	
2805	8F : 28xx 2-8-0 (1903)		To Newport (Pill) 5/51	6342	4MT : 43xx 2-6-0 (1911)		
2816	8F : 28xx 2-8-0 (1903)			6390	4MT : 43xx 2-6-0 (1911)		
2847	8F : 28xx 2-8-0 (1903)			8400	4F : 94XX 0-6-0T (1949)		
2853	8F : 28xx 2-8-0 (1903)			8405	4F : 94XX 0-6-0T (1949)		
2857	8F : 28xx 2-8-0 (1903)	Ex Stourbridge 10/51		8407	4F : 94XX 0-6-0T (1949)		
2863	8F : 28xx 2-8-0 (1903)		To Newport (Pill) 5/51	8452	4F : 94XX 0-6-0T (1949)	Ex Tyseley 6/51	
2883	8F : 28xx 2-8-0 (1903)		To Newport (Pill) 5/51	8459	4F : 94XX 0-6-0T (1949)	Ex Chester 6/51	
3020	7F : R.O.D. 2-8-0 (1917)			9425	4F : 94XX 0-6-0T (1949)		
3026	7F : R.O.D. 2-8-0 (1917)	Ex Croes Newydd 6/51		9426	4F : 94XX 0-6-0T (1949)		
3043	7F : R.O.D. 2-8-0 (1917)			9438	4F : 94XX 0-6-0T (1949)	New 3/51	
6963	5MT : MOD-HALL 4-6-0 (1944)			9449	4F : 94XX 0-6-0T (1949)	New 6/51	
6966	5MT : MOD-HALL 4-6-0 (1944)	Ex Shrewsbury 12/51		2256	3MT : 2251 0-6-0 (1930)		
6976	5MT : MOD-HALL 4-6-0 (1944)	Ex Wolverhampton 12/51		2295	3MT : 2251 0-6-0 (1930)		To Worcester 10/51
6979	5MT : MOD-HALL 4-6-0 (1944)	Ex Shrewsbury 12/51		3216	3MT : 2251 0-6-0 (1930)		
7800	5MT : MANOR 4-6-0 (1938)		To Tyseley 7/51	3218	3MT : 2251 0-6-0 (1930)		
7800	5MT : MANOR 4-6-0 (1938)	Ex Tyseley 10/51		3630	3F : 57xx 0-6-0T (1933)		
7811	5MT : MANOR 4-6-0 (1938)			3694	3F : 57xx 0-6-0T (1933)		
7823	5MT : MANOR 4-6-0 (1938)	Ex Chester 10/51		4631	3F : 57xx 0-6-0T (1933)		
4900	5MT : HALL 4-6-0 (1928)	Ex Newton Abbot 10/51		4646	3F : 57xx 0-6-0T (1933)		To Stourbridge 6/51
4918	5MT : HALL 4-6-0 (1928)			8787	3F : 57xx 0-6-0T (1933)		
4960	5MT : HALL 4-6-0 (1928)			9782	3F : 57xx 0-6-0T (1933)		To Stourbridge 7/51
4980	5MT : HALL 4-6-0 (1928)			5724	3F : 57xx 0-6-0T (1929)		
5930	5MT : HALL 4-6-0 (1928)			7763	3F : 57xx 0-6-0T (1929)		
5967	5MT : HALL 4-6-0 (1928)			8729	3F : 57xx 0-6-0T (1929)		To Chester 8/51
5994	5MT : HALL 4-6-0 (1928)			6418	2P : 64xx 0-6-0T (1932)		To Wolverhampton 7/51
6901	5MT : HALL 4-6-0 (1928)			5404	1P : 54xx 0-6-0T (1931)		
6906	5MT : HALL 4-6-0 (1928)			5407	1P : 54xx 0-6-0T (1931)		
6929	5MT : HALL 4-6-0 (1928)			5417	1P : 54xx 0-6-0T (1931)		To Gloucester 5/51
6803	5MT : GRANGE 4-6-0 (1936)		To Stourbridge 6/51	5424	1P : 54xx 0-6-0T (1931)		
6816	5MT : GRANGE 4-6-0 (1936)			1401	1P : 14xx 0-4-2T (1932)		
6819	5MT : GRANGE 4-6-0 (1936)			1411	1P : 14xx 0-4-2T (1932)		

Manor 4-6-0 'Fritwell Manor' of Machynlleth hauls the 10.10 Paddington to Aberystwyth and Pwllheli 'Cambrian Coast Express' through Sutton Bridge Junction, Shrewsbury, in 1960. Taking exactly eight hours the Pwllheli section of the train was the longest day journey one could undertake on the Great Western. There was an anomaly in the Saturday timings of the service the service avoided Shrewsbury by running direct from Abbey Foregate Junction to English Bridge Junction and omitted two stops on the Cambrian yet took twenty three minutes longer to reach Pwllheli.

"What's up, Mr Cartwright. You don't seem very happy?"

Slasher scratched the back of his head.

"D'you know, John, I cooked a couple of bacon sandwiches last night to bring to work and when I got up just now, they were gone."

"You can't trust a soul these days, Mr Cartwright, and that's a fact."

Having started their working careers only a few years after the old Queen finished hers, a surprising number of drivers failed to detect the passage of time or the benefits that the brave new world of the 1950's bestowed. One of these was the Black Prince, Tommy Burrows, who was still waiting for the safety razor, amongst other things, to be invented. It had never dawned on him that shaving in ones own bathroom had become a commonplace daily ritual and he continued to visit, as he had done for the past half-century, the local barber for the purpose. Unfortunately neither his timetable or pocket would permit the operation to be performed on a daily basis and he settled for a weekly visit, by which time he had all the appearance of an especially unsavoury vagrant. To add to his charms whenever he walked anywhere, he did so not on the pavement but in the gutter. "It's amazing what you find there," he would tell us with pieces of soggy string and God knows what else poking out of his pockets. He once dammed up the stream at the bottom of his garden to see what useful debris he could extricate from the flow and it all ended up in his pockets.

In his main line days he had had a reputation as a hard hitter – it was said that when he worked an express from Birmingham to Wol-verhampton the last coach went through the Snow Hill down main crossover like a wagon masters whip – but when I fired to him, he was enjoying a prelude to retirement in the local link.

For all his peculiar habits, Tom was very good to his firemen – his lads – and I recall working the 06.35 all stations Wellington to Lapworth with him one morning just as his weekly scrape was due. Conceding that the working was a rough one for fireman he proffered a tin of sugared almonds, inviting me to "have a couple if you like."

With Tom looking like a man whose last meal had been a bottle of methylated spirits and wondering where he had found the sweets, I refused as politely as I could whereupon Tom stirred the contents of the tin with a black oily finger, which probably hadn't been washed since his last shave, in the hope that it would somehow tempt me to change my mind. It took a stronger stomach than mine to swallow Tom's sugared almonds.

Now and again he would come to work accompanied by a piano accordion with which he would jump out onto the platform and entertain his passengers during station time. One day his audience included a reporter from one of the local papers who printed an account of Tom's impromptu concerts; a piece of publicity which had the effect of producing a prohibition from Paddington on 'playing musical instruments and similar devices from the footplate of a railway locomotive.' The Bilston Hornpipe was not, it seemed, synonymous with the dignity of the Great Western.

Occasionally you came across a hard hitter who had some sympathy for his fireman, one

such being George Clinch – known, for some mysterious reason as 'Sam' – whom I accompanied on a high speed departmental special to Newport and back. The object of the run was to work the permanent way coach which was designed to detect imperfections in the track and mark them with a splash of whitewash. To sustain the high maximum speeds necessary for the coach to work properly we had been allocated Castle 4-6-0 7019 'Fowey Castle' but at the last minute Stafford Road pinched it for one of their posh jobs and gave us 5927 'Guild Hall' instead. There was nothing wrong with the Hall but it had no speedometer which would not normally have mattered except that the loss of 7019 niggled Sam and brought out the cussed element in him.

We only had five coaches on but for some reason Sam would not extend the engine and the engineer complained bitterly every time we came to a stand. The excuse Sam gave was that to go any faster would knock his fireman up. With five coaches!

One incident that Sam drank on for years took place when the first multiple units had taken over some of the local Birmingham services. Booked for the early morning Lapworth – Wellington stopper, the diesel failed at the last minute and Sam had to make do with a 51xx 2-6-2T. Giving the details of the train, the guard remarked that he expected to see some time lost since the 2-6-2T could not be expected to maintain the diesel timings. Sam told him to hang on tight and eventually ran into Wellington bang on time. He waited until the guard approached and was ready for him.

47

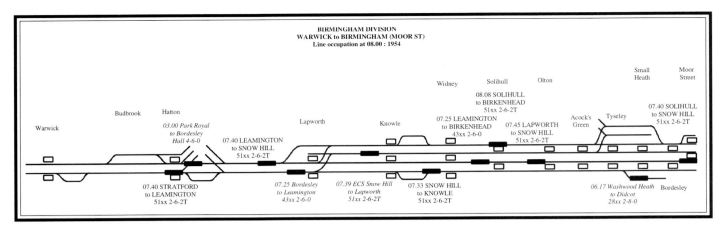

"There you are, kid," he jeered, swinging his watch from side to side, "you said it couldn't be done and here we are – on time!"

The guard failed to look abashed.

"Yes," he replied, "but all the other drivers on this job stop at New Hadley Halt…."

Being on the Great Western – 'Western Region' was just a meaningless political nonsense – and not a million miles from the border, it was inevitable that we should absorb a number of Welshmen and there is no question that Wales, the Great Western part of it at any rate, was the breeding ground of some very fine railwaymen. One of the best of them was Jack Wilkinson who came to us from Aberystwyth and brought with him a rich tenor singing voice that he would occasionally put to use on the footplate. Welshmen have been criticised as being prone to officiousness but Jack was untypical in this respect and would often let his fireman drive part of the way, using the privilege as a basis for tuition in rules and regulations; an essential qualification in the eventual jump from firing to driving.

Music was our mutual passion and we were standing in Fosse Road loop with a Bordesley – Banbury one day when he stood in the middle of the footplate to give a very animated version of the Cornish Floral Dance. A fine voice is a pleasure to listen to any day but on the footplate of a steam locomotive….the quintessence of business and pleasure! Inevitably I occasionally received both barrels of Land of my Fathers but, credit where due, I got it in both Welsh and English.

In passing it is curious that so many railwaymen take a deep interest in serious music: there is clearly some consonance between the disciplines of the timetable and the structure of a sonata although none took it quite as seriously as one fellow I knew, a station master who used to play Wagner over the announcing system to his passengers. Anyone who couldn't sit through five hours of Parsifal without a break was regarded with the contempt he thought they deserved…..

Another Welshman was a fireman who came to Tyseley from Oswestry and was smart enough to work out an unusually quick way up the promotional ladder. Because of the complexities of the job, Running Foremen were relieved on their days off by a group of firemen known as the panel which generally consisted of men who were interested in the wider aspects of motive power work. Most locomen were content to remain in the driving line of promotion but for the few who aspired to higher office the panel offered a rapid way to gain experience for senior salaried positions. 'Oswestry' spent as much time as he could on panel duties, absorbing every facet he could of managerial life until eventually he was accepted into the ranks of traffic management.

To those unfamiliar with the city, Birmingham, or rather its inhabitants, had a reputation which lay somewhere between the dour and the antisocial. Most generalisations have a grain of truth in them although it must be stressed that such a reputation belonged fairly and squarely with LMS Birmingham. The Great Western side of the city was different and in so far as the word genteel could be applied to the Black Country, it belonged with us. To prove it we had amongst our collection of characters at Tyseley a number of comedians: a breed unknown in the sombre halls of Bescot and Walsall.

Foremost amongst these was Reg 'Farmyard' Grafton who could amuse and embarrass at the same time. His speciality was farmyard noises and one of his party tricks was to hide in the shed and imitate a herd of cattle on the loose. Within ten minutes the place would be full of earnest looking men, sticks in hand, intent on driving the beasts off the premises.

He sometimes coloured his act with a touch of ventriloquism and I still cringe when I recall the time I returned with him in a passenger train from Banbury. Reg and I sat opposite each other, the only other seat in the compartment being taken by a gentlemen travelling alone. Innocuously Reg started to talk to me about commonplace railway matters, interjecting his words with the sound of a very distressed cat. It was so convincing that even I was unsure whether Reg was up to his tricks but by the time we were approaching Leamington – where I fled – Fred and the other passenger were pretty well stripping the compartment trying to locate a cat which seemed to have got stuck behind the heaters.

We also had our share of blue blood in the shape of Dai Davies whose predecessors were said to have disposed of their estates in order to assuage the tax man, leaving Dai with all the attributes, except money, of landed gentry. A senior driver in my early days at Tyseley, he certainly lived up to the image and when off-duty would appear garbed in a brown tweed jacket, jodhpurs and riding crop. A habitué of hunt balls and known to the titled, he was in every respect but one the personification of an English shire county gentleman. The missing element was the fact he was not actually English but came from Merioneth, cycnics claiming that he was a tax émigré from across the border who had gone native. Dai's version was that the ranks of the landed gentry were swollen with members who wanted to drive a steam engine : he was the only one who actually did so.

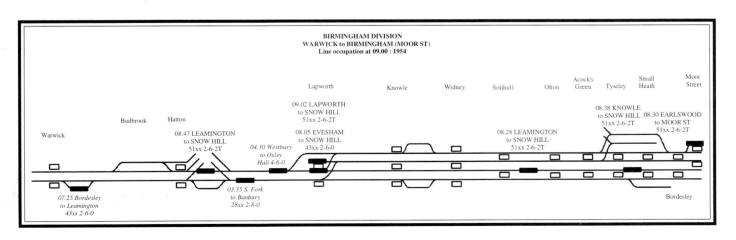

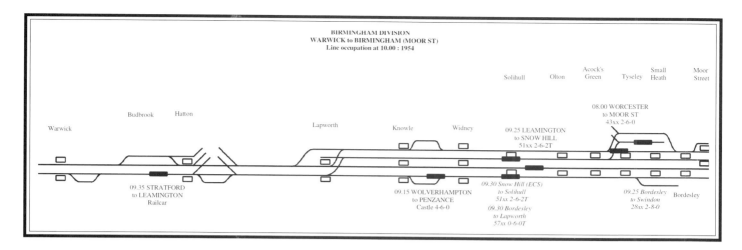

BIRMINGHAM DIVISION
WARWICK to BIRMINGHAM (MOOR ST)
Line occupation at 10.00 : 1954

Solihull　Olton　Acock's Green　Tyseley　Small Heath　Moor Street

Budbrook　Hatton

Warwick

Lapworth

Knowle　Widney

08.00 WORCESTER
to MOOR ST
43xx 2-6-0

09.25 LEAMINGTON
to SNOW HILL
51xx 2-6-2T

09.35 STRATFORD
to LEAMINGTON
Railcar

09.15 WOLVERHAMPTON
to PENZANCE
Castle 4-6-0

09.30 Snow Hill (ECS)
to Solihull
51xx 2-6-2T

09.30 Bordesley
to Lapworth
57xx 0-6-0T

09.25 Bordesley
to Swindon
28xx 2-8-0

Bordesley

From the point of view of both performance and appearance the Austerity 2-10-0 mineral engines were about as far removed from the Great Western ideal as it was possible to get. There were however sixty-four examples allocated to the region which took great care to distribute them in such a way as to minimise reaction. A large number of depots had them in one's and two's whilst the largest block allocation was at Ebbw Junction which had eleven examples. Similar numbers were allocated to Swansea Victoria and Shrewsbury for joint working over the LNWR . Almost unheard of was the ten-coupled version although 90757 came south from Grangemouth to Banbury for two months in the summer of 1952 for trials on the Iron Ore services as a prelude to the introduction of 9F 2-10-0's later in the decade.

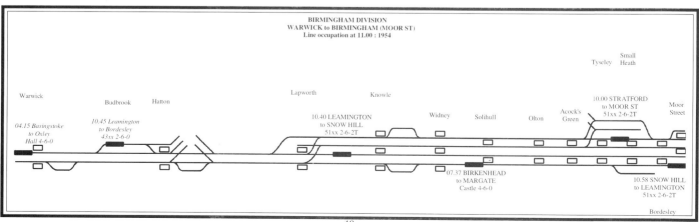

BIRMINGHAM DIVISION
WARWICK to BIRMINGHAM (MOOR ST)
Line occupation at 11.00 : 1954

Tyseley　Small Heath

Warwick

Budbrook　Hatton

Lapworth　Knowle

Widney　Solihull　Olton　Acock's Green

10.00 STRATFORD
to MOOR ST
51xx 2-6-2T

Moor Street

04.15 Basingstoke
to Oxley
Hall 4-6-0

10.45 Leamington
to Bordesley
43xx 2-6-0

10.40 LEAMINGTON
to SNOW HILL
51xx 2-6-2T

07.37 BIRKENHEAD
to MARGATE
Castle 4-6-0

10.58 SNOW HILL
to LEAMINGTON
51xx 2-6-2T

Bordesley

NEW LAMPS FOR OLD

The Britannia Pacifics were tinny, filthy things but would steam with a candle in the firebox. 70053 'Moray Firth' heads the 08.30 Snow Hill to Kingswear south of Toddington, between Stratford and Cheltenham, on the trip described in the text. The author is out of sight filling up the back corners.

One thing British Railways was not short of around the time of nationalisation was passenger engines, especially those at the upper end of the scale. The Southern and LNER were churning out express locomotives as though there was no tomorrow whilst at Swindon we were perpetuating the Castle 4-6-0's even though something like a quarter-century had elapsed since the type first appeared. Crewe had its hands full with rebuilding their large 4-6-0's and producing designs of smaller locomotives for rural and suburban work.

At the time no-one had any sensible idea how long the steam engine was going to remain in harness but it was certain that the types then being built were going to last for as long as needed. What was equally certain was that there was no immediate need for locomotives beyond the existing company designs yet the existence of a unified system free from the constraints of corporate responsibilities provided the temptation for a new set of designs; a temptation that was too hard to resist. Thus the first half of the 1950's saw the production of a dozen new classes, none of which represented much of an improvement over traditional design and whose place could more economically have been filled by an extension of pre-1948 types. It was a case of engineer turned bureaucrat with predictable results.

Great Western antipathy towards the Standard engines had less to do with conservatism than is generally supposed and much of the supposed bias was based on reason. The locomotives we had been used to were amongst the best in the world and any successors would have to possess qualities sufficient to put a Hall or a Castle 4-6-0 well in the shade. The Great Eastern which was just as individualistic as the Great Western were given Britannia Pacifics as a replacement for B17 4-6-0's - 4MT to 7MT in one bound - and there was no question that

they had been given a bargain. We on the other hand were expected to trade the sure footed and comfortable Castle 4-6-0 for a Pacific that was not only plagued with draughts but could barely keep its feet on level track. It was a very curious type of progress.

In their own right, there was not a great deal wrong with the standard classes as a whole provided close comparisons were not drawn with the company engines. One thing that has to be said in their support was that they could, with one or two exceptions, raise steam like nothing on earth.

As an enthusiast I enjoyed the novelty of working on these engines and because of this I was probably less conservative than many of my drivers although on at least one occasion I was able to transmit my zeal to the other side of the cab.

The best known of the standard engines were the Britannia Pacifics – handsome if rather tinny machines – of which the Great Western initially had an allocation of fifteen divided between Old Oak Common (5), Canton (5), Laira (4) and Newton Abbot (1). With their ability to slip on level track they were not well received in the West of England, where half the stations sit at the foot of inclines, and drivers very quickly grew impatient with having to report on delays they felt could have be avoided had they been allowed to retain their traditional engines. The popular notion that the Britannia's awoke some inexplicable West Country prejudice is pure nonsense: the Castle and Hall 4-6-0's had been lifting trains out of places like Totnes without fuss as a matter of routine and it seemed absurd that the most modern design in the country could not do the same.

The problem was eventually quietened by appointing an ex-LMS superintendent to Cardiff and sending all fifteen engines to Canton where, from 1957, they worked with reason-

able success the majority of South Wales expresses to and from Paddington.

Unfortunately they were virtually unknown in the Birmingham district and it was not until very late in my firing career that I came into contact with them. As an instance of how uncommon some of the BR Standards were in my locality, I have recorded elsewhere how I came to work 75045 from Banbury to Tyseley in August 1953 just after it had been built at Swindon. The next time I saw the engine was in July 1966 when I noticed it being hauled to Long Marston for scrapping.

Although we only took 75045 light engine and were unable to form a proper judgement of the type, we were disappointed at a number of features which were so elementary they should have been resolved early in the design stage. My driver tried to clean the front eyeglass but found to his surprise that it could not be opened. It was astonishing that on the most modern locomotive either of us had ever seen, polishing a window meant leaving the footplate and walking along the framing. Just as irritating was the fact that all the fittings were unreasonably stiff and although initially we took it as being a sign of a new engine, it turned out to be a feature of the standard engines throughout their lives. The comments my driver made about their designers does not bear repeating.

The political aspect of the standard engines did nothing to help matters. Had Swindon, for example, produced a batch of engines which needed improving they would simply have disappeared into the works to be modified into better machines. The Standards on the other hand had been built by the (very distant) Marylebone Road Junta to be dispersed amongst the regions whether they liked them or not. Comments on them were countered by the claim that Stratford never had any complaints.

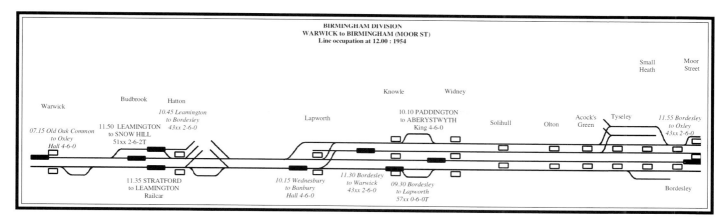

BIRMINGHAM DIVISION
WARWICK to BIRMINGHAM (MOOR ST)
Line occupation at 12.00 : 1954

Nowhere was the folly of centralised control better illustrated than in the case of the Snow Hill suburban service which for years had been worked by the very efficient 51xx 2-6-2 tanks. Instructed to make use of ten 82xxx standard 3MT 2-6-2T's, Paddington would liked to have hidden them in some South Wales backwater but were obliged to use them on the Birmingham suburban workings where they replaced a similar number of 51xx engines which in turn were dispatched to South Wales.

Paddington should have followed their initial instincts since the best that could be said of the new engines was that they were overloaded with five coaches and in the autumn of 1953 all ten were exported to Barry, their ranks being filled with 61xx 2-6-2T's – super 51xx's - from the London area.

Six years later we received half a dozen 4MT 4-6-0's from Swindon and Chester but found them to be very poor tools indeed. The 75xxx's may have been all right pottering between Oxford and Bletchley but on the altogether more demanding routes of the Great Western, the less said the better.

Whilst it is true that the 9F 2-10-0's were well received in other parts of the country, they did not achieve much of a reputation at Tyseley, partly because they came very late in the day when steam was being run down but also because their loadings were identical, being governed by the length of loops and sidings, to those of a 28xx. What, we asked, was the point in spending money on a new 2-10-0 that was no advance on the sixty-year old 2-8-0?

They were however good steamers with one of the class being exceptional and I remember working on it when firing the 21.15 Oxley – Bristol vacuum. I had a few words with the incoming fireman when I relieved him at Tyseley station and he told me that the engine steamed well but 'made a funny noise up the chimney!'

The engine was 92250 which had been fitted with the Giesel ejector and we had not been on the road long before I realised that the engine would make steam on a firebox of ballast. It was almost like firing a diesel and the driver was so impressed that he said he might have a bash at firing it himself. (Needless to say he didn't but the fact he was prepared to consider it spoke well of the engine).

"Get 92212 ready," said the outside foreman one day, pointing to the engine, "and take it down to Bordesley Old Yard to do some brake tests."

"What sort of tests?" I asked.

"Dunno. They'll tell you when you get there."

I prepared the engine and with Driver Jim Eames ran light to Bordesley to spend what I suspected would be a rather tedious shift testing brakes on new wagons. Jim wasn't unhappy since as a local Councillor with a meeting later that afternoon he was anxious for an early finish. On arrival we were coupled to a train of brand new vacuum-fitted loaded 21-ton mineral wagons whilst the guard, three carriage & wagon men and a traffic inspector climbed up onto the engine.

"Right, "announced the guard, "thirty-five equal sixty, running class C. Fully fitted. Relief at Gloucester."

"What?" said Jim getting off his seat.

"Thirty-five equ –"

"What did you say about Gloucester?"

"That's where we get relief."

Jim turned to the traffic inspector and told him it was the first he'd heard of having to work a train. The inspector thrust a circular under Jim's nose showing us to be a special test run to Bristol which we were to work as far as Gloucester. Jim could see his meeting being held in his absence but before he could react the carriage & Wagon men butted in, asking if they

could do some preliminary tests before leaving the yard.

With Jim chafing at the bit, we did some brake tests and shunted the trains up and down the siding until the C&W were satisfied that everything was working correctly. The traffic man then announced that we were ready for the main line and went off to telephone control to get us a path. Jim jumped off the engine and went with him, ready for a fight. In the meantime I assumed that whatever Jim succeeded in doing I should be doing some main line work and started to build a big fire in 92212's firebox.

Climbing back on the engine Jim announced that he had persuaded the controller to relieve us at Stratford and that he had already determined which train he was going to get back to Birmingham. I looked at my watch, shook my head but continued to make the fire up knowing that Jim was going to run the wheels off the train.

We got the right away and ran easily through Tyseley with a full boiler and the needle almost up to the mark. Running as a class C we should have a priority second only to an express passenger and with a combination of a clear road, the steep seven mile climb to Earlwood and Jims determination to beat the clock, I knew I was in for a rough time. As soon as the brake was clear of the main line Jim leant forward, gave the regulator a mighty tug and wound the reverser well forward whilst I started shovelling like a navvy which was murderous on the 9F's since a good deal of the heat came back into the cab and it was never very long before your overalls started to smoke. With the way Jim was going about the only thing that stopped mine from catching alight was the amount of perspiration I was producing and by Hall Green the racket 92212 was making was such as to make people stop in the tracks to turn and look at us.

Shovel, turn and fire. Shovel, turn and fire. It was simply a basic cycle of trying to get more

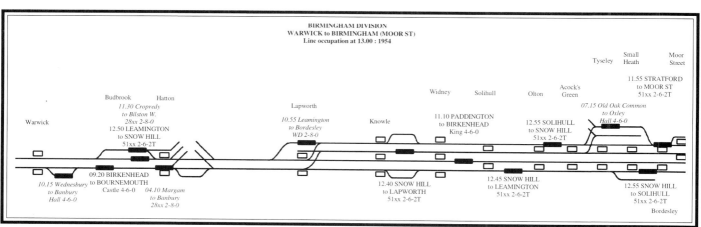

BIRMINGHAM DIVISION
WARWICK to BIRMINGHAM (MOOR ST)
Line occupation at 13.00 : 1954

51

None of the BR Standard engines showed an imporvement over existing Great Western designs whilst the 3MT 2-6-2T's disgraced the name of steam. Ten were sent in mid-1952 to replace some of the 51xx 2-6-2T's on the Snow Hill suburban workings but could barely keep time with four coaches. Obliged by politics to accept them, the Western moved them from Birmingham as soon as they decently could, 82005 being shunted around no less than seven sheds in as many years before being palmed off to the Midland.

in one end of the firebox than Jim was forcing out of the other although not everything I threw in was coal. Thundering up the straight toward Shirley I lost my balance for a second and clouted the smokeplate into the firebox. Normally I'd have made some effort to extricate it but any pause in my firing would have brought the needle down whilst the heat from the fire, especially now the door had been enlarged thanks to the loss of the smokeplate, was such that I couldn't have got near it anyway.

Charging over the top at Earlswood I was able to put the shovel down for a few minutes, not that I had time for a rest since the dust that the 9F's created made it necessary for me to swill the footplate down with the slacker pipe.

We hurtled down the other side of the bank, the stations a blur, having to keep a close look-out for hotboxes in the train: how on earth they stood up to the sort of speed we were doing is a tribute to the way wagons were built. Looking back at the train and seeing a long string of wagons shaking like jelly and oscillating from one side to the other was a sight to remember and I wondered what sort of a ride the guard was having.

Jim started to gather the wagons in on the tender buffers by applying the steam brake on the engine and whilst it made very little impression on our speed it prevented the train from snatching as we levelled out of the fall and climbed the short bank beyond Henley station.

As soon as we were over the slight hump and falling again, Jim released the brake and allowed speed to build up again to get as much momentum as possible for the climb to Wilmcote. I hadn't had to fire since we passed the top of Earlswood bank and this had allowed the tem-

perature around the firebox door to diminish enough for me to poke around with the shovel to see if anything remained of the smokeplate. Musing that 9F's doubled as a pretty efficient steel retort, I could see no trace of the plate and after deciding that it had melted away, covered all traces with a good layer of coal in the back end of the box.

As I put the shovel down we entered the 1 in 75 fall to Stratford and I was just beginning to wonder how much faster a ten-coupled engine could go when Jim dribbled a couple of inches of vacuum through the train bringing us down to a walking pace by the time Stratford East cleared the road for us into the station, well in time for Jim to catch his intended train home.

"Have we got any timings for this job?" said the Stratford man as he climbed up to relieve us.

"Fast for the first half," replied Jim, "and bloody fast for the second…"

One of the great cause celebres of the 1950's was the Rugby locomotive test plant which was a good idea thirty years after its time although it tended only to confirm what most people already knew in the first place. For all this, the loco research people took a great pride in it and I was pleased, when I was invited to pay a visit in early 1960, to find a Great Western man as engineer in charge of a joint LMS/LNER project. The Swindon spirit, it seemed, always shows in the end.

He outlined the purpose and workings of the plant over a cup of tea and then took me into the control room where 9F 92166 was moving slowly on the rollers; measurements being taken as comparative tests prior to it being fitted with a mechanical stoker. The fasci-

nation of seeing a locomotive at work without moving an inch was capped by the sight of the fireman being supervised on the footplate by a technician who would peer into the firebox through a piece of darkened glass every half minute and give an instruction as to where the next shovelful of coal should be directed.

The driver was similarly supervised and sat on his seat altering the regulator or cut-off at the whim of the technician. He and his fireman seemed rather bored by it all.

It was a very interesting and courteous introduction to a brave new world but the engineer's true spirit only revealed itself when he was seeing me off the premises. A train went by on the Great Central bridge and we both turned to look at it. As luck would have it, it was a Great Western Hall and the sight of it started a far keener flow of conversation that anything in the plant had provoked. The Hall had apparently been one of 'his' when it had been an oil burner at Swindon.

Although 92166 (together with 65 & 67) was eventually stoker-fitted for the Water Orton – Carlisle goods workings, in their early days they were used on some of the LM services which worked through to Banbury and became, for a short while, a regular sight on my part of the system. I rarely needed to identify them individually since a glance at the pall of dense black smoke was usually sufficient to recognise a stoker fired 2-10-0 long before the number came into sight.

Some of the Standard classes were only seen because they had been built at Swindon and, like 75045, had to be moved through the Western to their accepting region. I saw most of the 3MT 2-6-0's – surely one of the ugliest designs

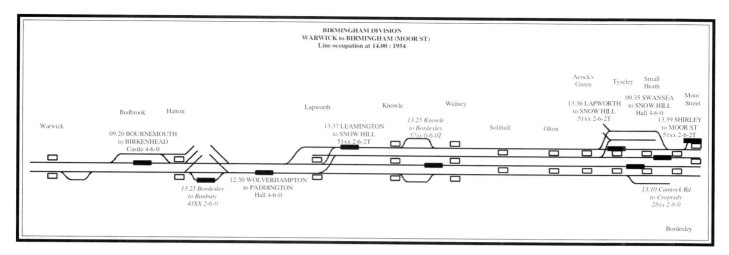

ever to grace a piece of track – in this way, some of them being utilised to work the 01.05 Swindon – Bordesley goods before be run light from Tyseley to the London Midland. Once they had passed through I never set eyes upon them again.

One of the first sheds on the Northern main line to have any Standards was Oxford and I recall waiting there in June 1957 when 75029 backed from the shed into the down bay. It had just come from a visit to Swindon works and was attractively painted in green lined livery. The livery was not the only thing different about it since it was emitting a most curious noise from its chimney and after a closer look I discovered it had been fitted with a double blastpipe and chimney, an alteration that did nothing for the appearance of the engine. Having produced one of the most useless engines of all time, the BTC were clearly trying to make it the ugliest and the fact that nothing more grand could be found for it than a local passenger from Oxford to Kingham suggested that Oxford did not place very much reliance in the class.

One positive thing to say about the 75xxx 4-6-0's was that they allowed me to carve a small niche in the book of posterity by being one of the few (so far as I know) who succeeded in getting the things to steam properly.

In mid-1959 a new working from Washwood Heath to Eastleigh was introduced and we were given a batch of 4MT's, mostly redundant engines from Chester, with which to work the duty. The train ran through three regions and since the engine worked through someone decided that the best way of avoiding any disputes as to which company's engines should be booked was to use a neutral Standard. After a week on the working I realised that it was an ill-founded compromise and any LM or SR engine would have been preferable to the ones actually used.

Any working from Birmingham to Eastleigh required an engine that could steam consistently and this the 4MT's simply could not do. We did the best we could but lost time hand over fist and in the end a gang of inspectors was delegated to accompany the working to see if they could come up with any ideas.

Someone produced what was referred to as Gold Dust which was supposed to clean the tubes after being sprinkled onto the fire. The problem was that it gave off such a noxious gas that the footplate had to be evacuated immediately after use whilst the tubes remained unaffected.

We relieved the working at Tyseley and took it as far as Banbury, struggling for steam night after night and heartily glad to be relieved even though we felt slightly guilty at having to hand on such a poor tool to the Banbury men whose faces fell when they saw a 4MT coming towards them.

Eventually it dawned on the inspectors that the fault lay with the engine and not with the firemen and as soon as the Southern agreed to let a Great Western engine work through with the train, they had it rediagrammed to a Manor 4-6-0 or 43xx 2-6-0.

Some of the 4MT's were transferred away to Machynlleth and Worcester but a handful remained, one of their workings being the 09.30 Bordesley to Stourbridge local goods.

On my first trip with the 09.30 I had double-chimney 75003 which had just come out of repair and was in such a filthy state that it took me most of the week clean it up. Its steaming was not as bad as it had been on the Eastleigh job – the Stourbridge train was nothing like as heavy – but it was far from good and on the Tuesday my driver, Jack Kitchen, took over the firing and confirmed that the class were a set of dead ducks.

On the Wednesday we took a good look inside the engine before leaving Tyseley and on opening the smokebox door came across the mesh cage which was supposed to act as a self cleaning device. The cage was nothing new to us but up to that point we had generally accepted the principle that if an engineer put something on (or in) an engine, it was there for a good purpose. Jack and I decided that any sort of obstruction in the smokebox was liable to prejudice steaming and, making sure no one was looking, we unscrewed it, threw it out and hid it.

The difference it made to 75003 was extraordinary and for probably the first time in its life the engine sprung to life with no steaming difficulties whatever. On the way back from Stourbridge Jack gave it the acid test by giving it full regulator and full forward gear on the 1 in 60 at Old Hill; treatment that should have had the needle falling like a brick.

75003 steamed on as though it was on level track and so far as we could tell it didn't matter how much steam you wanted, the boiler would supply it without the fireman having to slave like a navvy.

My claim to have changed the character of a class of engines is, of course, made more than slightly tongue in cheek and I find it hard to believe that men at other sheds afflicted with the class did not rise to the same fiddle. The Cambrian men did good work with them when they replaced the Manor 4-6-0's in North Wales whilst the Midland relied on them for much of their St Pancras – Bedford suburban service and it is hard to believe that this work was done with the self-cleaning cage in place.

From my admittedly rather limited experience if I had to make a choice from what were a pretty mediocre set of engines, I would probably plump for the Britannia's and the 76xxx 2-6-0's. The rest I would have turned into razor blades and I am often amused by the fact that

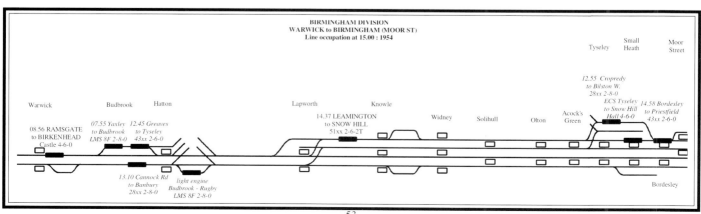

One word sums up the BR standard 4MT 4-6-0's as built : useless. If these engines were supposed to compete with the 43xx 2-6-0's - also class 4's - they failed miserably. The only way to get any work from the brutes was to open the smokebox door and sabotage the self-cleaning gear. 75045 stands at Tyseley on its first run from Swindon in August 1953 en route to Accrington.

the lavish praised directed at some of the standard engines is more often than not generated by people who never had to work them.

Tales of woe regarding the Britannia's had filtered down from Old Oak and the West of England and with these in mind I relieved 70014 'Iron Duke' one morning at Wolverhampton to take the 21.45 Eastleigh – Crewe Parcels as far as Wellington. It was no marathon run and when I saw the engine approach my first reaction was one of relief that I didn't have to work it through to Crewe. My second reaction, once we were on the move, was to wonder why Old Oak men had taken such a dislike to the class since 70014 simply purred along, making all the steam you wanted and treating the four mile 1 in 150 Shifnal bank as though it was level. I was sorry to hand the engine over at Wellington.

Not everyone disliked them and during its time on the Midland one colleague, Pat Webb of the Derby loco inspectorate, claimed that 70014 was the best engine he had ever had between St Pancras and Leicester. On the debit side though, the Britannia's could be highly unstable when starting a train whilst the footplate was very uncomfortable to ride in.

In mid-1965 ex Holyhead Pacifics 70045 and 70043 plus 70053 from Polmadie spent a few months at Oxley before being sent north to Carlisle and saw a considerable amount of use on our summer workings to the west of England.

Marked up one Saturday with Driver Teddy Bowe for the 08.35 Snow Hill to Kingswear, I expected to find the usual Hall (or, if I was lucky, a Castle) arriving with the stock and I was interested to see 70053 'Moray Firth' come oozing up 11 and 12 platforms. (Oozing in this case was the correct adjective for the engines' arrival since, like most Standards, steam was leaking from just about every joint. It occurred to me as I stowed my traps on the footplate that if half of it could be diverted through the cylinders a considerable saving in coal might result).

My first task was to locate the various controls and find out what they were for, a duty which started by banging my leg on, and almost falling over, the water regulating handle which for some unaccountable reason was placed just behind the fireman's seat. Other controls were identified through the expedient of trying them to see what happened.

LOCO	CLASS	IN	OUT	LOCO	CLASS	IN	OUT
			BANBURY ALLOCATION : 1952				
90192	8F : WD 2-8-0 (1943)		To Canton 7/52	6906	5MT : HALL 4-6-0 (1928)		
90312	8F : WD 2-8-0 (1943)		To Oxford 10/52	6929	5MT : HALL 4-6-0 (1928)		To Shrewsbury 7/52
90313	8F : WD 2-8-0 (1943)			6929	5MT : HALL 4-6-0 (1928)	Ex Shrewsbury 11/52	
90485	8F : WD 2-8-0 (1943)	Ex Oxley 1/52	To Southall 10/52	4900	5MT : HALL 4-6-0 (1924)		To Worcester 7/52
90572	8F : WD 2-8-0 (1943)	Ex Chester 6/52	To Canton 7/52	6816	5MT : GRANGE 4-6-0 (1936)		
90579	8F : WD 2-8-0 (1943)			6819	5MT : GRANGE 4-6-0 (1936)		
90757	8F : WD 2-10-0 (1943)	Ex Grangemouth 8/52	To Grangemouth 10/52	6833	5MT : GRANGE 4-6-0 (1936)	Ex Leamington 1/52	To Chester 7/52
2886	8F : 28xx 2-8-0 (1938)			6835	5MT : GRANGE 4-6-0 (1936)		To Chester 7/52
2897	8F : 28xx 2-8-0 (1938)			6839	5MT : GRANGE 4-6-0 (1936)		
2898	8F : 28xx 2-8-0 (1938)		To Bristol (SPM) 12/52	6854	5MT : GRANGE 4-6-0 (1936)		To Oxley 9/52
2899	8F : 28xx 2-8-0 (1938)		To Southall 4/52	6856	5MT : GRANGE 4-6-0 (1936)	Ex Oxley 4/52	To Oxley 9/52
3802	8F : 28xx 2-8-0 (1938)		To Oxley 4/52	6860	5MT : GRANGE 4-6-0 (1936)	Ex Oxley 10/52	
3819	8F : 28xx 2-8-0 (1938)			6879	5MT : GRANGE 4-6-0 (1936)	Ex Oxley 4/52	To Oxley 9/52
3820	8F : 28xx 2-8-0 (1938)		To Shrewsbury 10/52	6625	5MT : 56xx 0-6-2T (1927)	Ex Leamington 3/52	To Croes Newydd 10/52
3831	8F : 28xx 2-8-0 (1938)			6696	5MT : 56xx 0-6-2T (1927)		To Croes Newydd 10/52
3839	8F : 28xx 2-8-0 (1938)	Ex Worcester 7/52	To Tyseley 10/52	4102	4MT : 51xx 2-6-2T (1928)	Ex Leamington 1/52	To Leamington 3/52
3859	8F : 28xx 2-8-0 (1938)	Ex Chester 9/52		4102	4MT : 51xx 2-6-2T (1928)	Ex Leamington 4/52	
3861	8F : 28xx 2-8-0 (1938)		To Hereford 12/52	4149	4MT : 51xx 2-6-2T (1928)		
3863	8F : 28xx 2-8-0 (1938)		To Oxley 4/52	5141	4MT : 51xx 2-6-2T (1928)		w/d 10/52
2812	8F : 28xx 2-8-0 (1903)	Ex Chester 9/52		5307	4MT : 43xx 2-6-0 (1911)	Ex Oxley 6/52	
2816	8F : 28xx 2-8-0 (1903)			5317	4MT : 43xx 2-6-0 (1911)		
2817	8F : 28xx 2-8-0 (1903)	Ex Ebbw Jcn 10/52		5324	4MT : 43xx 2-6-0 (1911)		To Bristol (SPM) 10/52
2819	8F : 28xx 2-8-0 (1903)	Ex Ebbw Jcn 10/52		5332	4MT : 43xx 2-6-0 (1911)		
2823	8F : 28xx 2-8-0 (1903)	Ex Shrewsbury 9/52		5361	4MT : 43xx 2-6-0 (1911)		
2827	8F : 28xx 2-8-0 (1903)	Ex Oxford 7/52		5391	4MT : 43xx 2-6-0 (1911)		To Tyseley 9/52
2834	8F : 28xx 2-8-0 (1903)	Ex Ebbw Jcn 10/52		5399	4MT : 43xx 2-6-0 (1911)	Ex Croes Newydd 12/52	
2835	8F : 28xx 2-8-0 (1903)	Ex Canton 7/52		6332	4MT : 43xx 2-6-0 (1911)		To Stourbridge 4/52
2847	8F : 28xx 2-8-0 (1903)			6342	4MT : 43xx 2-6-0 (1911)		
2853	8F : 28xx 2-8-0 (1903)		To Croes Newydd 5/52	6390	4MT : 43xx 2-6-0 (1911)		To Bristol (SPM) 10/52
2857	8F : 28xx 2-8-0 (1903)			7315	4MT : 43xx 2-6-0 (1911)	Ex Wolverhampton 10/52	
3017	7F : R.O.D. 2-8-0 (1917)	Ex Old Oak C. 4/52	To Bristol (SPM) 10/52	8400	4F : 94XX 0-6-0T (1949)		
3020	7F : R.O.D. 2-8-0 (1917)			8405	4F : 94XX 0-6-0T (1949)		
3024	7F : R.O.D. 2-8-0 (1917)	Ex Didcot 11/52		8407	4F : 94XX 0-6-0T (1949)		
3026	7F : R.O.D. 2-8-0 (1917)			8452	4F : 94XX 0-6-0T (1949)		
3043	7F : R.O.D. 2-8-0 (1917)			8459	4F : 94XX 0-6-0T (1949)		
6963	5MT : MOD-HALL 4-6-0 (1944)		To Oxley 4/52	9425	4F : 94XX 0-6-0T (1949)		
6966	5MT : MOD-HALL 4-6-0 (1944)			9426	4F : 94XX 0-6-0T (1949)		
6976	5MT : MOD-HALL 4-6-0 (1944)			9438	4F : 94XX 0-6-0T (1949)		
6979	5MT : MOD-HALL 4-6-0 (1944)			9449	4F : 94XX 0-6-0T (1949)		
7800	5MT : MANOR 4-6-0 (1938)		To Tyseley 6/52	2256	3MT : 2251 0-6-0 (1930)		
7811	5MT : MANOR 4-6-0 (1938)		To Oxley 7/52	3216	3MT : 2251 0-6-0 (1930)		
7823	5MT : MANOR 4-6-0 (1938)			3218	3MT : 2251 0-6-0 (1930)		
4918	5MT : HALL 4-6-0 (1928)		To Wolverhampton 7/52	3630	3F : 57xx 0-6-0T (1933)		
4960	5MT : HALL 4-6-0 (1928)		To Wolverhampton 7/52	3694	3F : 57xx 0-6-0T (1933)		To Chester 1/52
4977	5MT : HALL 4-6-0 (1928)	Ex Oxley 2/52		4631	3F : 57xx 0-6-0T (1933)		
4980	5MT : HALL 4-6-0 (1928)			8787	3F : 57xx 0-6-0T (1933)		
4987	5MT : HALL 4-6-0 (1928)	Ex Leamington 10/52		5724	3F : 57xx 0-6-0T (1929)		
5930	5MT : HALL 4-6-0 (1928)			7763	3F : 57xx 0-6-0T (1929)		
5950	5MT : HALL 4-6-0 (1928)	Ex Tyseley 9/52		5404	1P : 54xx 0-6-0T (1931)		
5954	5MT : HALL 4-6-0 (1928)	Ex Leamington 1/52		5407	1P : 54xx 0-6-0T (1931)		
5967	5MT : HALL 4-6-0 (1928)		To Shrewsbury 7/52	5424	1P : 54xx 0-6-0T (1931)		
5967	5MT : HALL 4-6-0 (1928)	Ex Shrewsbury 11/52		1401	1P : 14xx 0-4-2T (1932)		
5994	5MT : HALL 4-6-0 (1928)		To Chester 1/52	1411	1P : 14xx 0-4-2T (1932)		To Stourbridge 1/52
6901	5MT : HALL 4-6-0 (1928)		To Chester 1/52				

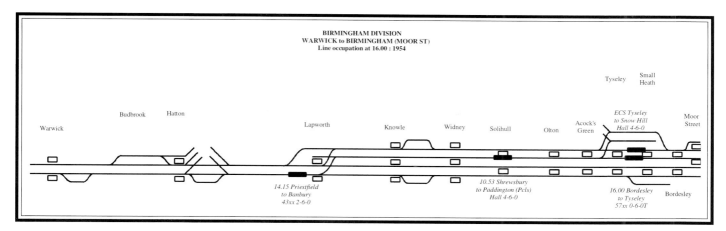

The second task was to give the thing the best clean I could whilst the large contingent of passengers scrambled into the coaches and fought for seats. I never came across a breed of engines that collected dirt quite as efficiently as the Standards and the Britannia's excelled in this respect. I managed to get the front windows reasonably transparent but the cab side windows were so begrimed they had to stay as they were.

Wretched as the external state of the engine was, the fire was in good shape as it might well have been since we had the maximum single engine line limit of twelve vehicles, about 450 tons, to get up the bank to Earlswood. I wondered if I was going to have to feed it as I had done 92212 but for the time being the needle was inching cheerfully towards the red mark and to keep 70053 from blowing off I eased the dampers shut, leaving the small ejector to bleed off any excess steam there was.

I learned before we turned a wheel how quickly the Britannia's responded to changes in controls and as the station staff slammed closed the last of the doors, I noticed that the fire had suddenly started to look rather lifeless although there was no sign of trouble on the pressure gauge. Before I could do anything the right away was passed down the platform and I opened the dampers as I shouted across to Teddy Bowe.

Teddy drew back on the regulator and 70053 went into a violent slip which took a good half minute to bring under control by which time we were nosing through Snow Hill tunnel and gaining speed on the falling gradient.

Whether it was the slipping or the opening of the dampers (or both), by the time we emerged from the tunnel the fire was once again in first class shape and all I had to do was to flick a couple of shovelfuls into the back corners. I also placed a good layer of coal under the fire-

box doors, not for steaming reasons but because it was the only way of reducing the amount of heat that radiated back into the cab. The engine responded at once by blowing off and I had to quieten it down by putting the injector on. There was no doubt that as steam raisers the Britannia's were in the class of their own: we had a boiler full of water, I had done virtually no firing, the cut-off was at 45%, we were making a musical beat as Teddy took the train up the 1 in 200 to Spring Road yet 70053 was still blowing off. I wondered what the result might have been had they put a Britannia's firebox and boiler on a Castle's frames: it would probably have made diesels more unnecessary than they actually were...

With no worries about steam production, the challenge was to prevent 70053 from blowing off and I found the best way of achieving this was to let the boiler level to fall to half a glass and thereafter cool things down with a touch of the injector whenever the valves threatened to lift. Firing was just a matter of keeping the back corners filled even though we were pounding along on full regulator and 25% cut-off and I even had time to take note of the many photographers who lined the route in expectation of seeing a Britannia, a class not normally associated with the North Warwicks.

At Earlswood Teddy eased the regulator and allowed 70053 to cruise down the bank at the limit of 60 mph with nothing more than a hint of steam. It was then we found out that some time had passed since the engine had last been in the shops as the riding became quite hard. This was exacerbated by cab being fixed to the boiler and not, as was usual, the frames and I developed an instant respect for the Polmadie men who for ten years had clung onto 70053 and its shedmates as they swept down Beattock and Shap banks.

However, with relatively little to do in the way of firing, I was able to sit down for longer than usual and with the blower on to keep the fire from licking back into the cab, the firedoors open and the injector keeping the boiler cool, I was able to take things easy and amuse myself by watching the fast-revolving motion which was quite a novelty to a Great Western man.

Even Teddy was impressed with my workload and when we got to Stratford and discovered that we had not even used enough water to make filling the tender worthwhile, he remarked that he was going to change the pace.

"Isn't it your last day as a fireman?" He asked and I nodded.

"I'll see you don't forget it in a hurry..."

We pulled away from Stratford and, forewarned, I started to build the back corners up and get a decent bed of fire across the firebox although it did not take long for me to realise that I was wasting my time since 70053 was blowing off long before the fire was in what I considered any sort of shape. I think if I'd have stuck a candle in the firebox, the needle would have touched the red mark.

I thought we might have a bit of a struggle on Long Marston bank but Teddy simply opened up, set the cut-off to 40% and we sailed up the incline, our exhaust startling a set of men on a 22xx 0-6-0 at Honeybourne East who raised their caps in mock deference.

It was not until we got onto the second half of the climb, the 1/150 from Honeybourne to Broadway, that 70053 showed signs of flagging although a little gentle firing, about a dozen rounds, cured matters instantly and as soon as we were over the top Teddy pulled the lever back a little and the Pacific simply leapt forward.

Toddington passed in a flash and then we were on the downhill to Cheltenham with 70053

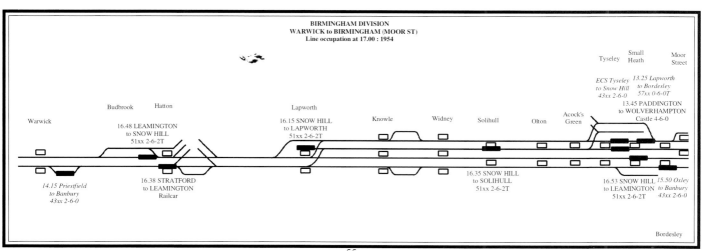

pitching quite madly with none of the graceful dignity that I was used to from Great Western engines. On the other hand there was none of the hard work usually needed to get a good turn of speed and about all the firing I did was to fill the back corners up as we shot through Gotherington. At Bishop's Cleeve, Ted, who had been enjoying himself, gave the regulator a last tug open and after a hundred yards or so shut off and put the reverser in the 45% position to allow a gentle cruise into Cheltenham.

As Teddy's road knowledge finished at Cheltenham, our train had been wired forward by Birmingham under the codeword 'Eger' and accordingly a pilotman was waiting for us as we came to a stand in Malvern Road.

"Never seen one of these before."

"Neither had I until this morning." responded Teddy, giving up his seat to let him take over.

This was a reversal of the normal procedure where the pilotman normally stood behind the driver to call out the signals and speed restriction but Teddy had an ulterior motive.

"Put your feet up," he called to me as I entered the cab after filling the tender, "and I'll do a bit of firing."

I had, I thought, come across some strange things since signing on that morning but a driver offering to do the firing capped everything. He had of course seen the easy trip I had had and probably thought it would be a piece of cake.

Poor old Teddy. The pilotman either had shares in the mining industry or was trying to knock the chimney off and even on the falling gradients to Gloucester he must have taken five years off the engine. By about Churchdown Teddy, who was no lightweight and hadn't stopped firing since the wheels started turning, pushed the shovel in my direction.

"Here……"

The problem was that the pilotman had no idea of the Britannia's valve settings and thought the bigger the engine, the longer the cut-off needed. It took a lot of coal to keep up with him but at no time was there any sign of the needle dropping below the red line. We slackened off for the avoiding line at Gloucester and then, with a noise like a machine gun from the chimney, we bounded away hotfoot for Bristol. Fortunately for my back, it started to dawn on the pilotman that the engine would work just as well – and certainly a lot more efficiently – with a shorter cut-off and gradually he started to wind back until he discovered that 35% did the same amount of work for less coal. With less firing to do and more time to look around, I scoured the four track section between Tuffley and Standish

hoping to see an LMS service that we could do battle with but, alas, there were no takers.

It was surprising that we had such a clear road for a summer Saturday, although leaving Birmingham at 08.30 we were probably leading the pack. We did not however give any following trains grounds for complaint which was hardly surprising from the way the pilotman was flogging the engine.

We slowed for the crossing to the Midland at Standish Junction and far from having to bring the engine round after so much pounding, it demonstrated its eagerness for more by blowing off furiously as the train snaked across the pointwork.

"Good engines, these" called the pilotman as he opened up, wound the engine back to 35% and tried to set a record for the run to Yate. The

LOCO	CLASS	IN	OUT	LOCO	CLASS	IN	OUT
				BANBURY ALLOCATION : 1953			
90313	8F : WD 2-8-0 (1943)			4102	4MT : 51xx 2-6-2T (1928)		
90579	8F : WD 2-8-0 (1943)			4149	4MT : 51xx 2-6-2T (1928)		
2886	8F : 28xx 2-8-0 (1938)			5170	4MT : 51xx 2-6-2T (1928)	Ex Stourbridge 5/53	
2897	8F : 28xx 2-8-0 (1938)			5317	4MT : 43xx 2-6-0 (1911)		
3819	8F : 28xx 2-8-0 (1938)			5332	4MT : 43xx 2-6-0 (1911)		
3831	8F : 28xx 2-8-0 (1938)			5361	4MT : 43xx 2-6-0 (1911)		
3859	8F : 28xx 2-8-0 (1938)			5399	4MT : 43xx 2-6-0 (1911)		
2812	8F : 28xx 2-8-0 (1903)			6342	4MT : 43xx 2-6-0 (1911)		To Tyseley 7/53
2816	8F : 28xx 2-8-0 (1903)			7315	4MT : 43xx 2-6-0 (1911)		
2817	8F : 28xx 2-8-0 (1903)			8400	4F : 94XX 0-6-0T (1949)		
2819	8F : 28xx 2-8-0 (1903)		To Banbury 3/53	8405	4F : 94XX 0-6-0T (1949)		
2823	8F : 28xx 2-8-0 (1903)			8407	4F : 94XX 0-6-0T (1949)		
2827	8F : 28xx 2-8-0 (1903)			8452	4F : 94XX 0-6-0T (1949)		
2834	8F : 28xx 2-8-0 (1903)			8459	4F : 94XX 0-6-0T (1949)		
2835	8F : 28xx 2-8-0 (1903)			9425	4F : 94XX 0-6-0T (1949)		
2847	8F : 28xx 2-8-0 (1903)			9426	4F : 94XX 0-6-0T (1949)		
2850	8F : 28xx 2-8-0 (1903)	Ex Westbury 12/53		9438	4F : 94XX 0-6-0T (1949)		
2857	8F : 28xx 2-8-0 (1903)			9449	4F : 94XX 0-6-0T (1949)		
3020	7F : R.O.D. 2-8-0 (1917)			2202	3MT : 2251 0-6-0 (1930)	Ex Oxford 7/53	
3024	7F : R.O.D. 2-8-0 (1917)		To Canton 9/53	2209	3MT : 2251 0-6-0 (1930)	Ex Croes Newydd 9/53	
3026	7F : R.O.D. 2-8-0 (1917)		To Canton 9/53	2246	3MT : 2251 0-6-0 (1930)	Ex Stourbridge 5/53	
3043	7F : R.O.D. 2-8-0 (1917)		To Canton 9/53	2256	3MT : 2251 0-6-0 (1930)		
6966	5MT : MOD-HALL 4-6-0 (1944)			2259	3MT : 2251 0-6-0 (1930)	Ex Croes Newydd 9/53	
6976	5MT : MOD-HALL 4-6-0 (1944)			2270	3MT : 2251 0-6-0 (1930)	Ex Stourbridge 5/53	
6979	5MT : MOD-HALL 4-6-0 (1944)			2297	3MT : 2251 0-6-0 (1930)	Ex Croes Newydd 9/53	
7823	5MT : MANOR 4-6-0 (1938)			3216	3MT : 2251 0-6-0 (1930)		To Stourbridge 5/53
4977	5MT : HALL 4-6-0 (1928)			3218	3MT : 2251 0-6-0 (1930)		To Stourbridge 5/53
4980	5MT : HALL 4-6-0 (1928)			3694	3F : 57xx 0-6-0T (1933)		To Tyseley 9/53
4987	5MT : HALL 4-6-0 (1928)			3694	3F : 57xx 0-6-0T (1933)	Ex Tyseley 11/53	
5930	5MT : HALL 4-6-0 (1928)			4631	3F : 57xx 0-6-0T (1933)		
5947	5MT : HALL 4-6-0 (1928)	Ex Old Oak C. 3/53		8787	3F : 57xx 0-6-0T (1933)		
5950	5MT : HALL 4-6-0 (1928)			5724	3F : 57xx 0-6-0T (1929)		To Tyseley 7/53
5954	5MT : HALL 4-6-0 (1928)			5724	3F : 57xx 0-6-0T (1929)	Ex Tyseley 11/53	
5967	5MT : HALL 4-6-0 (1928)			7763	3F : 57xx 0-6-0T (1929)		
6906	5MT : HALL 4-6-0 (1928)			5404	1P : 54xx 0-6-0T (1931)		
6929	5MT : HALL 4-6-0 (1928)			5407	1P : 54xx 0-6-0T (1931)		
6816	5MT : GRANGE 4-6-0 (1936)		To Landore 2/53	5424	1P : 54xx 0-6-0T (1931)		
6819	5MT : GRANGE 4-6-0 (1936)		To Swindon 8/53	1411	1P : 14xx 0-4-2T (1932)		
6839	5MT : GRANGE 4-6-0 (1936)			1473	1P : 14xx 0-4-2T (1932)	Ex Croes Newydd 9/53	To Neasden 11/53
6860	5MT : GRANGE 4-6-0 (1936)		To Laira 7/53				

noise was unbelievable – not for nothing were the Britannia's known as 'Clangers' – but in Wickwar tunnel the fury rose to a climax as we roared down the bank in pitch darkness and passed a northbound express which was also going like the clappers.

It proved to be the finale so far as high speeds were concerned since the main line was waiting to see the whites of our eyes before blocking the London – South Wales line for us, and we came to a stand for a few minutes at Yate, right at the foot of the climb up to Westerleigh. I looked into the firebox and judged that it would get us to Temple Meads without further attention.

I was interested to see how 70053 would behave itself on the curved climb to Westerleigh but instead of the expected bout of slipping, it started away quite quietly and took all the heavy handedness of the pilotman as it lifted the train up the bank. Once on the main line, the fun was over and we cruised by Stoke Gifford and Filton Junction to arrive in Temple Meads well before time.

We hooked off at Bristol and ran light to Barrow Road shed, passing on our way the

Warship diesel that was to take over our train.

"Brummie men off the 08.30?" asked the outside foreman and we confirmed the fact.

"6856 for the back working over on…."

My driver made a surprise interruption.

"Is the one we've just brought in going back to Wolverhampton today?"

The foreman looked down his sheet and nodded.

"Can you make my mate a happy man and swap them over. He'd like to take 70053 back with him?"

The poor man had probably spent the last ten years trying to persuade drivers to accept a Britannia and here was a bloke actually asking for one but the numbers were changed and he got a set of local men to run 70053 to Mangotsfield to turn it for us on the angle.

The run back was less frenetic than the outward trip had been since we were in the middle of a batch of northbound specials and were on the block for much of the time. It was not without its moments though, especially during the first stage on the climb out of Bristol with its 1 in 80 gradients up to Filton Junction. With twelve vehicles behind the tender none of us were sure of the single engine limit up the bank – it was actually eleven coaches for a class 7 – but we decided to risk it and Teddy made a rather impolite gesture to the crew of the Hall 4-6-0 that was waiting to bank us from Stapleton Road. 70053 coughed a bit but the rail was dry and we got up to Filton with no especial worries.

Teddy repeated the show at Stratford where the inspector asked us if we wanted assistance, the question being put in a tone of voice which suggested he was short of bankers and would be grateful if we didn't.

"We'll manage" said Teddy obligingly and blasted the Pacific and its train up to Wilmcote and Earlswood.

It had been a good day and I was glad that I had got some mileage in on the class. My judgement of them was broadly favourable at least so far as steam generation was concerned although on the debit side they were noisy, dirty and uncomfortable to work on and I wondered if my opinion of them would be sustained had I to work on them day in, day out. On balance I decided that they were not really a significant advance on the Great Western engines which I was used to and this, indeed, was true of the Standards as a whole. Some of them had a number of good points but they did not really advance the art of locomotive designing to the extent one was entitled to expect.

WESTERN MERRY-GO-ROUND

The 21.50 Snow Hill - Cheltenham - Swindon was one of Tyseley shed's star turns and Modified Hall 6971 'Athelhampton Hall' was for many years retained as the regular engine for the working. The engine is seen in the works yard at Swindon waiting for a tender after receiving a general overhaul in April 1956.

Returning to the present, having digressed to discuss BR standard engines, in March 1956 I moved into No. 5 'the Parcels' link with Driver Bert Watkins, who was known, for some reason, as Harold. The best turn in the link, and the working from which it got its name, was the 21.50 Snow Hill to Swindon parcels which ran outwards via Cheltenham and Gloucester but returned via Didcot, Oxford, Honeybourne Curve and Stratford. It was quite an extraordinary turn since not only did we box the whole of the west Midlands but we could go from Snow Hill to Moor Street, where the return working terminated, without either leaving or turning the engine. To complete a shift of over two hundred miles with the engine pointing the same way was probably unique.

The idea of what ought to have been a main line working running a rather devious course over the North Warwickshire seems strange but it saved a path over the heavily used route through Banbury which made the working of mineral traffic in the southern part of the division that little bit easier. We

were by no means the only main line train to be kept away from the Banbury area and in the down direction, for example, the North Warwicks was used by no less than five goods workings from the London area to Birmingham which came down the O.W.W. from Oxford to Honeybourne and then into Birmingham via Stratford on Avon.

I found myself on the Swindon parcels in my second week in the link, booking on at 20.50 and being given 6971 'Athelhampton Hall' which was the regular engine for the job. The extent to which specific engines were retained on particular jobs was the prerogative of the shedmaster – some thought it a good idea whilst to others one engine was very much the same as another – and at Tyseley it was the policy to keep regular engines on the more important daily duties wherever it could be done without upsetting the diagramming. 6971 was the usual engine for the job and when it was not available 5907 'Marble Hall', 5912 'Queen's Hall' or 7929 'Wyke Hall' would be selected.

For a short time a Stafford Road Castle was diagrammed to the job but since the parcels was an important train and the Castle had already done a days work before it coupled up, the working did not last long. With a nominated Tyseley Hall, at least there was no uncertainty about the condition of the engine that would be provided.

The sight of a four-vehicle parcels train was not one that would arouse much interest in the hearts and minds of spectators, especially as the engine was the same most nights, yet it was one of the Birmingham district's key services since it provided a direct parcels connection between the Black Country and the rest of the Great Western system.

9.50 p.m. Birmingham to Swindon due 12.33 a.m. (Saturdays excepted).	Bk. Van .... Birmingham	Penzance ..	3.45 p.m.	Penzance	SX
	Bk. Van 96 " or 186	Bristol	1.40 a.m.	Swindon	MX
	Bk. Van .... "	Weymouth	—	—	—
	Siphon G .. "	Fishguard Hr	4.15 p.m.	Fishguard Hbr. MWFO	Y

The 21.50 ex Snow Hill was a lightweight but important service which connected Birmingham with all points in the South West. The Bristol and Penzance BG's went forward after a tight connection at Swindon with the 22.40 Paddington to Penzance whilst the Weymouth vehicle went forward in the 04.30 Westbury local to be transferred to the 05.45 Bristol - Weymouth. The Fishguard Siphon was detached at Cheltenham and worked forward in the 23.55 to Gloucester and the 00.05 ex Swindon, reaching its destination late the following afternoon. It should be noted that parcels vehicles were diagrammed in exactly the same way that passenger vehicles were.

1.40 a.m. Swindon to Birmingham (Moor Street), due 4.20 a.m. (Mondays excepted.)	Flower, Fish and other Seasonal traffic.		West of England.	Birmingham ..	—		
	Bk. Van	TTaSO	Penzance	B'ham (M.St.)	9.50 p.m. ...	Birmingham	SX
	Siphon G. ..		Fishguard H.	"	"	"	SX
	Bk. Van 96 or 186.		Bristol	Birmingham ..	"	"	SX

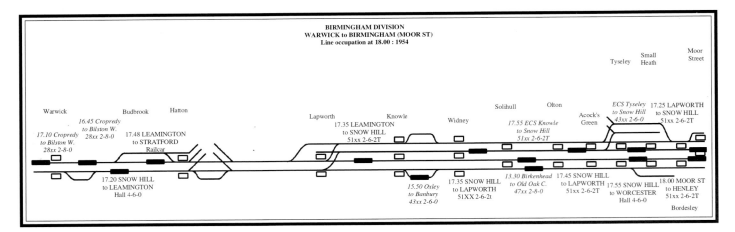

The destination of the vehicles were Penzance, Bristol, Weymouth and Fishguard and the arrangements laid down for the four vehicles never failed to impress me, especially that of the trailing van which ran via Cheltenham, Gloucester, Swansea, Felin Fran (of all places…) and Clarbeston Road. It served as many of the local stations as was possible before getting to Fishguard in time for the Irish Ferries to Rosslare and Waterford.

The Weymouth vehicle remained at Swindon for about four hours before going forward via Yeovil whilst the West of England vans had a tight connection at Swindon with the 22.40 express parcels from Paddington to Plymouth.

Each vehicle of every parcels train was strictly diagrammed but if traffic was especially heavy it was the duty of the station inspector not only to find additional vehicles but to make sure that the district control and connecting points knew the facts so that arrangements further up the line could be made.

Whether we had the booked four vehicles or not, no quarter was given where running was concerned and the 21.50 was in fact the fastest train of the day between Birmingham and Cheltenham, the seventy-five minute booking being three minutes better than that of the Castle-hauled Wolverhampton – Penzance 'Cornishman'.

Nor did we hang about and quite apart from pride in letting Swindon know that we of the northern line could give a reliable account of ourselves, any unexplained loss of time was liable to result in being met by a loco inspector on arrival at Swindon: not an interview to be relished.

Departure from Snow Hill was always punctual – the 21.50 was not held for anything – and after taking the relief line at Moor Street we would dash like mad for Stratford and onto Cheltenham, our first stop, where the Fishguard van

was removed. After leaving Lansdown Road we would take the South loop at Gloucester and join the old South Wales main line via the facing connection at Standish Junction.

Now and again we would come across a late running Midland express between Gloucester and Standish and invariably a race would take place although the contest between a Hall 4-6-0 and three vans versus a 5XP and ten or more passenger coaches was hardly an equal one. Still, it made the Midland fireman sweat a bit.

We paused for a couple of minutes at Stroud which gave me a chance to get the engine ready for the next stage, filling the boiler up to the whistle and getting it good and hot. Having done the equivalent of a trip from Birmingham to London we now had the hardest section ahead of us, nearly eight miles uphill; the steepest part being three and a half miles at 1 in 94.

To a stranger from the north, this line was a trap for the unwary. The section west of Stroud was a placid sort of line over which 14xx 0-4-2T's and their single auto coaches were at home and the sight of them could lull you into a sense of false security, making you forget the terrors of Sapperton bank. It was easy to see why, when it had been the direct line to South Wales, most trains had avoided it to run via Bath and Stapleton Road.

The rural atmosphere did not finish at Stroud and although you were climbing the side of a house, the track meandered to the left and right through pretty little halts and level crossings and only the labouring exhaust reminded one that it was one of the most difficult sections of the Great Western. The severity of the bank obliged freight trains to take assistance and a shed was provided at Brimscombe to ensure that a banker was at hand whenever needed.

Once over the top at Sapperton the books were balanced with a fine dash downhill. The regulator on 6971 would be cracked open to

allow the 4-6-0 to streak away through Kemble and Minety, the brakes being applied hard at the last minute for Swindon where we took the goods line to run past the station before backing into Platform 1 on the down side.

As soon as the shunter had released us we would cross over to the up side and couple up to the 01.50 which normally consisted of the Penzance and Bristol vans we had brought up the previous night plus, three times a week, the Fishguard siphon which came in with the 16.35 Neyland – Paddington Parcels.

The main parcels service from the West to the Midlands was the 23.20 Taunton – Wolverhampton which ran into Swindon whilst we were there and handed over any urgent traffic for Birmingham as we reached Moor Street a good two hours earlier. Normally the transfer was limited to the Penzance BG but in the flower season it could be very different, as I found out the hard way.

I had a small fire simmering in the box one morning in anticipation of our usual light load when the guard came up to give us the details.

"Mothering Sunday this weekend", he announced and I asked him what that had to do with anything.

"Bit of extra flower traffic off the Taunton this morning."

"Oh yes."

"Twenty-two plus the usual. Twenty-four in all."

Twenty-four vehicles! Two seconds later I was in the tender pulling coal down for all I was worth and getting 6971 as hot as I could.

Whether we had two or twenty-two vehicles behind the tender there could be no hanging about once we got the right away from Swindon since the West of England TPO was only a few minutes behind us as far as Didcot and Heaven help the train that delayed it. (The TPO did not waste any time either and it was interesting to

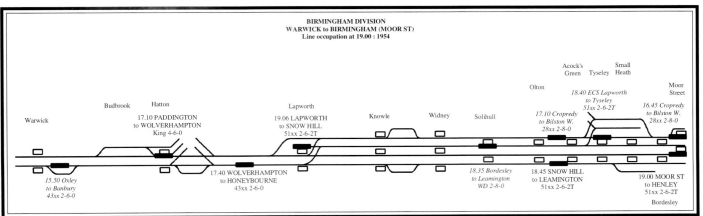

Main line goods workings between Oxford and Birmingham were normally worked by main line engines but the 21.15 Morris Cowley to Bordesley was an exception since the 24 modified passenger coaches which made up its load had little weight and could be handled by almost any engine that was available. The range of engines used on the service was extreme but perhaps never more than when 94xx 8410 was utilised. Since the train is seen at Acocks Green and it is still daylight, the 0-6-0T evidently had no difficulty in handling the train. 8410 was one of the first engines at Tyseley to be displaced by diesel power and was transferred to Port Talbot (Duffryn) in August 1951 from where it was withdrawn in February 1960.

see on the odd days when we were delayed at Swindon and had to follow it, the King went so well that we, even with our two vehicles, never got so much as a distant against us).

Our route back was only slightly less unusual than that of the outward trip since after Oxford, where we used to hope – usually unsuccessfully – for a clear run, we took the West Midlands line at Wolvercote Junction in order to keep Banbury free from non-stopping traffic.

If ever there was a dark piece of railway, the O.W.W. was it. Signalboxes were few and far between and those that did appear put one in mind of lighthouses, giving the succour of a small dot of light in a sea of darkness. On the other hand it was a fast road and Bert would usually have his watch out for the six-mile section between Handborough and Charlbury to ensure that we covered it in less than even time.

My attention was less on records than Charlbury troughs which I never found easy to find. Bert would suddenly shout "Down" and I would furiously lower the scoop, watch the float rise to the top of the gauge and just as furiously wind it back into place.

Adlestrop flashed by and brought with it schoolboy recollections of a poem, learned and subsequently forgotten, composed by somebody who woke up as his train called there and was inspired by the sleepiness of the country station. The poor fellow should have ridden on the Swindon parcels and generated an heroic saga instead: there was nothing placid about the way we flew up the no-man's lands which was neither Chilterns nor Cotswolds.

Unfortunately we missed the best racing section of all, the steep fall from Chipping Camden to Wyre, where it was said that trains could get up to three-figure speeds, and as soon as we reached the summit of the climb, Bert shut the regulator and applied the brake for the restriction over the Honeybourne curve which took us from the O.W.W to the more familiar metals of the North Warwicks.

It always seemed rather unjust to me that the Swindon parcels received no recognition for its nightly feats. Running a two hundred mile circuit from Birmingham to Birmingham with only three intermediate stops must have put the train high on the list of memorable 4-6-0 workings yet being a parcels train and running in the dead of night it went, alas, unnoticed.

This anonymity did not prevent the train from having a certain reputation amongst the footplate staff and to add to the challenge of a fast schedules, drivers would vie amongst themselves to see who could achieve the earliest arrival at Snow Hill.

So far as I know the record was held by Gerald Cleaver who succeeded in coming to a stand in Moor Street one morning at 03.56: no less than thirty minutes before time and fourteen minutes better than my best. He was, as they say, a goer and he frightened the life out of me one night when I was standing outside Kingham with a train of empty stock and Gerald and the down Swindon Parcels came through. The Great Western was unique in not specifying a maximum speed for passenger trains, the appendix merely stating that speeds could be as high as necessary and Gerald took greater advantage of this small print than anyone else. I don't know how his fireman, Jimmy Cullen, reacted but the sight of the parcels coming through Kingham – on a rising gradient - that morning made my hair stand on end. Interestingly there was no posturing so far as Gerald was concerned, he simply sat, leaning forward onto the lever rack, gazing immovably into the space ahead.

How one could pick up half an hour with the parcels is beyond my comprehension since on my trips we flogged the engine as hard as we could but never got near Gerald's achievement. Getting away from the Honeybourne slack we would go like mad before easing off for Stratford after which the sky would echo to the bark of 6971 as it pounded up to Wilmcote on second valve and a longish cut off. Having been on the road for something like six hours this last stretch was always the worst and, whether or not one's driver felt like setting a new record, there was no let up in the pace until Earlswood had been passed. One was always conscious that an engine like 6971, free steaming and free running, made the job a lot easier than it might otherwise have been.

On the run down through Grimes Hill and Shirley the shovel would be put aside for the last time and the cab cleaned, ready for Moor Street and a glance at the station clock to see how the run compared with others. It was hard work but it was worth it because the job took

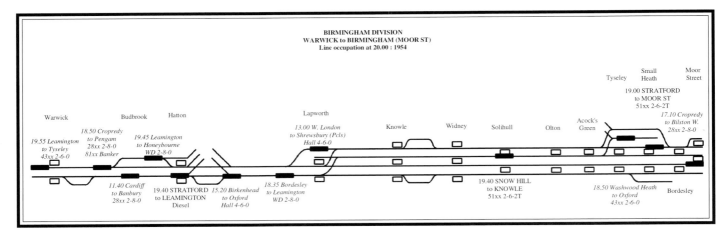

BIRMINGHAM DIVISION
WARWICK to BIRMINGHAM (MOOR ST)
Line occupation at 20.00 : 1954

you well away from workaday Birmingham and into countryside that was by any reckoning foreign. There was also a sense of pride and comfort in being at somewhere remote, such as Stroud, yet knowing that you were still on the Great Western. It was rather like travelling ten thousand miles and finding that the natives spoke English.

In some respects the working was harder for drivers than it was for their firemen - and we didn't have much time for a rest. Running for long distances non-stop and needing all the heat the fire could generate, it was a cold duty for the drivers and I remember Bill Timmis who made quite a sight when he turned up for the Swindon parcels. Slightly built, he would mount the engine in a large overcoat several sizes too big for him clutching a box of straw for his feet. Other drivers felt the cold so much that they well nigh stamped the floorboards out in their efforts to keep warm.

I only remember one instance of the Swindon Parcels being delayed and on that occasion we had a good excuse. We had had a late start from Swindon with further delays at Didcot and Oxford and as soon as we were beyond Wolvercote Bert spared neither engine nor fireman to recover what he could of the deficit.

Four miles into the O.W.W with 6971 going like the wind through Handborough cutting there was a sudden loud crash and the engine rolled as though it was going over on its side whilst pieces of debris flew past the cab like shrapnel. Suddenly the vacuum disappeared and, still on the rails, 6971 came to a stand with Bert and I breathing very heavily. Shaken, I got off the footplate to see what had happened and found the undersides of the coaches and their brake pipes badly smashed with lumps and pieces of yellow rock all over the place. Curious I walked a little further and discovered that the side of the cutting had collapsed onto the down line ahead of us.

The most immediate thing was to protect the opposite line but with the next signalbox, Charlbury, being six miles distant there was little to be gained by walking. Fortunately the train was still on the road and by pulling the brake strings and disconnecting the pipes between the engine and first vehicle we were able, after putting a red light on the front of the engine, to limp the six miles unfitted to advise the signalman that the road was blocked.

We eventually arrived at Moor Street, still unfitted, and for our labours received some pretty cutting remarks from the porters waiting to unload the train. 6971, fortunately, was undamaged and after a thorough clean was back on the job that same night. Bert's only comment was that we were lucky not have been derailed.

Whilst the Swindon Parcels was the star turn of the link it was not the only interesting duty we worked and one which came a close second was the 16.44 Wolverhampton – Oxford express which we worked from Snow Hill at 17.25. Running right away to Warwick and having either 5012 'Berry Pomeroy Castle' or 5033 'Broughton Castle', both being Oxford engines which alternated on the working, we would catch up with the 17.20 Leamington local by Solihull and treat the commuters to a race. The 51xx on the relief line had only a quarter of our weight behind him and it was

LOCO CLASS	IN	OUT	LOCO CLASS	IN	OUT
BANBURY ALLOCATION : 1954					
90313 8F : WD 2-8-0 (1943)		To Southall 4/54	6929 5MT : HALL 4-6-0 (1928)		
90579 8F : WD 2-8-0 (1943)			6839 5MT : GRANGE 4-6-0 (1936)		To Oxley 4/54
2886 8F : 28xx 2-8-0 (1938)			4102 4MT : 51xx 2-6-2T (1928)		
2897 8F : 28xx 2-8-0 (1938)			4149 4MT : 51xx 2-6-2T (1928)		
3819 8F : 28xx 2-8-0 (1938)			5170 4MT : 51xx 2-6-2T (1928)		
3829 8F : 28xx 2-8-0 (1938)	Ex Tyseley 9/54		5317 4MT : 43xx 2-6-0 (1911)		
3831 8F : 28xx 2-8-0 (1938)			5332 4MT : 43xx 2-6-0 (1911)		
3835 8F : 28xx 2-8-0 (1938)	Ex Oxford 9/54		5361 4MT : 43xx 2-6-0 (1911)		
3859 8F : 28xx 2-8-0 (1938)			5399 4MT : 43xx 2-6-0 (1911)		
2812 8F : 28xx 2-8-0 (1903)			7315 4MT : 43xx 2-6-0 (1911)		
2816 8F : 28xx 2-8-0 (1903)			8400 4F : 94XX 0-6-0T (1949)		
2817 8F : 28xx 2-8-0 (1903)			8405 4F : 94XX 0-6-0T (1949)		
2822 8F : 28xx 2-8-0 (1903)	Ex Shrewsbury 9/54		8407 4F : 94XX 0-6-0T (1949)		
2823 8F : 28xx 2-8-0 (1903)			8452 4F : 94XX 0-6-0T (1949)		
2827 8F : 28xx 2-8-0 (1903)			8459 4F : 94XX 0-6-0T (1949)		
2834 8F : 28xx 2-8-0 (1903)			9425 4F : 94XX 0-6-0T (1949)		
2835 8F : 28xx 2-8-0 (1903)			9426 4F : 94XX 0-6-0T (1949)		
2847 8F : 28xx 2-8-0 (1903)			9438 4F : 94XX 0-6-0T (1949)		To Gloucester 9/54
2850 8F : 28xx 2-8-0 (1903)		To Ebbw Jcn 11/54	9449 4F : 94XX 0-6-0T (1949)		
2857 8F : 28xx 2-8-0 (1903)			2202 3MT : 2251 0-6-0 (1930)		
2858 8F : 28xx 2-8-0 (1903)	Ex Southall 4/54		2209 3MT : 2251 0-6-0 (1930)		
2867 8F : 28xx 2-8-0 (1903)	Ex Tyseley 9/54		2246 3MT : 2251 0-6-0 (1930)		
3020 7F : R.O.D. 2-8-0 (1917)		w/d 6/54	2256 3MT : 2251 0-6-0 (1930)		
6966 5MT : MOD-HALL 4-6-0 (1944)			2259 3MT : 2251 0-6-0 (1930)		
6976 5MT : MOD-HALL 4-6-0 (1944)			2270 3MT : 2251 0-6-0 (1930)		
6979 5MT : MOD-HALL 4-6-0 (1944)			2297 3MT : 2251 0-6-0 (1930)		
7823 5MT : MANOR 4-6-0 (1938)		To Croes Newydd 1/54	3694 3F : 57xx 0-6-0T (1933)		To Oxley 1/54
4977 5MT : HALL 4-6-0 (1928)			3690 3F : 57xx 0-6-0T (1933)	Ex Oxley 3/54	
4980 5MT : HALL 4-6-0 (1928)			4631 3F : 57xx 0-6-0T (1933)		
4987 5MT : HALL 4-6-0 (1928)			8787 3F : 57xx 0-6-0T (1933)		
5930 5MT : HALL 4-6-0 (1928)			5724 3F : 57xx 0-6-0T (1929)		
5945 5MT : HALL 4-6-0 (1928)	Ex Oxley 7/54	To Oxley 9/54	7763 3F : 57xx 0-6-0T (1929)		
5947 5MT : HALL 4-6-0 (1928)			5404 1P : 54xx 0-6-0T (1931)		
5950 5MT : HALL 4-6-0 (1928)			5407 1P : 54xx 0-6-0T (1931)		
5954 5MT : HALL 4-6-0 (1928)			5424 1P : 54xx 0-6-0T (1931)		
5967 5MT : HALL 4-6-0 (1928)			1411 1P : 14xx 0-4-2T (1932)		
6906 5MT : HALL 4-6-0 (1928)					

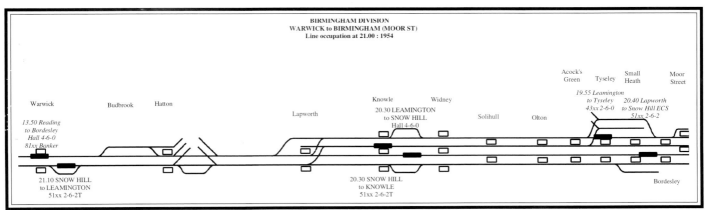

BIRMINGHAM DIVISION
WARWICK to BIRMINGHAM (MOOR ST)
Line occupation at 21.00 : 1954

Birmingham Moor Street was unusual in that engines were released by electrically worked traversers, one for the inner platforms and another for the outer platform and run-round road. Although an expensive piece of equipment to operate and maintain, it allowed relatively large engines to run-round their trains without the overhang obstructing the platform edges. At terminal stations with release crossovers there were usually severe restrictions placed upon the type of engines which could be released, 51xx 2-6-2T 5152, which left the Birmingham suburban area in September 1955 when it was moved to Banbury, is seen on the traverser after arriving with a local service.

surprising how hard we had to work a Castle to gain the advantage.

On reaching Warwick we would then repeat the racing, our opponent being the 18.00 LMS local to Rugby which generally had the advantage of a level line and a big 2-6-4 tank. Its crew invariably gave us a superior look as they romped away and, being a very light train, usually managed to show us a tail lamp.

The return working for was a train known as the 'Bocars', the 21.15 Morris Cowley to Bordesley, which consisted of twenty four passenger bogies adapted to carry motor car body frames. We would drop our Castle 4-6-0 on the loco, have a bite to eat and then travel passenger on our light engine which was worked up the Cowley branch by the crew of the local shunting pilot.

One of the most interesting aspects of the Bocar job was that the engine had no return working from Birmingham and consequently you never knew what sort of engine you were going to get since Oxford used anything that happened to be handy. It was not much of an exaggeration to say that if you never worked any other service but the Bocar, you would sooner or later experience almost anything that could turn a wheel and in my time I was given 28xx, Austerity and LMS 8F 2-8-0's, Hall and Grange 4-6-0's, 51xx 2-6-2T's and 72xx 2-8-2 mineral tanks. On one occasion I came close to being given a Dukedog 4-4-0 although the most extreme form of power was 3646, a 57xx 0-6-0 tank which actually handled the train very well. (And, it has to be said, there was nothing like a pannier tank on a main line working for teaching a fireman a few lessons in water economy…..). The bocars was a very light train and this accounted for some of the smaller engines used on it.

The length of the train tended to put the fear of God into the signalmen and as a result it usually got a good run since everyone was anxious to pass it on to the man in advance as quickly as possible. With clear signals everywhere and a decent engine it was not a difficult job to manage although you had to guard against complacency as I discovered one night when boarding a Grange 4-6-0 at Oxford loco.

Not knowing the local men who were working the engine I had nothing to say to them and spent the trip to Cowley watching the scenery from the cab window. When we backed onto the train at Cowley the Oxford men disappeared to their engine whilst I attended to the smokebox door and headlights.

LOCO	CLASS	IN	OUT	LOCO	CLASS	IN	OUT
			BANBURY ALLOCATION : 1955				
48402	8F 2-8-0 (1935)	Ex Canklow 7/55	To Bristol (SPM) 8/55	5170	4MT : 51xx 2-6-2T (1928)		
48412	8F 2-8-0 (1935)	Ex Toton 7/55		5306	4MT : 43xx 2-6-0 (1911)	Ex Swindon 10/55	
48419	8F 2-8-0 (1935)	Ex Toton 7/55		5317	4MT : 43xx 2-6-0 (1911)		
48471	8F 2-8-0 (1935)	Ex Kettering 7/55		5332	4MT : 43xx 2-6-0 (1911)		
90466	8F : WD 2-8-0 (1943)	Ex Shrewsbury 7/55		5361	4MT : 43xx 2-6-0 (1911)		
90579	8F : WD 2-8-0 (1943)		To Canton 8/55	5399	4MT : 43xx 2-6-0 (1911)		To Chester 9/55
90585	8F : WD 2-8-0 (1943)	Ex Ebbw Jcn 5/55		6331	4MT : 43xx 2-6-0 (1911)	Ex Chester 11/55	
90716	8F : WD 2-8-0 (1943)	Ex Shrewsbury 4/55		6362	4MT : 43xx 2-6-0 (1911)	Ex Croes Newydd 4/55	
2886	8F : 28xx 2-8-0 (1938)			6387	4MT : 43xx 2-6-0 (1911)	Ex Swindon 10/55	
2897	8F : 28xx 2-8-0 (1938)			7315	4MT : 43xx 2-6-0 (1911)		
3819	8F : 28xx 2-8-0 (1938)			8400	4F : 94XX 0-6-0T (1949)		To Cardiff (E. Dck) 8/55
3829	8F : 28xx 2-8-0 (1938)			8405	4F : 94XX 0-6-0T (1949)		To Duffryn 8/55
3831	8F : 28xx 2-8-0 (1938)			8407	4F : 94XX 0-6-0T (1949)		To Tyseley 5/55
3835	8F : 28xx 2-8-0 (1938)			8452	4F : 94XX 0-6-0T (1949)		
3836	8F : 28xx 2-8-0 (1938)	Ex Reading 7/55	To Reading 8/55	8459	4F : 94XX 0-6-0T (1949)		To Cardiff (E. Dck) 8/55
3859	8F : 28xx 2-8-0 (1938)			9425	4F : 94XX 0-6-0T (1949)		To Treherbert 9/55
2812	8F : 28xx 2-8-0 (1903)			9426	4F : 94XX 0-6-0T (1949)		To Tyseley 5/55
2816	8F : 28xx 2-8-0 (1903)			9449	4F : 94XX 0-6-0T (1949)		
2817	8F : 28xx 2-8-0 (1903)		To Chester 7/55	2202	3MT : 2251 0-6-0 (1930)		To Croes Newydd 7/55
2822	8F : 28xx 2-8-0 (1903)			2202	3MT : 2251 0-6-0 (1930)	Ex Croes Newydd 9/55	
2823	8F : 28xx 2-8-0 (1903)			2209	3MT : 2251 0-6-0 (1930)		To Croes Newydd 7/55
2827	8F : 28xx 2-8-0 (1903)			2209	3MT : 2251 0-6-0 (1930)	Ex Croes Newydd 9/55	
2834	8F : 28xx 2-8-0 (1903)		To Stourbridge 4/55	2246	3MT : 2251 0-6-0 (1930)		
2835	8F : 28xx 2-8-0 (1903)			2256	3MT : 2251 0-6-0 (1930)		To Westbury 7/55
2847	8F : 28xx 2-8-0 (1903)			2256	3MT : 2251 0-6-0 (1930)	Ex Westbury 9/55	
2850	8F : 28xx 2-8-0 (1903)			2259	3MT : 2251 0-6-0 (1930)		
2857	8F : 28xx 2-8-0 (1903)		To Tyseley 7/55	2270	3MT : 2251 0-6-0 (1930)		
2867	8F : 28xx 2-8-0 (1903)			2297	3MT : 2251 0-6-0 (1930)		
6966	5MT : MOD-HALL 4-6-0 (1944)			3646	3F : 57xx 0-6-0T (1933)	Ex Chester 10/55	
6976	5MT : MOD-HALL 4-6-0 (1944)			3694	3F : 57xx 0-6-0T (1933)		To Cardiff (E. Dck) 8/55
6979	5MT : MOD-HALL 4-6-0 (1944)			4631	3F : 57xx 0-6-0T (1933)		To Cardiff (E. Dck) 8/55
4942	5MT : HALL 4-6-0 (1928)	Ex Exeter 9/55		8787	3F : 57xx 0-6-0T (1933)		To Cardiff (E. Dck) 8/55
4977	5MT : HALL 4-6-0 (1928)			9774	3F : 57xx 0-6-0T (1933)	Ex Wellington 8/55	To Wellington 9/55
4980	5MT : HALL 4-6-0 (1928)		To Bristol (SPM) 12/55	5724	3F : 57xx 0-6-0T (1929)		To Cardiff (E. Dck) 8/55
4987	5MT : HALL 4-6-0 (1928)		To Reading 11/55	7763	3F : 57xx 0-6-0T (1929)		To Tyseley 10/55
5930	5MT : HALL 4-6-0 (1928)			5404	1P : 54xx 0-6-0T (1931)		
5947	5MT : HALL 4-6-0 (1928)			5407	1P : 54xx 0-6-0T (1931)		
5950	5MT : HALL 4-6-0 (1928)		To Westbury 5/55	5424	1P : 54xx 0-6-0T (1931)		
5954	5MT : HALL 4-6-0 (1928)			13105	0F : 350hp 0-6-0	New 3/55	
5967	5MT : HALL 4-6-0 (1928)		To Newton Abbot 1/55	13106	0F : 350hp 0-6-0	New 3/55	
6906	5MT : HALL 4-6-0 (1928)			13107	0F : 350hp 0-6-0	New 3/55	
6929	5MT : HALL 4-6-0 (1928)			13108	0F : 350hp 0-6-0	New 3/55	To Bristol (SPM) 8/55
4102	4MT : 51xx 2-6-2T (1928)		To Chester 5/55	13108	0F : 350hp 0-6-0	Ex Bristol (SPM) 9/55	
4149	4MT : 51xx 2-6-2T (1928)			13109	0F : 350hp 0-6-0	New 4/55	
5152	4MT : 51xx 2-6-2T (1928)	Ex Tyseley 9/55		13110	0F : 350hp 0-6-0	New 4/55	

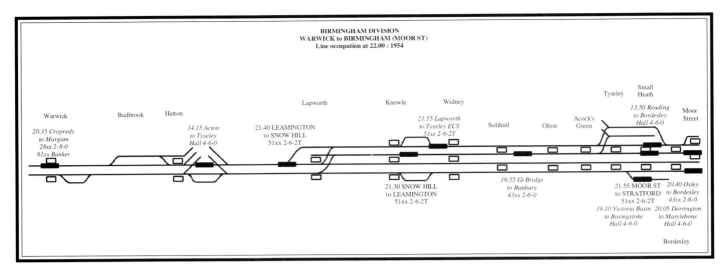

Back on the footplate, we got the right away and pulled onto the branch as I prepared for a night's work. My driver glanced across at me with a funny look on his face.

"Take the shirt off your back, these Oxford men."

I asked him what he meant.

"Well they've taken your shovel with them. How're you going to fire the engine?"

It was a question I answered by picking up a couple of pieces of coal with my hands and bunging them into the firebox. He pulled the train up at Kennington Junction and I called across to the signalman as I gave him the token.

"Tell the loco to send a shovel out, will you."

"What do want a bloody shovel for?"

"To fire the bloody engine."

To describe the signalman as an idiot would have been an injustice to the stupid.

"You bloody locomen. You'd leave your ***** behind on your honeymoon…."

We moved off and I picked up a shovel as we passed Oxford loco but we decided that the matter could not be left there. The signalman deserved a lesson in manners and the next day instead of handing him the staff, I dropped it on the cowhorn which drew from him an acidly worded lecture on how tokens were to be handed over. The day after I warmed it in the firebox and, handing it to him as requested, held onto it for a second or two longer than usual to let him get the full benefit of it.

The worst trip I had on the Bocars should have been the best since the Oxford foreman told me I was getting Dukedog 4-4-0 9023. Although they were relatively new engines, they looked old and I was rubbing my hands at the prospect when Austerity 2-8-0 90355 clanked off shed in its stead.

"Too low in steam to come off" said the Oxford driver when I asked him about the Dukedog and I looked quizzically at the 150lbs that 90355 was showing.

"We put the pricker through and it didn't feel too bad…."

When we got to Cowley I took a look at the tube plate and it was plastered. Heaven only knows when the tubes had last been cleaned and had we had a real train we should have had to ask for a change of engines at Oxford.

However badly off the Dukedog might have for steam it could hardly have been as bad as 90355 – not that Austerities were that good in any sort of condition – and we did the best we could on 140lb of steam as we clanked through Oxford, the needle dropping almost as quickly as my shovel was moving.

Although the ten miles from Oxford to Tackley is uphill, the gradient is not normally anything to worry about since the steepest section is the one and a half miles at 1 in 356 from Bletchington. 90355, however, seemed to regard it as a mountain and after a long painful slog managed to crawl past Tackley with about 100lb of steam on the gauge and, because even a touch of the injector would have finished things off, the water level well down in the glass.

Nor could we take advantage of the slight fall to Heyford since I needed all the time I could get to try and bring things round. With the engine continuing at a lazy walking pace, I managed to get some water into the boiler and still have enough steam to keep us on the move to Fritwell and eventually Banbury where we stopped for more time under the pretext of filling the tender.

By the time we were ready to move, the jungle telegraph had been at work and none of the signalmen were prepared to give us a run so we limped from one loop to the next with everything on the main line going round us. Never did anyone work so hard to get such a small return as I piled in the coal to get the needle to go up as far as the 150lb mark. I gave a quiet prayer of thanks that the Great Western had not had to accept very many of these dreadful locomotives and pitied the Great Northern who had been inundated with the wretched things.

By the time we shuffled our way into the Birmingham area, we had had enough and instead of working through to Bordesley, we forwarded a plea to the late turn running foreman at Tyseley who sent a set of men out to relieve us.

Run down Austerities were not the only things sent to try us on that particular turn and one November evening in 1955 we found ourselves on the 16.44 Wolverhampton to Oxford in a fog that was so thick it was impossible to see the smokebox from the cab which, given that most of the signals were my side of the engine, made life more than usually difficult since firing could only be done between spells of peering out of the cab window. The ATC was a considerable help when signals were clear but as soon as the horn went off to advise of a distant we had to shut off, come down to a crawl and peel our eyes, not only to get confirmation from the distant itself but for a sighting of the signal to which it referred. This, of course, caused time to be dropped but the signalmen were invariably helpful, leaning out of their boxes and giving us a hand signal to indicate the state of the section ahead. There was always the consolation that however bad it was for us, the other railways, lacking ATC, had it worse and I could understand the horror stories that used to circu-

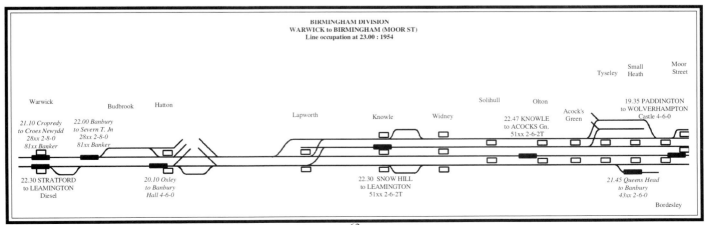

The London Midland services to London never achieved the prominence that was accorded to Liverpool, Manchester or Glasgow workings and most workings between New Street and Euston were handled by nothing larger than 5XP 4-6-0's. On the Great Western the principal workings were through trains from Birkenhead sometimes 40% heavier than the LM services and worked by class 8P Kings 4-6-0's. For a short time in 1955, as recounted in the text, the Kings were replaced by LMS Pacifics; a substitution which brought some very long faces to Old Oak Common. Blue liveried 6004 ' King George III' pulls away from Snow Hill with an express for Paddington in 1950.

late concerning six or more hours dropped between Glasgow and Euston because of fog.

On the Wolverhampton we lost time of course and reached Oxford well behind time although given the conditions it was not a bad performance. We arrived too late to take our engine up the branch and therefore had to wait at Oxford until a spare set of men worked the Bocars in for us.

Perhaps the most curious cause of delay to effect the Wolverhampton – Oxford occurred one afternoon when, in perfectly clear weather, we were pulled up at Wolvercote's home signal.

This was an unusual place to be stopped and I jumped off the engine as soon as we came to a stand and ran up to the box to carry out rule 55 and sign the register.

"And where do you think you're going?" boomed a voice as my foot touched the first step of the stairs. I looked up to find the way barred by a very large railway policeman who demanded that I identify myself which was easier said than done since footplatemen tend not to carry passports with them. In the end he accepted the argument that if I looked like a fire-

man then I probably was one but still would not let me into the signalbox.

"Grove special coming off the West Midland," he confided, "you'll have to wait until it's clear."

A minute later the Royal train, hauled by two shining Castles, appeared from the Worcester direction and was followed by the emergence from the box by half the court of St James whose presence at Wolvercote Junction someone deemed necessary to deal with any local traitorous intentions.

Fog and Royalty apart, the Wolverhampton – Oxford express was heaven compared to another Oxford job we had in the link which involved the 04.15 Bordesley to Newton Abbot goods, a working introduced in 1955, which we worked to Oxford via Stratford and Honeybourne in order to give some breathing space to the Banbury area.

The signing-on time for the duty was 02.55 which, given that I was courting at the time, was not a good time to start work and more often than not I would arrive home at midnight after a night on the tiles and wait up until it was time to set off for Tyseley where I would arrive yawning my head off.

Fortunately my driver had lived through the process himself and gave me more sympathy than I was entitled to expect. We would prepare the engine, pick up our train from Bordesley, get things running nicely and then, as soon as we were on the North Warwick line, he would tell me to get my head down for a while.

National service instilled in me the soldier's habit of being able to snatch a few minutes sleep at the drop of a hat but I don't think the writers

BANBURY ALLOCATION : 1956							
LOCO	CLASS	IN	OUT	LOCO	CLASS	IN	OUT
48412	8F 2-8-0 (1935)			5170	4MT : 51xx 2-6-2T (1928)		
48419	8F 2-8-0 (1935)			9303	4MT : 43xx 2-6-0 (1932)	Ex Tyseley 9/56	
48471	8F 2-8-0 (1935)			9312	4MT : 43xx 2-6-0 (1932)	Ex Oxley 9/56	
90466	8F : WD 2-8-0 (1943)			5306	4MT : 43xx 2-6-0 (1911)		
90585	8F : WD 2-8-0 (1943)			5317	4MT : 43xx 2-6-0 (1911)		To Tyseley 4/56
90716	8F : WD 2-8-0 (1943)			5332	4MT : 43xx 2-6-0 (1911)		
2886	8F : 28xx 2-8-0 (1938)			5361	4MT : 43xx 2-6-0 (1911)		
2897	8F : 28xx 2-8-0 (1938)		To Tyseley 11/56	5379	4MT : 43xx 2-6-0 (1911)	Ex Oxley 8/56	
3819	8F : 28xx 2-8-0 (1938)			6331	4MT : 43xx 2-6-0 (1911)		
3829	8F : 28xx 2-8-0 (1938)			6355	4MT : 43xx 2-6-0 (1911)	Ex Oxley 8/56	To Swindon 10/55
3831	8F : 28xx 2-8-0 (1938)			6362	4MT : 43xx 2-6-0 (1911)		
3835	8F : 28xx 2-8-0 (1938)		To Reading 12/56	6387	4MT : 43xx 2-6-0 (1911)		
3859	8F : 28xx 2-8-0 (1938)			7315	4MT : 43xx 2-6-0 (1911)		
2812	8F : 28xx 2-8-0 (1903)			8452	4F : 94XX 0-6-0T (1949)		
2816	8F : 28xx 2-8-0 (1903)			9449	4F : 94XX 0-6-0T (1949)		
2822	8F : 28xx 2-8-0 (1903)			2202	3MT : 2251 0-6-0 (1930)		To Machynlleth 3/56
2823	8F : 28xx 2-8-0 (1903)			2209	3MT : 2251 0-6-0 (1930)		To Croes Newydd 6/56
2827	8F : 28xx 2-8-0 (1903)		To Westbury 10/56	2246	3MT : 2251 0-6-0 (1930)		
2835	8F : 28xx 2-8-0 (1903)		To Reading 12/56	2256	3MT : 2251 0-6-0 (1930)		
2847	8F : 28xx 2-8-0 (1903)			2259	3MT : 2251 0-6-0 (1930)		
2850	8F : 28xx 2-8-0 (1903)		To Oxley 6/56	2270	3MT : 2251 0-6-0 (1930)		
2867	8F : 28xx 2-8-0 (1903)		To Reading 12/56	2297	3MT : 2251 0-6-0 (1930)		
6966	5MT : MOD-HALL 4-6-0 (1944)		To Swindon 8/56	3646	3F : 57xx 0-6-0T (1933)		
6976	5MT : MOD-HALL 4-6-0 (1944)			5404	1P : 54xx 0-6-0T (1931)		
6979	5MT : MOD-HALL 4-6-0 (1944)			5407	1P : 54xx 0-6-0T (1931)		
4942	5MT : HALL 4-6-0 (1928)			5424	1P : 54xx 0-6-0T (1931)		
4977	5MT : HALL 4-6-0 (1928)		To Laira 6/56	13105	0F : 350hp 0-6-0		To Old Oak C. 8/55
5930	5MT : HALL 4-6-0 (1928)			13105	0F : 350hp 0-6-0	Ex Old Oak C. 9/56	
5947	5MT : HALL 4-6-0 (1928)			13106	0F : 350hp 0-6-0		
5954	5MT : HALL 4-6-0 (1928)		To Laira 6/56	13107	0F : 350hp 0-6-0		
6906	5MT : HALL 4-6-0 (1928)			13108	0F : 350hp 0-6-0		
6929	5MT : HALL 4-6-0 (1928)			13109	0F : 350hp 0-6-0		
4149	4MT : 51xx 2-6-2T (1928)			13110	0F : 350hp 0-6-0		
5152	4MT : 51xx 2-6-2T (1928)						

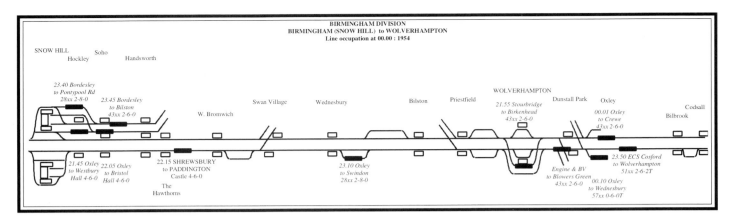

of military manuals ever envisaged forty winks being taken on the footplate of a moving 28xx 2-8-0 with a bucket for a pillow and an old overcoat as a blanket. It worked nevertheless and after half an hour or so in the land of nod I would get up as fresh as a daisy.

It was a lucky throw of the link arrangements that put me with Bert during that phase of my career and in many ways he was the most considerate of colleagues. Unlike some drivers who drove as though every inch of a line was uphill, Bert rarely flogged an engine and whenever possible let the road do the work although occasions did arise when he had to crack the whip in order to keep time.

One such occasion happened when the link was swollen with a number of summer passenger duties and we were given 7812 'Erlestoke Manor' to work the twelve coach 07.00 Snow Hill to Penzance. The Manors were good, free steaming engines and although officially in the same power class as a Hall (and, for all that, a Castle) with their relatively small driving wheels they were overloaded on heavy long distance workings and Bert had to make 7812 cough once or twice on the journey. How the driver who relieved us at St Philips Marsh got on, I can only imagine, since by the time he took over we were very low on coal whilst he was booked to run non-stop over the ninety-odd miles to Newton Abbot.

Normally we would have had a Hall 4-6-0 for the job but 7812 was being returned to Newton Abbot after a month at Tyseley and the shed thought it would be a convenient way of getting the engine home.

Variety was the name of the game at Tyseley with the diet of mixed traffic and goods engines being enhanced by summer express workings which could involve anything up to a Castle or, if we were on the main line, even the chance of a King. Not every shed enjoyed such varied motive power as I discovered one day after Bert and I had arrived at Weston-super-Mare with the 08.30 ex Snow Hill and 6803 'Bucklebury Grange'. We were sitting on the platform bench whiling away the last ten minutes before leaving with the 14.05 return working when the stock for the 13.57 to Paddington ran in on the opposite side of the platform behind 6026 'King John'.

It looked a picture with its paintwork and copper embellishments gleaming in the sunlight and more than put our workstained 6803 in the shade. The Old Oak men hopped off their engine and, all red neckerchiefs and goggles, wandered over to join us; the Cockney fireman complaining bitterly about how the double-chimney Kings were burning more coal than ever. He had told old 'so and so' at Swindon about it and what he thought of the modification. He stuck his thumb in the direction of 6803.

"What's this old camel like, then?"

"Very good. All the improved draughting engines steam very well."

He shook his head.

"Garn!"

"We got some 43's at Tyseley with improved dra-"

At this point it appeared we were speaking different languages and he looked at me as though I came from China.

"For'yfrees? For'yfrees? Wot sort of bleedin' engine's that then?"

Ye Gods, I thought to myself, when you spend your life on Castles and Kings, you just

BANBURY ALLOCATION : 1957

LOCO	CLASS	IN	OUT	LOCO	CLASS	IN	OUT
48412	8F 2-8-0 (1935)			9303	4MT : 43xx 2-6-0 (1932)		
48419	8F 2-8-0 (1935)			9312	4MT : 43xx 2-6-0 (1932)		
48471	8F 2-8-0 (1935)			5306	4MT : 43xx 2-6-0 (1911)		
90466	8F : WD 2-8-0 (1943)			5332	4MT : 43xx 2-6-0 (1911)		
90585	8F : WD 2-8-0 (1943)			5361	4MT : 43xx 2-6-0 (1911)		
90716	8F : WD 2-8-0 (1943)		To Shrewsbury 10/57	5379	4MT : 43xx 2-6-0 (1911)		
2886	8F : 28xx 2-8-0 (1938)			6331	4MT : 43xx 2-6-0 (1911)		
3819	8F : 28xx 2-8-0 (1938)			6362	4MT : 43xx 2-6-0 (1911)		To Canton 4/57
3829	8F : 28xx 2-8-0 (1938)		To Oxley 10/57	6387	4MT : 43xx 2-6-0 (1911)		
3831	8F : 28xx 2-8-0 (1938)			6392	4MT : 43xx 2-6-0 (1911)	Ex Chester 6/57	To Machynlleth 10/57
3859	8F : 28xx 2-8-0 (1938)			7308	4MT : 43xx 2-6-0 (1911)	Ex Hereford 6/57	
2812	8F : 28xx 2-8-0 (1903)			7315	4MT : 43xx 2-6-0 (1911)		
2816	8F : 28xx 2-8-0 (1903)		To Severn T. Jcn 12/57	8452	4F : 94XX 0-6-0T (1949)		To Worcester 3/57
2822	8F : 28xx 2-8-0 (1903)		To Taunton 8/57	8452	4F : 94XX 0-6-0T (1949)	Ex Worcester 6/57	
2823	8F : 28xx 2-8-0 (1903)			9449	4F : 94XX 0-6-0T (1949)		
2847	8F : 28xx 2-8-0 (1903)		To Severn T. Jcn 12/57	2246	3MT : 2251 0-6-0 (1930)		To Didcot 12/57
6976	5MT : MOD-HALL 4-6-0 (1944)			2256	3MT : 2251 0-6-0 (1930)		
6979	5MT : MOD-HALL 4-6-0 (1944)			2259	3MT : 2251 0-6-0 (1930)		
4924	5MT : HALL 4-6-0 (1928)	Ex Truro 10/57		2270	3MT : 2251 0-6-0 (1930)		
4942	5MT : HALL 4-6-0 (1928)			2297	3MT : 2251 0-6-0 (1930)		
4964	5MT : HALL 4-6-0 (1928)	Ex Canton 10/57		3646	3F : 57xx 0-6-0T (1933)		
5930	5MT : HALL 4-6-0 (1928)			5404	1P : 54xx 0-6-0T (1931)		w/d 12/57
5947	5MT : HALL 4-6-0 (1928)			5407	1P : 54xx 0-6-0T (1931)		
5989	5MT : HALL 4-6-0 (1928)	Ex Severn T. Jcn 10/57		5424	1P : 54xx 0-6-0T (1931)		
6906	5MT : HALL 4-6-0 (1928)			13105	0F : 350hp 0-6-0		
6929	5MT : HALL 4-6-0 (1928)			13106	0F : 350hp 0-6-0		
6823	5MT : GRANGE 4-6-0 (1936)	Ex Chester 9/57		13107	0F : 350hp 0-6-0		
6635	5MT : 56xx 0-6-2T (1927)	Ex Cathays 12/57		13108	0F : 350hp 0-6-0		
4149	4MT : 51xx 2-6-2T (1928)			13109	0F : 350hp 0-6-0		
5152	4MT : 51xx 2-6-2T (1928)			13110	0F : 350hp 0-6-0		
5170	4MT : 51xx 2-6-2T (1928)						

BIRMINGHAM DIVISION
BIRMINGHAM (SNOW HILL) to WOLVERHAMPTON
Line occupation at 01.00 : 1954

SNOW HILL — Soho — Hockley — Handsworth — W. Bromwich — Swan Village — Wednesbury — Bilston — Priestfield — WOLVERHAMPTON — Dunstall Park — Oxley — Codsall — Bilbrook

21.10 Paddington to Birkenhead 47xx 2-8-0
00.45 Bordesley to Oldbury 57xx 0-6-0T
21.10 Cropredy to Croes Newydd 28xx 2-8-0
00.25 Bordesley to Swan V. 57xx 0-6-0T
22.50 Stourbridge to Crewe 43xx 2-6-0.
19.45 Birkenhead to Paddington 47xx 2-8-0
The Hawthorns
00.01 Kidderminster to Bordesley 43xx 2-6-0
22.15 SHREWSBURY to PADDINGTON Castle 4-6-0
ECS Snow Hill to Tyseley 51xx 2-6-2T

don't know how the other half live. I was tempted to do a swap with him and show his driver how little coal you could get to London on but, alas, Bert beckoned.

I had another involvement with Old Oak men in early 1956 during the time the Kings had been temporarily taken out of traffic, their numbers being made up with borrowed engines which included four Pacifics from the LMS.

Bert and I were booked to travel passenger to Banbury for the 14.15 Acton – Bordesley and were standing on Snow Hill waiting for the 11.45 Birkenhead – Paddington which was normally a King working.

The train ran in ten minutes late hauled not by a King but by 46207 'Princess Arthur of Connaught' which I thought a splendid looking engine. Leaving Bert to look after himself, I ran up to the head of the train and asked the Cockney driver if he minded my riding with them as far as Banbury.

Stepping into the cab it was apparent that things were far from what they ought to have been. The footplate was in a complete mess – none of the fittings had seen a cloth for days – whilst both crewmen seemed weary and very dirty. Neither had anything complimentary to say about 46207.

The fireman bared his soul and gave me a long and sorry story about their down trip on the 09.10 ex Paddington, how they had been in trouble for steam from the word go and had dropped time hand over fist. To add to their woes, Stafford road had refilled the tender with Cardiff Briquettes, a rather poor quality patent fuel which had to be broken up before firing if the best results were to be obtained. I told the Old Oak man that I would lend a hand and put myself in charge of breaking the briquettes for him.

The five minute station stop at Snow Hill lengthened to ten before we got the tip to start and from the minute we began to move it was clear from the pressure gauge – 180lb – that it was going to be a difficult trip.

"A bleedin' Swindon man," moaned the driver as we passed Moor Street, "would never have designed a Camel like this…."

By Bordesley he had exhausted his stock of expletives on the designers' memory and turned instead to the engine.

"Whoever 'eard of a woman named Arfa? Arfa's a bleedin' blokes name…."

The needle seemed to be stuck at 180lb but worse was to come since Rowington troughs were frozen over and we decided to put the bag in at Leamington, a ploy that would at least disguise some of the time lost running. We stopped the engine in the right spot but the high sided tender obstructed the column and in the end we had to give it up as a bad job and press on. One side of the cab heaped renewed scorn on LMS engines whilst the other said a prayer for the speedy return of the Kings. Apparently this set of Old Oak men were not the only ones to have suffered misfortune at the hands of Crewe.

"A mate of mine 'ad one of these bleedin' Camels on the 10.30 down." The driver told me whilst we were trying to get a decent head of steam up before leaving Leamington. "They got to bleedin' Reading when his mate though he'd give the fire a bit of a root-up. 'e got the pricker out and accidentally knocked the

bleedin' coal pusher 'andle. Next thing he's got eight tons of bleedin' coal in the cab…."

As he finished the valves lifted and we started off for Banbury with the fireman heaving in briquette halves as fast as I could crack them. We both did our best but by the time the engine had hold of the train the needle was back to 180lb with the driver shaking his head sorrowfully.

We limped past Southam Road, having taken thirteen minutes instead of the usual nine and the driver started to worry about how they were going to get on south of Banbury.

"D'you want to come though to London with us?"

"I wouldn't mind." I replied but then pointed out I had a back working and there would be hell to pay if I didn't turn out for it. He offered to 'square things' – whatever that meant – but I had to decline although I would have given a great deal for the experience.

We ran into Banbury and I got off 'Arfur' rather reluctantly, not happy at leaving a job only half done. I was able however to give them a hand with the water column and with a little dexterity we managed to get it over the rear of the tender and get some water into the tank.

A little later I watched them storm past on their way to Paddington, valves lifting for once and the chimney laying a smoke screen over most of the county. It was unfair to place too much blame on them since they had a strange engine and rather poor coal. If they had had a chance to get used to the Princess Royal – plus some decent stuff in the tender – they might have put up quite a different performance.

A day or two later I was working a 28xx 2-8-0 on the 13.25 Bordesley to Banbury goods when we were overtaken near Olton by 46210 'Lady Patricia' at the head of the 11.35 ex Birkenhead. It seemed to be making a reasonable job of the working but the fireman leaned out as he went by and crossed his wrists, indicating that he wouldn't mind changing places with me. I surprised him by nodding in agreement although I doubt if he'd had a 28xx for many a year.

The annual City of Birmingham holiday express probably represented the best value anyone could get for money in the 1950's and for fifty shillings (£2.50) – roughly the equivalent of a days pay for most people – you could travel to a different seaside destination from Monday to Friday. For footplatemen – who received about the same amount for working the train – it was an interesting day out since it operated under a special arrangement by which you stayed with your engine at the destination and brought the return working back to Snow Hill. It was a long but not unprofitable day and you had the benefit of several hours at the seaside.

Bert and I found ourselves marked up to work the train on the Thursday of its week of operation when the destination was Weston-super-Mare. The engine, which was used for the train each day of the week and specially looked after, was a gleaming Modified Hall 4-6-0, 7918 'Rhose Wood Hall'.

We had a first class run down and little did I know it but I was about to discover an occupational Achilles heel.

We turned and stabled 7918 in Weston loco and made our way to the seafront where we

spent a couple of hours before returning to prepare the engine for the return leg. I got up from the sand, stretched and then jumped as a bolt of pain ran through my back.

"Good grief," I exclaimed, "that hurt."

"What hurt?" asked Bert without much interest and looking at his watch.

"My back."

He laughed.

"Your back can hurt as much as it likes. You're still firing all the way back."

We strolled back to the shed and I was relieved to find that the pain subsided as we walked. By the time we pulled out of the station, it had gone completely.

I started to fire in the usual manner but by the time we were passing Yatton not only had the pain returned but it stayed with a vengeance. As I hopped from one leg to another to see whether the pain could be eased by contortion, Bert started to take me seriously and suggested I called for relief at Bristol. I considered it but asking for relief would have entailed at least fifteen minutes delay to the train whilst I did not particularly want to be stranded a hundred miles from home. I told him I would carry on.

By Gloucester I was regretting my decision and by Cheltenham I was feeling like the ghost of Hamlets' father. All I could do was to experiment to see if there was any way I could fire and at the same time lessen the pain and eventually I discovered that if I lifted my left leg off the footplate and transferred as much weight as possible to my right hand side, I could just manage to get coal from the tender to the firebox. The problem was that I could only manage small amounts of coal at a time and therefore I had to fire more frequently than normal. Had I been paired with a younger driver I could have thrown the shovel in his direction but Bert had passed his threescore with his firing days well behind him. My only consolation, I didn't find it funny at the time, was his suggestion that I claim a world record for one-legged firing.

Eventually – after a nightmare of a trip – we reached Snow Hill where the shunter hooked off whilst I attended to the lamps. I tried to pull myself back on the footplate but couldn't. All the strength had gone from my arms whilst I stood, helpless, like a parody of Richard III. Bert watch me cavorting about and made what must be the most apposite suggestion I have heard in my life. Leaning from the cab he called down.

"Walk back along the sleepers to the platform ramp and I'll pick you up there. You won't have to climb from there."

I got rather more sympathy from the shunter who guided me back to the platform and somehow got me back onto the engine. He gave me a sad look.

"Your trouble is, you're too old for firing."

The doctor next morning agreed with him.

"Sciatica," he said, "an old man's complaint…"

The thing about sciatica is that its name does not reflect the pain involved although the doctor put me off work for a month and the loco, when I returned, were considerate enough – perhaps the shedmaster had had it in his day – to put me on the Swindon roundabout to see whether I would fall to pieces or not. One driver was so concerned, he even offered to do the firing for me.

DRIVERS : GOOD & BAD

The list of engines that brought an express train to its destination forty-three minutes early is a short one but includes County 4-6-0 1022 'County of Northampton' which not only pared nearly three-quarters of an hour off the 09.10 Birmingham - Weston-super-Mare but arrived with more than a thousand gallons of water to spare after running nonstop from Stratford. In its early days 1022 had been a West of England engine operating from Laira and Penzance sheds but in late 1951 it was moved to the Northern section spending most of the 1950's at Chester. The engine is seen waiting to enter Tyseley works.

After shaking off the sciatica and regaining my sealegs they put me with Fred Castle, a first class engineman who possessed every good quality but modesty.

"Jacks," he said to me when we first teamed up, "You have the great good fortune to be paired with the best driver at Tyseley."

"And you, Mr Castle," I responded – I thought it best not to be too familiar – "paired with the best fireman…"

His eyes narrowed and I knew he was about to put me to some sort of test.

What," he asked, "is the most important job you have to do?"

Heavens above, I said, I could think of several dozen although it was anyone's guess which was the most important. I blurted out a few of the most obvious – firing, injectors, keeping the footplate clean, etc – but he shook his head. Finally he looked at me in the same way that my old Latin master did when passing judgement of my declensions.

"The most important of your tasks," he roared, "is never to forget to warm my cup before you fill it with tea."

He burst into laughter and said we should get on very well together, which we did.

I looked forward to our first job together for in truth there was nothing like working for a really good driver, but our teamwork started in an anticlimax when the shed foreman asked us to pull a 51xx 2-6-2T off the factory road and get it ready to run to Leamington. It was in rather a sorry state, having been in a collision with a goods train at Budbrooke when returning to Leamington after banking a train to Hatton. We took it, buffers missing and damaged bun-

ker, up to the column and started to fill the tanks.

Ten minutes later we were making our excuses to the foreman.

"There's enough water coming out of the side tanks to float another ark."

"Leaking a bit, is it?"

"Leaking. Its leaking faster than we can fill it up."

"Ah well, I wanted to know if the tanks were watertight and now you've told me what I wanted to know. Take it back to the factory and then put your feet up."

So my first day with Fred Castle did not see any records set and in fact none ever were because shortly afterwards I was shifted to work for a short spell with 'Bless me' Burton and then with a driver, Arthur W, who did not set the best of examples for aspiring locomen.

As I saw things his problem was that he had done about fifteen years as a cleaner but only eight as a fireman which left him very short in terms of experience. He was also too keen on making overtime on the day turns which made him a rather reckless partner to be working with.

RUNNING TIMES : BIRMINGHAM : BANBURY						
Class	1	C	D	E	F	H
SNOW HILL	10.00	10.00				
Bordesley			10.00	10.00	10.00	10.00
Tyseley	10.06	10.07	10.06	10.06	10.06	10.06
Hatton	10.19				10.32	10.38
L. Spa	10.25	10.37	10.37	10.39	10.45	10.54
Southam Rd				10.51	10.56	11.05	11.16
BANBURY	10.49	11.11	11.17	11.26	11.39	11.50

The above tables shows the variance in speeds between different types of trains running nonstop from Birmingham to Banbury.

We once worked a coal train to Banbury with one of the LMS 8F 2-8-0's that Banbury shed had acquired from the Midland in July 1955 and shot past Claydon at a speed I thought irresponsible. Reminding Arthur that the gradient was now falling at about 1 in 300 I (respectfully) suggested he might ease up a little but he took no notice.

As usual the Cropredy distant was against us and although Arthur shut off as it came into sight, he had no hope whatsoever of drawing up at the home and, with the engine in reverse and the brake hard on, we streaked by the signalbox and ground to a halt by the distant for Banbury Ironstone Sidings.

It was not my place to berate him for failing to control the train but when he declared his intention to reverse the train back to Cropredy, my patience snapped and we had a thundering good argument there and then. In the end he gave way and moved forward to Ironstone Sidings and disappeared inside the box. What he told the signalman I never found out but somehow he managed to get away with it. Any other driver would have been hit with a form two and taken off the footplate for a week.

We trickled down to Banbury hump and were overtaken by the up Cambrian Coast whose Cockney fireman leant out of the King 4-6-0 and made it abundantly clear from his angry gesticulations that we had held them up and he was less that happy about it.

Of course had Arthur driven more responsibly we wouldn't have tied things up at Cropredy and we'd still have got to Banbury well ahead of the Cambrian. It was not good enough.

His efforts with an LMS 8F however were as nothing compared to what happened when he found himself at the controls of an Austerity. We were sent out to relieve a special class E from Birkenhead to Banbury which was running as an overload to the 15.20 Birkenhead - Oxford class C. A class E service was a partially fitted express goods in which approximately 10% of the vehicles were vacuum equipped allowing a maximum speed of 35 miles per hour.

Thirty-five miles per hour may not sound very much and with a normal engine – a Hall or 43xx 2-6-0 – it was a rather moderate rate. An Austerity, however, was uncomfortable at a walking pace and whoever dug it out to work a semi-fitted train should have been made to ride on it. To make matters worse Arthur was not too clear about the various categories of fitted trains and rather than familiarise himself with the difference between the highest (a class C which was allowed to run at 55 mph) and the lowest (a Class E), he assumed all fitted or partially fitted services came under the same heading and ran to class C timings.

Thus it was we left Tyseley like a King going over Dainton, roaring away up the main line with the 2-8-0 heaving and crashing all over the place and becoming positively dangerous down Hatton bank. Being just a fireman and allowed no opinion I kept my own counsel and hoped that the climb from Leamington, where we stopped for water, might slow us down a little but Arthur charged away like a madman and with every revolution I expected a rod to go through the firebox and kill the pair of us.

We eventually went in at Fenny Compton to clear the up main for the 20.00 Birmingham – Paddington and the 16.30 ex Birkenhead which followed it by six minutes. The first of the pair streaked by towards Claydon and I looked with interest for the signal to clear for the up Birkenhead. My surprise can be imagined when the signalman pulled off for us. He had evidently been following our progress on the block and decided to give us a run between the two Londons: clearly the sight of an Austerity meant little to him.

To Arthur however the clearing of the loop signal was a green light in more than one respect and knowing that an express was up our tail he did his best to run the wheels off the 2-8-0 until we went inside at Banbury. Other than the guard, I don't think that there could have been anyone more pleased than me when we stopped at the signal on Banbury Hump, journey's end.

I was even more pleased a week or two later when a pair of dead mens shoes sent me into No.5 link to be paired with Harry 'HJ' Mason who was as different from Arthur as chalk was

from cheese. Not only was he a craftsman with an engine but he was a scientist who evaluated and quantified almost every aspect of the job. He would experiment to the nth degree with different engines, comparing each type and trying them on different regulator and cut-off settings until he was satisfied that he had discovered the most efficient way of working that particular type. He measured the coal and water in the tender before and after each run and discussed with me, at length, how we could economise without impairing efficiency. To add to my delight – and Harry was a driver to whom I willingly and cheerfully gave of my best – the link included a number of London turns which he would often let me drive between Leamington and Birmingham.

This, of course, included the ascent of Hatton bank and it fascinated me to watch Harry firing and how he gently stroked the shovel just inside the firebox, letting the movement of the engine and the shape of the fire distribute the coal. This, truly, was firing with your head and not your back. Modestly he would give the inside band of his cap a wipe when we passed Knowle and declare that he could only stand it for twenty miles or so. In return I would say that it was not right for the driver to be firing over such a rough section and he would tell me to keep an eye on the road and not to lose any time to Snow Hill.

He was equally pedantic in his observance of the passing times in the working book and no matter how much they had been rounded up or down by the timing clerk, he insisted on sticking to them. Even the loss of a single half minute irritated him and one night when we were coming down with the 19.12 Paddington – Wolverhampton and were sailing rather close to the wind, instead of easing off at Tyseley he kept the King pounding until we were coming out of Moor Street tunnel and had to use quite a bit of vacuum to get the train, now on time, to stop in the proper place. Walking back down the train he helped an old lady alight from one of the coaches.

"I didn't think you were going to stop here tonight." She said as Harry took her arm.

"Neither, madam, did I…."

Where driving experience was concerned, most firemen had to take what crumbs came to them from the rich man's table but I was lucky in that Harry laid a place for me at the table. On the London jobs he allowed me to drive from Leamington to Birmingham but on goods trains, even if we were working to Gloucester, he would take the shovel for the entire trip. I think it helped him with his theories on the physics of the steam engine whilst I was more than happy to take over the regulator for long periods. I was even happier when he had to work a 43xx 2-6-0, his favourite engines, which I could never get to steam. Harry on the other hand had spent twenty-two years as a fireman with much of the time being spent on the class and had had plenty of time to master them.

The greatest surprise wrought by Harry was his argument that present day senior firemen had a far harder time of it than his generation: a viewpoint not easily – in fact not at all – accepted by his peers in the enginemen's cabin.

"In my time" he would say to them between howls of protest, "the loco's were well maintained, coal was good and…"

"Rubbish!"

"…and we lodged between turns."

"Tripe!"

"We used to work to Bristol, stay the night there and work back next day. Nowadays they fire to Weston, London, Aberystwyth and God knows where else – and work back the same day."

It was a well argued point but not, alas, one that took root with many of his generation who preferred to regard most young fireman as an unfortunate waste of space.

Of all the engines that we saw, the County 4-6-0's tended to be the most scarce and I was therefore more than usually interested to find a rather grimy 1022 'County of Northampton' standing dead outside that factory at Tyseley one morning. Harry and I, who happened to be spare that day, talked about it to the fitter.

"It failed coming down from London last night," he told us adding that the problem was one that could be solved after an hour or so resetting the valves. I said something to Harry about wishing we could have a turn with it.

The next day Harry and I were booked to a Weston out and home passenger excursion, something that we both agreed was a much more attractive proposition than kicking out heels at Tyseley all day.

We signed on, read the notices and, expecting the usual Hall 4-6-0 for the job, looked casually down the engine board for our loco.

"Harry, " I shouted, "look what we've got. 1022!"

The gods had smiled on me through Harry's intervention.

LOCO	CLASS	IN	OUT	LOCO	CLASS	IN	OUT
			BANBURY ALLOCATION : 1958				
92221	9F : 2-10-0 (1954)	New 7/58		6929	5MT : HALL 4-6-0 (1928)		
92222	9F : 2-10-0 (1954)	New 7/58		6949	5MT : HALL 4-6-0 (1928)	Ex Wolverhampton 9/58	
92223	9F : 2-10-0 (1954)	New 7/58		6823	5MT : GRANGE 4-6-0 (1936)		To Laira 6/58
92224	9F : 2-10-0 (1954)	New 8/58		6848	5MT : GRANGE 4-6-0 (1936)	Ex Laira 3/58	To Swindon 9/58
92225	9F : 2-10-0 (1954)	New 8/58		6635	5MT : 56xx 0-6-2T (1927)		To Radyr 3/58
92226	9F : 2-10-0 (1954)	New 8/58		4149	4MT : 51xx 2-6-2T (1928)		
92227	9F : 2-10-0 (1954)	New 8/58		5152	4MT : 51xx 2-6-2T (1928)		
92228	9F : 2-10-0 (1954)	New 8/58		5170	4MT : 51xx 2-6-2T (1928)		
92229	9F : 2-10-0 (1954)	New 9/58	To Old Oak C. 10/58	9303	4MT : 43xx 2-6-0 (1932)		
92230	9F : 2-10-0 (1954)	New 9/58	To Old Oak C. 10/58	9312	4MT : 43xx 2-6-0 (1932)		
48412	8F 2-8-0 (1935)		To Chester 6/58	5306	4MT : 43xx 2-6-0 (1911)		To Swindon 9/58
48419	8F 2-8-0 (1935)		To Swansea 2/58	5332	4MT : 43xx 2-6-0 (1911)		To Llanelly 10/58
48471	8F 2-8-0 (1935)		To Chester 6/58	5361	4MT : 43xx 2-6-0 (1911)		To Truro 10/58
90148	8F : WD 2-8-0 (1943)	Ex Shrewsbury 3/58		5379	4MT : 43xx 2-6-0 (1911)		w/d 5/58
90313	8F : WD 2-8-0 (1943)	Ex Southall 4/58		6311	4MT : 43xx 2-6-0 (1911)		
90466	8F : WD 2-8-0 (1943)			6331	4MT : 43xx 2-6-0 (1911)	Ex Oxley 11/58	
90585	8F : WD 2-8-0 (1943)			6387	4MT : 43xx 2-6-0 (1911)		
2886	8F : 28xx 2-8-0 (1938)		To Tyseley 4/58	7305	4MT : 43xx 2-6-0 (1911)	Ex Oxley 4/58	
2890	8F : 28xx 2-8-0 (1938)	Ex Southall 10/58		7308	4MT : 43xx 2-6-0 (1911)		
3819	8F : 28xx 2-8-0 (1938)		To Westbury 8/58	7315	4MT : 43xx 2-6-0 (1911)		
3820	8F : 28xx 2-8-0 (1938)	Ex Chester 6/58		8452	4F : 94XX 0-6-0T (1949)		
3831	8F : 28xx 2-8-0 (1938)		To Tyseley 4/58	9449	4F : 94XX 0-6-0T (1949)		
3856	8F : 28xx 2-8-0 (1938)	Ex Southall 10/58		2211	3MT : 2251 0-6-0 (1930)	Ex Croes Newydd 9/58	
3858	8F : 28xx 2-8-0 (1938)	Ex Chester 6/58		2230	3MT : 2251 0-6-0 (1930)	Ex Croes Newydd 9/58	
3859	8F : 28xx 2-8-0 (1938)		To Pontypool Rd 2/58	2234	3MT : 2251 0-6-0 (1930)	Ex Shrewsbury 9/58	
2812	8F : 28xx 2-8-0 (1903)		To Tyseley 8/58	2256	3MT : 2251 0-6-0 (1930)		
2816	8F : 28xx 2-8-0 (1903)	Ex Canton 9/58		2259	3MT : 2251 0-6-0 (1930)		To Neyland 12/58
2823	8F : 28xx 2-8-0 (1903)		To Ebbw Jcn 8/58	2270	3MT : 2251 0-6-0 (1930)		
2853	8F : 28xx 2-8-0 (1903)	Ex Southall 9/58		2297	3MT : 2251 0-6-0 (1930)		
2882	8F : 28xx 2-8-0 (1903)	Ex Chester 6/58	To Tyseley 8/58	3646	3F : 57xx 0-6-0T (1933)		
6976	5MT : MOD-HALL 4-6-0 (1944)			5407	1P : 54xx 0-6-0T (1931)		
6979	5MT : MOD-HALL 4-6-0 (1944)			5420	1P : 54xx 0-6-0T (1931)	Ex Southall 1/58	
4924	5MT : HALL 4-6-0 (1928)			5424	1P : 54xx 0-6-0T (1931)		
4942	5MT : HALL 4-6-0 (1928)			5815	1P : 14xx 0-4-2T (1932)	Ex Leamington 2/58	To Swindon 4/58
4964	5MT : HALL 4-6-0 (1928)			13105	0F : 350hp 0-6-0		
5921	5MT : HALL 4-6-0 (1928)	Ex Ebbw Jcn 1/58		13106	0F : 350hp 0-6-0		
5930	5MT : HALL 4-6-0 (1928)			13107	0F : 350hp 0-6-0		
5947	5MT : HALL 4-6-0 (1928)			13108	0F : 350hp 0-6-0		
5989	5MT : HALL 4-6-0 (1928)			13109	0F : 350hp 0-6-0		
6906	5MT : HALL 4-6-0 (1928)			13110	0F : 350hp 0-6-0		

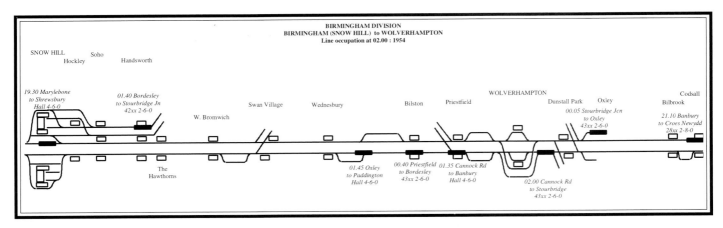

"I asked the foreman if he wanted it trying out by a couple of good chaps."

Not only had 1022 received the necessary mechanical attention but it had also had a thorough clean and looked very smart in its green livery although I could not help thinking that the rather squat double chimney detracted rather from the original. We jumped up and did a quick check of the engine which had a good fire in the box that was burning through very nicely. Harry tested the vacuum and declared himself ready to come off shed.

"They've changed all the rings on the valves," he told me, "so the lady ought to give us a really decent trip."

We collected our twelve coach set and made our way, tender first, down the relief road as a prelude to the rather tricky manoeuvring necessary to get southbound trains positioned at Snow Hill. We stood for a couple of minutes at Bordesley North to let a couple of suburbans by and then continued northwards towards Hockley where we had to run round the train, get the engine good and hot, and then bring it into Snow Hill for loading. Although we had only gone a mile or so, it was obvious from the way we went up the 1 in 45 between Moor Street and Snow Hill that the fitters had done a first class job with the engine.

When we got to Snow Hill it seemed that there was some trouble to the north of the station since we were brought to a stand at the north end where the signalman relayed a change of plans.

"Run round here," he shouted, "push back and then run forward into twelve."

There was no time or point in arguing so we did as he asked and eventually ran into platform twelve which was thick with passengers going for a day out by the sea. My difficulty was that I was now expected to bring the engine up to scratch in Snow Hill where the station brass were paranoid about smoke and engines blowing off. This was one of the advantages about running round at Hockley where you could make as much smoke and noise as you liked whilst making the fire up.

I did what I could with the fire, sprinkling coal carefully rather than ladling it in, and filled the boiler up to the top of the glass.

"Bordesley, Small Heath, Hall Green, Henley-in-Arden, Stratford then right away Weston." Shouted the guard from the platform.

"Righto," returned Harry and then after the guard had walked back, "look at that poor bugger...."

He was a Bordesley goods guard, poor man, whose wife had decided to keep him company for the day.

"Wonder if she goes with him when he's on the Bilston pilot."

As we spoke the 07.30 Shrewsbury – Paddington ran in, its King shining as usual from end to end, and as soon as the Stafford Road fireman saw 1022 he jumped down and came across to us.

"I wouldn't take that bloody thing off shed," he remonstrated kicking the cab side of our engine and giving us a colourful description of its failure two days earlier.

LOCO	CLASS	IN	OUT	LOCO	CLASS	IN	OUT
92212	9F 2-10-0 (1954)	New 11/59		5921	5MT : HALL 4-6-0 (1928)		
92213	9F 2-10-0 (1954)	Ex Bristol (SPM) 11/59		5930	5MT : HALL 4-6-0 (1928)		To Tyseley 11/59
92214	9F 2-10-0 (1954)	Ex Canton 11/59		5947	5MT : HALL 4-6-0 (1928)		To Fishguard 11/59
92215	9F 2-10-0 (1954)	New 12/59		5989	5MT : HALL 4-6-0 (1928)		
92221	9F 2-10-0 (1954)		To Laira 6/59	6906	5MT : HALL 4-6-0 (1928)		
92222	9F 2-10-0 (1954)		To Laira 6/59	6911	5MT : HALL 4-6-0 (1928)	Ex Penzance 11/59	
92223	9F 2-10-0 (1954)		To Laira 6/59	6929	5MT : HALL 4-6-0 (1928)		
92224	9F 2-10-0 (1954)		To Laira 6/59	6949	5MT : HALL 4-6-0 (1928)		
92225	9F 2-10-0 (1954)		To Laira 6/59	4149	4MT : 51xx 2-6-2T (1928)		
92226	9F 2-10-0 (1954)			5152	4MT : 51xx 2-6-2T (1928)		
92227	9F 2-10-0 (1954)			5170	4MT : 51xx 2-6-2T (1928)		w/d 12/59
92228	9F 2-10-0 (1954)			9312	4MT : 43xx 2-6-0 (1932)		
92232	9F 2-10-0 (1954)	Ex Canton 9/59		5337	4MT : 43xx 2-6-0 (1911)	Ex Canton 1/59	To Didcot 8/59
92233	9F 2-10-0 (1954)	Ex Canton 9/59		5351	4MT : 43xx 2-6-0 (1911)	Ex Swindon 5/59	To Didcot 8/59
92234	9F 2-10-0 (1954)	Ex Canton 9/59		5375	4MT : 43xx 2-6-0 (1911)	Ex Worcester 2/59	To Didcot 8/59
92250	9F 2-10-0 (1954)	New 2/59	To Ebbw Jcn 11/59	6311	4MT : 43xx 2-6-0 (1911)		
90148	8F : WD 2-8-0 (1943)			6331	4MT : 43xx 2-6-0 (1911)		w/d 4/59
90261	8F : WD 2-8-0 (1943)	Ex Leamington 8/59		6364	4MT : 43xx 2-6-0 (1911)	Ex Taunton 10/59	
90268	8F : WD 2-8-0 (1943)	Ex Southall 6/59		6387	4MT : 43xx 2-6-0 (1911)		
90313	8F : WD 2-8-0 (1943)			7305	4MT : 43xx 2-6-0 (1911)		
90466	8F : WD 2-8-0 (1943)		To Southall 2/59	7308	4MT : 43xx 2-6-0 (1911)		
90483	8F : WD 2-8-0 (1943)	Ex Leamington 8/59		7315	4MT : 43xx 2-6-0 (1911)		
90585	8F : WD 2-8-0 (1943)			7325	4MT : 43xx 2-6-0 (1911)		
7217	8FT : 72xx 2-8-2T (1934)	Ex Landore 6/59	To Oxley 9/59	8452	4F : 94XX 0-6-0T (1949)		
7237	8FT : 72xx 2-8-2T (1934)	Ex Severn T. Jcn 6/59		8498	4F : 94XX 0-6-0T (1949)	Ex Tondu 11/59	
2890	8F : 28xx 2-8-0 (1938)		To Swindon 11/59	9449	4F : 94XX 0-6-0T (1949)		
3816	8F : 28xx 2-8-0 (1938)	Ex Canton 6/59		2211	3MT : 2251 0-6-0 (1930)		To Tyseley 6/59
3820	8F : 28xx 2-8-0 (1938)		To Oxley 3/59	2230	3MT : 2251 0-6-0 (1930)		To Swindon 7/59
3856	8F : 28xx 2-8-0 (1938)		To Severn T. Jcn 12/59	2234	3MT : 2251 0-6-0 (1930)		To Didcot 9/59
3858	8F : 28xx 2-8-0 (1938)		To Reading 9/59	2256	3MT : 2251 0-6-0 (1930)		
3863	8F : 28xx 2-8-0 (1938)	Ex Oxley 6/59	To Severn T. Jcn 9/59	2270	3MT : 2251 0-6-0 (1930)		w/d 9/59
2804	8F : 28xx 2-8-0 (1903)	Ex Stourbridge 6/59	w/d 7/59	2297	3MT : 2251 0-6-0 (1930)		
2816	8F : 28xx 2-8-0 (1903)		w/d 10/59	3646	3F : 57xx 0-6-0T (1933)		
2841	8F : 28xx 2-8-0 (1903)	Ex Oxley 8/59	To Reading 9/59	6429	2P : 64xx 0-6-0T (1932)	Ex Croes Newydd 6/59	
2853	8F : 28xx 2-8-0 (1903)		To Stourbridge 1/59	5407	1P : 54xx 0-6-0T (1931)		
4078	7P : CASTLE 4-6-0 (1923)	Ex Wolverhampton 10/59		5420	1P : 54xx 0-6-0T (1931)		
5057	7P : CASTLE 4-6-0 (1923)	Ex Bristol 11/59		5424	1P : 54xx 0-6-0T (1931)		w/d 4/59
7011	7P : CASTLE 4-6-0 (1923)	Ex Shrewsbury 10/59		13105	0F : 350hp 0-6-0		
6976	5MT : MOD-HALL 4-6-0 (1944)			13106	0F : 350hp 0-6-0		
6979	5MT : MOD-HALL 4-6-0 (1944)			13107	0F : 350hp 0-6-0		
7905	5MT : MOD-HALL 4-6-0 (1944)	Ex Laira 11/59		13108	0F : 350hp 0-6-0		
4924	5MT : HALL 4-6-0 (1928)		To Taunton 6/59	13109	0F : 350hp 0-6-0		
4942	5MT : HALL 4-6-0 (1928)			13110	0F : 350hp 0-6-0		
4964	5MT : HALL 4-6-0 (1928)			D3108	0F : 350hp 0-6-0	Ex Reading 9/59	
4990	5MT : HALL 4-6-0 (1928)	Ex Wolverhampton 8/59	To Hereford 10/59				

Grange 4-6-0 6828 'Trellech Grange' of Stourbridge and 51xx 2-6-2T banker 5188 of Tyseley attack the climb from Stratford to Earlswood with the 14.05 Weston-super-Mare to Birmingham (Snow Hill) on 30th August 1952. 6828 stayed at Stourbridge - where it rarely if ever had its name pronounced correctly - until September 1957 when it moved to Llanelly. It ended the decade at Truro.

Ten minutes after the departure of the London, we got the right away and, freed from the constraints of Snow Hill, I quickly opened the door and banged a rapid dozen up the front, giving the blower a token touch to keep down smoke as best I could.

"One yellow, Harry." I called from my side of the cab. "Right away up the relief."

Harry jockeyed the brake and brought us to a stand at Bordesley where quite a crowd was waiting for us, as there was at all the local stations we called. For me the stops were a blessing since they gave me time to build the fire up and get the engine ready before the real work started. Our train was actually using the path of the 09.10 Saturdays working to Pembroke Dock which had sixteen minutes recovery time between Stratford and Cheltenham. This allowed us to call at the suburban stations and still be on time at Malvern Road.

By Shirley I had the engine pretty well as I wanted it and gave Harry the tip who opened up on second valve making 1022 leap ahead, We topped Earleswood with no trouble whatsoever and Harry eased back to first valve to let the train

sail down the bank at sixty until he had to brake for the stop at Henley. With a good fire and the right level of water in the boiler, working 1022 was like being on a diesel – only more interesting – and I had ample time to watch the countryside as it passed by, remembering the rather miserable time I spent in the area during the war.

We picked up what seemed to be half the population of Henley, how they got them in the train I cannot imagine, and after leaving Stratford we had a doddle of a run. I wondered why some people had such a rough time on the Coun-

ties since those I had worked on had been amongst the best engines I had known and this included 1009 'County of Carmarthen' during the time it had been fitted with an ugly stovepipe double chimney.

"Be all right if we get a clear run to Weston." called Harry as he opened up for the climb to Broadway. I told him it would be a miracle if we saw so much as a single distant off once we got onto the Midland who regarded us as an intrusion. Harry gave me a curious look.

"We'll see," he said rather mysteriously, "we'll see."

We had a pretty good run over the Great Western, the only blot on the landscape being Long Marston who, even if the road was clear, always left his distant until the last minute, keeping the gates in favour of road traffic far too late. We gave the bobby a frown and a cheery whistle to the 0-6-0 tank in the military sidings as 1022 with the needle just off the mark and a full boiler romped up the last stretch of the bank.

You had to be careful at Broadway since it was not actually the summit of the climb and although the track fell at 1 in 264 for a couple of miles as far

BANBURY ALLOCATION : 1960							
LOCO	CLASS	IN	OUT	LOCO	CLASS	IN	OUT
92212	9F 2-10-0 (1954)			5947	5MT : HALL 4-6-0 (1928)	Ex Fishguard 4/60	
92213	9F 2-10-0 (1954)			5988	5MT : HALL 4-6-0 (1928)	Ex Landore 3/60	
92214	9F 2-10-0 (1954)			5989	5MT : HALL 4-6-0 (1928)		
92215	9F 2-10-0 (1954)			5990	5MT : HALL 4-6-0 (1928)	Ex Landore 3/60	
92221	9F 2-10-0 (1954)	Ex Laira 3/60	To Laira 6/60	6906	5MT : HALL 4-6-0 (1928)		
92221	9F 2-10-0 (1954)	Ex Westbury 9/60		6911	5MT : HALL 4-6-0 (1928)		
92222	9F 2-10-0 (1954)	Ex Laira 3/60	To Laira 6/60	6929	5MT : HALL 4-6-0 (1928)		
92223	9F 2-10-0 (1954)	Ex Laira 3/60	To Laira 6/60	6949	5MT : HALL 4-6-0 (1928)		To Taunton 1/60
92226	9F 2-10-0 (1954)		To Southall 7/60	6952	5MT : HALL 4-6-0 (1928)	Ex Oxford 5/60	
92227	9F 2-10-0 (1954)			4149	4MT : 51xx 2-6-2T (1928)		
92228	9F 2-10-0 (1954)			4154	4MT : 51xx 2-6-2T (1928)	Ex Newton Abbot 4/60	
92232	9F 2-10-0 (1954)			5152	4MT : 51xx 2-6-2T (1928)		
92233	9F 2-10-0 (1954)			5167	4MT : 51xx 2-6-2T (1928)	Ex Tyseley 4/60	
92234	9F 2-10-0 (1954)			9312	4MT : 43xx 2-6-0 (1932)		
7207	8FT : 72xx 2-8-2T (1934)	Ex Landore 6/60		6311	4MT : 43xx 2-6-0 (1911)		w/d 2/60
7228	8FT : 72xx 2-8-2T (1934)	Ex Llanelly 2/60		6335	4MT : 43xx 2-6-0 (1911)	Ex Machynlleth 2/60	To Worcester 7/60
7236	8FT : 72xx 2-8-2T (1934)	Ex Landore 6/60		6364	4MT : 43xx 2-6-0 (1911)		To Tyseley 1/60
7244	8FT : 72xx 2-8-2T (1934)	Ex Duffryn 2/60		6387	4MT : 43xx 2-6-0 (1911)		
7247	8FT : 72xx 2-8-2T (1934)	Ex Oxley 1/60		7305	4MT : 43xx 2-6-0 (1911)		
90148	8F : WD 2-8-0 (1943)			7308	4MT : 43xx 2-6-0 (1911)		To Severn T. Jcn 1/60
90261	8F : WD 2-8-0 (1943)			7315	4MT : 43xx 2-6-0 (1911)		
90268	8F : WD 2-8-0 (1943)			7325	4MT : 43xx 2-6-0 (1911)		
90313	8F : WD 2-8-0 (1943)			7334	4MT : 43xx 2-6-0 (1911)		To Carmarthen 6/60
90315	8F : WD 2-8-0 (1943)	Ex Gloucester 6/60		8452	4F : 94XX 0-6-0T (1949)		To Wolverhampton 5/60
90483	8F : WD 2-8-0 (1943)			8498	4F : 94XX 0-6-0T (1949)		To Wolverhampton 5/60
90585	8F : WD 2-8-0 (1943)			9449	4F : 94XX 0-6-0T (1949)		w/d 6/60
3816	8F : 28xx 2-8-0 (1938)		To Stourbridge 4/60	2256	3MT : 2251 0-6-0 (1930)		w/d 6/60
3817	8F : 28xx 2-8-0 (1938)	Ex Canton 6/60		2297	3MT : 2251 0-6-0 (1930)		w/d 6/60
3843	8F : 28xx 2-8-0 (1938)	Ex Reading 6/60		3217	3MT : 2251 0-6-0 (1930)	Ex Worcester 3/60	
3846	8F : 28xx 2-8-0 (1938)	Ex Stourbridge 6/60	To Croes Newydd 6/60	3646	3F : 57xx 0-6-0T (1933)		
4078	7P : CASTLE 4-6-0 (1923)		To Old Oak C. 4/60	6403	2P : 64xx 0-6-0T (1932)	Ex Stourbridge 1/60	
5057	7P : CASTLE 4-6-0 (1923)		To Old Oak C. 4/60	6421	2P : 64xx 0-6-0T (1932)	Ex Laira 7/60	
7011	7P : CASTLE 4-6-0 (1923)		To Canton 4/60	6429	2P : 64xx 0-6-0T (1932)		
6976	5MT : MOD-HALL 4-6-0 (1944)			5407	1P : 54xx 0-6-0T (1931)		w/d 6/60
6979	5MT : MOD-HALL 4-6-0 (1944)			5417	1P : 54xx 0-6-0T (1931)	Ex Neasden 2/60	
7905	5MT : MOD-HALL 4-6-0 (1944)			5420	1P : 54xx 0-6-0T (1931)		
7929	5MT : MOD-HALL 4-6-0 (1944)	Ex St Blazey 9/60		13105	0F : 350hp 0-6-0		
4910	5MT : HALL 4-6-0 (1928)	Ex Carmarthen 3/60	To Tyseley 7/60	13106	0F : 350hp 0-6-0		
4910	5MT : HALL 4-6-0 (1928)	Ex Tyseley 9/60		13107	0F : 350hp 0-6-0		
4923	5MT : HALL 4-6-0 (1928)	Ex Landore 3/60	To Carmarthen 6/60	13108	0F : 350hp 0-6-0		
4942	5MT : HALL 4-6-0 (1928)		To Exeter 6/60	13109	0F : 350hp 0-6-0		
4964	5MT : HALL 4-6-0 (1928)			13110	0F : 350hp 0-6-0		
5921	5MT : HALL 4-6-0 (1928)		To Tyseley 6/60	D3108	0F : 350hp 0-6-0		
5933	5MT : HALL 4-6-0 (1928)	Ex Oxford 5/60					

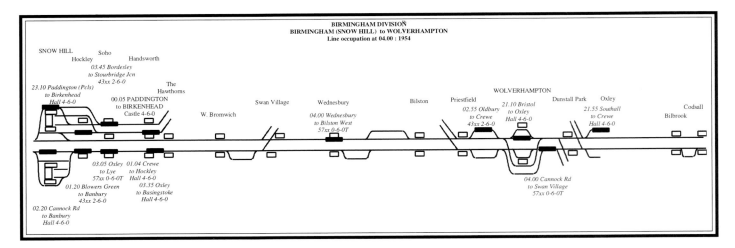

BIRMINGHAM DIVISION
BIRMINGHAM (SNOW HILL) to WOLVERHAMPTON
Line occupation at 04.00 : 1954

as Laverton, the following three and a half miles were uphill. It paid to keep filling the firebox until Hayles Abbey came into sight after which you could put the shovel down for the twelve miles to Cheltenham.

At Lansdown Junction we ran onto the Midland and whatever they may have thought of us, we were clearly something of a celebrity to the crowds of trainspotters to whom a County was a rarity. Unfortunately there was no opportunity to put on a show for them since the speed restriction at the junction was followed by a three-quarter mile 15 mph permanent way slack where we had to put up with the indignity of being overtaken by an LMS 4F 0-6-0 on a coal train.

The crew waved cheerily as they overhauled us but I felt sorry for them since their 4F sounded as though Swindon itself would have had its work cut out getting it back into shape.

After watching the brake van disappeared into the distance, I checked our water level and as we came off the restriction told Harry that we had no need to take water at Gloucester. He nodded, whistled up for the main line, and opened up 1022 in hot pursuit of the 4F to see if we could catch it by Tuffley.

The 4F 0-6-0's were rather poor tools, overtaking us had probably winded it, and we had no trouble roaring past it. 1022 was on second valve and a long cut-off and I was surprised that Harry was not easing off for Standish where the signalman could usually be relied upon to stop us whilst he found a Midland train to run in front of us. Seeing Harefield's distant against us and in anticipation of being stopped I pushed a few shovelfulls down the front of the box. Harry however kept 1022 running and, reaching for the cord, blew the whistle code for the Bristol route plus a long crow I didn't recognise.

I wondered what his game was but before I could say anything, the distant cleared and we were given a clear run onto the Bristol road.

"By George," I said to Harry, "I've never seen us get a road like that around here."

"Ah," he replied, "it's not a bad thing to have a brother who's in the box at Standish…."

CHALFORD CAR : 1955					
Arr	Station	Dep	Arr	Station	Dep
	Gloucester (C)	07.00		Chalford	06.33
07.47	Chalford	07.55	07.13	Gloucester (C)	07.40 ECS
08.34	Gloucester (C)	09.58	07.55	Stonehouse	08.42
10.58	Kemble	11.20	09.14	Chalford	09.30
12.15	Gloucester (C)	13.15	10.10	Gloucester (C)	11.15
13.56	Chalford	14.00	11.59	Chalford	12.55
14.40	Gloucester (C)	17.12	13.35	Gloucester (C)	15.12
17.54	Chalford	18.00	15.53	Chalford	16.00
18.40	Gloucester (C)		16.25	Stonehouse	16.40
			17.01	Brimscombe	17.06
			17.42	Gloucester (C)	18.15
			18.56	Chalford	19.00
			19.43	Gloucester (C)	20.15
			20.56	Chalford	21.00
			21.43	Gloucester (C)	21.35
			22.21	Chalford	

The Chalford Car which served the halts and small stations between Gloucester and Chalford consisted of two 14xx 0-4-2 tanks and their autocoaches, one based at each end of the route. The workings for both are given above.

Apparently Harry had telephoned him the night before and told him to keep an eye out for us.

His brother had done us proud and from the lie of signals at Standish it was clear he had reversed the tradition of a lifetime and put us in front of a Midland train that had been taking water at Gloucester but ought to have had priority. "We won't let him down," said Harry and got 1022 to make a noise that must have been audible several counties away. I couldn't see the Midland man booking any time against us the way we were flying and there is nothing more certain than the fact they had nothing that could keep up with a County.

Not for the first time I regretted that only thirty Counties had taken to the road: it was difficult to believe from the way we wear tearing through the countryside that these were only class 6 engines and I don't think a King could not have done any better. Heaven it was to be young and bliss it was to be on 1022's footplate with the exhaust injector cheerfully singing away and Harry in the mood to straighten out every curve on the way to Bristol. The firing was hard work but what a return I was getting.

Stonehouse, Frocester, Charfield and Wickwar passed in a blur and in much less time than usual Harry was shutting off for the connection between the two railways at Westerleigh. How far his brothers influence extended I do not know but, coincidence or not, we didn't see a single signal against us which for a cross country train at the height of the summer was pretty exceptional and made quite a contrast with the section to section start-stop method of working that was the hallmark of the Midland route from Birmingham to Bristol.

"How're we off for water?" Harry called to me as we crawled towards North Somerset Junction at Bristol and when I gave him the thumbs up he made a sign to the signalman and all signals came off. We accelerated off the avoiding line and onto the main line, Harry giving the 1022 full regulator and a long cut-off to finish the trip in a blaze of glory. I was amused to see a crowd of passengers at Yatton, waiting for a following train, move back like frightened sheep as we approached in a thunder of smoke and steam to crash through the station at high speed and bounce over the complicated trackwork at the west end of the station where the Cheddar and Clevedon branches diverged.

I gave a last look at the fire but in spite of the way we had been going, it was in good shape

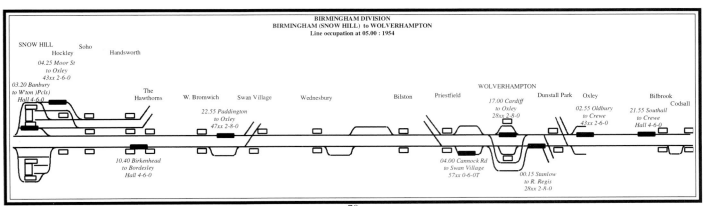

BIRMINGHAM DIVISION
BIRMINGHAM (SNOW HILL) to WOLVERHAMPTON
Line occupation at 05.00 : 1954

The North Warwick stations in the Birmingham area were serviced by the 09.45 trip from Bordesley which worked Shirley, Earlswood Lakes and Henley yards, finishing off with a run up the Henley goods branch. 57xx 0-6-0T 9733 is seen forming the 13.50 Henley - Tyseley return working after propelling up from Henley goods in the early 1950's.

and all I had to do was level it down with the pricker to make it easier for the Weston firedropper to clean it prior to our return. I left the firebox doors open and with 230lb on the gauge we slowed to come off the main line at Worle Junction and drew to a stand in the excursion platform at Weston with Harry keeping one eye on the buffer stops and the other on his watch.

Instantly the platform was black with passengers as they jumped from the coaches to push their way through the barrier.

"There'll be no complaints from them." Smiled Harry and I murmured something vaguely complimentary about his having hammered all the way from Stratford.

"This is our booked time," he showed me the special traffic notice, "and this is the time now."

No wonder they all looked so happy, we had given them almost an extra hour at the seaside. Harry had brought the train in no less than forty-three minutes ahead of time and although there was a little padding in the timings, to shave them by three quarters of an hour

was a tribute to the engine, Harry and, of course, his brother.

The homeward journey was unremarkable by contrast other than the fact it was a joy to fire on an engine like 1022. Having just had its valves relined and set, it was in the peak of mechanical condition and I shall always remember it for being able to run non-stop between Stratford and Weston, arriving with over a thousand gallons of water in the tender. Who said we needed diesels?

Although I had done scores of trips on the 21.50 Snow Hill – Swindon parcels and its unusual route, it was a source of regret that we had

no other workings over the Standish – Swindon section and by 1958 I had resigned myself to never seeing Sapperton in daylight.

"Fancy seeing a bit of the country?" Harry said after signing on 11.00 spare on morning. "We've got to travel passenger to Swindon and bring an engine back."

Ignoring my comments that I had left my camera at home, he led the way to Birmingham, walked me over to New Street and pushed me aboard the 09.50 Bradford - Paignton 'Devonian'.

"I thought we'd have a day out," he explained "and travel out via Gloucester. It'll give you a chance to see your route in daylight."

There weren't that many drivers who would have been so considerate, most would have gone to Swindon and back in the shortest possible time and I tried to thank him but he was engrossed in the way our driver was trying to knock the chimney off his Jubilee. There was a roar from the front end which was continuous other than on the descent of the Lickey. Harry wondered if he had shares in a coal mine.

We changed at Gloucester and walked

WOLVERHAMPTON (STAFFORD RD) ALLOCATION : 1950							
LOCO	CLASS	IN	OUT	LOCO	CLASS	IN	OUT
6004	8P : KING 4-6-0 (1927)			6924	5MT : HALL 4-6-0 (1928)		To Leamington 12/50
6005	8P : KING 4-6-0 (1927)			6942	5MT : HALL 4-6-0 (1928)	Ex Tyseley 11/50	To Oxley 12/50
6006	8P : KING 4-6-0 (1927)			6956	5MT : HALL 4-6-0 (1928)	Ex Oxley 12/50	
6008	8P : KING 4-6-0 (1927)			6812	5MT : GRANGE 4-6-0 (1936)		
6011	8P : KING 4-6-0 (1927)			6848	5MT : GRANGE 4-6-0 (1936)		
6020	8P : KING 4-6-0 (1927)			4103	4MT : 51xx 2-6-2T (1928)		
4000	7P : CASTLE 4-6-0 (1923)			4105	4MT : 51xx 2-6-2T (1928)		
4083	7P : CASTLE 4-6-0 (1923)	Ex Shrewsbury 12/50		4108	4MT : 51xx 2-6-2T (1928)		
4092	7P : CASTLE 4-6-0 (1923)	Ex Worcester 12/50		4115	4MT : 51xx 2-6-2T (1928)		
5008	7P : CASTLE 4-6-0 (1923)			5143	4MT : 51xx 2-6-2T (1928)		
5010	7P : CASTLE 4-6-0 (1923)			5151	4MT : 51xx 2-6-2T (1928)		
5015	7P : CASTLE 4-6-0 (1923)			4337	4MT : 43xx 2-6-0 (1911)		To Tyseley 12/50
5022	7P : CASTLE 4-6-0 (1923)			6321	4MT : 43xx 2-6-0 (1911)		
5031	7P : CASTLE 4-6-0 (1923)			6391	4MT : 43xx 2-6-0 (1911)		To Stourbridge 12/50
5045	7P : CASTLE 4-6-0 (1923)	Ex Old Oak C. 12/50		7315	4MT : 43xx 2-6-0 (1911)		
5053	7P : CASTLE 4-6-0 (1923)			3102	4MT : 31xx 2-6-2T (1938)		
5070	7P : CASTLE 4-6-0 (1923)			3104	4MT : 31xx 2-6-2T (1938)		
5088	7P : CASTLE 4-6-0 (1923)			3160	4MT : 3150 2-6-2T (1906)		
7026	7P : CASTLE 4-6-0 (1923)			8411	4F : 94XX 0-6-0T (1949)		
1016	6MT : COUNTY 4-6-0 (1945)			8423	4F : 94XX 0-6-0T (1949)	New 12/50	
1017	6MT : COUNTY 4-6-0 (1945)			8462	4F : 94XX 0-6-0T (1949)		
1024	6MT : COUNTY 4-6-0 (1945)		To Shrewsbury 11/50	9428	4F : 94XX 0-6-0T (1949)	New 12/50	
1025	6MT : COUNTY 4-6-0 (1945)		To Shrewsbury 11/50	3615	3F : 57xx 0-6-0T (1933)		
1029	6MT : COUNTY 4-6-0 (1945)			3756	3F : 57xx 0-6-0T (1933)		
4018	5P : STAR 4-6-0 (1907)			3778	3F : 57xx 0-6-0T (1933)		
4031	5P : STAR 4-6-0 (1907)			9621	3F : 57xx 0-6-0T (1933)		
4049	5P : STAR 4-6-0 (1907)			5701	3F : 57xx 0-6-0T (1929)		
4053	5P : STAR 4-6-0 (1907)			5739	3F : 57xx 0-6-0T (1929)		
4058	5P : STAR 4-6-0 (1907)			5780	3F : 57xx 0-6-0T (1929)		
4060	5P : STAR 4-6-0 (1907)		To Bristol (BR) 12/50	8705	3F : 57xx 0-6-0T (1929)		
4061	5P : STAR 4-6-0 (1907)	Ex Shrewsbury 11/50		8726	3F : 57xx 0-6-0T (1929)		
6964	5MT : MOD-HALL 4-6-0 (1944)			8734	3F : 57xx 0-6-0T (1929)		
7915	5MT : MOD-HALL 4-6-0 (1944)			6422	2P : 64xx 0-6-0T (1932)		
4960	5MT : HALL 4-6-0 (1928)		To Banbury 12/50	2061	2F : 2021 0-6-0T (1897)		
5942	5MT : HALL 4-6-0 (1928)		To Oxley 11/50	2095	2F : 2021 0-6-0T (1897)		
5944	5MT : HALL 4-6-0 (1928)		To Oxley 12/50	2109	2F : 2021 0-6-0T (1897)		
5995	5MT : HALL 4-6-0 (1928)		To Oxley 11/50	1410	1P : 14xx 0-4-2T (1932)		To Stourbridge 10/50
6901	5MT : HALL 4-6-0 (1928)		To Banbury 12/50	1410	1P : 14xx 0-4-2T (1932)	Ex Stourbridge 12/50	

The 09.25 Bordesley to Swindon via Stratford, Cheltenham and Gloucester was a useful train for juggling engines. One April morning in 1951 saw 28xx 2-8-0 2801 of Pontypool Road in the working so that a Tyseley engine, ex works, could bring back the return working. 2801 continued its way to South Wales on one of the many workings from Swindon via Sapperton.

over the bridge from Eastgate to Central to pick up the 16.00 Cheltenham – Paddington, the equivalent of the pre-war Cheltenham Flyer, which came in behind a little 45xx 2-6-2T and left behind 5017 'The Gloucestershire Regiment', one of Horton Road's beautifully kept Castles.

What a difference a good engine made and in contrast to the vulgar roar of the Jubilee, 5017 picked up its train with a dignified purr: plenty of speed and very little fuss. I hoped that we would find something to race with on the four track route between Tuffley Junction and Standish but the early afternoon was a quiet period for the Midland and we had the section to ourselves.

We paused at Stroud, Harry pointing out that his brother – another one – was the Mayor of the place, and then started out on the climb to Sapperton. The other occupants of the compartment probably though it strange that a railwayman with thousands of miles under his belt should take such a boyish interest in a train journey but the truth was railways was not just a job, it was something of a vocation and the only time I could cease to marvel at the

sight and sound of a Castle pounding its way to Sapperton would be when I was dead.

To me, coming from industrial Birmingham, the line was a world apart from the Great Western I was familiar with. Snow Hill and Bordesley had their charms but lacked the postcard atmosphere of Chalford and Frampton and there could have been no greater contrast between our local trains with their 51xx 2-6-2T's and the Chalford Cars: a pair of 14xx 0-4-2T auto cars which spent the day running between Gloucester Central and Chalford.

Although we had been climbing ever since leaving Gloucester, at Brimscombe, where a 2-

6-2 tank stood by as the goods banker, the bank starts to turn really nasty and I could hear from the deepening exhaust of 5017 that the driver was extending the cut-off as he hit the 1 in 111 to Chalford. Even this was not the steepest part of the climb and as we slogged up the last section – three and a half miles at 1 in 94 – and into Sapperton tunnel, I wondered how the fireman was coping and what it was like to work over the route on a Britannia which were not renown for keeping their feet on heavy gradients.

On the far side of the bank 5017 took every advantage of the falling gradient and I could see why the Cheltenham Flyer had got its reputation for high speed even though the records had been broken east of Swindon. All too soon we were running into Swindon where, Harry reminded me, it was time to start work.

Our job was to take 3839, one of the later 28xx 2-8-0's, back to Tyseley. The engine had been in Swindon for an overhaul and, newly painted, was a picture internally and externally. When we were ready to come off shed I asked Harry which way we were going to go back and, of course, he knew what I was thinking.

LOCO	CLASS	IN	OUT	LOCO	CLASS	IN	OUT
\multicolumn{8}{c}{WOLVERHAMPTON (STAFFORD RD) ALLOCATION : 1951}
6004	8P : KING 4-6-0 (1927)			6848	5MT : GRANGE 4-6-0 (1936)		
6005	8P : KING 4-6-0 (1927)			4103	4MT : 51xx 2-6-2T (1928)		
6006	8P : KING 4-6-0 (1927)			4105	4MT : 51xx 2-6-2T (1928)		
6008	8P : KING 4-6-0 (1927)			4108	4MT : 51xx 2-6-2T (1928)		
6011	8P : KING 4-6-0 (1927)			4115	4MT : 51xx 2-6-2T (1928)		
6020	8P : KING 4-6-0 (1927)			5143	4MT : 51xx 2-6-2T (1928)		w/d 12/51
4000	7P : CASTLE 4-6-0 (1923)			5151	4MT : 51xx 2-6-2T (1928)		To Tyseley 4/51
4083	7P : CASTLE 4-6-0 (1923)			5151	4MT : 51xx 2-6-2T (1928)	Ex Tyseley 5/51	
4092	7P : CASTLE 4-6-0 (1923)			6321	4MT : 43xx 2-6-0 (1911)		
5008	7P : CASTLE 4-6-0 (1923)			7315	4MT : 43xx 2-6-0 (1911)		
5010	7P : CASTLE 4-6-0 (1923)			3102	4MT : 31xx 2-6-2T (1938)		
5015	7P : CASTLE 4-6-0 (1923)			3104	4MT : 31xx 2-6-2T (1938)		
5022	7P : CASTLE 4-6-0 (1923)			3160	4MT : 3150 2-6-2T (1906)		
5027	7P : CASTLE 4-6-0 (1923)	Ex Chester 12/51		8411	4F : 94XX 0-6-0T (1949)		
5031	7P : CASTLE 4-6-0 (1923)			8423	4F : 94XX 0-6-0T (1949)		To Chester 1/51
5032	7P : CASTLE 4-6-0 (1923)	Ex Shrewsbury 12/51		8462	4F : 94XX 0-6-0T (1949)		
5045	7P : CASTLE 4-6-0 (1923)			9428	4F : 94XX 0-6-0T (1949)		
5053	7P : CASTLE 4-6-0 (1923)			9435	4F : 94XX 0-6-0T (1949)	New 1/51	
5061	7P : CASTLE 4-6-0 (1923)	Ex Shrewsbury 1/51	To Chester 7/51	3615	3F : 57xx 0-6-0T (1933)		
5070	7P : CASTLE 4-6-0 (1923)			3658	3F : 57xx 0-6-0T (1933)	Ex Tyseley 5/51	To Stourbridge 6/51
5088	7P : CASTLE 4-6-0 (1923)			3664	3F : 57xx 0-6-0T (1933)	Ex Tyseley 6/51	
7026	7P : CASTLE 4-6-0 (1923)			3756	3F : 57xx 0-6-0T (1933)		
1004	6MT : COUNTY 4-6-0 (1945)	Ex Penzance 11/51	To Shrewsbury 12/51	3778	3F : 57xx 0-6-0T (1933)		
1016	6MT : COUNTY 4-6-0 (1945)			4605	3F : 57xx 0-6-0T (1933)	Ex Tyseley 5/51	To Wellington 6/51
1017	6MT : COUNTY 4-6-0 (1945)		To Shrewsbury 12/51	9621	3F : 57xx 0-6-0T (1933)		
1029	6MT : COUNTY 4-6-0 (1945)			5701	3F : 57xx 0-6-0T (1929)		
4018	5P : STAR 4-6-0 (1907)		w/d 4/51	5739	3F : 57xx 0-6-0T (1929)		
4031	5P : STAR 4-6-0 (1907)		w/d 6/51	5780	3F : 57xx 0-6-0T (1929)		
4049	5P : STAR 4-6-0 (1907)			8705	3F : 57xx 0-6-0T (1929)		
4053	5P : STAR 4-6-0 (1907)			8726	3F : 57xx 0-6-0T (1929)		
4058	5P : STAR 4-6-0 (1907)		w/d 4/51	8734	3F : 57xx 0-6-0T (1929)		
4061	5P : STAR 4-6-0 (1907)			6418	2P : 64xx 0-6-0T (1932)	Ex Banbury 7/58	
6964	5MT : MOD-HALL 4-6-0 (1944)			6422	2P : 64xx 0-6-0T (1932)		
6966	5MT : MOD-HALL 4-6-0 (1944)	Ex Laira 10/51	To Banbury 12/51	2061	2F : 2021 0-6-0T (1897)		
7915	5MT : MOD-HALL 4-6-0 (1944)		To Oxley 5/51	2095	2F : 2021 0-6-0T (1897)		w/d 4/51
6940	5MT : HALL 4-6-0 (1928)	Ex Laira 10/51		2109	2F : 2021 0-6-0T (1897)		To Gloucester 1/51
6956	5MT : HALL 4-6-0 (1928)			1410	1P : 14xx 0-4-2T (1932)		To Croes Newydd 7/51
6812	5MT : GRANGE 4-6-0 (1936)		To Oxley 6/51	1426	1P : 14xx 0-4-2T (1932)	Ex Neasden 7/51	To Croes Newydd 9/51

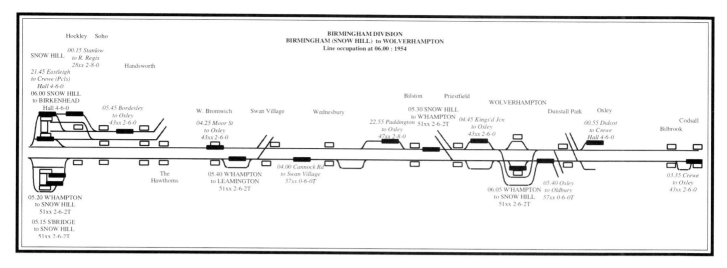

BIRMINGHAM DIVISION
BIRMINGHAM (SNOW HILL) to WOLVERHAMPTON
Line occupation at 06.00 : 1954

"I'll see what I can do for you," he announced and strode off to find a telephone whilst I mentally prepared for a record attempt on Sapperton.

"Sorry, mate," Harry said when he returned, "Control won't wear it. Back light via Banbury."

We turned the engine and filled the tender with Harry taking careful measurements since the engine was new and he wanted to make an accurate assessment of it on its first trip ex works. I worked on the fire until Harry said those three words that gladden the heart of every fireman worth his salt:

"You can drive…."

We had a good run to begin with. I trickled up the Highworth loop and got the road in the wake of a Paddington-bound flyer. There was no chance of catching it up but I gave it a try all the same and in no time we were taking the Oxford road at Didcot where matters changed considerably.

Why, I don't know, but the signalmen that afternoon seemed to think we were some sort of cripple and weaved us in and out of every loop for no obvious reason. Perhaps they though we might shine the rails a little although it became obvious that no-one knew what our destination was when we were turned off the main line at Oxford and put onto the shed.

"Just keep going" said Harry and I kept moving through the shed yard until we came to the outlet.

"Tyseley loco," Harry shouted to the bobby, "not Oxford – any route you like."

The board came off and I ran gently down to Wolvercote, hoping that he would pull off for the West Midland route which would add even more variety to the day but the signalman was not in a mood to oblige and set the road for the Banbury line which I took, plodding along from signal to signal until we got to Banbury where the signalman brought us to a stand and asked us if we were for the shed.

I don't know what had happened to the system on that particular day but regulating us from Swindon to Tyseley should not have been much of a task. At the time of starting the controller was supposed to make a train card out for us, showing the engine number, crew details and where we were going and make sure the key signalmen on the line knew well in advance who we were.

'3829 light to Tyseley loco' was all anyone needed to say yet for some reason no one seemed to know much about us. Usually light engines were grist to the mill for district controllers and advance information that an engine was running light from Swindon to Birmingham would normally have the controllers at Didcot, Oxford and Banbury looking to see if they could make up a train for us to work.

Banbury eventually got the message, pulled off and sent us northwards where once again we went in and out of goods loops without being overtaken until reaching Leamington South where the bobby held out a red flag. I shut off and came to an abrupt halt: red flags spell trouble.

"Could you give my mate a ride to Knowle? He's just missed the passenger."

I looked at Harry and he nodded.

"Having a signalman up here is about the only thing that will guarantee us a good run…"

The signalman climbed up, the board cleared and, as Harry had predicted, we not only got a clear run but were turned main line at Lapworth as far as Knowle. As soon as we had dropped our passenger, sure enough, we were turned in to the relief line even though there was nothing following us on the main.

In spite of the delays coming back it had been a good day for both of us; I with my tour of the country and a long stint at the regulator and Harry who had happily compiled a report on 3829 that would have satisfied a team of statisticians. As we signed off he mesmerised me with a broadside of figures concerning the water and oil that had been used and the temperature of bearings at various stages of the trip.

Harry's depth of interest in his job and his enquiring mind were too valuable for him to remain as a driver and when, in later years, main line diesels started to appear he was sent to Swindon on an instructors course and came back as an inspector, qualified to convert drivers from steam to diesel.

This training consisted of classroom lectures on diesel traction and electrical transmissions plus a thorough examination of a diesel locomotive on shed followed by driving experience on the main line which was usually done on a special train which operated between Tyseley and Honeybourne. This last element required a fireman to keep the footplate clean, couple and uncouple when we ran round the train, tend the train heating boiler and, naturally, to keep the students well supplied with tea.

It was very profitable work since we ran three trips to Honeybourne and back each day which brought me into the mileage band and, almost, the supertax bracket for a week; something that drew a few caustic remarks from one of the instructors who, being salaried, did not receive any daily perks.

When Harry was the only instructor on the trip and there was only one trainee he would remember my interest in the job and allow me to

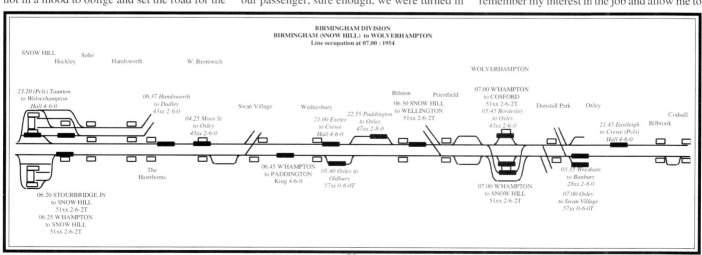

BIRMINGHAM DIVISION
BIRMINGHAM (SNOW HILL) to WOLVERHAMPTON
Line occupation at 07.00 : 1954

Normally worked by a 43xx 2-6-0, the 01.05 Swindon to Bordesley via Didcot, Oxford, Honeybourne and Shirley was used to clear any residual West Midlands empties and when things were tight could be worked by a smaller engine. Nonetheless the use of a Dukedog was unusual, especially at a time when many of the class were in store, and 9011 of Swindon which seen working the train through Tyseley in June 1956 made an interesting sight. Finding a suitable return working did not make life any easier for Tyseley shed.

handle the engine for a short distance. It was a novel experience to be at the front – literally – of a train without twenty feet or so of boiler to protect you but after a few trips it dawned on me that it was not very much different from driving a car or a bus and that all the skill and teamwork developed on the steam engine was missing. When Harry told me that the day was coming when there would be only one footplateman on each engine, I thought he was pulling my leg until I reflected that diesel shunters and multiple units had dispensed with firemen and it probably wouldn't be long before expresses went the same way.

Much as I would have liked it to, the link system saw to it that my partnership with Harry did not last forever and to my dismay I found myself paired with the one driver no-one seemed to get on with. I had had a short spell with him some time earlier and discovered that he was one of those people whose only object in life seemed to be stabbing as many people in the back as he could. He was a man who revered management but lacked the character to join it and,

like so many of the managerially inadequate, compensated for his weakness by making life a misery for those over whom he had a measure of dominion.

One of his favourite tricks was to watch his firemen like a hawk, twist any minor shortcoming into a deliberate act of sabotage and go running, report in hand, to the shedmaster over whom he seemed to exert some influence. What this influence was I have no idea but it was suggested that because he had worked during the 1955 ASLEF strike – and he was an ASLEF member – it had somehow given him some leverage. How he got away with it, I could not

understand since it was common knowledge that he had a severe drink problem.

You also had to watch everything you said since he was just as likely to twist an off hand expression into an act of heresy and see that it was reported. A casual remark, for example, that the controls on the BR standards were stiff to operate would be transmitted as a furious diatribe on contemporary management and even though it was unlikely to get one the sack, you never knew what the accumulative effect of such reports might be at the end of the day. It was a very uncomfortable situation and could only be kept in check by limiting conversation to the minimum necessary in the line of duty and, when travelling passenger, to use a different compartment. (One of the reasons he was a non-starter for management circles was his inability to detect dumb insolence….).

He had a number of discomfiting personal habits, the worst of which was flicking quantities of snuff in his firemans face. Sometimes he played a variation on the theme as witnessed by a colleague of mine who was firing to him on the Handsworth pilot. Filling the tank from the column he happened to notice the driver cooking the

WOLVERHAMPTON (STAFFORD RD) ALLOCATION : 1952							
LOCO	CLASS	IN	OUT	LOCO	CLASS	IN	OUT
6004	8P : KING 4-6-0 (1927)			4103	4MT : 51xx 2-6-2T (1928)		
6005	8P : KING 4-6-0 (1927)			4105	4MT : 51xx 2-6-2T (1928)		
6006	8P : KING 4-6-0 (1927)			4108	4MT : 51xx 2-6-2T (1928)		
6008	8P : KING 4-6-0 (1927)		To Laira 7/52	4115	4MT : 51xx 2-6-2T (1928)		
6011	8P : KING 4-6-0 (1927)			4147	4MT : 51xx 2-6-2T (1928)	Ex Tyseley 10/52	
6016	8P : KING 4-6-0 (1927)	Ex Laira 7/52		5106	4MT : 51xx 2-6-2T (1928)	Ex Tyseley 11/52	
6020	8P : KING 4-6-0 (1927)			5151	4MT : 51xx 2-6-2T (1928)		
4000	7P : CASTLE 4-6-0 (1923)			5187	4MT : 51xx 2-6-2T (1928)	Ex Tyseley 7/52	
4079	7P : CASTLE 4-6-0 (1923)	Ex Gloucester 10/52		5188	4MT : 51xx 2-6-2T (1928)	Ex Tyseley 10/52	
4083	7P : CASTLE 4-6-0 (1923)			5190	4MT : 51xx 2-6-2T (1928)	Ex Tyseley 10/52	
4092	7P : CASTLE 4-6-0 (1923)			6321	4MT : 43xx 2-6-0 (1911)		To Tyseley 10/52
5008	7P : CASTLE 4-6-0 (1923)			7315	4MT : 43xx 2-6-0 (1911)		To Banbury 10/52
5010	7P : CASTLE 4-6-0 (1923)			3102	4MT : 31xx 2-6-2T (1938)		
5015	7P : CASTLE 4-6-0 (1923)			3104	4MT : 31xx 2-6-2T (1938)		
5022	7P : CASTLE 4-6-0 (1923)			3160	4MT : 3150 2-6-2T (1906)		
5027	7P : CASTLE 4-6-0 (1923)			8411	4F : 94XX 0-6-0T (1949)		
5031	7P : CASTLE 4-6-0 (1923)			8462	4F : 94XX 0-6-0T (1949)		
5032	7P : CASTLE 4-6-0 (1923)			9428	4F : 94XX 0-6-0T (1949)		
5045	7P : CASTLE 4-6-0 (1923)			9435	4F : 94XX 0-6-0T (1949)		
5053	7P : CASTLE 4-6-0 (1923)			3615	3F : 57xx 0-6-0T (1933)		
5070	7P : CASTLE 4-6-0 (1923)			3664	3F : 57xx 0-6-0T (1933)		
5088	7P : CASTLE 4-6-0 (1923)			3756	3F : 57xx 0-6-0T (1933)		
7026	7P : CASTLE 4-6-0 (1923)			3778	3F : 57xx 0-6-0T (1933)		
1016	6MT : COUNTY 4-6-0 (1945)		To Laira 10/52	9621	3F : 57xx 0-6-0T (1933)		
1029	6MT : COUNTY 4-6-0 (1945)			9798	3F : 57xx 0-6-0T (1933)	Ex Tyseley 7/52	To Tyseley 11/52
4049	5P : STAR 4-6-0 (1907)			5701	3F : 57xx 0-6-0T (1929)		
4053	5P : STAR 4-6-0 (1907)			5738	3F : 57xx 0-6-0T (1929)	Ex Tyseley 7/52	
4061	5P : STAR 4-6-0 (1907)			5739	3F : 57xx 0-6-0T (1929)		
6964	5MT : MOD-HALL 4-6-0 (1944)			5780	3F : 57xx 0-6-0T (1929)		
4918	5MT : HALL 4-6-0 (1928)	Ex Banbury 7/52		7735	3F : 57xx 0-6-0T (1929)	Ex Tyseley 7/52	To Tyseley 11/52
4960	5MT : HALL 4-6-0 (1928)	Ex Banbury 7/52	To Reading 10/52	8705	3F : 57xx 0-6-0T (1929)		
4991	5MT : HALL 4-6-0 (1928)	Ex Oxley 7/52		8726	3F : 57xx 0-6-0T (1929)		
5944	5MT : HALL 4-6-0 (1928)	Ex Oxley 7/52		8734	3F : 57xx 0-6-0T (1929)		
6940	5MT : HALL 4-6-0 (1928)		To Oxley 1/52	6418	2P : 64xx 0-6-0T (1932)		
6956	5MT : HALL 4-6-0 (1928)		To Oxley 1/52	6422	2P : 64xx 0-6-0T (1932)		
6848	5MT : GRANGE 4-6-0 (1936)			2061	2F : 2021 0-6-0T (1897)		To Gloucester 3/52
				2061	2F : 2021 0-6-0T (1897)	Ex Gloucester 5/52	

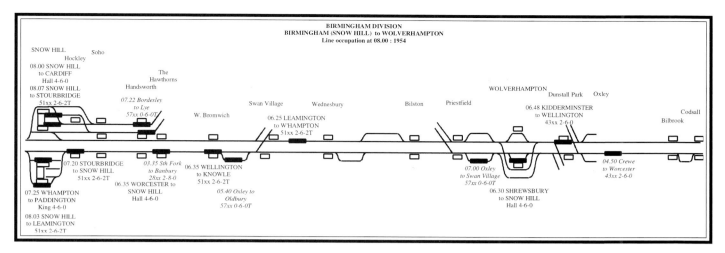

BIRMINGHAM DIVISION
BIRMINGHAM (SNOW HILL) to WOLVERHAMPTON
Line occupation at 08.00 : 1954

firemans eggs and bacon on the shovel and then, when they were done, coating them in snuff.

When the fireman returned to the footplate the driver casually announced that his breakfast had been prepared with not a word about the snuff. For once he almost got his deserts and it was all the fireman could do to prevent himself from throwing eggs, bacon and driver into the fourfoot.

When my turn came I had to stomach the unpalatable sight of him eating a lobster and cold chips with a bottle of beer whilst I struggled to retain sufficient appetite to address my own breakfast. God knows where the lobster came from but from the stink of the thing I suspected it had surrendered rather than been caught. Eventually I had to get off the engine and continue my meal upwind.

In spite of his snuff and eating habits I did my best to get on with him, making sure I didn't foot a single foot wrong, but some how this seemed to increase his determination to trip me up and in the end he succeeded in engineering an incident in which, of course, I came off second best.

We were booked to relieve the 16.30 Birkenhead – Paddington at Snow Hill and work it as far as Reading via Oxford, returning with the 00.05 goods (the Biscuits) to Bordesley. In passing, the up Birkenhead was a curious working which transferred part of its formation at Birmingham to the 20.00 ex Wolverhampton which ran to Paddington via Bicester, saving through passengers the rather tedious detour via Oxford.

There had been some trouble with engines that day and instead of the booked Castle, our train ran in behind a BR 4MT 4-6-0 which had been having difficulty ever since leaving Wolverhampton and was declared a failure by the Stafford Road men as soon as they arrived in Snow Hill.

Naturally there was a delay changing engines but we took the south pilot, 4-6-0 6861 'Cynant Grange' and I wasted no time in getting it ready for the road. Why he should hold me responsible for the affair, I have no idea but whilst I was doing my best to get the Grange up to the mark I could sense that my driver was going to take it out on me and, once we eventually pulled away, it didn't take long for my suspicions to be confirmed.

If he had treated a dog the way he treated 6861 he would have been thrown into prison – no bad thing really – but we had a light load with the engine in good nick and I found I could (just)

keep up with him. In fairness we reduced the delay quite appreciably although I had a pretty good idea that his running had less to do with time recovery than making life miserable for his fireman. Had the engine been a whit off form however, his treatment of it would have caused it to sit down on the main line, blocking everything.

We handed over the train to a set of Cockneys at Reading where we were given 5965 'Woollas Hall' which was not only due for a visit to Swindon but only just fit for traffic. Coupling up the guard gave us '67 = 67' and listened to my driver for a few minutes whilst he told him what a useless ornament I was. (This, after having kept up with him on 6861).

Sixty-seven was a heavy load for any engine so I ladled as much as I could into the front end whilst waiting for the rightaway and hoped for the best. My driver's mood was even blacker than it had been in the up direction and, revelling in the green fire and poor engine, ran on full regulator and the longest cutoff he could get away with until I was literally fighting for steam and water.

By Didcot pressure was down to 120lb with the water level all but disappearing from the bottom of the glass; neither factor having the slightest effect of the occupant of the right-hand seat who continued to drive as though he was on a diesel. By Appleford I could see the end of any progress in sight and went across to him.

"If you don't ease up, we shall come to a stand."

His response was curious.

"You wait. I'll fix you, you wait."

He followed this strange acknowledgement of our predicament with a torrent of abuse that made me wonder about his state of mind. Indeed it was sympathy for his mental condition as much as job security that prevented me from giving him the hiding of his life. I let him rant and rave whilst I did my best with the engine and eventually we pulled up at Hincksey North where he jumped from the engine and disappeared into the box. I took the opportunity to get the fire into some sort of order and waited for him to come back.

Five minutes later he returned and we moved on.

"I've settled you, you bastard. I've settled you." He muttered but I took no notice until we came to a stand opposite Oxford loco where the shift foreman came onto the footplate.

"Now then. What this all about?"

"He can't make steam, the water's been out of sight since we left Reading and at Hinksey he threatened to hit me."

I was speechless and before I could gather my wits the foreman had ordered me off the engine and to make my own way back to Tyseley. He didn't even have sufficient common justice to ask for my side of the story and, seething with indignation, I walked to the rear of the train and boarded the brakevan.

"I'll have to ride with you: I've been kicked off the job." I told the guard.

"Why."

"He" - I indicated the driver – "told the Oxford foreman I couldn't make steam."

"That's rubbish. You knocked two minutes off the timings between Reading and Didcot – and that's more than you're paid to do."

To add insult to injury, when we got to Banbury the driver had the train reduced to 45 wagons to curry favour with the Oxford man who was now firing for him. With justice of this sort I wondered what is was we had fought two world wars for.

At Tyseley the foreman told me to make a written report out before leaving duty and I went home assuming that when someone in authority was able to amass the facts, I would get an apology and perhaps some compensation for what had happened. In that respect I underestimated the influence the driver had with the shed master for not only did they fail to give me an opportunity to present a defence but I found myself limited to engine preparing and disposal.

The railway management were no help at all. I had several interviews with minor officials who seemed determined to support the driver's point of view whilst the union, which had been weakened by the 1955 strike, did nothing except offer moral support.

After seven weeks of engine preparing and nursing a grievance, I was marked up to fire a high speed special to Newport and back with an Inspector to assess me for competence. With 5927 'Guild Hall' and only five vehicles, it was a piece of cake and we managed to touch 84 mph between Honeybourne and Milcote. Jack Jones, the Inspector, knew me well and expressed his surprise at finding me to be the subject of his report. I gave him my side of the story and he told me to stop worrying.

The next day I was back on the main line with, I was glad to discover, a different – and decent – driver. I heard afterwards that in my absence they could only get a volunteer fireman to work with my protagonist.

75

Like most very large locomotives, firing the Kings required special skill and it was very easy to become a navvy with little to show for results. What was needed was a huge fire in the main part of the box with a much more shallow fire on the sloping front end. Once this was understood the engines became much easier to manage and understand. 6014 'King Henry VII' pounds a Paddington - Wolverhampton express towards the summit of Hatton bank in 1960. This particular engine could be easily identified by the wedge-shaped cab front, a remnant of a semi-steamlining experiment of the 1930's.

To most drivers and firemen one train was very much like another and so long as the quantity of work at their shed did not diminish, they did not complain much. In this respect I was an odd-man out since I resented the fact that Tyseley was excluded from the key Wolverhampton – Paddington expresses which were shared by Old Oak and Stafford Road. All we had in the way of London workings was the Sunday 10.00 Snow Hill (08.10 ex Shrewsbury) to Paddington and the 16.10 return which we worked as far as Birmingham. On summer Saturdays we also had the 10.10 Snow Hill to Margate as far as North Acton, returning north with the 14.10 from Paddington.

Occasionally we would ask for a greater share in the working of the weekday trains but would be told it was not a practicable proposition since very few Tyseley drivers signed the road into Paddington. (Because, of course, they had very few workings into London…).

Amongst the other objections to sharing some of the work at Tyseley was the fact that very few London trains started from Birmingham and that it made operational sense to work the Wolverhampton – Paddington workings by crews from the starting points.

The prospect of starting a series of London trains from Birmingham was impracticable since the stock would have to run from Tyseley carriage sidings to Snow Hill via Handsworth and would raise innumerable line occupation difficulties. (When we responded that we could take the stock straight from Tyseley to Snow Hill and run round in the station, we were told that the movement would block two roads and could not be countenanced. No one mentioned using Moor Street as a starting point….).

Thus, as the years passed, I worked to almost every point on the system – Chester, Aberystwyth, Crewe, Reading, Gloucester, Swindon and Weston-super-Mare – except London which to me seemed rather absurd.

We pressed our point at length and were eventually rewarded by being given the 09.00 Paddington to Wolverhampton – between

WOLVERHAMPTON (STAFFORD RD) ALLOCATION : 1953					
LOCO CLASS	IN	OUT	LOCO CLASS	IN	OUT
6004 8P : KING 4-6-0 (1927)			4105 4MT : 51xx 2-6-2T (1928)		To Oxford 5/53
6005 8P : KING 4-6-0 (1927)			4108 4MT : 51xx 2-6-2T (1928)		
6006 8P : KING 4-6-0 (1927)			4115 4MT : 51xx 2-6-2T (1928)		To Chester 7/53
6011 8P : KING 4-6-0 (1927)			4147 4MT : 51xx 2-6-2T (1928)		To Oxford 6/53
6016 8P : KING 4-6-0 (1927)			5106 4MT : 51xx 2-6-2T (1928)		
6020 8P : KING 4-6-0 (1927)			5112 4MT : 51xx 2-6-2T (1928)	Ex Tyseley 8/53	
4000 7P : CASTLE 4-6-0 (1923)			5151 4MT : 51xx 2-6-2T (1928)		
4079 7P : CASTLE 4-6-0 (1923)			5187 4MT : 51xx 2-6-2T (1928)		
4083 7P : CASTLE 4-6-0 (1923)			5188 4MT : 51xx 2-6-2T (1928)		
4090 7P : CASTLE 4-6-0 (1923)	Ex Old Oak C. 9/53		5190 4MT : 51xx 2-6-2T (1928)		To Weymouth 6/53
4092 7P : CASTLE 4-6-0 (1923)			7309 4MT : 43xx 2-6-0 (1911)	Ex Tyseley 6/53	
5008 7P : CASTLE 4-6-0 (1923)			3102 4MT : 31xx 2-6-2T (1938)		
5010 7P : CASTLE 4-6-0 (1923)			3104 4MT : 31xx 2-6-2T (1938)		w/d 6/53
5015 7P : CASTLE 4-6-0 (1923)			3160 4MT : 3150 2-6-2T (1906)		
5022 7P : CASTLE 4-6-0 (1923)			8411 4F : 94XX 0-6-0T (1949)		
5027 7P : CASTLE 4-6-0 (1923)			8462 4F : 94XX 0-6-0T (1949)		To Tyseley 9/53
5031 7P : CASTLE 4-6-0 (1923)			8462 4F : 94XX 0-6-0T (1949)	Ex Tyseley 10/53	
5032 7P : CASTLE 4-6-0 (1923)			9428 4F : 94XX 0-6-0T (1949)		
5045 7P : CASTLE 4-6-0 (1923)			9435 4F : 94XX 0-6-0T (1949)		To Wellington 10/53
5053 7P : CASTLE 4-6-0 (1923)			9435 4F : 94XX 0-6-0T (1949)	Ex Wellington 11/53	
5070 7P : CASTLE 4-6-0 (1923)			3615 3F : 57xx 0-6-0T (1933)		
5088 7P : CASTLE 4-6-0 (1923)			3664 3F : 57xx 0-6-0T (1933)		
7026 7P : CASTLE 4-6-0 (1923)			3756 3F : 57xx 0-6-0T (1933)		
1004 6MT : COUNTY 4-6-0 (1945)	Ex Shrewsbury 2/53		3778 3F : 57xx 0-6-0T (1933)		
1018 6MT : COUNTY 4-6-0 (1945)	Ex Shrewsbury 1/53		3792 3F : 57xx 0-6-0T (1933)	Ex Oxley 5/53	
1019 6MT : COUNTY 4-6-0 (1945)	Ex Shrewsbury 1/53		3793 3F : 57xx 0-6-0T (1933)	Ex Oxley 5/53	
1029 6MT : COUNTY 4-6-0 (1945)		To Neyland 12/53	8798 3F : 57xx 0-6-0T (1933)	Ex Oxley 5/53	
4049 5P : STAR 4-6-0 (1907)		w/d 6/53	9621 3F : 57xx 0-6-0T (1933)		
4053 5P : STAR 4-6-0 (1907)			5701 3F : 57xx 0-6-0T (1929)		To Bristol (BR) 10/53
4061 5P : STAR 4-6-0 (1907)			5738 3F : 57xx 0-6-0T (1929)		To Tyseley 3/53
6964 5MT : MOD-HALL 4-6-0 (1944)		To Oxley 10/53	5739 3F : 57xx 0-6-0T (1929)		
6964 5MT : MOD-HALL 4-6-0 (1944)	Ex Oxley 11/53		5780 3F : 57xx 0-6-0T (1929)		
4918 5MT : HALL 4-6-0 (1928)		To Oxley 6/53	8705 3F : 57xx 0-6-0T (1929)		
4991 5MT : HALL 4-6-0 (1928)		To Pontypool Rd 11/53	8726 3F : 57xx 0-6-0T (1929)		
4997 5MT : HALL 4-6-0 (1928)	Ex Neyland 12/53		8734 3F : 57xx 0-6-0T (1929)		
5944 5MT : HALL 4-6-0 (1928)		To Oxley 1/53	6418 2P : 64xx 0-6-0T (1932)		
6956 5MT : HALL 4-6-0 (1928)		To Shrewsbury 1/53	6422 2P : 64xx 0-6-0T (1932)		
4103 4MT : 51xx 2-6-2T (1928)		To Tyseley 10/53	2061 2F : 2021 0-6-0T (1897)		To Wellington 2/53
4103 4MT : 51xx 2-6-2T (1928)	Ex Tyseley 11/53				

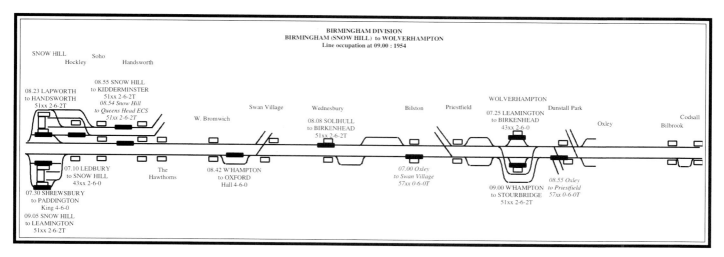

BIRMINGHAM DIVISION
BIRMINGHAM (SNOW HILL) to WOLVERHAMPTON
Line occupation at 09.00 : 1954

SNOW HILL
Hockley   Soho   Handsworth

08.23 LAPWORTH
to HANDSWORTH
51xx 2-6-2T

08.55 SNOW HILL
to KIDDERMINSTER
51xx 2-6-2T
08.54 Snow Hill
to Queens Head ECS
51xx 2-6-2T

W. Bromwich   Swan Village   Wednesbury   Bilston   Priestfield

WOLVERHAMPTON
Dunstall Park
07.25 LEAMINGTON
to BIRKENHEAD
43xx 2-6-0
Oxley   Codsall
Bilbrook

08.08 SOLIHULL
to BIRKENHEAD
51xx 2-6-2T

07.10 LEDBURY
to SNOW HILL
43xx 2-6-0
The
Hawthorns
08.42 W'HAMPTON
to OXFORD
Hall 4-6-0

07.00 Oxley
to Swan Village
57xx 0-6-0T

08.55 Oxley
to Priestfield
57xx 0-6-0T

07.30 SHREWSBURY
to PADDINGTON
King 4-6-0

09.00 W'HAMPTON
to STOURBRIDGE
51xx 2-6-2T

09.05 SNOW HILL
to LEAMINGTON
51xx 2-6-2T

Snow Hill and Wolverhampton! It was not much of a concession – 13 miles - but at least the train was worked by a King.

I worked the service with Mickey Tolley, one of Tyseley's noted hard-hitters, and relieved a set of Old Oak men who ran in with 6012 'King Edward VI'. They had very little to say to us, they were probably still grieving at having to hand over some of their work to Tyseley, but had left a fire that could have taken us all stations to Birkenhead without being touched. The footplate was in the usual mess that Old Oak men managed to make and prompted my driver to comment in tones loud enough to be heard by the departing crew:

"If you want me I'll be standing on this pile of coal in the corner."

The difference between a King and any other Great Western engine was apparent from the moment that Mick opened the regulator after getting the right away when we stormed away through the tunnel to Hockley as though running light. By the time we came back into daylight we were going so well that Mick had to pull the lever up a bit. I noticed that the vigorous start cost us something in steam pressure but was surprised to see how quickly the needle went back to the red mark when Mick eased off.

There was no point in adding anything to the fire but to get the best out of it on the climb to Handsworth I took the pricker down and levelled the coal over the firebars. Beyond West Bromwich the line falls all the way to Wolverhampton and there was little for me to do other than sit and listen to the music from the front end. Watching Wednesbury, Bilston and Priestfield flash by with the injector singing and the fire looking after itself, I was almost persuaded that a fireman's work fell in inverse proportion to the size of his engine.

All too soon we were running into the Low Level where we got rid of our passengers, took the stock to Cannock Road sidings and 6012

onto Stafford Road where the local staff would get it ready for the 16.35 return to Paddington. They only had to say the word and I would have waited and gone back with it – all the way to London.

Shortly afterwards Tyseley was given a third London job which took a night parcels train to Paddington via Oxford and Reading. Unfortunately the booked engine was a Hall and not a King but it did mean that more Tyseley men

had to learn the road to London which not only augured well for the future but stood us in good stead when we fought for an allocation of work in the addition services created in 1959 when the workings between New Street and Euston were thinned out to allow preparatory engineering work to start on the LNW electrification.

Our express service had always been pretty good but from 1959 it was amazing with a train from Paddington at ten minutes past every hour from 09.10 to 20.10 with an 08.30 and 09.00 in addition. New Warship diesels were sent to Laira to release enough King 4-6-0's to handle the six new trains whilst we at Tyseley were booked to work the 18.10, 19.10 and 20.10 departures from Paddington. These new diagrams were not conceded without some opposition from Old Oak and for a time we worked the 20.10 ex Paddington by double-heading the up Inter City (16.35 Wolverhampton – London) and returning with our own engine. (Later the

duty was amended so that we worked the Inter-City with its Old Oak King from Snow Hill).

Every coin has two sides and having won the case for Tyseley to have a greater proportion of the London express work, I suddenly realised that the matter was no longer academic and that I was going to have to fire a King from London to Birmingham.

This was a sobering reality since the Kings were huge engines by any reckoning and I had never worked one for any great distance. In addition the London trains were both fast and heavy and any failure by Tyseley men to time them would be seized upon by Old Oak and Stafford Road as a sign that all we were fit for were 28xx 2-8-0's and unfitted coal trains. It was therefore with some trepidation that I saw myself booked on duty at 13.55 to travel passenger to London and bring back the 18.10 Birkenhead express as far as Snow Hill.

Bert Watkins, my driver, and I reached Paddington punctually at 17.20 and, after brewing up, walked to the far end of our stock in No. 4 platform only to discover that we had no engine. The peak service was in full swing and I idled the time away by watching the comings and going of local trains. I also observed the departure of the 17.55 'Red Dragon' to Carmarthen with its Britannia Pacific which, like most Canton engines, shone as though new.

Bang on time the driver pulled back on the regulator and the Pacific, still quite a novelty on the Great Western, started off with the usual bout of slipping, making quite a contrast with 'our' engines which took the heaviest loads out of Paddington without the slightest fuss. The ups and downs engine which had brought the stock in, followed the train to the end of the platform, paused briefly until the route was reset and then disappeared towards Old Oak for another set of coaches.

I learned in time to be wary of the ups and downs engines (as the Paddington pilots were

LOCO	CLASS	IN	OUT	LOCO	CLASS	IN	OUT
6001	8P : KING 4-6-0 (1927)	Ex Old Oak C. 9/54		4997	5MT : HALL 4-6-0 (1928)		
6004	8P : KING 4-6-0 (1927)		To Laira 3/54	6949	5MT : HALL 4-6-0 (1928)	Ex Swindon 2/54	
6005	8P : KING 4-6-0 (1927)			6956	5MT : HALL 4-6-0 (1928)	Ex Shrewsbury 3/54	
6006	8P : KING 4-6-0 (1927)			5634	5MT : 56xx 0-6-2T (1924)	Ex Shrewsbury 2/54	
6011	8P : KING 4-6-0 (1927)			4103	4MT : 51xx 2-6-2T (1928)		
6014	8P : KING 4-6-0 (1927)	Ex Laira 3/54		4108	4MT : 51xx 2-6-2T (1928)		
6016	8P : KING 4-6-0 (1927)		To Old Oak C. 12/54	4140	4MT : 51xx 2-6-2T (1928)	Ex Gloucester 9/54	
6020	8P : KING 4-6-0 (1927)			5106	4MT : 51xx 2-6-2T (1928)		
7220	8F : 72xx 2-8-2T (1934)	Ex Neath 3/54	To Pontypool Rd 9/54	5112	4MT : 51xx 2-6-2T (1928)		
4000	7P : CASTLE 4-6-0 (1923)		To Chester 10/54	5151	4MT : 51xx 2-6-2T (1928)		
4000	7P : CASTLE 4-6-0 (1923)	Ex Chester 12/53		5187	4MT : 51xx 2-6-2T (1928)		
4079	7P : CASTLE 4-6-0 (1923)			5188	4MT : 51xx 2-6-2T (1928)		
4083	7P : CASTLE 4-6-0 (1923)			9312	4MT : 43xx 2-6-0 (1932)	Ex Oxley 8/54	
4090	7P : CASTLE 4-6-0 (1923)			5391	4MT : 43xx 2-6-0 (1911)	Ex Oxley 6/54	
4092	7P : CASTLE 4-6-0 (1923)			7309	4MT : 43xx 2-6-0 (1911)		To Shrewsbury 3/54
4094	7P : CASTLE 4-6-0 (1923)	Ex Bristol (BR) 7/54		3102	4MT : 31xx 2-6-2T (1938)		
5008	7P : CASTLE 4-6-0 (1923)			3104	4MT : 31xx 2-6-2T (1938)		
5010	7P : CASTLE 4-6-0 (1923)			8411	4F : 94XX 0-6-0T (1949)		
5015	7P : CASTLE 4-6-0 (1923)			8462	4F : 94XX 0-6-0T (1949)		
5022	7P : CASTLE 4-6-0 (1923)			9428	4F : 94XX 0-6-0T (1949)		
5027	7P : CASTLE 4-6-0 (1923)		To Bristol (BR) 6/54	9435	4F : 94XX 0-6-0T (1949)		
5031	7P : CASTLE 4-6-0 (1923)		To Chester 11/54	9496	4F : 94XX 0-6-0T (1949)	New 10/54	
5032	7P : CASTLE 4-6-0 (1923)			3615	3F : 57xx 0-6-0T (1933)		
5045	7P : CASTLE 4-6-0 (1923)			3664	3F : 57xx 0-6-0T (1933)		
5047	7P : CASTLE 4-6-0 (1923)	Ex Newton Abbot 11/54		3756	3F : 57xx 0-6-0T (1933)		
5053	7P : CASTLE 4-6-0 (1923)		To Laira 12/54	3778	3F : 57xx 0-6-0T (1933)		
5070	7P : CASTLE 4-6-0 (1923)			3792	3F : 57xx 0-6-0T (1933)		
5088	7P : CASTLE 4-6-0 (1923)			3793	3F : 57xx 0-6-0T (1933)		
7026	7P : CASTLE 4-6-0 (1923)			8798	3F : 57xx 0-6-0T (1933)		
1004	6MT : COUNTY 4-6-0 (1945)		To Swindon 3/54	9621	3F : 57xx 0-6-0T (1933)		
1018	6MT : COUNTY 4-6-0 (1945)		To Laira 9/54	5739	3F : 57xx 0-6-0T (1929)		To Chester 11/54
1019	6MT : COUNTY 4-6-0 (1945)		To Swindon 3/54	5780	3F : 57xx 0-6-0T (1929)		
4053	5P : STAR 4-6-0 (1907)		w/d 7/54	8705	3F : 57xx 0-6-0T (1929)		
4061	5P : STAR 4-6-0 (1907)			8726	3F : 57xx 0-6-0T (1929)		
6964	5MT : MOD-HALL 4-6-0 (1944)			8734	3F : 57xx 0-6-0T (1929)		
6975	5MT : MOD-HALL 4-6-0 (1944)	Ex Oxley 8/54		6404	2P : 64xx 0-6-0T (1932)	Ex Croes Newydd 11/54	
4912	5MT : HALL 4-6-0 (1928)	Ex Swindon 3/54		6418	2P : 64xx 0-6-0T (1932)		
4926	5MT : HALL 4-6-0 (1928)	Ex Oxley 8/54		6422	2P : 64xx 0-6-0T (1932)		

WOLVERHAMPTON (STAFFORD RD) ALLOCATION : 1954

King 6005 'King George II' heaves the fourteen coaches of the 08.30 Birkenhead - Paddington up the 1 in 57 gradient at Swan Village between Wolverhampton and Birmingham in 1948. The stock of the train (eight vehicles from Birkenhead and six from Wolverhampton) put in a high daily mileage, the train returning as the 18.10 Paddington - Birkenhead the same day.

known) which could creep up on you unawares. I once coupled an engine to a train in Paddington and stepped out onto the adjacent track as soon as the train on it had cleared. The next thing I was aware of was an 0-6-0 Pannier bearing down upon me and the only thing which saved the Jacks' race from extinction was its driver who stopped before any damage could be done. I gave him a thumbs-up sign and he responded with some good-natured but unrepeatable advice reminding me that trains at Paddington have engines at both ends.

With less than ten minutes to go before departure time, our engine, 6011 'King James 1', backed into the station, its late arrival being aggravated by the departure box routing it into the wrong platform. A quick shunt corrected the matter but left me with no time to both couple up and check the state of the engine before departure and the best I could do was to glance into the firebox and confirm that the cheery Old Oak men who had brought the engine in had bequeathed me a pretty massive fire.

At 18.14. four minutes late, we got the Orange RA to start and Bert opened up to get us on the move, peering into the firebox as we passed Royal Oak.

"Be all right for a while with that." I said confidently but he frowned.

"Give it a good root up. The first few miles are uphill."

I couldn't see why such an effort was called for but obediently I brought the irons down and, thinking we'd got enough coal to last us until Banbury, lifted the fire as he wanted.

That done that I performed a quick check – 240lb of pressure and the glass full – and decided that the Kings were an absolute doddle to work. I casually threw half a dozen shovelfulls of coal to the front of the box – which brought home to me exactly how long a King's firebox was – and, to keep the water level constant, put on the right hand feed.

As I finished, we turned the corner at Old Oak West, Bert opened up to second valve and I suddenly realised that 6011 had set a trap into which I had walked open-eyed. 6011 suddenly needed a great deal of steam and the action of the injector was preventing the boiler from generating an adequate supply. The needle started to drop alarmingly and putting the blower on only made matters worse by using up more steam. There was only one thing to do and I picked up the shovel and started to work like a navvy, sending eight down at a time but managing to stabilise the pressure gauge at 200lb by the time we passed Greenford.

I put the pricker in to test the fire and the end came out red hot – a fairly reliable acid test of a good fire – yet there was nothing I could do to get the needle anywhere near the red mark. With a train like the 18.10 there was no question of Bert easing off to give a few minutes respite and for the rest of the climb through Gerrards Cross and up to Saunderton I was banging in eight at time and keeping the firebox door closed as much as possible to prevent cold air from getting in. Bert, good chap that he was, left me to fire uninterrupted whilst he looked after the scoop on Denham troughs, saying nothing about the pressure gauge which was indicating 160lbs. The Kings, I reflected sorrowfully, were not quite the doddle I had thought.

Then, all of a sudden, things changed. We passed Beaconsfield and started to run downhill towards Ashendon and as soon as Bert eased the regulator, the needle, helped a little by the blower, went back to the red line so quickly you could almost see it move. I took advantage of the easing to fill the boiler up and as we cruised through the High Wycombe restriction at 45 mph, 6011 blew off, reminding me that you had to take care with the Stafford Road Kings not to overfill the boiler.

Because of local water conditions they had

LOCO	CLASS	IN	OUT	LOCO	CLASS	IN	OUT
6001	8P : KING 4-6-0 (1927)			4108	4MT : 51xx 2-6-2T (1928)		
6005	8P : KING 4-6-0 (1927)			4140	4MT : 51xx 2-6-2T (1928)		
6006	8P : KING 4-6-0 (1927)			5106	4MT : 51xx 2-6-2T (1928)		
6011	8P : KING 4-6-0 (1927)			5112	4MT : 51xx 2-6-2T (1928)		w/d 10/55
6014	8P : KING 4-6-0 (1927)			5151	4MT : 51xx 2-6-2T (1928)		
6020	8P : KING 4-6-0 (1927)			5187	4MT : 51xx 2-6-2T (1928)		
4000	7P : CASTLE 4-6-0 (1923)			5188	4MT : 51xx 2-6-2T (1928)		To Carmarthen 7/55
4079	7P : CASTLE 4-6-0 (1923)			5188	4MT : 51xx 2-6-2T (1928)	Ex Carmarthen 9/55	
4083	7P : CASTLE 4-6-0 (1923)			9312	4MT : 43xx 2-6-0 (1932)		
4090	7P : CASTLE 4-6-0 (1923)		To Old Oak C. 12/55	5391	4MT : 43xx 2-6-0 (1911)		To Oxley 10/55
4092	7P : CASTLE 4-6-0 (1923)			3102	4MT : 31xx 2-6-2T (1938)		
4094	7P : CASTLE 4-6-0 (1923)			3104	4MT : 31xx 2-6-2T (1938)		
5008	7P : CASTLE 4-6-0 (1923)			8411	4F : 94XX 0-6-0T (1949)		
5010	7P : CASTLE 4-6-0 (1923)			8462	4F : 94XX 0-6-0T (1949)		
5015	7P : CASTLE 4-6-0 (1923)			9428	4F : 94XX 0-6-0T (1949)		
5022	7P : CASTLE 4-6-0 (1923)			9435	4F : 94XX 0-6-0T (1949)		
5031	7P : CASTLE 4-6-0 (1923)	Ex Chester 2/55		9496	4F : 94XX 0-6-0T (1949)		
5032	7P : CASTLE 4-6-0 (1923)			3615	3F : 57xx 0-6-0T (1933)		
5045	7P : CASTLE 4-6-0 (1923)			3664	3F : 57xx 0-6-0T (1933)		
5047	7P : CASTLE 4-6-0 (1923)			3756	3F : 57xx 0-6-0T (1933)		
5070	7P : CASTLE 4-6-0 (1923)			3778	3F : 57xx 0-6-0T (1933)		
5088	7P : CASTLE 4-6-0 (1923)			3792	3F : 57xx 0-6-0T (1933)		
7026	7P : CASTLE 4-6-0 (1923)			3793	3F : 57xx 0-6-0T (1933)		
4061	5P : STAR 4-6-0 (1907)			8798	3F : 57xx 0-6-0T (1933)		
6964	5MT : MOD-HALL 4-6-0 (1944)			9621	3F : 57xx 0-6-0T (1933)		
6975	5MT : MOD-HALL 4-6-0 (1944)		To Oxley 9/55	5780	3F : 57xx 0-6-0T (1929)		
4912	5MT : HALL 4-6-0 (1928)			8705	3F : 57xx 0-6-0T (1929)		
4926	5MT : HALL 4-6-0 (1928)			8726	3F : 57xx 0-6-0T (1929)		
4997	5MT : HALL 4-6-0 (1928)		To Oxley 9/55	8734	3F : 57xx 0-6-0T (1929)		
6949	5MT : HALL 4-6-0 (1928)			6404	2P : 64xx 0-6-0T (1932)		To Croes Newydd 1/55
6956	5MT : HALL 4-6-0 (1928)			6418	2P : 64xx 0-6-0T (1932)		
5634	5MT : 56xx 0-6-2T (1924)		To Shrewsbury 6/55	6422	2P : 64xx 0-6-0T (1932)		
4103	4MT : 51xx 2-6-2T (1928)						

WOLVERHAMPTON (STAFFORD RD) ALLOCATION : 1955

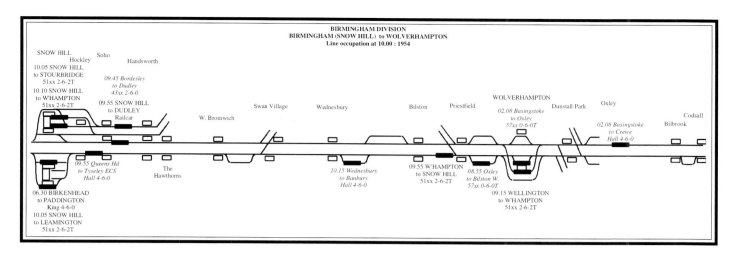

been fitted with 'Afloc' water treatment which, when the boiler was full and blowing off, could result in water being ejected through the safety valves.

It was a good sign for the coming few miles which included the fairly stiff climb to Saunderton, five miles at an average of 1 in 204, but I was mindful of what had happened earlier in the trip and wondered whether the needle would fall again as soon as Bert opened up.

In the event 6011 romped up the bank with the pressure holding good at 230lb. Bert shouted across to me.

"You all right?"

"Yes. I've got the hang of it now."

He yanked the regulator into second valve, pulled the lever up and my face fell almost as quickly as the needle dropped from the red mark. I rooted the fire with the pricker, put the blower on and did some pretty heavy firing but with no result except to see pressure drop to 150lb with very little water in the glass. I shovelled furiously, wondering where all the steam and water had gone, until Bert shut off for the Bicester stop where I was able to get some water in the boiler.

"A dozen in there might not be a bad idea."

Bert looked into the firebox and I did as he suggested only to find 6011 blowing off by the time I put the shovel down. This, I reflected, was an extraordinary state of affairs. Every time the engine did any work the needle fell through the bottom of the gauge yet as soon as you shut off, everything went back to normal in the wink of an eye.

We got the right away, Bert opened up on second valve and the needle fell to 160lb. It made no difference how much I hurled into the box, it would not climb back towards the red mark and I started to get concerned since the road we had covered so far was far less severe

than that north of Leamington. Bert didn't help by reminding me that we still had the four minute late start to make up.

By the time we came to a stand in Banbury all I had succeeded in doing was making a large hole in the tender and had to spent most of the station stop moving coal from the centre to the front. The Banbury passenger pilot, a Hall 4-6-0, was standing across the platform and the fireman who had heard that Tyseley had gained a foothold in the London jobs, walked across to see how we were coping. I was too busy in the tender to spare time for conversation but 6011 had got itself back to the red mark and gave the young Banbury man the impression that we were on top of the job. How looks can deceive.

The six uphill miles to Claydon promised to be difficult and 6011 did not disappoint me. Bert got the train moving, I shovelled like a man possessed yet the needle dropped alarmingly. I gave the fire another root with the pricker and this time discovered clinker forming on the bars. There was not enough to effect steaming but it was something I could have done without and I was beginning to tire. Where the needle stood as we roared past Cropredy, I had no idea; I was too busy to look up and in any case I was already depressed enough.

We stormed over Claydon and Bert took advantage of the drop to Fosse Road to recover some time and put paid to any ideas I had about him cruising downhill to let me get some water in the boiler and the needle back on the mark. Shovelling for all I was worth, 6011 flew down the gradient yet all the signs on the footplate indicated an engine that was in trouble. At Fosse Road Bert sensed my concern and, having picked up a minute or two, eased the engine onto first valve so that I could get the fire and boiler into some sort of order for the slog out of Leamington and up Hatton Bank. On the showing so far

I doubted whether we would make it but never-theless belted twelve up the far end of the box and put both injectors on.

As soon as 6011 came to a stand in Leamington the needle came up to the red mark as though it was on a piece of elastic but I knew that it was no guide as to how we were going to survive on Hatton. I started firing furiously as soon as we started away but by Warwick the needle had fallen to 200lb and it was only by virtue of hard and continuous firing that I managed to pass Hatton with as much as 160lb on the clock. I had turned the injectors off at Leamington to avoid foaming through the safety valves and by the time we were half way up the bank, the level was beginning to fall yet there was nothing I could do about it.

Firing like mad I managed to keep the needle around the 160 mark for the climb and was then struck by the realisation that, unlike the goods trains I was used to working, there would be no easing off at the summit. Bert still had some time to recover and he would, quite properly, run helter-skelter until the last minute. How on earth I was supposed to get some water in the boiler without killing the engine was a problem I couldn't resolve. Bert shouted that he thought we'd be all right but I didn't share his confidence.

Rowington troughs came into view, I moved over to the handle and dropped the scoop. The gauge rose to full but when I tried to wind the scoop back up, my strength had evaporated and instead of the normal deft movement, I had to fight for every turn with the result that several thousand gallons of water shot through the vents and onto the footplate. I did my best to clean things up but with the pressure gauge falling from 150lb at Lapworth to 140 at Knowle, things looked rather bleak and even the imperturbable Bert started to look worried.

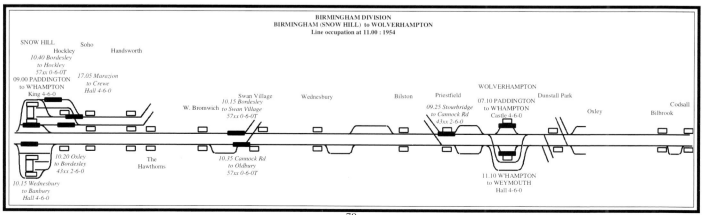

Banbury had six pilot engines at work each day plus an LM engine from Bletchley which tripped goods traffic to and from Merton Street in the late afternoon. The most familiar of these pilots was the passenger pilot which spent 24 hours a day shunting at Banbury General, worked by a mixed traffic engine as an insurance against failures on the main line. Hall 4-6-0 6906 'Chicheley Hall' shunts stock in the up platform of the rebuilt station whilst acting as pilot in 1958.

He suggested that I give the fire another root through with the pricker which, in my state, was easier said than done and by the time I'd finished it was as much as I could do to send a few pounds of coal past the back end of the fire. The well practised swing had gone and after a few efforts with the shovel I had to retire to my seat, fully spent and wholly dejected.

"I'll shut off at Olton and we'll run in from there." Bert announced with a tinge of disappointment in his voice.

"Blast it," I thought. "I'm not going to let him down." And I remembered how hard we had argued for a share in this work. We had to show the world that whatever Old Oak and Stafford Road could do, Tyseley could match them and whether it was the prospect of failure or the fact that I'd had a two minute rest, I suddenly came back to life.

I brought the pricker down, gave the fire a thorough root-up and started to fire like a man inspired. For the first time since leaving London I actually managed to get the needle to rise whilst the engine was steaming and we succeeded in passing Solihull with as much as 180lb on the clock. Bert cheered up a little and kept the engine going until we reached Solihull which we

passed at 70 mph whilst I swept up the footplate, put the injectors on, half-closed the doors and put my feet up just like the regular chaps who did this job day in day out.

We rolled into platform 5 at Snow Hill and came to a stand, Bert looking at his watch and declaring a right-time arrival. Our relief clambered up and took stock.

"What's it like?"

"All right, mate."

"I say, Jacksy, you're looking a bit black, aren't you?"

"You have to work for a living on these London jobs…."

Travelling back in the local to Tyseley I told Bert that I thought I had made a right hack of the

job. He told me not to worry. "They're big engines and take some getting used to. You'll be able to have another go tomorrow night."

We had 6011 on the two days following and each time I managed to improve on my performance. On the Thursday we had 6008 'King James II', almost fresh out of Swindon, and had such a magnificent trip that at the end of it I didn't feel as though I'd been to work.

The key to understanding the Kings was to appreciate that although they had the same basic design of firebox as any other Great Western engine, they needed a different kind of fire. You had to have a large – very large – body of fire on the level section of firebars with a much thinner bed of fire on the sloping bars at the front end. Once that sort of fire had been built up then you needed to feed it by keeping the back end well filled together with the front and middle portions of the fire. There was no question of firing little and often since the boiler needed to have the injector on continuously: the evaporation rate was tremendous when a heavy train was being worked.

You also had to be very careful not to fall into the trap of getting too much coal

WOLVERHAMPTON (STAFFORD RD) ALLOCATION : 1956							
LOCO	CLASS	IN	OUT	LOCO	CLASS	IN	OUT
6001	8P : KING 4-6-0 (1927)			4103	4MT : 51xx 2-6-2T (1928)		
6005	8P : KING 4-6-0 (1927)			4108	4MT : 51xx 2-6-2T (1928)		
6006	8P : KING 4-6-0 (1927)			4140	4MT : 51xx 2-6-2T (1928)		
6011	8P : KING 4-6-0 (1927)			5106	4MT : 51xx 2-6-2T (1928)		
6014	8P : KING 4-6-0 (1927)			5151	4MT : 51xx 2-6-2T (1928)		
6020	8P : KING 4-6-0 (1927)			5187	4MT : 51xx 2-6-2T (1928)		
4000	7P : CASTLE 4-6-0 (1923)		To Carmarthen 9/56	5188	4MT : 51xx 2-6-2T (1928)		
4079	7P : CASTLE 4-6-0 (1923)			3102	4MT : 31xx 2-6-2T (1938)		
4083	7P : CASTLE 4-6-0 (1923)			3104	4MT : 31xx 2-6-2T (1938)		
4092	7P : CASTLE 4-6-0 (1923)			9312	4MT : 43xx 2-6-0 (1932)		To Oxley 1/56
4094	7P : CASTLE 4-6-0 (1923)			8411	4F : 94XX 0-6-0T (1949)		
5008	7P : CASTLE 4-6-0 (1923)		To Old Oak C. 11/56	8462	4F : 94XX 0-6-0T (1949)		
5010	7P : CASTLE 4-6-0 (1923)			9428	4F : 94XX 0-6-0T (1949)		
5015	7P : CASTLE 4-6-0 (1923)			9435	4F : 94XX 0-6-0T (1949)		
5022	7P : CASTLE 4-6-0 (1923)		To Old Oak C. 2/56	9496	4F : 94XX 0-6-0T (1949)		
5022	7P : CASTLE 4-6-0 (1923)	Ex Old Oak C. 3/56		3615	3F : 57xx 0-6-0T (1933)		
5031	7P : CASTLE 4-6-0 (1923)			3664	3F : 57xx 0-6-0T (1933)		
5032	7P : CASTLE 4-6-0 (1923)			3756	3F : 57xx 0-6-0T (1933)		
5045	7P : CASTLE 4-6-0 (1923)			3769	3F : 57xx 0-6-0T (1933)	Ex Tyseley 2/56	
5047	7P : CASTLE 4-6-0 (1923)			3778	3F : 57xx 0-6-0T (1933)		
5070	7P : CASTLE 4-6-0 (1923)			3792	3F : 57xx 0-6-0T (1933)		
5075	7P : CASTLE 4-6-0 (1923)	Ex Chester 5/56		3793	3F : 57xx 0-6-0T (1933)		
5088	7P : CASTLE 4-6-0 (1923)			8798	3F : 57xx 0-6-0T (1933)		
7026	7P : CASTLE 4-6-0 (1923)			9621	3F : 57xx 0-6-0T (1933)		
4061	5P : STAR 4-6-0 (1907)			5780	3F : 57xx 0-6-0T (1929)		
6964	5MT : MOD-HALL 4-6-0 (1944)			8705	3F : 57xx 0-6-0T (1929)		To Aberbeeg 3/56
4912	5MT : HALL 4-6-0 (1928)			8726	3F : 57xx 0-6-0T (1929)		
4926	5MT : HALL 4-6-0 (1928)			8734	3F : 57xx 0-6-0T (1929)		
4986	5MT : HALL 4-6-0 (1928)	Ex Oxley 6/56		6418	2P : 64xx 0-6-0T (1932)		
6949	5MT : HALL 4-6-0 (1928)			6422	2P : 64xx 0-6-0T (1932)		
6956	5MT : HALL 4-6-0 (1928)						

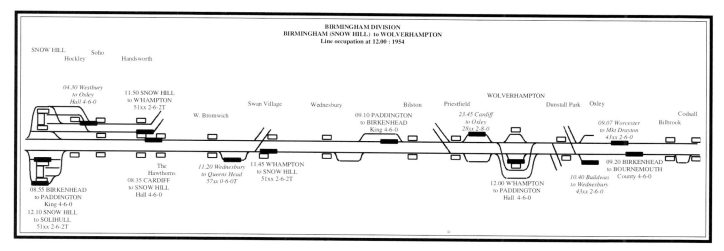

BIRMINGHAM DIVISION
BIRMINGHAM (SNOW HILL) to WOLVERHAMPTON
Line occupation at 12.00 : 1954

under the brick arch, something easily done with Welsh coal, which affected steaming quite seriously.

Once I had mastered the Kings, I came to look forward to the London jobs which of course were quite unlike any other work we had at the shed. It was nice to cruise through the Birmingham suburbs and arrive at Snow Hill in charge of one of the line's most important trains and, equally, it was satisfying to mingle at Paddington with footplatemen who worked such trains as a matter of daily routine. The London men didn't seem to harbour any resentment at our presence and when we pulled out of Paddington the Cockneys on the Paddington pilots would shout encouragement as though, being Tyseley men, we needed it. Of the engines used, I preferred the Old Oak Kings as opposed to the Stafford Road allocation since the latter had the Afloc water treatment which somehow made the engines a little less free running than the unaltered Old Oak ones.

In addition to their engines, I had more than a healthy respect for Old Oak crews who, in my opinion, were amongst the finest enginemen in the land and I could sit at Paddington and listen to their tales, and the way they told them, for hours. I recall one driver who had been telling me of a trip with the 10.30 Cornish Riviera – first stop Plymouth – the previous week. They were barely half an hour into the trip when it became clear that all was not well with the engine. The fireman had the long pricker out by Reading to root the fire up, the needle was falling, the blower was on and the water level was well down in the glass. The fireman looked across for advice.

"Tell you what," proposed the driver, "I'll ease off when we get to Newton Abbot and give you a chance to get some water in the boiler….."

It wasn't all a bed of roses and there were times when the Kings could be rough as I discovered when I travelled up to London one afternoon to bring the 19.10 express down. Running into Paddington I spotted 6003 'King George IV', gleaming bright from one end to the other, acting as the Ranelegh Bridge stand-by pilot which was not normally the sort of job a King was used for.

Standing at the platform end half an hour later, I was surprised to see the same 6003 back down from the Bridge since our train was diagrammed for a Castle. The incoming crew explained that 6003 was waiting the call to go into Swindon and was being kept on relatively short trips for the time being. He also added, with reference to the engine's gleaming external state, that a book shouldn't be judged by its cover.

My mate and I soon found out that we had both the best and worst of worlds in 6003. Its steaming was beyond reproach, or would have been had the engine stayed steady enough for me to put anything in the firebox. It banged and crashed over every piece of pointwork as though it had square wheels whilst we clung on for dear life. Several times we got it up to around 80 mph when it started to roll like a schooner; a sensation eased by my driver who, by lengthened the cut off, managed to persuaded the engine to nose its way to some sort of stability. The noise from the chimney was symphonic and Leamington, our first stop, was the first point from Paddington where the engine eased its antics enough to allow my mate to sit down. It was all very exciting and being an old hand with Kings, I was able to handle it. Had it been my first run though I suspect we would have been lucky to get as far as High Wycombe.

It has to be said that King duties were rather bitty at Tyseley. We either travelled passenger

to London and worked an express down to Birmingham or did an odd and sods job by working the down Inter-City from Snow Hill to Wolverhampton, which was very small beer compared to coming down from Paddington. The trouble with the Inter-City turn was that when we got to Wolverhampton, the rest of the shift was spent in lowly engine preparation before working back to Snow Hill with the 16.33 Paddington. I would much rather have worked a King to London and back.

One evening I travelled up to London with Cliff 'Biscuit' Hughes to work the 18.10 Birkenhead during the period when it was booked non-stop to Leamington. It happened to be his last steam working since he was moving into one of the local links the following week. Whilst he was looking forward to spending his last few years in the warmth and comfort of a diesel cab, he was nevertheless sad to be saying farewell to steam.

"What," he suddenly asked, "about a hundred?"

"Do you mean pounds of steam?" I replied assuming he was referring to a recent trip where we had been in trouble for steam. He wasn't sure whether I was pulling his leg or not.

"No – miles per hour! And that'll need more than a hundred pounds of steam…."

At Paddington I counted the coaches of our train and noted that the normal rake of eleven had been increased by two, the additional vehicles being reserved for the Electrical Study Society.

"I'll show them…." muttered Biscuit as we climbed on board 6008 'King James II' and busied ourselves with last minute preparations, much of which consisted of Biscuit telling electricians of his plans and turning down requests for footplate trips.

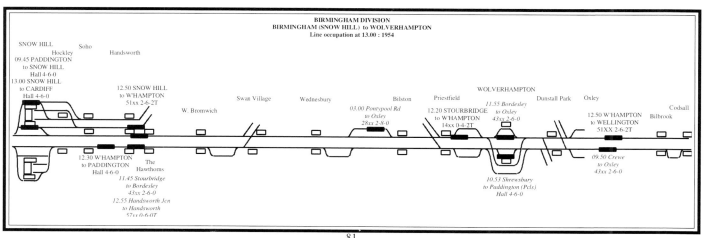

BIRMINGHAM DIVISION
BIRMINGHAM (SNOW HILL) to WOLVERHAMPTON
Line occupation at 13.00 : 1954

Most of the two hour expresses between Snow Hill and Paddington were shared between Old Oak Common and Stafford Road sheds with Tyseley crews seeing very little of the work until additional services were introduced in 1959 because of the engineering works taking place between New Street and Euston. Up to that time one of the few opportunities for Tyseley men to get their hands on a King came with the 09.00 Paddington - Wolverhampton 'Inter-City' which they relieved at Snow Hill and worked to Wolverhampton. The diagrammed engine was an Old Oak King 4-6-0 and 6025 is seen in May 1960 preparing to leave Stafford Road for the stock of the return working, the 16.35 Wolverhampton - Paddington.

6008 was in good shape but Biscuit took things fairly carefully at first, our extra coaches costing us a couple of minutes to High Wycombe. He tested the engine (and fireman) up Saunderton and after Risborough pulled the regulator onto second valve and, with the cut-off well back, started a pretty impressive firework display. By this time I had enough experience on Kings to keep up with him – and more – and although it was heavy work, the needle stuck to the red mark giving Biscuit had all the steam he needed.

Princes Risborough to Haddenham is mostly downhill and Biscuit took full advantage of the fact, tearing through Haddenham as though something unpleasant was after him.

"There you are," he shouted above the din, pointing furiously at the speedometer. "One hundred!"

The last thing I had was time to put the shovel down and check for myself and to this day I have no idea whether his claim was justified or not. What I do know is that we were travelling at an astonishingly high speed – really trotting them along – and if Biscuit said we had done a hundred, it was good enough for me.

The conclusion of the falling gradi-

ent did not mark the end of our speeding by any means and as soon as we hit the seven mile climb from Blackthorn through Bicester and up to Ardley, Biscuit merely dropped the lever down a little to rattled half the windows in Bicester as we rocketed through the station. What a contrast, I thought, to my first trip on a London. Here we were scorching through Oxfordshire at speeds that probably hadn't been touched for years, with the safety valves simmering and everything in tip top order. Ardley tunnel flashed by like a bridge and for a few minutes I was able to set the shovel aside whilst I concentrated on the scoop and Aynho troughs.

"Shan't be stopping at Banbury for a pilot," called Biscuit, "only slow us up..." and with the whistle shrieking we roared through

the station, spurred on by a set of Tyseley men waiting on the platform for a down working. Our momentum virtually flattened the bank to Claydon and gave Biscuit the opportunity to make the most of the bank down to Fosse Road where he sighed as he shut the regulator for the stop at Leamington.

Eighty-seven miles at the rate we had been going had made quite a hole in the tender – the Kings had a healthy appetite at ordinary speeds – and I had to use the station time to pull some coal forward since Biscuit seemed bent on emptying the tender and we still had Hatton bank to contend with. Struggling back to the footplate I found Biscuit nodding to a passenger who had come off the train to have a look at the engine.

"Goodnight," shouted Biscuit as the passenger returned to his coach, adding as an aside to me: "I reckon he'd come down to see what the second engine was."

We pulled out of the station and Biscuit opened up in the style to which he had become accustomed in the last couple of hours whilst I started to make inroads into the coal so hurriedly moved forward during the station stop. Biscuit was certainly fortunate to have been given 6008 for his swan song; it was steaming perfectly and as soon as the water level dropped

WOLVERHAMPTON (STAFFORD RD) ALLOCATION : 1957							
LOCO	CLASS	IN	OUT	LOCO	CLASS	IN	OUT
6001	8P : KING 4-6-0 (1927)			6956	5MT : HALL 4-6-0 (1928)		
6005	8P : KING 4-6-0 (1927)			4103	4MT : 51xx 2-6-2T (1928)		To Leamington 11/57
6006	8P : KING 4-6-0 (1927)			4108	4MT : 51xx 2-6-2T (1928)		
6011	8P : KING 4-6-0 (1927)			4140	4MT : 51xx 2-6-2T (1928)		
6014	8P : KING 4-6-0 (1927)			5106	4MT : 51xx 2-6-2T (1928)		To Laira 10/57
6020	8P : KING 4-6-0 (1927)			5151	4MT : 51xx 2-6-2T (1928)		
4079	7P : CASTLE 4-6-0 (1923)		To Bristol (BR) 6/57	5187	4MT : 51xx 2-6-2T (1928)		
4083	7P : CASTLE 4-6-0 (1923)			5188	4MT : 51xx 2-6-2T (1928)		To Bristol (BR) 8/57
4092	7P : CASTLE 4-6-0 (1923)			3102	4MT : 31xx 2-6-2T (1938)		
4094	7P : CASTLE 4-6-0 (1923)		To Landore 6/57	3104	4MT : 31xx 2-6-2T (1938)		w/d 6/57
5010	7P : CASTLE 4-6-0 (1923)			8411	4F : 94XX 0-6-0T (1949)		
5015	7P : CASTLE 4-6-0 (1923)			8462	4F : 94XX 0-6-0T (1949)		
5022	7P : CASTLE 4-6-0 (1923)			9428	4F : 94XX 0-6-0T (1949)		
5031	7P : CASTLE 4-6-0 (1923)			9435	4F : 94XX 0-6-0T (1949)		
5032	7P : CASTLE 4-6-0 (1923)			9496	4F : 94XX 0-6-0T (1949)		
5045	7P : CASTLE 4-6-0 (1923)			3615	3F : 57xx 0-6-0T (1933)		
5047	7P : CASTLE 4-6-0 (1923)			3664	3F : 57xx 0-6-0T (1933)		
5070	7P : CASTLE 4-6-0 (1923)			3756	3F : 57xx 0-6-0T (1933)		
5075	7P : CASTLE 4-6-0 (1923)			3769	3F : 57xx 0-6-0T (1933)		
5088	7P : CASTLE 4-6-0 (1923)			3778	3F : 57xx 0-6-0T (1933)		
7026	7P : CASTLE 4-6-0 (1923)			3792	3F : 57xx 0-6-0T (1933)		
4061	5P : STAR 4-6-0 (1907)		w/d 3/57	3793	3F : 57xx 0-6-0T (1933)		
6964	5MT : MOD-HALL 4-6-0 (1944)		To Shrewsbury 6/57	9621	3F : 57xx 0-6-0T (1933)		
4901	5MT : HALL 4-6-0 (1928)	Ex Carmarthen 9/57		5780	3F : 57xx 0-6-0T (1929)		
4912	5MT : HALL 4-6-0 (1928)			8726	3F : 57xx 0-6-0T (1929)		
4926	5MT : HALL 4-6-0 (1928)			8734	3F : 57xx 0-6-0T (1929)		
4986	5MT : HALL 4-6-0 (1928)			6418	2P : 64xx 0-6-0T (1932)		
4990	5MT : HALL 4-6-0 (1928)	Ex Penzance 4/57		6422	2P : 64xx 0-6-0T (1932)		
5926	5MT : HALL 4-6-0 (1928)	Ex St Blazey 4/5					
6949	5MT : HALL 4-6-0 (1928)						

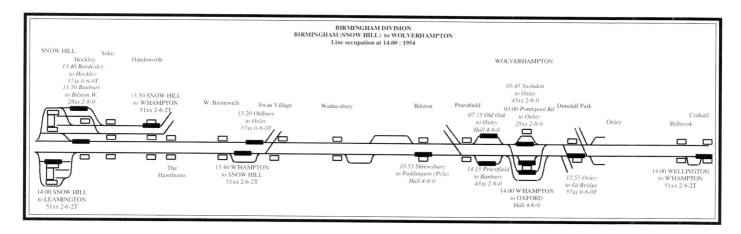

into sight in the glass I was able to put the injector on and leave it on.

We thundered through Warwick, the roar of 6008 echoing back but not so loudly that it drowned the cheers from the crew on the Banker crew as we swept past them in their bay siding. Biscuit still had the bit between his teeth and although our speed dropped off towards the top of the three mile climb, we were still travelling at a fine rate and I hoped the electrical crowd were taking good note. I put the shovel down to top the tender up at Rowington and then got back into my firing rhythm since the eight miles to Solihull were just as bad as the climb from Warwick to Hatton.

I think Biscuit and 6008 could have carried on all night – certainly the engine was in first class condition, steaming like a dream with the water only half way down the glass – but at Olton he had to ease back and he ended his steam career with a cheerful ride through the Birmingham suburbs; 6008 on first valve and 45% cut-off to give us plenty of momentum for the bank into Snow Hill.

"Right time, mate," he announced as we came to a stand. "Not bad for my last trip."

I wiped my brow and the perspiration from my eyes.

"Not bad for whom…"

The electrical men treated Biscuit like a returning hero and almost carried him off the station when he told then he had 'got a hundred from the old girl'.

"Coming for some tonsil varnish?" asked Biscuit after his fan club had dispersed. "I'll pay."

Who could refuse an offer like that?

Biscuit was lucky to have had 6008 for his trip. A few weeks later I was on the same train when 5029 'Nunney Castle' backed down and the Old Oak man, with a broad grin, said he

hoped we were wearing trusses. Ye Gods, I thought, if the engine's given him a rough ride the few yards from Ranelagh Bridge, what is it going to be like for us on the main line?

We soon found out and it was, not to put too fine a point on it, as rough as an old boot. If they'd have used monkeys to fire engines like 5029, the Western would have been prosecuted by the RSPCA and it was one trip when I was more than usually thankful to see Snow Hill.

The drivers I fired with on the London turns were, if anything, more varied than the engines and sometimes considerably more temperamental. I came down on the 18.10 one night with Vic Herbert, who could really run the wheels off them. We had 6011 'King James I' and a tender full of eggs – a compound of slack and a moulding agent - which was good coal provided you had the firebed good and hot at the start of the run. The drawback was that, until you had shovelled a couple of tons of them into the firebox, they would roll all over the place creating a thick dusty fog that made your eyes sting quite severely. I had to keep spraying the tender down and every now and again Vic would glare at me and pull his collar up around the back of his neck which was the signal for me to splash some more water in the tender.

The turbulence from Harbury tunnel, which Vic tore through far faster than most, brought a fresh attack of dust and another glare so I reached down for the watering pipe only to find that it had become disconnected and had disappeared over the side of the engine, probably because it had not been secured very well at Old Oak. Vic cursed me soundly for failing to ensure that it had not been properly checked before starting and with a particularly aggressive adjustment to his collar, conversation ceased for the night.

Although things like uncontrollable coal dust made some drivers a little prickly, when the

occasion demanded an extra effort, most responded to the call as happened when Teddy (Baden) Powell and I were on the up Inter-City one afternoon with 6022 'King Edward III'; the engine having about as much life in it as its namesake.

When we took over at Snow Hill the incoming Stafford Road man told us the engine was no good and by the time we got to Small Heath we found he hadn't been exaggerating. At Leamington we wired ahead for the pilot to take over from Banbury.

Reaching Banbury after a devil of a struggle, we hooked off, ran to the loco and were given Modified Hall 7905 'Fowey Hall' which had been quickly nobbed up but was in good nick. We did our best to pull round some of the lost time and by the time we were approaching High Wycombe we though we might get into Paddington at a time not too far removed from that quoted in the timetable. We were just starting to congratulate ourselves when we were brought to a stand and told to draw past the station on the through road and back into the platform because of a points failure at the North box.

After the messing around involved, all hope of a reasonable arrival at Paddington disappeared and we ran in exactly an hour late, just in time to step down from 7905 and board our King on the 20.10 down. We could, I suppose, have sat on our rights and demanded a break but Teddy and I thought it would just make a bad situation worse and the best we could do was to get the 20.10 off to a punctual start.

Somehow drivers manage to perpetuate the myth that to work on the footplate eyesight of a superhuman nature was called for. It was certainly true that keen sight was called for but in certain circumstances the rules were diluted to allow drivers to wear spectacles of an accepted type and one of these was Joe Smith

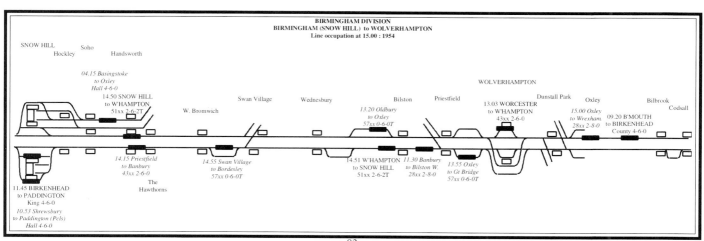

No higher calling.... The author, footplate left, finds himself at Leamington firing 6018 'King Henry VI'

who, when he was working the up Inter-City, would always peer through his lenses at the speedometer as we went through Bicester and claim one hundred miles per hour. At that speed I was too tied up with feeding the firebox to have a look for myself but Joe's glasses were always so covered in filth, I wondered how he could find his engine let alone read the fine calibration on the clock. Still, he certainly did his best to straighten a few curves out. He was also a student of the Malaprop: "Look over there," he would shout excitedly as we tore through Gerrards Cross on the way to London, "There's the Metrolopis…"

Because of the weight, speed and importance of the evening expresses from Paddington, we rarely received anything but a King (or a Castle on the 19.10) although on the 19.10 one night we arrived to find County 1002 'County of Berks', a former Penzance engine which had recently moved to Didcot, backing onto the train. Fred Salmon, my driver, moaned like anything as he climbed aboard only to have a complete change of mind before we'd covered more than half a dozen miles. Didcot, which usually had nothing larger than

a Hall 4-6-0, were evidently proud of this 'large' engine and took pains to look after it well.

Occasionally I would find myself paired with Doctor Iodine, so named because of his activities with the St John's Ambulance Brigade, who, I hoped, treated his patients more compassionately than he did his engines and firemen. As an individual I liked him very much but I needed every breath in my body when firing to him.

We were working the 18.10 Birkenhead one night and had Tommy Figget riding with us to refresh the road as he was having his maiden trip out of Paddington the following day. We set off with the Doc shouting out the name of

every station and signalbox together with a brief description of the signalling, Tommy taking conscientious notes of everything that was said. I, of course, was too busy with the shovel to take part in Tommy's education although I had to bite my lip at one point.

"On these Londons," shouted the Doc as he flogged the engine to pieces, "you can do it all on first valve…."

I doubt if old Iodine even knew what the first valve was, much less what it was for since, except when slowing down and stopping, he drove the Londons on second valve plus a pretty savage cut-off all the way from Paddington until shutting off at Olton.

In addition to good eyesight, a further requirement for drivers – not that it was mentioned anywhere officially – was a strong set of nerves since reflecting, for example, on the effect that a broken connecting rod would have at high speed was not something conducive to peace of mind. Once you started dwelling on the things that could go wrong with a steam engine and the injuries that could result, you

| WOLVERHAMPTON (STAFFORD RD) ALLOCATION : 1958 |||||||
LOCO	CLASS	IN	OUT	LOCO	CLASS	IN	OUT
6001	8P : KING 4-6-0 (1927)			5926	5MT : HALL 4-6-0 (1928)		
6005	8P : KING 4-6-0 (1927)			6926	5MT : HALL 4-6-0 (1928)	Ex Oxley 6/58	To Shrewsbury 11/58
6006	8P : KING 4-6-0 (1927)			6949	5MT : HALL 4-6-0 (1928)		To Banbury 9/58
6011	8P : KING 4-6-0 (1927)			6956	5MT : HALL 4-6-0 (1928)		To Shrewsbury 11/58
6014	8P : KING 4-6-0 (1927)			4108	4MT : 51xx 2-6-2T (1928)		To Newton Abbot 6/58
6016	8P : KING 4-6-0 (1927)	Ex Old Oak C. 12/58		4140	4MT : 51xx 2-6-2T (1928)		To Stourbridge 1/58
6020	8P : KING 4-6-0 (1927)		To Laira 1/59	4161	4MT : 51xx 2-6-2T (1928)	Ex Tyseley 10/58	
6027	8P : KING 4-6-0 (1927)	Ex Laira 12/58		5151	4MT : 51xx 2-6-2T (1928)		
4083	7P : CASTLE 4-6-0 (1923)		To Newton Abbot 4/58	5187	4MT : 51xx 2-6-2T (1928)		
4092	7P : CASTLE 4-6-0 (1923)		To Reading 4/58	3102	4MT : 31xx 2-6-2T (1938)		w/d 10/58
5010	7P : CASTLE 4-6-0 (1923)		To Old Oak C. 4/58	8411	4F : 94XX 0-6-0T (1949)		
5015	7P : CASTLE 4-6-0 (1923)		To Bristol (BR) 4/58	8425	4F : 94XX 0-6-0T (1949)	Ex Laira 10/58	
5019	7P : CASTLE 4-6-0 (1923)	Ex Bristol (BR) 4/58		8426	4F : 94XX 0-6-0T (1949)	Ex Laira 10/58	
5022	7P : CASTLE 4-6-0 (1923)			8462	4F : 94XX 0-6-0T (1949)		To Oxley 9/58
5026	7P : CASTLE 4-6-0 (1923)	Ex Oxford 4/58		8462	4F : 94XX 0-6-0T (1949)	Ex Oxley 10/58	
5031	7P : CASTLE 4-6-0 (1923)			9428	4F : 94XX 0-6-0T (1949)		
5032	7P : CASTLE 4-6-0 (1923)		To Newton Abbot 4/58	9435	4F : 94XX 0-6-0T (1949)		
5045	7P : CASTLE 4-6-0 (1923)			9496	4F : 94XX 0-6-0T (1949)		
5046	7P : CASTLE 4-6-0 (1923)	Ex Canton 4/58		3615	3F : 57xx 0-6-0T (1933)		
5047	7P : CASTLE 4-6-0 (1923)			3664	3F : 57xx 0-6-0T (1933)		
5059	7P : CASTLE 4-6-0 (1923)	Ex Newton Abbot 4/58		3756	3F : 57xx 0-6-0T (1933)		
5063	7P : CASTLE 4-6-0 (1923)	Ex Bristol (BR) 4/58		3769	3F : 57xx 0-6-0T (1933)		To Wrexham (GC) 10/58
5070	7P : CASTLE 4-6-0 (1923)			3778	3F : 57xx 0-6-0T (1933)		
5072	7P : CASTLE 4-6-0 (1923)	Ex Laira 4/58		3792	3F : 57xx 0-6-0T (1933)		
5075	7P : CASTLE 4-6-0 (1923)		To Laira 4/58	3793	3F : 57xx 0-6-0T (1933)		w/d 9/58
5088	7P : CASTLE 4-6-0 (1923)			8796	3F : 57xx 0-6-0T (1933)	Ex Worcester 9/58	
5089	7P : CASTLE 4-6-0 (1923)	Ex Laira 4/58		8798	3F : 57xx 0-6-0T (1933)		
7026	7P : CASTLE 4-6-0 (1923)			9621	3F : 57xx 0-6-0T (1933)		To Croes Newydd 12/58
6975	5MT : MOD-HALL 4-6-0 (1944)	Ex Oxley 12/58		5780	3F : 57xx 0-6-0T (1929)		To Taunton 6/58
4901	5MT : HALL 4-6-0 (1928)			8726	3F : 57xx 0-6-0T (1929)		
4912	5MT : HALL 4-6-0 (1928)		To Shrewsbury 11/58	8734	3F : 57xx 0-6-0T (1929)		To Wrexham (GC) 10/58
4926	5MT : HALL 4-6-0 (1928)		To Worcester 2/58	6418	2P : 64xx 0-6-0T (1932)		
4986	5MT : HALL 4-6-0 (1928)			6422	2P : 64xx 0-6-0T (1932)		
4990	5MT : HALL 4-6-0 (1928)						

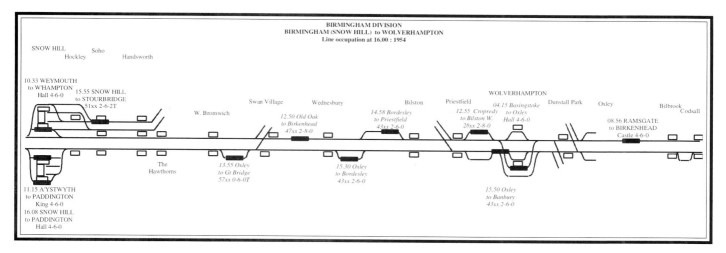

BIRMINGHAM DIVISION
BIRMINGHAM (SNOW HILL) to WOLVERHAMPTON
Line occupation at 16.00 : 1954

were on a slippery slope and most of the drivers I worked with were, in that sense, sensibly unimaginative.

There is an exception to every rule and I fired to him on one of the down expresses one night: an experience that promised to see both of us in the psychiatric ward. He took duty with all the signs of a man who had slept badly the night before and spent an inordinate amount of time reading the notices and temporary instructions before walking down to catch the train to London.

On the way home we came over the top at Beaconsfield where he shut the regulator for the run down to Wycombe. Having been climbing continuously for twenty miles with the engine now nose-down it was only natural that the water level in the glass should be well down, although I had the situation well in hand. My driver caught sight of the glass and danced all a twitter across the cab.

"Put the other feed on, put the other feed on!"

"It IS on."

"Oh my God, we'll drop a plug…"

I shepherded him back to his seat and as soon as the engine hit a stretch of level track, showed him a full glass. It kept him quiet for a while but for most of the trip there was a crisis at every other signal. He was one of those people who spend their lives worrying themselves sick about things that never actually happen.

He was at least consistent in his moods which was more than can be said for a certain Old Oak driver who worked the up Inter-City during the period when we used to double-head it from Snow Hill to Paddington.

With a King as the train engine and a Castle as pilot there was enough power at the head of the service to make it one of the easiest runs imaginable and, in very rough terms, we provided something like four thousand five hundred horsepower which, with nine coaches, was about the same power to weight ratio as a modern HST.

'Bicycle' Davis and I backed on one afternoon with Castle 4-6-0 5082 'Swordfish' and coupled up to the King at the head of the train. With, as one wit put it, 15P power there was no shortage of power yet the Old Oak man behind drove as though he was trying to get in front. The noise from the King was incredible and at Wycombe the Old Oak man jumped off his engine and walked forward to us.

"Now then driver," he said to Bicycle as though he was addressing a cleaner on his first day, "the bit from here to London is tightly timed, so don't hold us back. Get your skates on."

"Righto," answered Bicycle and gave the performance of a lifetime, streaking like a maniac through Denham and Ruislip and cruising into Paddington well before time. The Cockneys limped onto the platform and lurched past us, white as sheets. The fireman looked at me as he went by.

"You're bloody mad, the pair of you."

It wasn't often you got one across Old Oak men who regarded themselves as the cats whiskers and probably were. In their company you had to be a good listener —there was no danger of getting a word in – and their tales could have filled a book. I envied them in many respects and particularly because of their range of route-knowledge. We at Tyseley, for example, simple went to and from London whilst they covered every route from Paddington except, for some reason, Worcester.

In time I amassed a considerable mileage on Kings but until 1961 it was all as a fireman and whilst that was exciting enough, it was not the same as being the man in charge. This changed in the summer of 1961 when as a passed fireman and eligible to cover driver's vacancies, I was instructed to travel up to Lapworth and pilot the down Inter-City over the down relief as far as Snow Hill. This unusual requirement arose because of planned engineering works on the down fast – a rather unusual development at that time – and the fact some Old Oak men signed to Wolverhampton via the main line only.

I travelled up in the 10.20 multiple unit from Snow Hill and reported to the signalman who seemed to take the stopping of the Inter-City as some sort of a personal slight. It was disgraceful, he complained, that an express driver should have to have his hand held down the relief and added that such an important train should not be given out of course stops for any reason. By the time he was halfway through a diatribe concerning the civil engineer's seeming inability to complete his work within the compass of a weekend, I had had enough and told him I should be on the platform until the train arrived. His parting shot was that they should have sent an older driver to work on such an important train.

I sat on a seat happily watching trains for a while until I heard an engine whistling up from the south, the signalman opening his window and pointed meaningfully in its direction. A few minutes later 6024 'King Edward I' came to a stand in the platform and gave me an attack of butterflies.

"Up you come, me old mate," said the Old Oak man moving over to his firemans seat. "Ten on."

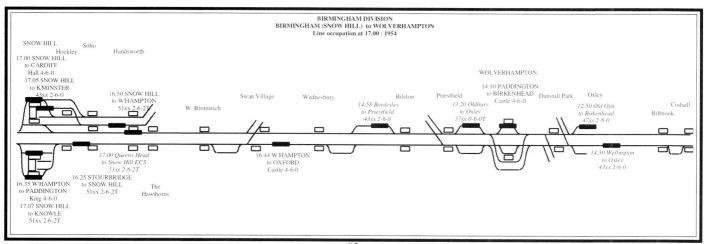

BIRMINGHAM DIVISION
BIRMINGHAM (SNOW HILL) to WOLVERHAMPTON
Line occupation at 17.00 : 1954

A King had always looked a huge engine to me but never so much as at that moment and I felt very young, small and inexperienced to be driving one. The drivers seat seemed enormous and in going over to it I tripped over the raised platform on the floor, which was not a good start in full view of my audience.

Trying to look as though I did this sort of thing every day of the week, I opened the large ejector, checked the signals and after confirming the right-away with the guard, opened the regulator. 6024 moved and, glory be, kept going and once I had the engine and train safely on the down relief road, felt confident enough to open the second valve and notch back a little. By the time we were halfway to Knowle I was revelling in it and started to really open the engine up, although the fireman didn't seem to be working especially hard.

According to the special traffic notice the possession on the down main only extended as far as Widney Manor and I expected to have to take the train from relief to main at Solihull where I would hand the regulator back to the Londoner. The signalmen however had done some conferring and decided to keep us on the relief line throughout which was a bonus for me since I could keep hold of the reigns right through to Snow Hill. I eased the engine back to first valve to p r e v e n t overspeeding on the falling gradient and revelled in the doubly pleasing experience of hearing 6024 blow off whilst the driver sarcastically criticised his fireman for overdoing things. The fireman's reply was unprintable.

Two things occupied my mind at that point. One was whether any of my colleagues at Tyseley would notice me in charge of a King as I sped by the shed whilst the other was the notorious climb into Snow Hill which acted as a trap for the unwary. Mindful that even Old Oak men top link men had come to grief in Moor Street tunnel, I shut off at Small Heath and dropped the lever down to 45%, letting 6024 ease itself down to 25 mph for the relief to main crossover at Moor Street.

I gathered from his expression that the Old Oak man though 25 mph a little slow and as we approached Moor Street he asked me if we were going to get up the bank without sticking. By way of a reply I dropped the lever to 60% and gave the regulator first valve and then second. It was better than conducting an orchestra: 6024 dug its heels in and with the most satisfying possible noise pounded its way up the bank and into Snow Hill where I brought it to the gentlest of stops in No.5 platform. I wondered if my career had anything more to offer.

The Kings had been at the forefront of Great Western affairs for thirty-five years before any of the class was withdrawn and it was a considerable shock when they started to go. Eventually only one of the class, 6018 'King Henry VI' remained and I recall seeing it visit the area in April 1963 when it was used to work an enthusiasts excursion from Snow Hill to Swindon and back.

Most express workings to and from Paddington had been in the hands of diesels for about a year by that time but there was still a backlog of drivers to train on the new engines and for this reason our link included the 17.28 commuter express from Snow Hill to Solihull which was worked by a D1xxx 'Western' hydraulic to give drivers the opportunity to be trained within the link.

Naturally the fireman had very little to do on this turn, especially as he tended to be crowded out with instructors, trainee drivers and inspectors, and it was without much enthusiasm I signed on with Joe Hackett one afternoon for the turn. As we walked across the tracks I noticed 6018 standing on the shed and looked at it rather wistfully as we boarded our brand-new red Western diesel.

The next day we were told by the foreman that our turn had been cancelled – the diesel had either fallen to bits or been used vice another that had come to grief – and as Joe signed the

road we were instructed to take 6018 light to Swindon for scrapping.

Joe and I, it seemed, were the only ones who had been unaware of the event and from the moment we went over to the engine there were photographers everywhere. It was naturally a rather melancholy occasion but I consoled myself that if the last of the Kings had to make a final journey, it was something for me to be part of the ceremony.

We ran up the relief line through the outer Birmingham suburbs and drew level with an up express hauled by a Western diesel. The fireman pointed an enquiring finger at 6018 and in response I drew a finger across my throat to indicate it was going for the chop. He closed his window and the diesel pulled ahead, the passengers taking a considerable interest in us as they were drawn by.

We were stopped by signals several times – chiefly I suspect to allow the photographers to get a good look at us – and at Knowle, with cameras going off like machine guns, we allowed one of the photographers to come up on the footplate. He said he had never been on a King before and since this was certainly going to be his last opportunity, neither Joe nor I had the heart to refuse him.

At Leamington one of the signalmen held us until he had photographed the engine from every conceivable angle and at Banbury we received a salute of whistles from every engine on the loco. Normally Kings were prohibited from the old road but a concession was made for engines going to and from Swindon and thus we ran via Oxford where we stood, bright and shiny, next to a grubby and travel-stained Hymech diesel. Old and new!

I would have liked to have continued through to Swindon but Joe, who never liked to make a minute's overtime, started grumbling at the delay we had suffered and arranged to be relieved by a set of Didcot men at Foxhall.

As it pulled away, we took a long, hard look, taking in for the last time the crisp beat of the exhaust, the tick of the vacuum pump and the whistle being blown: everything very Great Western. Watching the tail-lamp fade in the dusk that had now descended, I had quite a lump in my throat and even Joe, who was 100 per cent diesel, confided that he never thought 'they' would go. It was a sad day.

LOCO	CLASS	IN	OUT	LOCO	CLASS	IN	OUT
			WOLVERHAMPTON (STAFFORD RD) ALLOCATION : 1959				
6001	8P:KING 4-6-0 (1927)			4918	5MT:HALL 4-6-0 (1928)	Ex Shrewsbury 6/59	
6005	8P:KING 4-6-0 (1927)			4938	5MT:HALL 4-6-0 (1928)	Ex Oxley 12/59	
6006	8P:KING 4-6-0 (1927)			4954	5MT:HALL 4-6-0 (1928)	Ex Oxley 12/59	
6007	8P:KING 4-6-0 (1927)	Ex Laira 9/59		4986	5MT:HALL 4-6-0 (1928)		To Stourbridge 6/59
6008	8P:KING 4-6-0 (1927)	Ex Laira 1/59		4986	5MT:HALL 4-6-0 (1928)	Ex Stourbridge 12/59	
6011	8P:KING 4-6-0 (1927)			4990	5MT:HALL 4-6-0 (1928)		To Banbury 8/59
6014	8P:KING 4-6-0 (1927)			5926	5MT:HALL 4-6-0 (1928)		
6016	8P:KING 4-6-0 (1927)		To Laira 1/59	6926	5MT:HALL 4-6-0 (1928)	Ex Shrewsbury 6/59	
6017	8P:KING 4-6-0 (1927)	Ex Laira 2/59		6930	5MT:HALL 4-6-0 (1928)	Ex Stourbridge 12/59	
6020	8P:KING 4-6-0 (1927)			4161	4MT:51xx 2-6-2T (1928)		To Stourbridge 3/59
6022	8P:KING 4-6-0 (1927)	Ex Old Oak C. 6/59		5151	4MT:51xx 2-6-2T (1928)		
6027	8P:KING 4-6-0 (1927)			5187	4MT:51xx 2-6-2T (1928)		
4078	7P:CASTLE 4-6-0 (1923)	Ex Bristol (BR) 6/59	To Banbury 10/59	8411	4F:94XX 0-6-0T (1949)		
5019	7P:CASTLE 4-6-0 (1923)			8425	4F:94XX 0-6-0T (1949)		
5022	7P:CASTLE 4-6-0 (1923)			8426	4F:94XX 0-6-0T (1949)		
5026	7P:CASTLE 4-6-0 (1923)			8461	4F:94XX 0-6-0T (1949)	Ex Swindon 9/59	
5031	7P:CASTLE 4-6-0 (1923)			8462	4F:94XX 0-6-0T (1949)		To Oxley 1/59
5045	7P:CASTLE 4-6-0 (1923)			9428	4F:94XX 0-6-0T (1949)		
5046	7P:CASTLE 4-6-0 (1923)			9435	4F:94XX 0-6-0T (1949)		
5047	7P:CASTLE 4-6-0 (1923)			9496	4F:94XX 0-6-0T (1949)		w/d 12/59
5059	7P:CASTLE 4-6-0 (1923)		To Shrewsbury 6/59	3615	3F:57xx 0-6-0T (1933)		
5063	7P:CASTLE 4-6-0 (1923)			3664	3F:57xx 0-6-0T (1933)		
5070	7P:CASTLE 4-6-0 (1923)			3756	3F:57xx 0-6-0T (1933)		
5072	7P:CASTLE 4-6-0 (1923)			3778	3F:57xx 0-6-0T (1933)		
5088	7P:CASTLE 4-6-0 (1923)			3792	3F:57xx 0-6-0T (1933)		
5089	7P:CASTLE 4-6-0 (1923)			8796	3F:57xx 0-6-0T (1933)		
7015	7P:CASTLE 4-6-0 (1923)	Ex Bristol (BR) 6/59	To Shrewsbury 11/59	8798	3F:57xx 0-6-0T (1933)		
7026	7P:CASTLE 4-6-0 (1923)			8726	3F:57xx 0-6-0T (1929)		
6975	5MT:MOD-HALL 4-6-0 (1944)		To Oxley 5/59	6418	2P:64xx 0-6-0T (1932)		
6987	5MT:MOD-HALL 4-6-0 (1944)	Ex Stourbridge 12/59		6422	2P:64xx 0-6-0T (1932)		
4901	5MT:HALL 4-6-0 (1928)						

THE HOLIDAY TRADE

Foreign engines came from far and wide to assist with the Birmingham holiday peak traffic and produced the sight of Penzance-based Grange 4-6-0 6860 'Aberporth Grange' on the 12.18 Hastings to Birmingham (Snow Hill), seen climbing Hatton bank in the final stages of its journey. The 12.18 Hastings enjoyed a variety of motive power, starting off with a St Leonards Schools 4-4-0 and continuing from Brighton to Redhill with a Bricklayers Arms LMS 4MT 2-6-4T. The Great Western engine, booked to be a 43xx 2-6-0, took over at Redhill after arriving with a local from Reading South and worked through to Birmingham.

One of the features of life in the Midlands (and much of the North of England) up to the 1960's was that most of the factories closed down for holidays at the same time and created an exodus of people that the Old Testament would not have been ashamed of. Since of the three railways in Birmingham the Great Western had the best links to the most popular resorts, most of the travelling thousands would descend upon Snow Hill and, because Snow Hill was badly arranged for heavy volumes of southbound traffic, Moor Street from where numerous unadvertised long distance trains used to start.

The factories and workshops would close simultaneously at about four o'clock on a Friday afternoon and within an hour a vast queue would be forming outside Moor Street, its tail disappearing into the large goods shed by the side of the station which was used as an alternative to paralysing half the roads in the city.

On any Friday evening the system was stretched but on these post-war holiday Fridays matters all but reached breaking point with the ordinary suburban peak being threatened by the presence of a dozen or more twelve coach trains, each of which had to be worked into Moor Street by one engine and worked away by another. The light engine movements alone amassed a considerable mileage.

Assessments of the trains required would be made by local stationmasters and their estimates translated into trains by Paddington who would have the stock sent down to Tyseley for cleaning a fortnight before the event. The trains would then be farmed out to a variety of sidings and stabling points to wait until being worked empty on the Friday in question to Moor Street.

Every movement, empty or loaded, would have an engine and crew diagrammed to it and each would be stepped up so that the engine for the second departure ran light to collect the stock for the first train, coupling to its own train when the first train had departed behind its booked engine. It was planned very carefully on paper but with dozens of engines, crews and coaches involved it was inevitable that something would go wrong and the district controller would be watching – by telephone reports and his mind's eye – every movement and extemporising before trouble threatened.

Seats on the trains were regulated with the colour of tickets corresponding to a par-

WOLVERHAMPTON (STAFFORD RD) ALLOCATION : 1960						
LOCO CLASS	IN	OUT	LOCO CLASS		IN	OUT
6001 8P : KING 4-6-0 (1927)			5926 5MT : HALL 4-6-0 (1928)			
6005 8P : KING 4-6-0 (1927)			5983 5MT : HALL 4-6-0 (1928)		Ex Swindon 7/60	
6006 8P : KING 4-6-0 (1927)			6926 5MT : HALL 4-6-0 (1928)			
6007 8P : KING 4-6-0 (1927)			6930 5MT : HALL 4-6-0 (1928)			
6008 8P : KING 4-6-0 (1927)			6931 5MT : HALL 4-6-0 (1928)		Ex St Blazey 7/60	
6011 8P : KING 4-6-0 (1927)			6933 5MT : HALL 4-6-0 (1928)		Ex Penzance 3/60	
6014 8P : KING 4-6-0 (1927)			6934 5MT : HALL 4-6-0 (1928)		Ex Oxley 7/60	
6017 8P : KING 4-6-0 (1927)			6945 5MT : HALL 4-6-0 (1928)		Ex Penzance 3/60	
6020 8P : KING 4-6-0 (1927)			5151 4MT : 51xx 2-6-2T (1928)			
6022 8P : KING 4-6-0 (1927)			5187 4MT : 51xx 2-6-2T (1928)			
6027 8P : KING 4-6-0 (1927)	Ex Old Oak C. 1/60		8411 4F : 94XX 0-6-0T (1949)			w/d 6/60
5019 7P : CASTLE 4-6-0 (1923)			8425 4F : 94XX 0-6-0T (1949)			To Canton 7/60
5022 7P : CASTLE 4-6-0 (1923)			8426 4F : 94XX 0-6-0T (1949)			To Worcester 9/60
5026 7P : CASTLE 4-6-0 (1923)			8452 4F : 94XX 0-6-0T (1949)		Ex Banbury 5/60	
5031 7P : CASTLE 4-6-0 (1923)			8461 4F : 94XX 0-6-0T (1949)			To Pontypool Rd 9/60
5045 7P : CASTLE 4-6-0 (1923)			8498 4F : 94XX 0-6-0T (1949)		Ex Banbury 5/60	
5046 7P : CASTLE 4-6-0 (1923)			9428 4F : 94XX 0-6-0T (1949)			w/d 6/60
5047 7P : CASTLE 4-6-0 (1923)			9435 4F : 94XX 0-6-0T (1949)			
5063 7P : CASTLE 4-6-0 (1923)			9470 4F : 94XX 0-6-0T (1949)		Ex Shrewsbury 7/60	
5070 7P : CASTLE 4-6-0 (1923)		To Shrewsbury 2/60	3615 3F : 57xx 0-6-0T (1933)			
5072 7P : CASTLE 4-6-0 (1923)		To Canton 9/60	3664 3F : 57xx 0-6-0T (1933)			
5088 7P : CASTLE 4-6-0 (1923)			3715 3F : 57xx 0-6-0T (1933)		Ex Southall 2/60	
5089 7P : CASTLE 4-6-0 (1923)			3756 3F : 57xx 0-6-0T (1933)			To Croes Newydd 8/60
7026 7P : CASTLE 4-6-0 (1923)			3778 3F : 57xx 0-6-0T (1933)			
6987 5MT : MOD-HALL 4-6-0 (1944)			3792 3F : 57xx 0-6-0T (1933)			
4901 5MT : HALL 4-6-0 (1928)		To Oxley 7/60	8796 3F : 57xx 0-6-0T (1933)			
4918 5MT : HALL 4-6-0 (1928)			8798 3F : 57xx 0-6-0T (1933)			To Swansea (E. Dck) 5/60
4923 5MT : HALL 4-6-0 (1928)	Ex Carmarthen 7/60		8726 3F : 57xx 0-6-0T (1929)			To Llanelly 7/60
4938 5MT : HALL 4-6-0 (1928)			6418 2P : 64xx 0-6-0T (1932)			
4954 5MT : HALL 4-6-0 (1928)			6422 2P : 64xx 0-6-0T (1932)			
4986 5MT : HALL 4-6-0 (1928)						

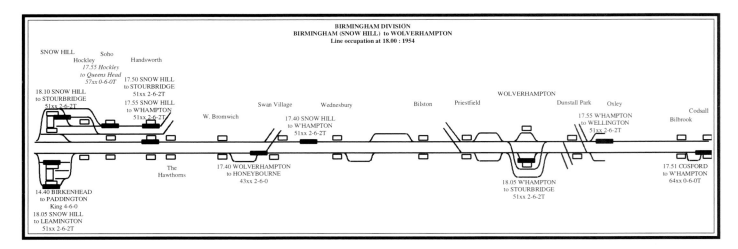

BIRMINGHAM DIVISION
BIRMINGHAM (SNOW HILL) to WOLVERHAMPTON
Line occupation at 18.00 : 1954

ticular train. It was a clean and simple form of organisation which worked well except for an incident one year when a barrier was manned by a colour blind ticket collector…..

The provision of engines was a problem and although they were needed for a couple of weekends when goods traffic was quiet, not all the Tyseley allocation was suitable for long distance express work and up to twenty big engines would be drafted in from a variety of foreign sheds to assist with the additional trains. Fortunately the Great Western was well stocked with reliable middle-range 4-6-0's and it was unusual to find anything smaller on the services at least until late on Saturday when the sheds would have to start scraping the bottom of some very murky barrels. The 43xx 2-6-0's were not reckoned to be ideal engines for this traffic: they were not really up to the job and, on a personal note, I was never happy with them.

As the foreign engines arrived at Tyseley they would have their fires, ashpans and smokeboxes thoroughly cleaned out, be fully coaled and watered and then turned to face uphill (towards London). Most of them would be stabled in and around the shed with as many as possible standing on the middle pits either side of the coalstage where the foreman fitter would give them a thorough examination and see to any running repairs that presented themselves. All the tools would be taken off and locked away in the tool stores since to find twenty extra sets of tools at the drop of a hat would be asking too much for any depot.

One thing that could be taken for granted was that each of the foreigners would be as rough as a pair of old boots. Cardiff, Bristol, Worcester, Gloucester, Shrewsbury and Wolverhampton would each get an order to send a D class (Hall, Grange, Manor or Castle) 4-6-0 to Tyseley and, knowing that the engine would be away for at least a fortnight, would earmark the roughest engine in their possession. I never recall seeing an ex-works engine amongst any of the imports although there were plenty of engines waiting to go into Swindon and one's greatest fear was to be booked to a foreign Castle 4-6-0 since no-one would send one to Tyseley for the excursion traffic unless it was in particularly bad shape.

On the Wednesday prior to the exodus all the locos involved would be lit up so that by the Friday they would be well warmed through by the time the preparation crews descended upon them. There would be a certain amount of shunting done to get them in the right order to go off the shed. Some of the locos were prepared by the crews that were going to work these trains but this depended on how far they would be working and the length of time they were on duty.

The final element of preparation was overseen by the toolman whose responsibility it was to ensure that each engine had a full set of tools before ringing off shed. In earlier days the responsibility for tools had rested with each

OXLEY ALLOCATION : 1950						
LOCO CLASS	IN	OUT	LOCO CLASS		IN	OUT
90141 8F : WD 2-8-0 (1943)		To Wakefield 11/50	6645 5MT : 56xx 0-6-2T (1927)			
7207 8F : 72xx 2-8-2T (1934)			5606 5MT : 56xx 0-6-2T (1924)			To Stourbridge 11/50
7226 8F : 72xx 2-8-2T (1934)			5624 5MT : 56xx 0-6-2T (1924)			
7227 8F : 72xx 2-8-2T (1934)			5657 5MT : 56xx 0-6-2T (1924)			
7238 8F : 72xx 2-8-2T (1934)			9312 4MT : 43xx 2-6-0 (1932)			
7243 8F : 72xx 2-8-2T (1934)			9314 4MT : 43xx 2-6-0 (1932)			
2825 8F : 28xx 2-8-0 (1903)		To Reading 9/50	5300 4MT : 43xx 2-6-0 (1911)		Ex Stourbridge 11/50	
2830 8F : 28xx 2-8-0 (1903)			5307 4MT : 43xx 2-6-0 (1911)		Ex Canton 10/50	
2832 8F : 28xx 2-8-0 (1903)			5309 4MT : 43xx 2-6-0 (1911)			
2833 8F : 28xx 2-8-0 (1903)			5313 4MT : 43xx 2-6-0 (1911)			
2854 8F : 28xx 2-8-0 (1903)			5341 4MT : 43xx 2-6-0 (1911)		Ex Landore 11/50	
3031 7F : R.O.D. 2-8-0 (1917)			5379 4MT : 43xx 2-6-0 (1911)			
3033 7F : R.O.D. 2-8-0 (1917)			5386 4MT : 43xx 2-6-0 (1911)			
4708 7F : 47xx 2-8-0 (1919)			5390 4MT : 43xx 2-6-0 (1911)			
6967 5MT : MOD-HALL 4-6-0 (1944)			6335 4MT : 43xx 2-6-0 (1911)			
6975 5MT : MOD-HALL 4-6-0 (1944)			6361 4MT : 43xx 2-6-0 (1911)			
4919 5MT : HALL 4-6-0 (1928)	Ex Shrewsbury 12/50		6362 4MT : 43xx 2-6-0 (1911)			
4950 5MT : HALL 4-6-0 (1928)	Ex Newton Abbot 11/50		7311 4MT : 43xx 2-6-0 (1911)			
4955 5MT : HALL 4-6-0 (1928)			8417 4F : 94XX 0-6-0T (1949)			
4977 5MT : HALL 4-6-0 (1928)	Ex Gloucester 12/50		9408 4F : 94XX 0-6-0T (1948)			
4991 5MT : HALL 4-6-0 (1928)			3744 3F : 57xx 0-6-0T (1933)			
5921 5MT : HALL 4-6-0 (1928)			3745 3F : 57xx 0-6-0T (1933)			
5942 5MT : HALL 4-6-0 (1928)	Ex Wolverhampton 11/50		3792 3F : 57xx 0-6-0T (1933)			
5944 5MT : HALL 4-6-0 (1928)	Ex Wolverhampton 12/50		3793 3F : 57xx 0-6-0T (1933)			
5945 5MT : HALL 4-6-0 (1928)			8798 3F : 57xx 0-6-0T (1933)			
5991 5MT : HALL 4-6-0 (1928)			9714 3F : 57xx 0-6-0T (1933)			
5995 5MT : HALL 4-6-0 (1928)	Ex Wolverhampton 11/50		9715 3F : 57xx 0-6-0T (1933)			
6920 5MT : HALL 4-6-0 (1928)			9730 3F : 57xx 0-6-0T (1933)			
6942 5MT : HALL 4-6-0 (1928)	Ex Wolverhampton 12/50		9739 3F : 57xx 0-6-0T (1933)			
6956 5MT : HALL 4-6-0 (1928)		To Wolverhampton 12/50	9742 3F : 57xx 0-6-0T (1933)			
6856 5MT : GRANGE 4-6-0 (1936)			9747 3F : 57xx 0-6-0T (1933)			
6862 5MT : GRANGE 4-6-0 (1936)			9752 3F : 57xx 0-6-0T (1933)			
6879 5MT : GRANGE 4-6-0 (1936)			9768 3F : 57xx 0-6-0T (1933)			
5684 5MT : 56xx 0-6-2T (1927)			9769 3F : 57xx 0-6-0T (1933)			
6600 5MT : 56xx 0-6-2T (1927)			5748 3F : 57xx 0-6-0T (1929)			
6609 5MT : 56xx 0-6-2T (1927)		To Stourbridge 12/50	7759 3F : 57xx 0-6-0T (1929)			
6610 5MT : 56xx 0-6-2T (1927)			7796 3F : 57xx 0-6-0T (1929)			
6638 5MT : 56xx 0-6-2T (1927)			7797 3F : 57xx 0-6-0T (1929)			
6640 5MT : 56xx 0-6-2T (1927)						

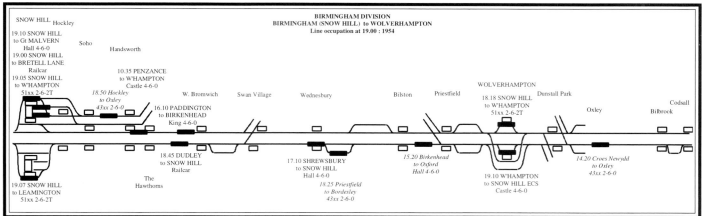

BIRMINGHAM DIVISION
BIRMINGHAM (SNOW HILL) to WOLVERHAMPTON
Line occupation at 19.00 : 1954

The northern approach to Snow Hill. Modified Hall 4-6-0 6974 'Bryngwyn Hall' of Old Oak Common runs through Hockley on the up main with empty stock to form a southbound service from Snow Hill in 1957. Hockley station was unusual in that it lacked a platform face on the down main line.

fireman, who locked the tools in the box on the engine and left the key with the timekeeper. Predictably keys went astray – many travelling far afield in the pockets in forgetful firemen – and after a number of incidents in which engines were delayed whilst their crews foraged for tools, the system was changed and the toolman introduced.

Being the height of the summer, rain was almost certain to appear just as the working got under way; a deluge which not only dampened the waiting passengers but made a bad start for train crews who had to work in tender first to Moor Street before taking over a service to Bristol or beyond. It could also be rather chilly and I recall the time when Joe Smith and I worked the 02.00 Moor Street to Weymouth on a particularly cold and wet summers night.

We worked in the empty stock for the preceding train and after it had departed, ran forward and coupled up to the Weymouth stock. Wet and irritable from having worked tender-first from Tyseley in a rain shower, Joe and I sat for a while in the leading compartment of the first coach trying to

dry out. In spite of it being August, the compartment was no warmer than the footplate and after shivering for a while, Joe told me to couple up the pipes and turn the steam heating on.

We started to dry out and were getting quite comfortable when a traffic inspector presented himself and demanded to know why the train heating was on.

"Because its bloody cold," said Joe whose idea of fun was running over a traffic man.

"You know very well that heating is not applied until the beginning of the winter season. It says so in the appendix. Turn it off."

"What about the passengers?"

"Never you mind about the passengers…"

They exchanged views in a way that raised the temperature far more efficiently that the steam heating system but after a few minutes Joe capitulated and we went back to the engine and disconnected the heating pipes.

Grumbling about the brass – and Moor Street was swarming with them – Joe pulled away at departure time and crawled up the relief as far as Bordesley South where we were stopped by signals. He was determined to have the last word in the matter.

"Get those bloody pipes connected – quick!" he ordered made me nip between the tender and first coach to restore the heating.

At Oxford, where we stopped for water, Joe walked back along the train and noted with satisfaction that the compartment windows were all misted up with heat and that

LOCO	CLASS	IN	OUT	LOCO	CLASS	IN	OUT
				OXLEY ALLOCATION : 1951			
90010	8F WD 2-8-0 (1943)	Ex Immingham 10/51	To Leamington 11/51	6610	5MT 56xx 0-6-2T (1927)		
90069	8F WD 2-8-0 (1943)	Ex Immingham 10/51		6638	5MT 56xx 0-6-2T (1927)		
90125	8F WD 2-8-0 (1943)	Ex Motherwell 9/51		6640	5MT 56xx 0-6-2T (1927)		
90152	8F WD 2-8-0 (1943)	Ex Motherwell 9/51	To Southall 11/51	6645	5MT 56xx 0-6-2T (1927)		
90485	8F WD 2-8-0 (1943)	Ex Immingham 10/51		5624	5MT 56xx 0-6-2T (1924)		
7207	8F 72xx 2-8-2T (1934)			5657	5MT 56xx 0-6-2T (1924)		
7226	8F 72xx 2-8-2T (1934)			9312	4MT 43xx 2-6-0 (1932)		
7227	8F 72xx 2-8-2T (1934)			9314	4MT 43xx 2-6-0 (1932)		
7238	8F 72xx 2-8-2T (1934)			5300	4MT 43xx 2-6-0 (1911)		
7243	8F 72xx 2-8-2T (1934)			5307	4MT 43xx 2-6-0 (1911)		
3825	8F 28xx 2-8-0 (1938)	Ex Croes Newydd 10/51		5309	4MT 43xx 2-6-0 (1911)		
3860	8F 28xx 2-8-0 (1938)	Ex Chester 7/51		5313	4MT 43xx 2-6-0 (1911)		
2830	8F 28xx 2-8-0 (1903)			5315	4MT 43xx 2-6-0 (1911)	Ex Croes Newydd 3/51	To Croes Newydd 5/51
2832	8F 28xx 2-8-0 (1903)			5341	4MT 43xx 2-6-0 (1911)		
2833	8F 28xx 2-8-0 (1903)			5379	4MT 43xx 2-6-0 (1911)		
2854	8F 28xx 2-8-0 (1903)			5386	4MT 43xx 2-6-0 (1911)		
3028	7F R.O.D. 2-8-0 (1917)	Ex Croes Newydd 6/51	To Stourbridge 10/51	5390	4MT 43xx 2-6-0 (1911)		
3031	7F R.O.D. 2-8-0 (1917)			6335	4MT 43xx 2-6-0 (1911)		
3033	7F R.O.D. 2-8-0 (1917)		To Croes Newydd 9/51	6338	4MT 43xx 2-6-0 (1911)	Ex Shrewsbury 6/51	
4708	7F 47xx 2-8-0 (1919)			6361	4MT 43xx 2-6-0 (1911)		
6967	5MT MOD-HALL 4-6-0 (1944)	To Laira 1/51		6362	4MT 43xx 2-6-0 (1911)		
6967	5MT MOD-HALL 4-6-0 (1944)	Ex Laira 10/51	To Bristol (BR) 11/51	6363	4MT 43xx 2-6-0 (1911)	Ex Reading 1/51	
6975	5MT MOD-HALL 4-6-0 (1944)			7311	4MT 43xx 2-6-0 (1911)		
4919	5MT HALL 4-6-0 (1928)			8417	4F 94XX 0-6-0T (1948)		
4943	5MT HALL 4-6-0 (1928)	Ex Reading 1/51		8428	4F 94XX 0-6-0T (1948)	New 3/51	
4950	5MT HALL 4-6-0 (1928)			9408	4F 94XX 0-6-0T (1948)		
4955	5MT HALL 4-6-0 (1928)			3744	3F 57xx 0-6-0T (1933)		
4977	5MT HALL 4-6-0 (1928)			3745	3F 57xx 0-6-0T (1933)		
4991	5MT HALL 4-6-0 (1928)			3792	3F 57xx 0-6-0T (1933)		
5921	5MT HALL 4-6-0 (1928)		To Newport (Pill) 5/51	3793	3F 57xx 0-6-0T (1933)		
5942	5MT HALL 4-6-0 (1928)			8798	3F 57xx 0-6-0T (1933)		
5944	5MT HALL 4-6-0 (1928)			9714	3F 57xx 0-6-0T (1933)		
5945	5MT HALL 4-6-0 (1928)			9715	3F 57xx 0-6-0T (1933)		
5991	5MT HALL 4-6-0 (1928)			9730	3F 57xx 0-6-0T (1933)		
5995	5MT HALL 4-6-0 (1928)			9739	3F 57xx 0-6-0T (1933)		
6920	5MT HALL 4-6-0 (1928)			9742	3F 57xx 0-6-0T (1933)		To Wellington 4/51
6942	5MT HALL 4-6-0 (1928)			9747	3F 57xx 0-6-0T (1933)		
6812	5MT GRANGE 4-6-0 (1936)	Ex Wolverhampton 6/51		9752	3F 57xx 0-6-0T (1933)		
6844	5MT GRANGE 4-6-0 (1936)	Ex Birkenhead 10/51		9768	3F 57xx 0-6-0T (1933)		
6856	5MT GRANGE 4-6-0 (1936)			9769	3F 57xx 0-6-0T (1933)		
6860	5MT GRANGE 4-6-0 (1936)	Ex Birkenhead 10/51		5748	3F 57xx 0-6-0T (1929)		
6862	5MT GRANGE 4-6-0 (1936)			7759	3F 57xx 0-6-0T (1929)		
6879	5MT GRANGE 4-6-0 (1936)			7796	3F 57xx 0-6-0T (1929)		
5684	5MT 56xx 0-6-2T (1927)			7797	3F 57xx 0-6-0T (1929)		
6600	5MT 56xx 0-6-2T (1927)		To Canton 5/51	2579	2MT 2301 0-6-0 (1883)	Ex Didcot 5/51	

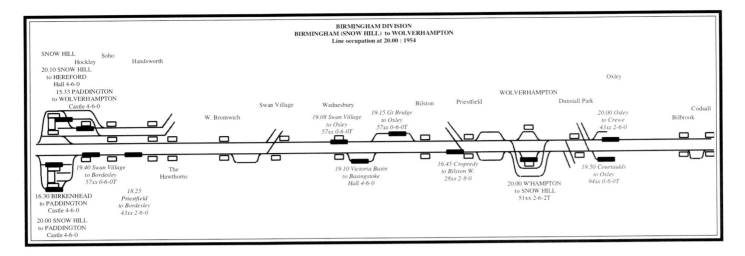

SNOW HILL   Soho
Hockley   Handsworth

20.10 SNOW HILL
to HEREFORD
Hall 4-6-0

15.33 PADDINGTON
to WOLVERHAMPTON
Castle 4-6-0

W. Bromwich   Swan Village   Wednesbury   Bilston   Priestfield   WOLVERHAMPTON   Oxley

Dunstall Park   Codsall   Bilbrook

19.08 Swan Village
to Oxley
57xx 0-6-0T

19.15 Gt Bridge
to Oxley
57xx 0-6-0T

20.00 Oxley
to Crewe
43xx 2-6-0

19.40 Swan Village
to Bordesley
57xx 0-6-0T

The Hawthorns

19.10 Victoria Basin
to Basingstoke
Hall 4-6-0

16.45 Cropredy
to Bilston W.
28xx 2-8-0

19.50 Courtaulds
to Oxley
94xx 0-6-0T

16.30 BIRKENHEAD
to PADDINGTON
Castle 4-6-0

18.25
Priestfield
to Bordesley
43xx 2-6-0

20.00 W'HAMPTON
to SNOW HILL
51xx 2-6-2T

20.00 SNOW HILL
to PADDINGTON
Castle 4-6-0

---

the passengers seemed warm and contented.

"If I hadn't done that," he remarked getting back on the engine, "they'd have been frozen solid by now."

It was a small victory of common-sense over gold braid and it restored Joe's good humour and prompted him to come out with some his tales about the old days when he was a fireman. His favourite concerned a Bordesley shunting driver – a crusty old boy as Joe described him – who for years had come to work carrying a stone jar sealed by a big end cork. What was contained in the jar was a closely guarded secret and the closest Joe got to it was when he was ordered to clean it at the end of the shift; an instruction accompanied by warnings of dire consequences should he so much as scratch the thing.

Joe, of course, dropped it and it fell to the footplate floor, smashing into a hundred small pieces. The driver was furious and did everything he could to Joe short of stuffing him into the firebox. Whilst the attack was going on Joe was on his knees, cleaning up the mess in the midst of which he found a small skeleton of something like a mouse which he gleefully showed to his persecutor.

The next thing the driver threw himself off the engine to be violently sick, presenting Joe with half a crown when he returned. "I never went from anyone's bad books to their good books quite as quickly as I did with him." Joe chuckled, adding, "If whatever was in the bottle did that to a mouse, imagine what it did to the old boy's insides….".

The volume of traffic over the North Warwickshire route was heavy on a summer Saturday and I did a lot of work with Joe on the West of England jobs, always looking forward to them since once you were beyond Cheltenham you were on a different planet whilst there was the added interest of finding yourself working an engine from an unusual shed. Excluding services run by special traffic notice, thirteen long distance workings were booked to operate on summer Saturdays between Cheltenham and Birmingham: five from Paignton, three from Penzance and one each from St Austell, Weston-super-Mare, Ilfracombe, Kingswear and Newquay.

One Saturday we were sent passenger to Temple Meads to bring back the 14.55 Paignton – Wolverhampton, booked to leave Bristol at 18.00 with stops at Cheltenham and Stratford. We arrived at Temple Meads in good time and spent the late afternoon chatting to other waiting locomen and the engine cleaners from Bath Road and St Philips Marsh; the latter spending a twelve hour shift on the station pushing coal forward and watering tenders whilst trains paused for relief in either direction. The man in charge was the arranger who made sure he had his crews on hand and kept an eye, via the controller, on the running of trains.

"Ten on, 4086 and passed Bridgwater," he told Joe, "and you're the second one down."

"Ah," said Joe, "a Castle – just the job for the top men."

The other crews who had been told their trains were running in behind Granges were more than a little envious but as Joe pointed out with curious logic, he was the senior man and therefore entitled to the best engine.

The first train ran in and the cleaners jumped on the engine, pushing coal forward and filling the tank. The boards came off and the Grange pulled out, Joe telling them to keep going and to "keep out of our way."

We started to gather our bags, expecting to see our Castle come round the bend at any moment but as we were getting into position the arranger came running up to Joe.

"You'll be third in. Your engines had trouble but it's on the move now. You'll follow the 15.05 Paignton."

"It'll be short of steam. My mate'll fix it when it comes."

The 15.05 Paignton ran in and departed behind its Grange and then our working rolled down the platform, hauled not by 4086 but a 28xx 2-8-0, 2851. The incoming driver told us that 4086 had blown a steam pipe at Highbridge and been replaced by the 2-8-0 which happened to be on a nearby empty stock train.

As we climbed aboard the engine the arranger reappeared, anticipating an argument about having to take a 2-8-0 on an express service. Joe stopped him dead in his tracks.

"We'll take it. Don't worry about us."

"All the way?"

"All the way to Brum."

The poor fellow had been worrying himself daft about where he

OXLEY ALLOCATION : 1952						
LOCO CLASS	IN	OUT	LOCO CLASS	IN	OUT	
90069 8F : WD 2-8-0 (1943)			6854 5MT : GRANGE 4-6-0 (1936)	Ex Banbury 9/52		
90284 8F : WD 2-8-0 (1943)	Ex Worcester 4/52		6856 5MT : GRANGE 4-6-0 (1936)		To Banbury 4/52	
90466 8F : WD 2-8-0 (1943)	Ex Colwick 2/52		6856 5MT : GRANGE 4-6-0 (1936)	Ex Banbury 9/52		
90485 8F : WD 2-8-0 (1943)		To Banbury 1/52	6860 5MT : GRANGE 4-6-0 (1936)		To Banbury 10/52	
7207 8F : 72xx 2-8-2T (1934)			6862 5MT : GRANGE 4-6-0 (1936)	Ex Landore 7/52		
7208 8F : 72xx 2-8-2T (1934)	Ex Leamington 1/52	To Canton 10/52	6879 5MT : GRANGE 4-6-0 (1936)		To Banbury 4/52	
7218 8F : 72xx 2-8-2T (1934)	Ex Leamington 1/52	To Duffryn 7/52	6879 5MT : GRANGE 4-6-0 (1936)	Ex Banbury 9/52		
7226 8F : 72xx 2-8-2T (1934)		To Neath 10/52	5684 5MT : 56xx 0-6-2T (1927)			
7227 8F : 72xx 2-8-2T (1934)		To Ebbw Jcn 11/52	6610 5MT : 56xx 0-6-2T (1927)			
7238 8F : 72xx 2-8-2T (1934)			6638 5MT : 56xx 0-6-2T (1927)		To Tondu 10/52	
7243 8F : 72xx 2-8-2T (1934)		To Ebbw Jcn 11/52	6640 5MT : 56xx 0-6-2T (1927)			
3802 8F : 28xx 2-8-0 (1938)	Ex Banbury 4/52		6645 5MT : 56xx 0-6-2T (1927)			
3813 8F : 28xx 2-8-0 (1938)	Ex Severn T. Jcn 7/52		5624 5MT : 56xx 0-6-2T (1924)		To Tondu 10/52	
3825 8F : 28xx 2-8-0 (1938)			5657 5MT : 56xx 0-6-2T (1924)		To Neyland 6/52	
3860 8F : 28xx 2-8-0 (1938)			5657 5MT : 56xx 0-6-2T (1924)	Ex Neyland 10/52	To Llanelly 11/52	
3863 8F : 28xx 2-8-0 (1938)	Ex Banbury 4/52		9312 4MT : 43xx 2-6-0 (1932)		To Stourbridge 5/52	
2830 8F : 28xx 2-8-0 (1903)			9312 4MT : 43xx 2-6-0 (1932)	Ex Stourbridge 6/52		
2832 8F : 28xx 2-8-0 (1903)		To Shrewsbury 11/52	9314 4MT : 43xx 2-6-0 (1932)		To Shrewsbury 6/52	
2833 8F : 28xx 2-8-0 (1903)			5300 4MT : 43xx 2-6-0 (1911)			
2854 8F : 28xx 2-8-0 (1903)			5300 4MT : 43xx 2-6-0 (1911)	Ex Shrewsbury 9/52		
2858 8F : 28xx 2-8-0 (1903)	Ex Ebbw Jcn 7/52	To Southall 11/52	5309 4MT : 43xx 2-6-0 (1911)		To Banbury 6/52	
2865 8F : 28xx 2-8-0 (1903)	Ex Ebbw Jcn 7/52	To Stourbridge 12/52	5309 4MT : 43xx 2-6-0 (1911)		To Stourbridge 5/52	
2868 8F : 28xx 2-8-0 (1903)	Ex Canton 7/52	To Stourbridge 11/52	5309 4MT : 43xx 2-6-0 (1911)	Ex Stourbridge 6/52		
2882 8F : 28xx 2-8-0 (1903)	Ex Severn T. Jcn 7/52		5313 4MT : 43xx 2-6-0 (1911)		To Stourbridge 1/52	
3016 7F : R.O.D. 2-8-0 (1917)	Ex Tyseley 7/52		5341 4MT : 43xx 2-6-0 (1911)			
3031 7F : R.O.D. 2-8-0 (1917)		To Worcester 10/52	5379 4MT : 43xx 2-6-0 (1911)		To Stourbridge 1/52	
3047 7F : R.O.D. 2-8-0 (1917)	Ex Reading 12/52		5386 4MT : 43xx 2-6-0 (1911)		To Tyseley 10/52	
4708 7F : 47xx 2-8-0 (1919)		To Old Oak C. 10/52	5390 4MT : 43xx 2-6-0 (1911)		To Reading 4/52	
6963 5MT : MOD-HALL 4-6-0 (1944)	Ex Banbury 4/52		5390 4MT : 43xx 2-6-0 (1911)	Ex Reading 7/52		
6975 5MT : MOD-HALL 4-6-0 (1944)		To Chester 7/52	5391 4MT : 43xx 2-6-0 (1911)	Ex Tyseley 11/52		
7915 5MT : MOD-HALL 4-6-0 (1944)			6335 4MT : 43xx 2-6-0 (1911)			
7811 5MT : MANOR 4-6-0 (1938)	Ex Banbury 7/52		6338 4MT : 43xx 2-6-0 (1911)		To Reading 4/52	
7818 5MT : MANOR 4-6-0 (1938)	Ex Gloucester 7/52		6361 4MT : 43xx 2-6-0 (1911)			
4919 5MT : HALL 4-6-0 (1928)			6362 4MT : 43xx 2-6-0 (1911)		To Chester 1/52	
4924 5MT : HALL 4-6-0 (1928)	Ex Tyseley 11/52		6363 4MT : 43xx 2-6-0 (1911)			
4926 5MT : HALL 4-6-0 (1928)	Ex Westbury 12/52		6383 4MT : 43xx 2-6-0 (1911)	Ex Reading 7/52	To Oswestry 10/52	
4943 5MT : HALL 4-6-0 (1928)			7311 4MT : 43xx 2-6-0 (1911)		To Taunton 10/52	
4950 5MT : HALL 4-6-0 (1928)			8417 4F : 94XX 0-6-0T (1948)			
4955 5MT : HALL 4-6-0 (1928)			8428 4F : 94XX 0-6-0T (1948)			
4959 5MT : HALL 4-6-0 (1928)	Ex Tyseley 10/52		9408 4F : 94XX 0-6-0T (1948)			
4977 5MT : HALL 4-6-0 (1928)		To Banbury 2/52	3744 3F : 57xx 0-6-0T (1933)			
4991 5MT : HALL 4-6-0 (1928)		To Wolverhampton 7/52	3745 3F : 57xx 0-6-0T (1933)		To Wolverhampton 7/52	
5942 5MT : HALL 4-6-0 (1928)		To Reading 7/52	3792 3F : 57xx 0-6-0T (1933)			
5944 5MT : HALL 4-6-0 (1928)		To Wolverhampton 7/52	3793 3F : 57xx 0-6-0T (1933)			
5945 5MT : HALL 4-6-0 (1928)			8798 3F : 57xx 0-6-0T (1933)			
5966 5MT : HALL 4-6-0 (1928)	Ex Leamington 10/52		9714 3F : 57xx 0-6-0T (1933)			
5972 5MT : HALL 4-6-0 (1928)	Ex Tyseley 10/52		9715 3F : 57xx 0-6-0T (1933)			
5991 5MT : HALL 4-6-0 (1928)			9730 3F : 57xx 0-6-0T (1933)			
5993 5MT : HALL 4-6-0 (1928)	Ex Tyseley 4/52	To Reading 7/52	9739 3F : 57xx 0-6-0T (1933)			
5995 5MT : HALL 4-6-0 (1928)			9747 3F : 57xx 0-6-0T (1933)			
5997 5MT : HALL 4-6-0 (1928)	Ex Tyseley 4/52	To Laira 7/52	9752 3F : 57xx 0-6-0T (1933)			
6920 5MT : HALL 4-6-0 (1928)			9768 3F : 57xx 0-6-0T (1933)			
6940 5MT : HALL 4-6-0 (1928)	Ex Wolverhampton 1/52	To Laira 7/52	9769 3F : 57xx 0-6-0T (1933)			
6942 5MT : HALL 4-6-0 (1928)			5748 3F : 57xx 0-6-0T (1929)			
6812 5MT : GRANGE 4-6-0 (1936)			7759 3F : 57xx 0-6-0T (1929)			
6844 5MT : GRANGE 4-6-0 (1936)		To Llanelly 7/52	7796 3F : 57xx 0-6-0T (1929)			
6848 5MT : GRANGE 4-6-0 (1936)	Ex Wolverhampton 1/52	To Llanelly 7/52	7797 3F : 57xx 0-6-0T (1929)			

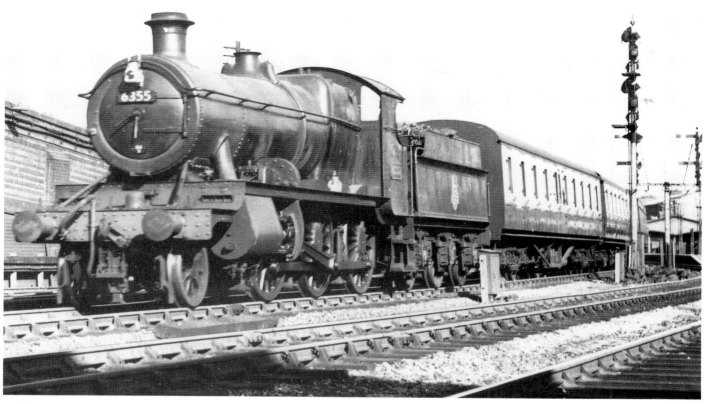

43xx 2-6-0 6355 of Oxley passes Hockley with a local train for Stourbridge Junction in July 1955.

would get a replacement engine from but Joe had disarmed him by solving the problem before it had arisen. The board cleared, Joe whistled up and we started away only to come to a stand at Dr Days Junction as something came off the Marsh ahead of us.

"Are we going to take the banker up to Filton?" I asked him but he shook his head.

"This ole girl'll get up, no trouble…"

In the event it was just as well because as we romped past Stapleton Road, there was no banker in sight. It was probably assisting the train that had stopped us at Dr Days which seemed to having a bad run since we subsequently received plenty of signal checks although 2851 ran pretty cheerfully in between; its rods and wheels revolving merrily away.

Joe said he hoped we'd be sent into Gloucester Eastgate so that he could show the LMS that we could run expresses with any sort of engine but to his disappointment we were crossed over to the Western at Standish Junction; a Midland train being signalled as soon as we had crossed over.

For some reason Joe's attitude to the Midland was sectarian in the extreme and he was far from amused when a Bristol – Leeds express came roaring by, its driver showing us his watch and suggesting that we had held him up at Standish. Joe ignored him and commented to me that the trouble with Midland men was that they had no fathers.

"If we'd had 4086, they wouldn't so much have smelt us."

We stopped at Gloucester South to fill the tank and joined the four road section at Engine Shed Junction just as they were pulling off for a Midland train. The same 5XP and crew stormed by with a shout of 'old iron', prompting Joe to drop the level in a forlorn attempt to keep up

with them as they roared northwards leaving a trail of black smoke.

We made our way onto the North Warwicks, running nicely where we could but guessing that the preceding Grange-hauled trains were having a rough time of it since we were checked time and time again until being brought to a complete stand at Toddington for signals. After quite a wait we got on the move again and it became evident that whatever had been holding us up had finally got a move on as we fairly ratted down the bank to Honeybourne where the sight and sound of the 18.45 Paddington – Hereford as it swept by on the O.W.W reminded me of the livelier side of the Great Western: far removed from the juggernaut-like Saturday afternoon holiday expresses that trudged a very weary road from Bristol northwards.

By the time we arrived at Stratford Joe was more than happy with 2851 and announced he would go up the bank to Wilmcote without the banker, a decision which threw the Station Inspector into a quandry. On the one hand he was happy to keep a banker up his sleeve but on the other he had visions of Joe coming to grief in mid-section and blocking the line. Joe, however, insisted and the Inspector compromised by saying that he would get the banker to give us a shove out of the platform. Joe grumbled to me, complaining that he wanted to see exactly how well 2851 would do on its own.

The Inspector proved to be the more pessimistic of the two since 2851 not only pounded the train up to Wilmcote but managed to accelerate on the climb to Bearley West, giving us an excellent start on the ten mile grind to Earlswood. To my mind it demonstrated what good all-rounders the 28xx's were and they were a certainly a fireman's engine. Whilst I had been firing steadily for much of the trip, I cannot say

I was overworked although the passengers and crew of the multiple-unit in the bay at Henley may have thought otherwise as Joe put on a show for their benefit and stormed through the station, rattling windows and laying a smoke screen as we passed.

By Danzey the gradient began to tell and 2851 started to lose pace on the steeper parts. Joe casually dropped the lever and not only succeeded in checking the decline but, with the 2-8-0 roaring like a set of timpani, so impressed the signalman that he stuck his head out of the box and gave us an admiring nod as we stormed by. We went over the top at Earlswood in great style but instead of shutting off, Joe, who was in his element, merely shortened the cut-off and in the process probably set a speed record for the class.

Not everyone recognised the work we were doing and on passing the box at Shirley the signalman indicated to us that we should get a move on, a sure sign that we had a queue of trains behind us. Anyone, I thought, who knew enough about railways to fill the back of a postage stamp should realise there wasn't much more you could expect from a 2-8-0.

We joined the London main line at Tyseley South and were turned out onto the main line, which pleased Joe since we were just that bit more conspicuous to the crowd of trainspotters who, as ever, were thronging the bridge over the line. I was able to record their expressions of surprise, initially at seeing a 28xx on an express and latterly on realising that 2851 was a stranger from far-off Taunton. A double scoop.

Joe would like to have entertained them further by opening out 2851 as we went by but we had signals against us all the way and eventually came to a stand at Bordesley North, waiting for a platform at Snow Hill. Joe took the opportu-

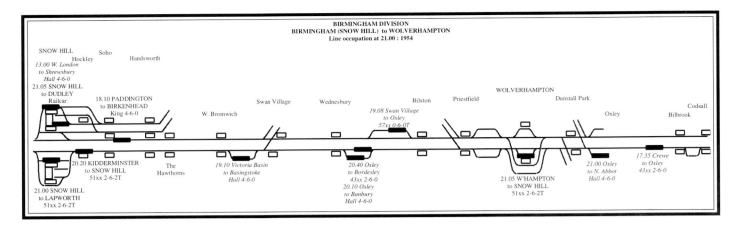

nity to have a look round the engine to see how it had stood up to the trip and when he came back he announced that not only had nothing dropped off but 2851 was as cool as a cucumber.

"You couldn't do this sort of work with one of them Midland class 8's," he added.

The signals cleared and we moved forward on the last leg of the journey, the sharp climb through Moor Street tunnel into Snow Hill. Joe gave an unusually long blast on the whistle to ensure that no-one on Snow Hill missed the sight of a 28xx arriving with an express and with a great grin from ear to ear brought 2851 and its train to a stand in 5 and 6 platforms, its late arrival having nothing to do with the engine.

Where the Great Western was concerned Joe was nothing if not a loyalist and there was nothing he liked better than to get one over the Midland, which he regarded as a rather grubby concern having no business to operating in the West of England.

We worked up to Bristol one day during the holiday rush and came back with the down Cornishman which had a Stafford Road Castle 4-6-0, 4092 'Dunraven Castle', and a heavy thirteen-coach load. The engine was fresh from Swindon works and not only did it look a picture but the Bristol men we relieved described it as a dream.

We were booked to call at Gloucester Eastgate (LMS) station and the closer we got, the more agitated Joe became about putting on the show to impress the Midland.

"Whatever you do, don't let the valves lift in Eastgate…."

"No, Joe."

"And don't take water. We don't want them thinking we have to fill the tank every time a wheel stops turning."

"No, Joe."

Under the gaze of several admiring glances, we rolled down the platform and came to a stand in Eastgate where the platform Inspector and his men immediately busied them-selves with loading and unloading several tons of goods from the front brake. The Inspector clearly had no time to spare for anything but parcels but this did not stop Joe from getting off the engine and trying to impress him with 4092.

"….you won't see many engine like this on your railway."

"What?"

"That engine'll move this lot without a slip."

"What?"

"You won't see an engine like mine for many a day."

The Inspector wiped his brow and turned to Joe telling him that it was just another bloody engine and not much different, so far as he could tell, from the hundreds of engines he saw every day of the week. And now would Joe mind if he got on with the paying business….

Abashed Joe backed off and then, spying a set of men waiting to relieve a train, walked over to them and, from the arm waving and other gesticulations, I could tell that his audience was being given a voluble lesson in the merits of the Great Western Castle class. A Black 5 ran by on a westbound service and, pointing first at one and then the other, it was pretty clear an animated comparison was being given. One of the drivers said something and all of a sudden Joe's arms fell to his side and he walked back to 4092 with a rather glum look on his face.

He didn't say a word to me and I could sense that something had embarrassed him and that it was not a time for conversation. We got the right away and, aided with a discrete pull on the leading sand lever, Joe executed a copybook start without an inch of slip. We hammered by the Great Western shed and blew a long couple of crows as we passed the Midland shed to draw the attention of anyone around to the sight of a real engine. By Churchdown Joe thawed out a little and started to talk again.

"You know them Midland men I was talking to?"

"Yes."

"I went to a lot of trouble to tell them what splendid engines these Castles were."

"Yes."

"Well they let me ramble on – and then they let on they were GW men from the Great Western shed at Gloucester. You'd have thought they'd have told me before I started."

It didn't look to me as though they could have got a word in but I laughed and said nothing.

Not all the trains I worked with Joe were long distance holiday workings although I did have another 28xx run with him that sticks in my mind. Our job was to work the 16.30 Birkenhead to Paddington between Snow Hill and Oxford, travel with the train to Reading and work back with the midnight 'Biscuits' from Reading to Tyseley. The latter was a fast, heavy class D service which loaded up to 68 vehicles and called only at Banbury where it put off and picked up Great Central loads. As a yardstick, the 18.10 Paddington – Birkenhead express with a King was allowed fifty-seven minutes from Banbury to Snow Hill with a stop at Leamington. The Biscuits was allowed sixty-three minutes nonstop and that meant a lot of work for the fireman.

On reaching Reading shed Joe and I reported to the foreman and were allocated 2842 which was not only an unusual type

OXLEY ALLOCATION : 1953						
LOCO CLASS	IN	OUT	LOCO CLASS	IN	OUT	
90069 8F : WD 2-8-0 (1943)		To Shrewsbury 2/53	6861 5MT : GRANGE 4-6-0 (1936)	Ex Pontypool Rd 4/53		
90284 8F : WD 2-8-0 (1943)		To Bristol (SPM) 9/53	6862 5MT : GRANGE 4-6-0 (1936)			
90466 8F : WD 2-8-0 (1943)		To Shrewsbury 9/53	6879 5MT : GRANGE 4-6-0 (1936)			
7238 8F : 72xx 2-8-2T (1934)		To Duffryn 2/53	5684 5MT : 56xx 0-6-2T (1927)			
3802 8F : 28xx 2-8-0 (1938)			6610 5MT : 56xx 0-6-2T (1927)			
3813 8F : 28xx 2-8-0 (1938)			6640 5MT : 56xx 0-6-2T (1927)			
3825 8F : 28xx 2-8-0 (1938)			6645 5MT : 56xx 0-6-2T (1927)			
3860 8F : 28xx 2-8-0 (1938)			9307 4MT : 43xx 2-6-0 (1932)	Ex Reading 5/53		
3863 8F : 28xx 2-8-0 (1938)			9312 4MT : 43xx 2-6-0 (1932)			
3865 8F : 28xx 2-8-0 (1938)	Ex Shrewsbury 11/53		9314 4MT : 43xx 2-6-0 (1932)			
2830 8F : 28xx 2-8-0 (1903)			9317 4MT : 43xx 2-6-0 (1932)	Ex Oxford 5/53		
2833 8F : 28xx 2-8-0 (1903)			9318 4MT : 43xx 2-6-0 (1932)	Ex Reading 5/53		
2841 8F : 28xx 2-8-0 (1903)	Ex Shrewsbury 12/53		5300 4MT : 43xx 2-6-0 (1911)		w/d 1/53	
2854 8F : 28xx 2-8-0 (1903)			5309 4MT : 43xx 2-6-0 (1911)		w/d 1/53	
2882 8F : 28xx 2-8-0 (1903)			5336 4MT : 43xx 2-6-0 (1911)	Ex Gloucester 7/53		
3016 7F : R.O.D. 2-8-0 (1917)			5341 4MT : 43xx 2-6-0 (1911)			
3028 7F : R.O.D. 2-8-0 (1917)	Ex Stourbridge 9/53		5375 4MT : 43xx 2-6-0 (1911)	Ex Reading 2/53		
3029 7F : R.O.D. 2-8-0 (1917)	Ex Worcester 1953		5378 4MT : 43xx 2-6-0 (1911)	Ex Llanelly 3/53		
3031 7F : R.O.D. 2-8-0 (1917)	Ex Worcester 2/53		5381 4MT : 43xx 2-6-0 (1911)	Ex Didcot 3/53		
3047 7F : R.O.D. 2-8-0 (1917)		w/d 6/53	5390 4MT : 43xx 2-6-0 (1911)			
6964 5MT : MOD-HALL 4-6-0 (1944)	Ex Wolverhampton 10/53	To Wolverhampton 11/53	5391 4MT : 43xx 2-6-0 (1911)			
6975 5MT : MOD-HALL 4-6-0 (1944)			6302 4MT : 43xx 2-6-0 (1911)	Ex Reading 4/53	To Reading 5/53	
7915 5MT : MOD-HALL 4-6-0 (1944)			6335 4MT : 43xx 2-6-0 (1911)			
7811 5MT : MANOR 4-6-0 (1938)		To Shrewsbury 1/53	6338 4MT : 43xx 2-6-0 (1911)	Ex Reading 4/53	To Reading 5/53	
7818 5MT : MANOR 4-6-0 (1938)		To Tyseley 3/53	6361 4MT : 43xx 2-6-0 (1911)		To Pontypool Rd 4/53	
4918 5MT : HALL 4-6-0 (1928)	Ex Wolverhampton 6/53		6363 4MT : 43xx 2-6-0 (1911)		To Bristol (SPM) 4/53	
4919 5MT : HALL 4-6-0 (1928)			6396 4MT : 43xx 2-6-0 (1911)	Ex Worcester 2/53	To Worcester 6/53	
4924 5MT : HALL 4-6-0 (1928)			8417 4F : 94XX 0-6-0T (1948)			
4926 5MT : HALL 4-6-0 (1928)			8428 4F : 94XX 0-6-0T (1948)			
4934 5MT : HALL 4-6-0 (1928)	Ex Swindon 3/53	To Tyseley 6/53	9408 4F : 94XX 0-6-0T (1948)			
4943 5MT : HALL 4-6-0 (1928)		To Old Oak C. 7/53	3744 3F : 57xx 0-6-0T (1933)			
4950 5MT : HALL 4-6-0 (1928)		To Laira 5/53	3745 3F : 57xx 0-6-0T (1933)			
4955 5MT : HALL 4-6-0 (1928)			3792 3F : 57xx 0-6-0T (1933)		To Wolverhampton 5/53	
4959 5MT : HALL 4-6-0 (1928)			3793 3F : 57xx 0-6-0T (1933)		To Wolverhampton 5/53	
5944 5MT : HALL 4-6-0 (1928)	Ex Wolverhampton 1/53		8798 3F : 57xx 0-6-0T (1933)		To Wolverhampton 5/53	
5945 5MT : HALL 4-6-0 (1928)			9714 3F : 57xx 0-6-0T (1933)			
5966 5MT : HALL 4-6-0 (1928)			9715 3F : 57xx 0-6-0T (1933)			
5972 5MT : HALL 4-6-0 (1928)			9730 3F : 57xx 0-6-0T (1933)			
5991 5MT : HALL 4-6-0 (1928)			9739 3F : 57xx 0-6-0T (1933)			
5995 5MT : HALL 4-6-0 (1928)			9748 3F : 57xx 0-6-0T (1933)			
6920 5MT : HALL 4-6-0 (1928)		To Oxford 4/53	9752 3F : 57xx 0-6-0T (1933)			
6924 5MT : HALL 4-6-0 (1928)	Ex Gloucester 3/53		9768 3F : 57xx 0-6-0T (1933)			
6926 5MT : HALL 4-6-0 (1928)	Ex Severn T. Jcn 3/53		9769 3F : 57xx 0-6-0T (1933)			
6942 5MT : HALL 4-6-0 (1928)			9748 3F : 57xx 0-6-0T (1929)			
6951 5MT : HALL 4-6-0 (1928)	Ex Worcester 4/53	To Canton 8/53	7759 3F : 57xx 0-6-0T (1929)			
6854 5MT : GRANGE 4-6-0 (1936)			7796 3F : 57xx 0-6-0T (1929)			
6856 5MT : GRANGE 4-6-0 (1936)			7797 3F : 57xx 0-6-0T (1929)			

On loan to Tyseley for the peak of the summer season, 5921 'Bingley Hall' of Newport (Ebbw Junction) approaches Leamington with a relief to the 11.50 Bournemouth - Birmingham (Moor Street) in 1955. The fascination lies in the carriage stock which includes concertinas and a pair of clerestories.

of engine for an express goods but one that I had seen on the scrap road at Swindon only a few weeks earlier. I asked the foreman if he had got the right number but in return I got a sort of look that was intended to keep firemen in their place: seen and not heard.

It was as well I didn't try to be clever with him for, sure enough, the engine waiting for us was indeed 2842 which I had not only marked off as being withdrawn but had photographed on the Swindon dump. When I had last seen it, 2842 had been in a wretched state and after years of work based at Newport (Ebbw Junction) there seemed no doubt that its days had come to an end. Clearly it was one of the few engines to have been granted a last minute reprieve and before being sent to Reading shed it had been given an intermediate repair with no expense spared. The smokebox shone, the buffer beam was bright red and looking like new, the firebox backplate had been neatly painted whilst the cab floorboards were white and new. Ebbw Junction would never have recognised it as the engine they sent for scrap.

The work done at Swindon was far more than skin deep and in spite of the fact the 2-8-0 was working a Hall diagram, 2842 ran like a sewing machine and gave me, without any doubt, my best run on the Biscuits.

Now and again I would be called upon to come off the main line jobs and cover for summer holiday leave in the local links, working with 51xx 2-6-2T's on the suburban workings from Snow Hill to Leamington, Stratford, Kidderminster and Wellington. It was very busy work but lacked the advantages of overtime since on passenger trains you almost always knew when you were going to sign off. I felt sorry for the regular firemen in the local links since most of them were married and had a lean time with no mileage or overtime payments.

Each 2-6-2T was allocated to two sets of men and kept in spotless condition. The tools were always kept safely locked up and preparing them was a piece of cake except for the leading sandboxes which were very difficult to fill and generally overlooked by the regular men.

The Snow Hill suburban service was one of the first in the country to be fully dieselised with multiple-units taking over a number of workings from June 1957. It was not an immediate success since the units frequently failed in service – there were two main line failures in the first day of operation: something unknown with the 51xx's – with a 2-6-2T being used in lieu. Since the diesel timings included a tightening of point to point running times, the steam substitutes had a hard time of it although one 51xx driver claimed to have beaten the new schedules until it was pointed out that he had missed a station.

If there was anything good to be said on behalf of the diesels it was the fact that they were single manned and this ensured that I remained on main line steam work, boxing the compass rather than shuttling up and down between Snow Hill and Leamington. Not all my colleagues, it has to be said, shared this point of view.

The most remote part of the world Tyseley men worked to was the Cambrian system which was so distant the locals didn't even speak English whilst the signalling was done by single line tokens which had to be collected and delivered by the fireman at speed. Some people got it off to a fine art but I, being used to main line signalling, never really mastered it and the dual problems of keeping a rough engine in steam and dealing with the tokens at the same time did not add up to my idea of a good day out.

Nonetheless when my turn came I had to accept it and in September 1960 I was marked to accompany 'Biscuit' Hughes on the 07.55

Snow Hill to Aberystwyth which we worked as far as Machynlleth. There was quite a healthy demand by holiday makers for the Cambrian Coast and the Western responded by running two expresses on summer Saturdays; the 07.55 running through to Aberystwyth followed by the 08.05 which ran to Barmouth. This made quite a change from the ordinary weekday service where passengers had to rise early for the 06.00 ex Snow Hill which still reached the coast at the same time as the Saturday through trains.

It might be thought that having mastered the King class on the London expresses I would take any other engine on my stride but when I found that we had been given 2-6-0 6338 for the Aberystwyth job, I was far from happy. Quite apart from the fact that 6338 was overdue for shopping and in a filthy external condition, I had never found the 43xx's to be easy engines to fire and always experienced the greatest difficulty in maintaining sufficient steam for anything but the lightest of jobs. 6338 was a Severn Tunnel Junction engine caught at Tyseley between workings and I suppose the foreman thought it a good move to utilise it whilst he had the opportunity.

We picked up our seven coach train – quite a respectable load for a 43xx – in Tyseley carriage sidings, ran to Snow Hill and backed into No.4 bay platform where we made ourselves ready for the run ahead.

"Commit this lot to memory," said Biscuit handing me a scroll which resembled something from a long forgotten classical period. I unravelled it to find the names of every station, signalbox, passing point and taxi rank between Birmingham and Aberystwyth. I pointed to a couple of them.

"How are you supposed to pronounce this...and this?"

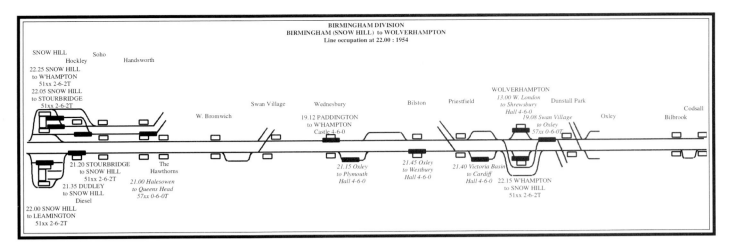

"Caersws," Biscuit replied, "and Llanbrynmair."

If they want me to learn the road, I told him, they should do it in English and carefully returned his scroll to his bag.

Whilst waiting for our passengers to board I did what I could to get the fire into shape and we got to Wolverhampton without too much trouble although the engine was extremely rough riding. We then had a long run of about fifty miles to Welshpool which developed into a nightmare as all 6338's energies seem to be aimed at rocking the engine violently from side to side whilst steam was in short supply. The blower and fireirons all worked overtime.

Biscuit said very little but his frequent anxious glances at the pressure gauge and water level whilst going up the bank from Sutton Bridge Junction to Westbury spoke volumes and tended to put me off my stroke. Coming downhill into Welshpool I managed to get some water in the boiler but I was very concerned about Talerddig bank which starts two miles west of Welshpool and lasts for no less than twenty-five miles, the worst section being four miles at 1 in 162 between Pontdolgoch and Carno.

We left Welshpool and, with Biscuit looking more and more anxious, I was keeping a more than normally careful watch on the gauge glass. I poked my head out to drop the staff off at Forden and, thinking I had time to check the injector before sticking my head out again to collect the token for the next section, jumped to the middle of the footplate and back again. I was too late and I had to compound Biscuit's troubles by shouting to him to stop the train, telling him why and then walking back down the train to retrieve the staff.

Most drivers would have considered ladling me into the firebox but Biscuit, who was a good natured soul most of the time, thought I had suffered enough at the hands of the passengers. As I walked back, every window opened and every head seemed to know why we had stopped and whose fault it was. I doubt if there was a railwayman amongst them, yet from the shouted advice they seemed to know a great deal about token working.

Back on the footplate it occurred to me that I could have chosen a better spot to stop the train since we were at the very foot of the climb to Talerddig and had lost the opportunity to take a run at it. To make things worse 6338 started to go off the boil – not that it had been particularly hot at any stage in the journey – and no matter how I slaved to reverse things, the needle refused to rise and eventually we limped into Carno, well behind time with only 120lb of steam on the clock.

The signalman took the staff off me with some anxiety. The big event of the day was the passing of the Cambrian Coast Express, which we were supposed to cross at Talerddig, and we had been in danger of stopping it. From the time taken climbing the bank, Carno had guessed we were in trouble and decided to keep us with him until the up Cambrian had gone through. Perspiring freely, I was relieved to be free to regain my breath and glad of the opportunity to do something with 6338 before we tackled the final two miles of the climb.

Perversely, 6338 decided to behave itself whilst we were standing and in practically no time I had the water level up the gauge glass and the needle on the red mark. I wondered, rather pessimistically, if it would remain like that for the rest of the climb to the summit.

It was clear that the fireman on the up Cambrian was having a better time of things than I was and after a jangle of bell codes in the signalbox, the express came storming through behind a very picturesque Manor 4-6-0 which, from the plume of steam at its valves, had clearly not suffered any difficulties on the exceptionally cruel grind from Machynlleth to Talerddig.

After the dust had settled we were given the staff and set off again, the needle and water falling as we picked up speed. It was a rough struggle but thanks to the breather at Carno, we eventually limped into Machynlleth and handed over the train, without any reluctance, to a set of Aberystwyth boys.

After the pounding we had had, Biscuit, who had a strong presbyterian element to his character, was half afraid I might wander off into the town and not return so he suggested that we had our sandwiches on the platform seat whilst we waited for our return working, the 12.30 Aberystwyth – Snow Hill.

"Sit there," he said, "and I'll get you a drink."

I sat and nursed a vision of a pint of whatever they drank in the Welsh mountains and five minutes later he returned, presenting me with a bottle of milk.

"That'll do you more good than the local demon drink. You don't want any of that sort of thing, do you?"

"No, Mr Hughes," I responded, just short of sarcasm, "that's what I don't want…"

On time, our train ran in behind another 43xx, 5369 of Tyseley, although any similarly between it and 6338 was masked by the condition of 5369, which was excellent, and the fact

LOCO	CLASS	IN	OUT	LOCO	CLASS	IN	OUT
3802	8F : 28xx 2-8-0 (1938)			9312	4MT : 43xx 2-6-0 (1932)		To Wolverhampton 8/54
3813	8F : 28xx 2-8-0 (1938)			9314	4MT : 43xx 2-6-0 (1932)		
3825	8F : 28xx 2-8-0 (1938)			9316	4MT : 43xx 2-6-0 (1932)	Ex Oxford 6/54	
3860	8F : 28xx 2-8-0 (1938)			9317	4MT : 43xx 2-6-0 (1932)		
3861	8F : 28xx 2-8-0 (1938)	Ex Stourbridge 9/54		9318	4MT : 43xx 2-6-0 (1932)		To Stourbridge 9/54
3863	8F : 28xx 2-8-0 (1938)			5312	4MT : 43xx 2-6-0 (1911)	Ex Worcester 5/54	
3865	8F : 28xx 2-8-0 (1938)			5336	4MT : 43xx 2-6-0 (1911)		
2819	8F : 28xx 2-8-0 (1903)	Ex Didcot 9/54		5341	4MT : 43xx 2-6-0 (1911)		
2830	8F : 28xx 2-8-0 (1903)			5375	4MT : 43xx 2-6-0 (1911)		
2833	8F : 28xx 2-8-0 (1903)			5378	4MT : 43xx 2-6-0 (1911)		
2841	8F : 28xx 2-8-0 (1903)			5381	4MT : 43xx 2-6-0 (1911)		
2854	8F : 28xx 2-8-0 (1903)			5390	4MT : 43xx 2-6-0 (1911)		
2882	8F : 28xx 2-8-0 (1903)			5391	4MT : 43xx 2-6-0 (1911)		To Wolverhampton 6/54
3016	7F : R.O.D. 2-8-0 (1917)			6324	4MT : 43xx 2-6-0 (1911)	Ex Worcester 2/54	
3028	7F : R.O.D. 2-8-0 (1917)			6335	4MT : 43xx 2-6-0 (1911)		
3029	7F : R.O.D. 2-8-0 (1917)			6355	4MT : 43xx 2-6-0 (1911)		
3031	7F : R.O.D. 2-8-0 (1917)			6355	4MT : 43xx 2-6-0 (1911)	Ex Gloucester 1/54	
6975	5MT : MOD-HALL 4-6-0 (1944)		To Wolverhampton 8/54	6362	4MT : 43xx 2-6-0 (1911)	Ex Hereford 6/54	To Croes Newydd 9/54
7915	5MT : MOD-HALL 4-6-0 (1944)			6367	4MT : 43xx 2-6-0 (1911)	Ex Chester 6/54	To Chester 7/54
4918	5MT : HALL 4-6-0 (1928)			8417	4F : 94XX 0-6-0T (1948)		
4919	5MT : HALL 4-6-0 (1928)			8428	4F : 94XX 0-6-0T (1948)		
4924	5MT : HALL 4-6-0 (1928)			8449	4F : 94XX 0-6-0T (1948)	New 9/54	
4926	5MT : HALL 4-6-0 (1928)		To Wolverhampton 8/54	9408	4F : 94XX 0-6-0T (1948)		
4955	5MT : HALL 4-6-0 (1928)			3694	3F : 57xx 0-6-0T (1933)		To Banbury 3/54
4959	5MT : HALL 4-6-0 (1928)			3694	3F : 57xx 0-6-0T (1933)	Ex Banbury 1/54	
4963	5MT : HALL 4-6-0 (1928)	Ex Laira 9/54		3744	3F : 57xx 0-6-0T (1933)		To Wellington 3/54
4966	5MT : HALL 4-6-0 (1928)	Ex Laira 9/54		3745	3F : 57xx 0-6-0T (1933)		To Stourbridge 4/54
5944	5MT : HALL 4-6-0 (1928)			9714	3F : 57xx 0-6-0T (1933)		To Neyland 5/54
5945	5MT : HALL 4-6-0 (1928)		To Banbury 7/54	9715	3F : 57xx 0-6-0T (1933)		
5945	5MT : HALL 4-6-0 (1928)	Ex Banbury 9/54		9730	3F : 57xx 0-6-0T (1933)		To Pontypool Rd 4/54
5966	5MT : HALL 4-6-0 (1928)			9739	3F : 57xx 0-6-0T (1933)		
5972	5MT : HALL 4-6-0 (1928)		To Truro 7/54	9747	3F : 57xx 0-6-0T (1933)		To Cathays 2/54
5991	5MT : HALL 4-6-0 (1928)			9752	3F : 57xx 0-6-0T (1933)		
5995	5MT : HALL 4-6-0 (1928)			9768	3F : 57xx 0-6-0T (1933)		
6924	5MT : HALL 4-6-0 (1928)			9769	3F : 57xx 0-6-0T (1933)		To Cardiff (E. Dck) 2/54
6926	5MT : HALL 4-6-0 (1928)			5748	3F : 57xx 0-6-0T (1933)		To Chester 2/54
6942	5MT : HALL 4-6-0 (1928)			5748	3F : 57xx 0-6-0T (1929)	Ex Chester 3/54	To Neyland 5/54
6839	5MT : GRANGE 4-6-0 (1936)	Ex Banbury 4/54		7759	3F : 57xx 0-6-0T (1929)		
6854	5MT : GRANGE 4-6-0 (1936)			7796	3F : 57xx 0-6-0T (1929)		To Pontypool Rd 4/54
6856	5MT : GRANGE 4-6-0 (1936)			7797	3F : 57xx 0-6-0T (1929)		To Shrewsbury 2/54
6861	5MT : GRANGE 4-6-0 (1936)			7797	3F : 57xx 0-6-0T (1929)	Ex Shrewsbury 9/54	
6862	5MT : GRANGE 4-6-0 (1936)			13034	0F : 350hp 0-6-0	New 1/54	
6879	5MT : GRANGE 4-6-0 (1936)			13035	0F : 350hp 0-6-0	New 1/54	
5684	5MT : 56xx 0-6-2T (1927)			13036	0F : 350hp 0-6-0	New 1/54	
6610	5MT : 56xx 0-6-2T (1927)			13037	0F : 350hp 0-6-0	New 1/54	
6640	5MT : 56xx 0-6-2T (1927)			13038	0F : 350hp 0-6-0	New 1/54	
6645	5MT : 56xx 0-6-2T (1927)			13039	0F : 350hp 0-6-0	New 3/54	
9307	4MT : 43xx 2-6-0 (1932)						

Tyseley South with the North Warwickshire line running in on the right and the Banbury/Paddington main line curving round to the left. 51xx 2-6-2T 5156 takes the down relief line with a local from Stratford-upon-Avon in July 1956, a year before diesel multiple units started to take over the suburban workings. 5156 moved to Hereford in October 1957.

most of the route was downhill. We cruised down to Welshpool where an unbalanced 43xx was waiting to double-head us as far as Wolverhampton. This meant that he was able to make the running while I still had to take care of the tokens and Biscuit, anxious to avoid a repetition of the morning's episode, did the worst thing imaginable by going up to the Stafford Road men on the leading engine.

"Take it easy through the staff stations. My mate's not used to them."

Both men looked back at me on 5369 and grinned broadly. I wished Biscuit would learn when to keep quiet.

Needless to say the Wolverhampton men made sure I had to deliver and collect each token at full tilt whilst Biscuit reminded me several times that the honour of Tyseley was in my hands. I managed to collect and release them all, exactly how I cannot recall, but Biscuit was happy and both he and the Wolverhampton men celebrated by storming up the main line as though going for a record. What sort of impression we made on the bystanders at Wellington as we pounded through, two 43xx's going hell for leather, I cannot imagine but I wished I'd been on the platform to take a photograph of it. Neither could I begin to estimate the speed we did coming down Shifnal bank; both engines were flying all over the place and watching the leading engine, I wondered what sort of ride the Wolverhampton crew were getting. Still, they set the pace and we did nothing to hinder them and the final stage of the run from Wolverhampton to Snow Hill seemed very quiet after they had left us on our own.

Perhaps the most unlikely trip I participated in was a passenger special from Wigan (NW) to Windsor which came onto the Great Western at Leamington and ran via Oxford and Reading. The details of how we came to get the job have been lost with time but normally it would have gone to Leamington shed since work was generally allocated to the point of origin. Influencing factors included the fact that at the time, May 1961, Leamington had no suitable engines and since a 4-6-0 had to be provided by Tyseley, the crew concerned might just as well work the train. To kill any final objections that Leamington may have had about work being stolen from them, the list clerk even managed to find a Tyseley driver, Frank Williams, who signed the road thus saving Slough the expense and trouble of providing a pilotman.

Frank had a reputation as a hard-hitter and when I signed on I was relieved to be given an engine that would both stand the pace and allow me to keep up with him. We were given 5927 'Guild Hall' which had just been received from Swindon having had a general overhaul.

The run light to Leamington gave me a chance to confirm that 5927 was equal to anything Frank could throw at it and we took over our seven coach special from a Black 5 4-6-0 on the LMS goods line which ran alongside Leamington Spa General.

The load was much lighter than I had anticipated and even though we were booked non-stop I had no trouble either with the engine or keeping up with Frank. The interest in the trip lay in seeing strange places for, whilst I knew the road to London via Bicester and to Reading via Oxford like the back of my hand, I was new to the stretch in between.

We left the main line at Slough Curve and a few minutes later eased into what must have been the neatest and tidiest station on the system. Our stock was pulled off us by the Windsor pilot and we made our way light to Slough loco, turning en route on the angle.

I prepared 5927 for the return journey, not that there was much to do since, in spite of the distance we had covered, the fire was clean and in good shape. With over five hours to kill before heading back, Frank did not particularly want to spend the day in Slough – although I was quite happy to watch trains there – and persuaded the foreman to let us run back to Windsor and sit on the stock until it was time to leave. The foreman was not too happy about it at first but Frank persisted.

"All right. But," and the Foreman pointed a stern finger at us. "If you make any smoke – any smoke – at Windsor….."

Frank assured him we wouldn't.

"'They'll' come and take you over to the castle – and that will be the last anyone'll see of you."

I wasn't sure whether he was joking or not and in fact I would have preferred to have remained at Slough. Keeping an engine quiet for five hours and then expecting it to do a long trip was not going to be easy but Frank was the boss. I put a few shovelfuls on the back end before we came off the loco and was relieved to find that the smoke had cleared by the time we reached Windsor. The last thing I wanted was to be hauled away by 'Them'.

After walking around Windsor for a couple of hours – when I could have been watching traffic on the main line – we returned to the station and I started to get 5927 ready for the trip. Much to my surprise there was very little to do. There was plenty of steam on the clock, enough fire to get us out of the danger zone and it was sufficient, a few minutes before starting, to open the damper and level the coal along the bars with the pricker. The main firing I left until we were approaching the main line and by the time Frank was ready to crack the whip I had all the fire we needed.

The run back to Leamington was as uneventful as the up trip had been and the main point of interest took place when we handed the train over to the LM since there was no direct connection and we had to run through the down

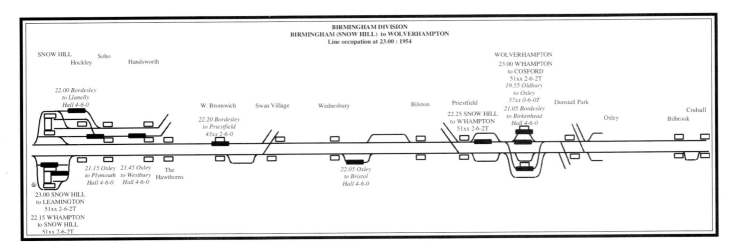

BIRMINGHAM DIVISION
BIRMINGHAM (SNOW HILL) to WOLVERHAMPTON
Line occupation at 23.00 : 1954

middle, set back onto the up main and then draw forward onto the goods line where we handed over to another Black 5. The passengers must have wondered where we were taking them. (So did I since it appeared the timing office had forgotten that the train could quite easily have been routed via Wellington and Crewe).

For years the Bicester line had featured in the performance section of the railway press as a high speed route but the emphasis had generally been on feats on haulage rather than maximum speeds and a number of drivers at Tyseley thought we ought to try and give the LNER – which seemed to hold all the laurels – a run for its money.

This desire for fame increased as the opportunity to produce something exceptional from a steam engine diminished and in the summer of 1963 Eric Wynne – a driver who could really straighten curves out – and myself decided to have a once and for all crack at a record. Unfortunately, as it turned out, we had left it too late in the day but at least we had declared an intention to hit the headlines.

The train, a Saturday Margate working, was an unlikely one but our decision was taken at Snow Hill as we saw the engine heading towards us. It was none other than 7018 'Drysllwyn Castle', the Castle responsible for a number of records on the Bristolian during its stay at Bath Road between July 1956 and August 1960.

We climbed aboard and discussed our strategy, Winnie deciding that he would go for one hundred miles per hour through Bicester. I rubbed my hands in anticipation and got the engine good and hot.

We set off and by the time we had got to Olton we were having serious doubts. 7018 was steaming well enough but its riding was terrible – and a rough riding Castle is a very rough engine indeed. It bucked all over the place and giving us a pretty nerve racking ride on first valve, it was soon mutually agreed that any records would have to

wait for another day and another engine.

If we failed to get into the record books we did at least impress the people standing on Princes Risborough platform as we stormed the bank from Ashendon to Saunderton. "If it won't run downhill," Winnie said lengthening the cut off as we hit the foot of the bank, "By golly it'll have to run uphill."

And run we did, scattering the crowds and making the most glorious noise as we thundered through the station.

Most of the summer workings were highly enjoyable events, even if the record books remained unchanged, but there were a couple of seasonal workings I used to try and avoid like the plague. One of these was the Sunday 07.10 'Worcester Fisherman' Snow Hill to Worcester via Shirley, Stratford and Honeybourne and the 17.50 return. The trains were pleasant enough but the interminable wait at Worcester was enough to drive one to distraction. Fortunately I only fell for the job once, which was quite enough, and not only did I have to kick my heels aimlessly in Worcester but it rained all day. The anglers were delighted, it was just the weather they had been praying for, but from my point of view it was too dark for photography, to wet to wander round the town and I had never been so bored with a job.

The Fisherman was not, by a short hair, the worst summer job we had. That accolade went to the 'Stratford Mop' which was a late night local from Stratford to Birmingham used by returning revellers who had been attending the annual Mop Fair.

Most of the respectable visitors returned on the booked evening stopping trains and the Mop ran for the benefit of the hard cases who had spent the day drinking their way through every pub in the town, the working being booked to leave shortly after closing time.

On the Mop Day of 1959 Fred Smith and I were given 7821 'Ditcheat Manor', a Tyseley engine on the point of being transferred to Newton Abbot, and we took an eight coach set down to Long Marston, turned on Honeybourne Angle and rejoined the stock, leaving to reach Stratford at about 22.00.

By the time last orders had been called in the town's pubs, the last thing any of our liquid assets had was a sense of time – if indeed they had any senses left at all – and they would roll up to the station in dribs and drabs, determined to keep the revelling spirit alive as long as a semblance of consciousness remained.

Departure time came and went. Every time I though we were ready to leave another pair of drinkers would appear on the horizon and Stratford, anxious not to have them for the night, would hold us back.

With the inside of the train resembling one of Falstaff's louder bawdy houses and the two policemen assigned to the service having trouble keeping law and order, it was decided half an hour after we should have departed that it was time to go and finally we got the right away.

We pulled out of the station only to come to a stand at the East box with a communication cord pulled. I walked back, conferred with the guard, reset the butterfly and restarted the train, coming to

OXLEY ALLOCATION : 1955						
LOCO	CLASS	IN	OUT	LOCO	CLASS	IN	OUT
7247	8F : 72xx 2-8-2T (1934)	Ex Ebbw Jcn 2/55		6856	5MT : GRANGE 4-6-0 (1936)		
3802	8F : 28xx 2-8-0 (1938)			6861	5MT : GRANGE 4-6-0 (1936)		To Tyseley 11/55
3813	8F : 28xx 2-8-0 (1938)			6862	5MT : GRANGE 4-6-0 (1936)		To Oxford 3/55
3825	8F : 28xx 2-8-0 (1938)		To Stourbridge 1/55	6864	5MT : GRANGE 4-6-0 (1936)	Ex Reading 2/55	To Oxford 3/55
3837	8F : 28xx 2-8-0 (1938)	Ex Didcot 5/55		6879	5MT : GRANGE 4-6-0 (1936)		
3845	8F : 28xx 2-8-0 (1938)	Ex Didcot 5/55		5684	5MT : 56xx 0-6-2T (1927)		
3860	8F : 28xx 2-8-0 (1938)			6610	5MT : 56xx 0-6-2T (1927)		
3861	8F : 28xx 2-8-0 (1938)			6640	5MT : 56xx 0-6-2T (1927)		
3863	8F : 28xx 2-8-0 (1938)			6645	5MT : 56xx 0-6-2T (1927)		
3865	8F : 28xx 2-8-0 (1938)			9307	4MT : 43xx 2-6-0 (1932)		
2819	8F : 28xx 2-8-0 (1903)			9314	4MT : 43xx 2-6-0 (1932)		
2830	8F : 28xx 2-8-0 (1903)			9316	4MT : 43xx 2-6-0 (1932)		To Worcester 1/55
2833	8F : 28xx 2-8-0 (1903)			9317	4MT : 43xx 2-6-0 (1932)		
2841	8F : 28xx 2-8-0 (1903)			5312	4MT : 43xx 2-6-0 (1911)		
2854	8F : 28xx 2-8-0 (1903)			5313	4MT : 43xx 2-6-0 (1911)	Ex Stourbridge 5/55	
2882	8F : 28xx 2-8-0 (1903)		To Stourbridge 1/55	5325	4MT : 43xx 2-6-0 (1911)	Ex Taunton 7/55	
3016	7F : R.O.D. 2-8-0 (1917)			5336	4MT : 43xx 2-6-0 (1911)		
3028	7F : R.O.D. 2-8-0 (1917)			5341	4MT : 43xx 2-6-0 (1911)		
3029	7F : R.O.D. 2-8-0 (1917)			5375	4MT : 43xx 2-6-0 (1911)		
3031	7F : R.O.D. 2-8-0 (1917)			5378	4MT : 43xx 2-6-0 (1911)		
6975	5MT : MOD-HALL 4-6-0 (1944)	Ex Wolverhampton 9/55		5381	4MT : 43xx 2-6-0 (1911)		
7915	5MT : MOD-HALL 4-6-0 (1944)			5391	4MT : 43xx 2-6-0 (1911)	Ex Wolverhampton 10/55	
4918	5MT : HALL 4-6-0 (1928)		To Landore 7/55	6324	4MT : 43xx 2-6-0 (1911)		
4919	5MT : HALL 4-6-0 (1928)			6335	4MT : 43xx 2-6-0 (1911)		
4924	5MT : HALL 4-6-0 (1928)		To Landore 7/55	6365	4MT : 43xx 2-6-0 (1911)	Ex Gloucester 5/55	To Gloucester 6/55
4955	5MT : HALL 4-6-0 (1928)		To Exeter 7/55	7305	4MT : 43xx 2-6-0 (1911)	Ex Croes Newydd 3/55	
4959	5MT : HALL 4-6-0 (1928)		To Bristol (BR) 5/55	8417	4F : 94XX 0-6-0T (1948)		
4963	5MT : HALL 4-6-0 (1928)			8428	4F : 94XX 0-6-0T (1948)		
4965	5MT : HALL 4-6-0 (1928)	Ex Laira 9/55		8449	4F : 94XX 0-6-0T (1948)		
4966	5MT : HALL 4-6-0 (1928)			9408	4F : 94XX 0-6-0T (1948)		
4986	5MT : HALL 4-6-0 (1928)	Ex Old Oak C. 3/55		9715	3F : 57xx 0-6-0T (1933)		
4997	5MT : HALL 4-6-0 (1928)	Ex Wolverhampton 9/55		9739	3F : 57xx 0-6-0T (1933)		
5900	5MT : HALL 4-6-0 (1928)	Ex Tyseley 11/55		9752	3F : 57xx 0-6-0T (1933)		
5944	5MT : HALL 4-6-0 (1928)			9768	3F : 57xx 0-6-0T (1933)		
5945	5MT : HALL 4-6-0 (1928)		To Oxford 5/55	7759	3F : 57xx 0-6-0T (1929)		
5966	5MT : HALL 4-6-0 (1928)		To Oxford 5/55	7797	3F : 57xx 0-6-0T (1929)		
5991	5MT : HALL 4-6-0 (1928)			13034	0F : 350hp 0-6-0		
5995	5MT : HALL 4-6-0 (1928)			13035	0F : 350hp 0-6-0		
6907	5MT : HALL 4-6-0 (1928)	Ex Laira 9/55		13036	0F : 350hp 0-6-0		
6924	5MT : HALL 4-6-0 (1928)		To Oxford 5/55	13037	0F : 350hp 0-6-0		
6925	5MT : HALL 4-6-0 (1928)	Ex Laira 9/55		13038	0F : 350hp 0-6-0		
6926	5MT : HALL 4-6-0 (1928)			13039	0F : 350hp 0-6-0		
6934	5MT : HALL 4-6-0 (1928)	Ex Laira 9/55		13191	0F : 350hp 0-6-0	New 11/55	
6942	5MT : HALL 4-6-0 (1928)		To Shrewsbury 8/55				
6839	5MT : GRANGE 4-6-0 (1936)						
6854	5MT : GRANGE 4-6-0 (1936)		To Oxford 3/55				

Firing continuously from Birmingham to Taunton may have entitled the author to claim a record for distance at Tyseley especially as the service concerned was routed via Stourbridge and Worcester. The author recorded the occasion by leaving the cab at Bristol on the outward journey to take a photograph of his engine, Modified Hall 4-6-0 7929 'Wyke Hall', which was in a better condition than appearances suggest.

a halt after a train length because of another cord being pulled. I repeated the process of resetting but when it happened a third time we decided that there had to be a better way of working the train. So far we had travelled about three hundred yards and I calculated I was going to have to reset the vacuum four hundred and forty times before we got to Snow Hill, if we ever did.

The matter was not helped by the guard and one of the policemen barricading themselves into a brake compartment and in the end I decided to break all the rules and run non-vacuum which was the only way we were going to get to Birmingham. I extricated the guard, told him to complete the journey on the engine, and together we pulled all the carriage strings and disconnected the vacuum pipes between the tender and first coach.

"We'll be moving in a minute." I assured the East signalman on the telephone.

"You bloody Birmingham people shouldn't be allowed into Stratford…."

There was no arguing with that and I returned to the engine to find the guard and his police escorts crowding the footplate. Fred grumbled a little but let them stay so long as they kept out of the way.

We got to Henley in Arden without further difficulty to be treated to the spectacle of a well lubricated passenger alighting from the train, climbing the home signal and giving us an unre-

hearsed aria, quite the equal for tunelessness to anything Schoenberg could have come up with sober. We decided to leave well alone and started away only for his song to change to a chant of "Wait for me, wait for me…."

As the journey proceeded the noise from the train gradually diminished, the police presence at most of the intermediate stations having had a sobering effect, and eventually we ran into Snow Hill where the first thing I did was to recouple the vacuum pipes so that everything would look in order when the shunter arrived. Fred tried to create a vacuum but could only manage a couple of inches although it, along with the guards handbrake, was sufficient to hold the stock whilst we ran round to take it back to Tyseley.

After coupling up I walked the length of the train to reset the butterflies to allow Fred to get the right amount of vacuum before we left and I discovered that every coach had had its cord pulled. It seemed that we had made the

OXLEY ALLOCATION : 1956					
LOCO CLASS	IN	OUT	LOCO CLASS	IN	OUT
7247 8F : 72xx 2-8-2T (1934)			6610 5MT : 56xx 0-6-2T (1927)		
3802 8F : 28xx 2-8-0 (1938)			6640 5MT : 56xx 0-6-2T (1927)		
3813 8F : 28xx 2-8-0 (1938)			6645 5MT : 56xx 0-6-2T (1927)		
3837 8F : 28xx 2-8-0 (1938)			73033 5MT : 4-6-0 (1951)	Ex Shrewsbury 10/56	
3845 8F : 28xx 2-8-0 (1938)			73034 5MT : 4-6-0 (1951)	Ex Shrewsbury 10/56	
3860 8F : 28xx 2-8-0 (1938)			73035 5MT : 4-6-0 (1951)	Ex Shrewsbury 10/56	
3861 8F : 28xx 2-8-0 (1938)			9307 4MT : 43xx 2-6-0 (1932)	(r/n 7329)	
3863 8F : 28xx 2-8-0 (1938)			9311 4MT : 43xx 2-6-0 (1932)	Ex Oxford 11/56	To Truro 12/56
3865 8F : 28xx 2-8-0 (1938)			9312 4MT : 43xx 2-6-0 (1932)	Ex Wolverhampton 1/56	To Banbury 9/56
2819 8F : 28xx 2-8-0 (1903)			9314 4MT : 43xx 2-6-0 (1932)		
2830 8F : 28xx 2-8-0 (1903)			9317 4MT : 43xx 2-6-0 (1932)	(r/n 7339)	
2833 8F : 28xx 2-8-0 (1903)			9319 4MT : 43xx 2-6-0 (1932)	Ex Tyseley 7/55	
2841 8F : 28xx 2-8-0 (1903)			5312 4MT : 43xx 2-6-0 (1911)		
2850 8F : 28xx 2-8-0 (1903)	Ex Banbury 6/56		5313 4MT : 43xx 2-6-0 (1911)		
2854 8F : 28xx 2-8-0 (1903)		To Shrewsbury 2/56	5325 4MT : 43xx 2-6-0 (1911)		To Tyseley 7/56
3016 7F : R.O.D. 2-8-0 (1917)			5336 4MT : 43xx 2-6-0 (1911)		To Laira 12/56
3024 7F : R.O.D. 2-8-0 (1917)	Ex Pontypool Rd 6/56	To Carmarthen 11/56	5341 4MT : 43xx 2-6-0 (1911)		
3028 7F : R.O.D. 2-8-0 (1917)		W/D 8/56	5375 4MT : 43xx 2-6-0 (1911)		
3029 7F : R.O.D. 2-8-0 (1917)		W/D 5/56	5378 4MT : 43xx 2-6-0 (1911)		To St Blazey 12/56
3031 7F : R.O.D. 2-8-0 (1917)		W/D 5/56	5379 4MT : 43xx 2-6-0 (1911)	Ex Shrewsbury 6/56	To Banbury 9/56
3043 7F : R.O.D. 2-8-0 (1917)	Ex Pontypool Rd 5/56	W/D 9/56	5381 4MT : 43xx 2-6-0 (1911)		
6975 5MT : MOD-HALL 4-6-0 (1944)			5390 4MT : 43xx 2-6-0 (1911)		
7915 5MT : MOD-HALL 4-6-0 (1944)			5391 4MT : 43xx 2-6-0 (1911)		To Reading 1/56
4919 5MT : HALL 4-6-0 (1928)		To Old Oak C. 7/56	6324 4MT : 43xx 2-6-0 (1911)		
4963 5MT : HALL 4-6-0 (1928)		To Carmarthen 6/56	6335 4MT : 43xx 2-6-0 (1911)		To Oswestry 5/56
4963 5MT : HALL 4-6-0 (1928)	Ex Carmarthen 9/56		6355 4MT : 43xx 2-6-0 (1911)		To Banbury 9/56
4965 5MT : HALL 4-6-0 (1928)		To Old Oak C. 7/56	7305 4MT : 43xx 2-6-0 (1911)		
4966 5MT : HALL 4-6-0 (1928)			8417 4F : 94XX 0-6-0T (1948)		
4984 5MT : HALL 4-6-0 (1928)	Ex Carmarthen 9/56		8428 4F : 94XX 0-6-0T (1948)		
4986 5MT : HALL 4-6-0 (1928)		To Wolverhampton 6/56	8449 4F : 94XX 0-6-0T (1948)		
4997 5MT : HALL 4-6-0 (1928)			9408 4F : 94XX 0-6-0T (1948)		
5900 5MT : HALL 4-6-0 (1928)			9715 3F : 57xx 0-6-0T (1933)		To Landore 8/56
5944 5MT : HALL 4-6-0 (1928)			9739 3F : 57xx 0-6-0T (1933)		
5958 5MT : HALL 4-6-0 (1928)	Ex Carmarthen 9/56		9752 3F : 57xx 0-6-0T (1933)		
5991 5MT : HALL 4-6-0 (1928)			9768 3F : 57xx 0-6-0T (1933)		
5995 5MT : HALL 4-6-0 (1928)			7759 3F : 57xx 0-6-0T (1929)		
6907 5MT : HALL 4-6-0 (1928)			7797 3F : 57xx 0-6-0T (1929)		
6925 5MT : HALL 4-6-0 (1928)			8713 3F : 57xx 0-6-0T (1929)	Ex Bristol (SPM) 1/56	To Tyseley 2/56
6926 5MT : HALL 4-6-0 (1928)			13034 0F : 350hp 0-6-0		
6934 5MT : HALL 4-6-0 (1928)			13035 0F : 350hp 0-6-0		
6806 5MT : GRANGE 4-6-0 (1936)	Ex Penzance 11/56		13036 0F : 350hp 0-6-0		
6839 5MT : GRANGE 4-6-0 (1936)			13037 0F : 350hp 0-6-0		
6856 5MT : GRANGE 4-6-0 (1936)		To Taunton 12/56	13038 0F : 350hp 0-6-0		
6879 5MT : GRANGE 4-6-0 (1936)			13039 0F : 350hp 0-6-0		
5684 5MT : 56xx 0-6-2T (1927)			13191 0F : 350hp 0-6-0		

right decision although trying to justify it, had we been found out, would probably have been difficult.

In subsequent years, and I was unfortunate enough to fall for the Mop three years in succession, the departure time was moved forward and more police were added. We also became less fussy about leaving people behind and to some extent the job became a little easier to work. We all, however, agreed that running the train unbraked was the best guarantee of a reasonable arrival in Birmingham.

The holiday season also saw additions to the London service and although most Paddington specials came through from Wolverhampton, where Stafford Road was better equipped to deal with them, some started from Snow Hill to be worked by Tyseley Halls, the largest passenger engine we had.

Dave Jones and I booked on one night to work the first portion of the 20.00 London and were mildly surprised to find we had been given 6834 'Dummer Grange' of St Philips Marsh, Bristol.

It was unusual to have a Grange on a working that was normally covered by either a Hall or a Castle but 6834 had been fitted with an improved draughting system and someone may have wanted to know how it would handle the working, which returned with the 00.05 Paddington night mail. At the end of the day, of course, a Grange was essentially a variation on the Hall theme, the chief difference being a slightly smaller driving wheel since they had been constructed before the war from parts of withdrawn 43xx engines.

So far as I could tell in the preparation stages 6834 seemed to be in good condition and gave us no trouble as we collected our nine vehicles from Tyseley carriage sidings and ran them to Snow Hill via Queens Head, Handsworth. I placed a dozen shovelfuls on the front of the fire and at 20.00 we pulled out with a heavy complement of passengers who were off for the August bank holiday.

As we started I gave the back end of the fire a good lift with the bar, Dave very quickly got 6834 onto second valve and we were away, enjoying what promised to be a good and comfortable run up to Leamington and London.

We were up to 65 mph by Solihull and seventy at Lapworth. Hatton was passed at sixty but Davey opened all stops on the run down the bank and 6834 tore away in remarkable style until being eased at Warwick for the stop at Leamington.

It was not unusual for an engine to vibrate slightly when the regulator is closed at full speed but when Dave shut off, 6834, which had been behaving perfectly up to that point, gave a excessively violent wobble which required a touch of the brake to steady. Neither had any idea as to a diagnosis and Dave simply shrugged his shoulders and brought the train normally into

Leamington up platform.

We got the right away and Dave opened the regulator only to find the train moving in reverse. We got off the engine and peered at the motion but, finding nothing amiss, tried again but still 6834 wanted to go backwards.

"Tell him we're a cripple and to wire us a fresh engine," Dave said and I went to find the station inspector who arranged for the up side pilot to drag 6834 off the train and onto Leamington loco. I was wondering what Leamington would have as a replacement since its role as a shed had recently been diminished because of the influx of multiple units on the local workings.

The foreman was almost apologetic.

"That's all I've got," he said pointing to 7334, a very grubby Banbury-based 2-6-0 which had arrived not much earlier after finishing a days work. "But I've told Banbury to turn their pilot and have it ready for you."

In theory the 73xx 2-6-0's with their larger cabs, side windows and screw reversers were reckoned to be a deluxe version of the 43xx's but in practice they were the weakest of all the 2-6-0's and I would have groaned had I been given one that had been freshly prepared.

We backed onto the train, coupled up and left twenty-six minutes late which, as Dave pointed out, was not too bad considering we'd had to change engines. Everyone who happened to be on hand at Leamington loco was at the lineside to see us off: they'd probably opened a book on the chances of us getting to Banbury within the hour.

As we pulled away, I would not have put any money on us. I had to root up the fire for at least the second time since getting on the engine and even with the blower hard on there was only 160lb on the clock. Dave was pounding away at Claydon bank but with careful firing of about five shovelfuls at a time to build up the back end I managed to hold the needle steady.

I tried the exhaust injector and much to my surprise it worked first time. We pounded up the bank past Fosse with the blower still on whilst I built the fire up and at Fenny Compton, with the worst of the climbing behind us, Dave came across to check our position.

"What do you think about taking this engine through to London?"

I looked at the gauge and saw that pressure had risen a little.

"Well," I replied, "its not as bad as I thought it would be."

Finally we agreed that if we had the road through Banbury we would keep going. Dave was concerned that by stopping for another change of engine, we would not only lose more time ourselves but would further delay the main portion of the train which was behind us.

We slogged our way over Fenny Compton and then began to develop some speed, not that 7334's riding was anything to shout about. I put a few more shovelfulls of coal inside the doors, checked the injector and then strained to get a sighting of the Banbury distants.

They were all off and with a blast on the whistle we roared through the station much to the astonishment of the crew on the pilot who were expecting us to change engines. The fireman, who had probably been having a easy shift until being stirred to assist in what everyone thought was an emergency, gave us a sign that Churchill might have recognised but not necessarily interpreted as we flew through, but everyone else entered into the spirit of the thing, not least the crew of a goods train in Astrop loop who cheered us on as we overtook them.

I paused from firing long enough to get a full tank of water on Aynho troughs and then started a cycle of hard firing, six at a time using the flap to cover the firehole to minimise the amount of cold air allowed to enter the firebox. This resulted in the needle rising to 170lb and permitted Dave to use full regulator and a lengthened cut-off on the climb to Ardley.

The noise was impressive and although the effort caused the gauge to fall to 140lb, we got over the top in pretty good shape whilst Dave was able to ease the engine on the run down to Bicester. Whilst cruising thus I gave the fire a pull round with the pricker, which brought the needle round to 180lb, and took the opportunity to fill the boiler with the righthand injector.

Things were not looking too bad but we still had the climb from Blackthorn to Saunderton ahead of us. Dave gave me a chance to bring things round by letting 7334 run on easy steam as far as Ashendon but then opened up on second valve, the signal for me to turn off the injector and attacked the fire with the irons. Speed fell – not quite as quickly as the pressure needle – but we slogged our way through Risborough and eventually, under the visibly worried eye of the signalman, went over the top at Saunderton where Dave closed the regulator and sat down for the first time since leaving Leamington.

There was now only one difficult section remaining and that was the five mile stretch of 1 in 663 between High Wycombe and Beaconsfield. It was not a bank that caused any concern with a large engine in good condition but

OXLEY ALLOCATION : 1957						
LOCO CLASS	IN	OUT		LOCO CLASS	IN	OUT
7247 8F : 72xx 2-8-2T (1934)				6839 5MT : GRANGE 4-6-0 (1936)		
3802 8F : 28xx 2-8-0 (1938)				6857 5MT : GRANGE 4-6-0 (1936)	Ex Chester 9/57	
3813 8F : 28xx 2-8-0 (1938)				6879 5MT : GRANGE 4-6-0 (1936)		
3829 8F : 28xx 2-8-0 (1938)	Ex Banbury 10/57			5684 5MT : 56xx 0-6-2T (1927)		
3837 8F : 28xx 2-8-0 (1938)				6610 5MT : 56xx 0-6-2T (1927)		
3845 8F : 28xx 2-8-0 (1938)		To Canton 1/57		6640 5MT : 56xx 0-6-2T (1927)		
3848 8F : 28xx 2-8-0 (1938)	Ex Worcester 6/57			6645 5MT : 56xx 0-6-2T (1927)		
3860 8F : 28xx 2-8-0 (1938)		To Canton 1/57		73033 5MT : 4-6-0 (1951)		
3861 8F : 28xx 2-8-0 (1938)				73034 5MT : 4-6-0 (1951)		
3863 8F : 28xx 2-8-0 (1938)				73035 5MT : 4-6-0 (1951)		
3865 8F : 28xx 2-8-0 (1938)				9314 4MT : 43xx 2-6-0 (1932)		
2809 8F : 28xx 2-8-0 (1903)	Ex Gloucester 6/57	To Tyseley 12/57		9319 4MT : 43xx 2-6-0 (1932)	(r/n 7341)	
2819 8F : 28xx 2-8-0 (1903)				5312 4MT : 43xx 2-6-0 (1911)		
2830 8F : 28xx 2-8-0 (1903)				5313 4MT : 43xx 2-6-0 (1911)		
2833 8F : 28xx 2-8-0 (1903)		To Chester 9/57		5341 4MT : 43xx 2-6-0 (1911)		To Tyseley 9/57
2841 8F : 28xx 2-8-0 (1903)		To Tyseley 1/57		5375 4MT : 43xx 2-6-0 (1911)		To Stourbridge 10/57
2850 8F : 28xx 2-8-0 (1903)				5381 4MT : 43xx 2-6-0 (1911)		To Didcot 12/57
6975 5MT : MOD-HALL 4-6-0 (1944)				5390 4MT : 43xx 2-6-0 (1911)		To Reading 12/57
7915 5MT : MOD-HALL 4-6-0 (1944)				6324 4MT : 43xx 2-6-0 (1911)		
4901 5MT : HALL 4-6-0 (1928)	Ex Canton 1/57	To Carmarthen 6/57		7305 4MT : 43xx 2-6-0 (1911)		
4913 5MT : HALL 4-6-0 (1928)	Ex Canton 1/57	To Shrewsbury 10/57		7339 4MT : 43xx 2-6-0 (1911)		
4913 5MT : HALL 4-6-0 (1928)	Ex Shrewsbury 11/57			8417 4F : 94XX 0-6-0T (1949)		
4951 5MT : HALL 4-6-0 (1928)	Ex Ebbw Jcn 2/57	To Reading 3/57		8428 4F : 94XX 0-6-0T (1949)		
4963 5MT : HALL 4-6-0 (1928)				8449 4F : 94XX 0-6-0T (1949)		To Shrewsbury 12/57
4966 5MT : HALL 4-6-0 (1928)				9408 4F : 94XX 0-6-0T (1948)		
4984 5MT : HALL 4-6-0 (1928)				9739 3F : 57xx 0-6-0T (1933)		
4997 5MT : HALL 4-6-0 (1928)				9752 3F : 57xx 0-6-0T (1933)		
5900 5MT : HALL 4-6-0 (1928)				9768 3F : 57xx 0-6-0T (1933)		
5916 5MT : HALL 4-6-0 (1928)	Ex Ebbw Jcn 2/57			7759 3F : 57xx 0-6-0T (1929)		
5944 5MT : HALL 4-6-0 (1928)				7797 3F : 57xx 0-6-0T (1929)		
5958 5MT : HALL 4-6-0 (1928)				13034 0F : 350hp 0-6-0		
5959 5MT : HALL 4-6-0 (1928)	Ex Landore 6/57	To Exeter 7/57		13035 0F : 350hp 0-6-0		
5991 5MT : HALL 4-6-0 (1928)				13036 0F : 350hp 0-6-0		
5995 5MT : HALL 4-6-0 (1928)				13037 0F : 350hp 0-6-0		To Tyseley 3/57
6907 5MT : HALL 4-6-0 (1928)				13037 0F : 350hp 0-6-0	Ex Tyseley 4/57	
6925 5MT : HALL 4-6-0 (1928)				13038 0F : 350hp 0-6-0		
6926 5MT : HALL 4-6-0 (1928)				13039 0F : 350hp 0-6-0		
6934 5MT : HALL 4-6-0 (1928)				13191 0F : 350hp 0-6-0		
6806 5MT : GRANGE 4-6-0 (1936)						

There may have been more uncomfortable engines to work on than the Austerity 2-8-0 although it is difficult to think what they might have been. Fortunately the Western managed to shed most of its quota soon after nationalisation and although some remained on the system, they were relatively small in number. 78714 (later 90656), still fitted with a Westinghouse pump, waits for the road at Stourbridge with an eastbound goods in 1948. Shortly afterwards it was transferred to the Lancashire & Yorkshire, working from Belle Vue shed, Wakefield.

with 7334 there was no room for complacency. I restored the injector, worked some magic with the fireirons and was rewarded by seeing 7334 actually blow off with 190lb as we went through West Wycombe. Dave opened up again and my efforts did the trick although by the time we got to Beaconsfield the needle had dropped to 150lb whilst the fire was beginning to look very dirty. None of this mattered now since it was downhill all the way and with a clear run through the suburbs, we ran into No.14 platform at Paddington and came to a halt.

"Well," remarked Dave looking at his watch. "Twenty-six late from Leamington. Twenty-six late into Paddington. They can't ask for more than that."

"Not, " I agreed, "with a nag like this."

There was not enough fire in the box to brew a decent pot of tea and the Paddington arranger must have sensed it without being told."

"Where the hell have you been?" he asked as he always did of any late arrival, adding rather weakly, "I don't suppose you want to double-head the Northern Mail with this ruddy thing?"

The look on our faces answered his question.

Some days later, Dave Jones contacted me about 6834. It appeared that the left hand hanging link broke whilst we were running down Hatton at speed with the regulator shut and as a result the quadrant block dropped to the bottom of the quadrant link, putting the lefthand side into back gear. When this took place, speed was well over 70 m.p.h., and the whole of the motion must have been subjected to a great deal of stress and strain. 6834 was repaired at Leamington loco and was soon back in service.

Complete engine failures were quite rare until the arrival of diesels but after the episode with 6834, I had two more in close succession. A month later I was working the fully loaded 20.30 Leamington - Bordesley with 0-6-0T 3673, the

first stop being Lapworth where we had a wagon to detach. To that point the trip was quite normal, we used the banker from Warwick to Hatton and trickled down to Lapworth where we shunted out his load.

Resuming our journey, we set off along the down relief and had only just passed the Lapworth starter when we heard a terrific roar from the front end, 3673 coming to a stand. I lit a paraffin lamp and had a look at the motion but finding nothing wrong tried again only to hear the very loud roar repeated with no movement.

Deciding we were a cripple, I protected the train and set off for Bentley Heath – Knowle box was switched out – with a wrong line order, cursing as I went the engineers who determined that the distance between sleepers was such as to make walking by the track such a misery. Eventually, after a three mile hike, I arrived and arranged for the Warwick banker to come down, pick me up and then drag our train to Tyseley.

The next morning I made a special detour to take a look at 3673 and found that the lefthand piston had disintegrated, much of it disappearing up the chimney and coming to rest in the countryside around Lapworth.

OXLEY ALLOCATION : 1958						
LOCO CLASS	IN	OUT	LOCO CLASS	IN	OUT
7247 8F : 72xx 2-8-2T (1934)			6863 5MT : GRANGE 4-6-0 (1936)	Ex Bristol (SPM) 4/58	To Laira 6/58
3802 8F : 28xx 2-8-0 (1938)			6879 5MT : GRANGE 4-6-0 (1936)		To Laira 6/58
3813 8F : 28xx 2-8-0 (1938)			5684 5MT : 56xx 0-6-2T (1927)		To Radyr 1/58
3829 8F : 28xx 2-8-0 (1938)			6610 5MT : 56xx 0-6-2T (1927)		
3837 8F : 28xx 2-8-0 (1938)			6640 5MT : 56xx 0-6-2T (1927)		
3848 8F : 28xx 2-8-0 (1938)		To Gloucester 3/58	6645 5MT : 56xx 0-6-2T (1927)		
3861 8F : 28xx 2-8-0 (1938)			73033 5MT : 4-6-0 (1951)		To Chester 5/58
3863 8F : 28xx 2-8-0 (1938)			73034 5MT : 4-6-0 (1951)		To Shrewsbury 6/58
3865 8F : 28xx 2-8-0 (1938)			73035 5MT : 4-6-0 (1951)		To Shrewsbury 6/58
2819 8F : 28xx 2-8-0 (1903)		To Didcot 11/58	9314 4MT : 43xx 2-6-0 (1932)	(r/n 7336)	
2830 8F : 28xx 2-8-0 (1903)			5312 4MT : 43xx 2-6-0 (1911)		W/D 10/58
2841 8F : 28xx 2-8-0 (1903)	Ex Stourbridge 9/58		5313 4MT : 43xx 2-6-0 (1911)		W/D 5/58
2850 8F : 28xx 2-8-0 (1903)			5375 4MT : 43xx 2-6-0 (1911)		To Worcester 8/58
6975 5MT : MOD-HALL 4-6-0 (1944)		To Wolverhampton 12/58	6311 4MT : 43xx 2-6-0 (1911)	Ex Croes Newydd 10/58	To Banbury 11/58
7915 5MT : MOD-HALL 4-6-0 (1944)			7305 4MT : 43xx 2-6-0 (1911)		To Banbury 4/58
4913 5MT : HALL 4-6-0 (1928)			7329 4MT : 43xx 2-6-0 (1911)		To Shrewsbury 6/58
4957 5MT : HALL 4-6-0 (1928)	Ex Ebbw Jcn 1/58		7339 4MT : 43xx 2-6-0 (1911)		
4963 5MT : HALL 4-6-0 (1928)			7341 4MT : 43xx 2-6-0 (1911)		To Shrewsbury 6/58
4966 5MT : HALL 4-6-0 (1928)			7341 4MT : 43xx 2-6-0 (1911)	Ex Shrewsbury 8/58	
4984 5MT : HALL 4-6-0 (1928)			8417 4F : 94XX 0-6-0T (1949)		
4997 5MT : HALL 4-6-0 (1928)			8428 4F : 94XX 0-6-0T (1949)		
5900 5MT : HALL 4-6-0 (1928)			8462 4F : 94XX 0-6-0T (1949)	Ex Wolverhampton 9/58	To Wolverhampton 10/58
5916 5MT : HALL 4-6-0 (1928)			9408 4F : 94XX 0-6-0T (1949)		
5944 5MT : HALL 4-6-0 (1928)			9739 3F : 57xx 0-6-0T (1933)		
5958 5MT : HALL 4-6-0 (1928)		To Shrewsbury 1/58	9752 3F : 57xx 0-6-0T (1933)		
5985 5MT : HALL 4-6-0 (1928)	Ex Penzance 4/58		9768 3F : 57xx 0-6-0T (1933)		
5991 5MT : HALL 4-6-0 (1928)			7759 3F : 57xx 0-6-0T (1929)		
5995 5MT : HALL 4-6-0 (1928)			7797 3F : 57xx 0-6-0T (1929)		
6907 5MT : HALL 4-6-0 (1928)			13034 0F : 350hp 0-6-0		
6925 5MT : HALL 4-6-0 (1928)			13035 0F : 350hp 0-6-0		
6926 5MT : HALL 4-6-0 (1928)		To Wolverhampton 6/58	13036 0F : 350hp 0-6-0		
6934 5MT : HALL 4-6-0 (1928)			13037 0F : 350hp 0-6-0		
6806 5MT : GRANGE 4-6-0 (1936)			13038 0F : 350hp 0-6-0		
6817 5MT : GRANGE 4-6-0 (1936)	Ex Croes Newydd 7/58		13039 0F : 350hp 0-6-0		
6839 5MT : GRANGE 4-6-0 (1936)			13191 0F : 350hp 0-6-0		
6857 5MT : GRANGE 4-6-0 (1936)			D3431 0F : 350hp 0-6-0	New 5/58	

When all else failed, the 43xx 2-6-0's could be found on holiday expresses, especially to North Wales, although they were not the ideal type of engine for such jobs since they were just a little too small for the sustained steaming needed. 5369 of Tyseley, seen at Stow Heath with a Bordesley - Oxley goods in August 1958, once gave the author an electrifying run from Machynlleth to Birmingham although it had the benefit of assistance by another 43xx between Newtown and Wolverhampton.

The engine remained immobile at Tyseley for some time whilst the hierarchy pondered whether repairs were worthwhile but eventually it was restored to traffic and lasted another three years, being withdrawn in May 1964 as one of the last of its type at Tyseley.

Both failures had occurred on the 20th of successive months and on the 20th of the third month I was firing to Joe Hiccox on the 22.05 Oxley – Bristol class D vacuum goods with 6975 'Capesthorne Hall' and a full load. The booked time up the bank to Earlswood was fourteen minutes and Joe was pushing the engine to keep time, something that was rarely achieved on these fast and heavy workings. There was a need for urgency however since we were followed by the 20.00 Lye – Moreton and the 23.10 Oxley – Swindon whilst the 23.30 Bordesley – Swindon was waiting at Earlswood to follow us. It was a complex system of train paths and unless everyone pulled their weight, the timetable could very easily disintegrate.

6975 was steaming well and we pounded through Shirley and up the bank in fine style until we got to Whitlocks End, two miles below the summit, when there was a terrific bang from the right hand front end with the entire driver's side of the engine being enveloped in steam. We started to lose momentum very quickly and it was only the fact that we had been going so well that allowed us to carry on to the summit and get to Earlswood platform

where we found that the righthand cylinder cover had blown out and was hanging on by no more than a couple of studs.

On any other night of the year we should have been able to make use of the 23.30 Bordesley – Swindon engine but it had left ahead of schedule and instead we had to call for a fresh engine from Tyseley with the Stratford banker being summoned to shunt us clear of the main line.

Eventually we got straightened out, completed our turn to Gloucester and came back passenger, our booked return working having left long before we arrived.

Joe, who lived in terror of being blamed for something, spoke to me about the failure in the train on the way back.

"You," he said conversationally, "will very likely get the sack for that lot, y'know."

I asked him what on earth he was talking about.

"You had got the boiler solid."

Absolute rubbish but there was no point in telling him since he had made it up. Joe had his good points but sometimes he exhibited all the character of a dead chicken and it worried me that someone in authority might accept his word without question. It had happened to me before but in this instance no questions were asked and the fault with 6975 was put down to a mechanical defect.

No-one had more respect for Earlswood bank than I had and the idea of going up there with a full glass let alone a full boiler was something I was too experienced to do. Whether anyone would accept my word for it against Joe's, though, was not something I was keen to put to the test. Rank had its privileges on the railway.

I was firing to Joe when for the first and only time in my career I had to fail an engine through being short of steam. We were on the 19.10 ex Paddington with a very troublesome 7020 'Gloucester Castle' and just managed to limp into Gerrards Cross where I did my best to get the fire to produce some heat. In spite of my protests that I could rally things, Joe insisted on my going to the box to tell Banbury that we should want assistance when we got there. As I made my way up the steps I saw Joe put a dozen shovelfulls in 7020's firebox and then, when I returned, had

OXLEY ALLOCATION : 1959							
LOCO	CLASS	IN	OUT	LOCO	CLASS	IN	OUT
7217	8F : 72xx 2-8-2T (1934)	Ex Banbury 9/59	To Ebbw Jcn 12/59	6907	5MT : HALL 4-6-0 (1928)		
7247	8F : 72xx 2-8-2T (1934)			6925	5MT : HALL 4-6-0 (1928)		
2888	8F : 28xx 2-8-0 (1938)	Ex Llanelly 2/59	To Stourbridge 3/59	6934	5MT : HALL 4-6-0 (1928)		
3802	8F : 28xx 2-8-0 (1938)			6806	5MT : GRANGE 4-6-0 (1936)		
3813	8F : 28xx 2-8-0 (1938)			6817	5MT : GRANGE 4-6-0 (1936)		
3820	8F : 28xx 2-8-0 (1938)	Ex Banbury 3/59		6839	5MT : GRANGE 4-6-0 (1936)		
3829	8F : 28xx 2-8-0 (1938)			6857	5MT : GRANGE 4-6-0 (1936)		
3837	8F : 28xx 2-8-0 (1938)		To Ebbw Jcn 3/59	6610	5MT : 56xx 0-6-2T (1927)		To Wrexham (GC) 2/59#
3842	8F : 28xx 2-8-0 (1938)	Ex Pontypool Rd 9/59		6640	5MT : 56xx 0-6-2T (1927)		
3854	8F : 28xx 2-8-0 (1938)	Ex Pontypool Rd 9/59		6645	5MT : 56xx 0-6-2T (1927)		
3861	8F : 28xx 2-8-0 (1938)			4146	4MT : 51xx 2-6-2T (1928)	Ex Stourbridge 9/59	
3863	8F : 28xx 2-8-0 (1938)		To Banbury 6/59	6353	4MT : 43xx 2-6-0 (1911)	Ex Gloucester 3/59	
3865	8F : 28xx 2-8-0 (1938)			7336	4MT : 43xx 2-6-0 (1911)		To Shrewsbury 1/59
2830	8F : 28xx 2-8-0 (1938)		To Banbury 8/59	7339	4MT : 43xx 2-6-0 (1911)		
2841	8F : 28xx 2-8-0 (1903)			7341	4MT : 43xx 2-6-0 (1911)		To Croes Newydd 11/59
2850	8F : 28xx 2-8-0 (1903)			8417	4F : 94XX 0-6-0T (1949)		W/D 3/59
2857	8F : 28xx 2-8-0 (1903)	Ex Pontypool Rd 2/59	To Pontypool Rd 3/59	8428	4F : 94XX 0-6-0T (1949)		
2859	8F : 28xx 2-8-0 (1903)	Ex Canton 2/59	To Pontypool Rd 12/59	8462	4F : 94XX 0-6-0T (1949)	Ex Wolverhampton 1/59	W/D 8/59
6975	5MT : MOD-HALL 4-6-0 (1944)	Ex Wolverhampton 5/59		8464	4F : 94XX 0-6-0T (1949)	Ex Canton 11/59	
6980	5MT : MOD-HALL 4-6-0 (1944)	Ex Shrewsbury 5/59		9408	4F : 94XX 0-6-0T (1948)		
7915	5MT : MOD-HALL 4-6-0 (1944)			3698	3F : 57xx 0-6-0T (1933)	Ex Llanelly 1/59	
4912	5MT : HALL 4-6-0 (1928)	Ex Shrewsbury 3/59		9739	3F : 57xx 0-6-0T (1933)		
4913	5MT : HALL 4-6-0 (1928)		To Laira 6/59	9752	3F : 57xx 0-6-0T (1933)		
4957	5MT : HALL 4-6-0 (1928)			9768	3F : 57xx 0-6-0T (1933)		
4963	5MT : HALL 4-6-0 (1928)			7759	3F : 57xx 0-6-0T (1929)		
4966	5MT : HALL 4-6-0 (1928)			7797	3F : 57xx 0-6-0T (1929)		W/D 10/59
4984	5MT : HALL 4-6-0 (1928)			13034	0F : 350hp 0-6-0		
4997	5MT : HALL 4-6-0 (1928)			13035	0F : 350hp 0-6-0		
5900	5MT : HALL 4-6-0 (1928)			13036	0F : 350hp 0-6-0		
5916	5MT : HALL 4-6-0 (1928)			13037	0F : 350hp 0-6-0		
5919	5MT : HALL 4-6-0 (1928)	Ex Bristol (BR) 3/59		13038	0F : 350hp 0-6-0		
5944	5MT : HALL 4-6-0 (1928)			13039	0F : 350hp 0-6-0		
5965	5MT : HALL 4-6-0 (1928)	Ex Oxford 3/59		13191	0F : 350hp 0-6-0		
5985	5MT : HALL 4-6-0 (1928)			D3431	0F : 350hp 0-6-0		
5991	5MT : HALL 4-6-0 (1928)			D3752	0F : 350hp 0-6-0	Ex Danygraig 10/59	
5995	5MT : HALL 4-6-0 (1928)						

to listen to him telling me that I had too much coal up front.

"In future," he whined, "when you're firing to me on these jobs, you only fire five at a time."

The next night I followed his instruction to the letter and predictably our King very quickly sat down for lack of steam.

I wondered sometimes – most of the time – where people like Joe had gained their experience. I discovered a week before my difficulty with 7020 that Joe had come to grief with the 19.10 Paddington when his advice had caused a senior fireman, whose experience and skill was beyond question, to run short of steam. The engine had been 7020 'Gloucester Castle' and it was obvious to any experienced hand that a special touch was needed to keep it going. Joe, alas, lacked that special touch.

Fortunately, albeit painfully, fate stepped in and took a hand in matters before I was provoked to do something unpleasant to Joe with the pricker. We had 5050 'Earl of St Germans' on the 19.10 Paddington and had had a rough trip getting to Solihull. With about 180lb on the clock and the journey all but over, Joe took it into his head to tell me to give the fire a pull through with the pricker.

Although I couldn't see the necessity for it, I did as he ordered and turned to bring the pricker down. 5050 was one of the Castles with the awkward straight sided tenders that had inward opening doors and since the coal was rather well back, I had had to keep the doors open whilst firing. Bringing the pricker from its housing I managed to wedge my hand between the handle and the tender doors causing a spilt finger and a great deal of blood.

It was the end of any effort from me that night yet we got into Snow Hill without loss of time, making me wonder why Joe had thought the fireirons were needed in the first place. After being relieved the General Hospital put six stitches in my hand and I had a months respite from firing which at least got Joe out of my hair for good since I was paired with a different driver when I resumed main line firing.

London, Chester and Bristol were the normal main line limits for Tyseley crews but when the holiday crowds arrived, the rules could change as happened on Easter Monday 1965 when I worked what I think was a (Tyseley) record for mileage in a single shift.

It was during the depressing period when diesels had yet to get on top of the job whilst steam was being run down, although when I looked down the duty lists I was pleased to see that I had been rostered to one of the remaining steam turns.

The job was a circuitous trip to Weston-super-Mare going, not via Stratford and Cheltenham, but via Stourbridge, Worcester, over the Midland to Gloucester and then by the normal route to Bristol. After arrival at Weston we were to take the stock empty to Bridgwater and

then run light to Taunton to prepare for the return trip.

Firing to Jack Roberts, who was an émigré from Cardiff Canton, with 7929 'Wyke Hall' we had an uneventful trip and, with some help from a very talkative pilotman from Bristol, the limit of Jack's road knowledge, we completed the outward part of the diagram without incident. We were probably in a more cheerful frame of mind than our passengers who had picked one of the rainiest days possible for their seaside outing.

At Taunton we met up with a set of Oxley men, who had worked down to Weston via Stratford with Black 5 4-6-0 45006, and after a few beers with them returned to the loco to get ready for the journey back to Birmingham. The West of England had been dieselised for some time and one thing we noticed was the way their firemen's waist measurements had adapted to the new style of working. When the foreman instructed a couple of them to prepare 7929 and 45006 it was as though he had set them one of the labours of Hercules. The chap who prepared 7929 seemed to have forgotten what a steam engine looked like and I had never seen anyone in such a lather of sweat as he pushed my coal forward in the tender. He told me he hoped that 7929 would be the last steam engine he ever saw at Taunton or anywhere else.

I am sure he did his best for 7929 but I deemed it prudent not to take any chances and cleaned the fire and ashpan out myself. My colleague on 45006 took a different line and decided that whatever the Taunton men did to his engine, it would be sufficient.

We left the shed coupled to 45006 and gathered quite a crowd to witness our departure. A Black 5 and a Hall together would have been rare at any time and quite a number of photographs of the unusual pairing were taken.

At Bridgwater we coupled up to our respective trains and spent an hour waiting, chatting to the Oxley men who were far from happy. 45006, they complained, was steaming badly and its injectors were acting up. If this, I reflected, was what they had discovered on the short run from Taunton, what sort of trip were they in for to Birmingham? I kept quiet but I thought that most of their problems would never have arisen if the fireman had prepared his own engine. Unfortunately he had had a long spell on diesels and, like 45006, was not in the pink of condition.

We had a good run back with nothing of note happening; the only point of interest being assisted from the front by the Stourbridge banker as far as Rowley.

Running down the bank at Handsworth with only a short distance to go I saw the lamps of a northbound train coming from the Snow Hill direction and saw, with quiet satisfaction, our Oxley friends going north and making a real fist of the bank. From the way they were going I wondered if they were going to even get as far as Handsworth.

Some time later I saw the Oxley fireman concerned, now all smiles in the cab of a diesel. He told me what a terrible trip they had had back to Wolverhampton and what he called steam engines cannot be recorded here. He was surprised when I told him that I had had a good trip back and put it down to the fact that I had had a Great Western engine. Silently I put it down to the fact that I had serviced my side of the engine at Taunton.

Perhaps the habit of taking care of my engines had been inculcated as a result of working on the 'Big Pilot' turn, where we took a 49xx or 68xx 4-6-0 from Tyseley to Snow Hill at 02.40 each morning and remained with it until relieved. The purpose of the pilot was to do a share of the ordinary shunting at Snow Hill – including pulling stalled goods trains out of the tunnel – whilst acting as standby for any main line failures. We generally assumed that any such failure would take place on an up train and therefore always kept the pilot facing towards London. It goes without saying that the engine had to be kept in the peak of condition with plenty of coal pulled forward and the cab spotless although, because we were working in a passenger station, you had to keep the fire small and only build it up when the word arrived that an express was in trouble. When the word came that a 'four cylinder' was in trouble then you had to build the fire up and raise steam in record time: it sorted the men from the boys.

When the pilot was used to replace a failure, whenever possible the crippled engine would take over the Big Pilot's duties until a replacement came down from Tyseley after which arrangements would be made to have the failed engine repaired and returned to its home shed. When we had one of our better engines on the pilot, it was surprising how quickly word got around and how soon we would be told to "get the pilot ready."

Not all the laughs resulted from dramatic events on epic runs and one of best happened in the dead of night when I was on a spare turn, sitting and twiddling my thumbs in the mess room at Tyseley. The foreman poked his head round the door and saw me sitting there: I hoped he'd got something interesting for me, such as a two-hour Paddington with a King (at two in the morning?).

"Nip round to Bernard B's place and tell him they're off the road at Tyseley."

Bernard was a member of the breakdown gang and on call twenty-four hours a day. Disappointed at not being given a train to work, I jumped on my bike and peddled as fast as I could. A few minutes later I was standing outside Bernards house and hammering for all I was worth on his door. Ten minutes later a very old and tired gentleman opened the door and blinked at me.

"Will you tell Bernard they're off the road at Tyseley and they want the vans out."

"Tell him your bloody self. He lives next door...."

Through excursions from the LNW to Stratford-upon-Avon introduced LMS locomotives to the Great Western from the late 1950's. Generally the workings travelled overnight to Stratford and returned north in the evening, the engines and stock being serviced at Tyseley. 5XP 4-6-0 45584 'North West Frontier' of Blackpool passes with Lapworth in August 1959 with a northbound return special.

An interesting development of the late 1950's was the introduction of special overnight trains from the Glasgow area to Stratford-upon-Avon with through LMS engines. Up to that time regional boundaries – which were little different from the pre-nationalisation borders – had been pretty well sacrosanct and it was virtually unknown for engine to cross borders with any degree of regularity. The specials from Glasgow however ran quite frequently and it suddenly dawned on someone in the diagramming office that it would not be the end of the world if the North Western was asked to work them through, especially as the services were re-engined at Crewe. The engines were quite an assorted bunch although, because the trains were heavy and often made up of sleeping cars, rebuilt Scots predominated. The LM engine would work through to Stratford and then take its stock to Tyseley, running via Long Marston so that the engine could turn on the Honeybourne angle. The engine would remain at Tyseley for the day before returning North with the back working that night.

The routing was either via Shrewsbury or the Wellington branch with GW pilotmen conducting the North Western men to Stratford.

On paper the through working was no doubt a good idea but it did not take account of the differing operating methods of the two railways

and considerable trouble was experienced by North Western men on the return workings after coaling up with GW soft coal. 46100 'Royal Scot' was itself a casualty on one occasion when its brick arch collapsed at Stratford, the engine remaining there for several days before being dragged to Tyseley for repairs.

Coming back one night with a goods from Gloucester to Birmingham, we passed the stock of one of the specials at Marston and managed to get as far as Earlswood before being shunted for it. We got inside, the main line signals cleared and then we waited and waited. The signalman was pacing anxiously up and down his frame with frequent glances out of the window to see if he could hear the special climbing the bank.

After a time he came up to us and warned us to make ready to examine the line to Henley but as he spoke we heard the sound of a train in the distance, climbing very slowly and making very heavy weather of the bank.

Eventually a Rebuilt Scot reached the summit and drew to a stand level with us, all four men on the footplate looking as though they had had enough for one day.

"What's up?" I asked the driver, who told me they had stopped to blow up.

"Oy Jacks," called the Tyseley pilotman, "Have you got a long bar?"

I brought the implement from my engine to theirs and, seeing that the fireman was all in, volunteered to do the necessary. The firebox was full of half burnt coal so I gave it a couple of good lifts with the bar and within five minutes the needle was rising and I was able to put the injector on. As a reward the driver passed me a cup of 'Crewe' tea.

With the fire now burning well, a good head of steam and the boiler full, I swung a couple of shovelfulls down the front end which was enough to get the Scot blowing off.

"If my mate," the Crewe driver indicated his fireman, "doesn't get the hang of firing blind coal, we'll be lucky to get home."

I nodded sympathetically and told him to keep the long bar in case they needed it again.

"D'you fancy a trip to Crewe?" I was asked and it was tempting to add it to my list of conquests. However I had already been on duty for ten hours and was approaching the limit.

He raised his hand in farewell, opened the regulator and the train moved off downhill towards Birmingham.

"These LMS engines shouldn't be allowed on our railway," said the signalman. "They're not suited."

"Ah," replied my driver. "They just want manning properly."

A few days later I bumped into the pilotman and he told me they hadn't done too badly although it had been touch and go on Handsworth bank. I also came across the driver who had prepared the Scot at Tyseley and asked him in which position he had stopped the big ends in order to get inside and oil the centre motion. I was keen to learn something about oiling a Scot but there was a long silence before he replied.

"Oh, I didn't know they'd got one inside as well…."

Working frequently across to Gloucester on goods trains, the limit of the working day often ruled out a back working and instead we had to return passenger, often riding back over the Midland with its relatively frequent service of trains via Bromsgrove. My colleagues generally rode in the train but I regarded it as an opportunity to broaden my horizons and would travel back on the engine, the Midland crew often pleased to have a Great Western audience to show off to.

Most drivers that I rode with were quite enthusiastic footplatemen whilst their firemen tended to be the opposite and this resulted in me being offered the shovel, the fireman more often than not retiring to the train.

One early morning, Bert and I had worked the 19.15 Bordesley to Stoke Gifford as far as Gloucester, with orders to travel home passenger on the Mail that left Gloucester (Eastgate) just after 02.00. Bert and I went into the locoman's cabin on the up platform, every nook and cranny hiding Midland men. There was the usual amount of sarcasm towards us but, ignoring it, I sought out Joe Spooner of Saltley who I knew was working the Mail and asked if I could ride back with them.

"Aye, if you want a trip on a real engine. We've got 45512 and it's a right camel."

I wondered at first whether he had the correct number since 45512 was a Carlisle-based rebuilt Patriot and I had never heard of one working the west of England line before.

'Bunsen' ran in with steam oozing from every joint. Joe and his mate put the bag in the tender whilst I stepped up on the footplate and started to pull some coal forward. I thought we should probably need it as Joe's reputation as a hard hitter had crossed the border to Tyseley: many a Saltley fireman was glad to see the diesels come about after firing for a spell to Joe.

Once the tank was filled, we made ready for the sprint to Cheltenham. The fireman ladled about forty shovelfuls into No.45512's firebox, closed the firehole doors, put the blower on, sat down and lit a cigarette. The injector was turned off when the gauge glass which, like the footplate generally, was very dirty and illuminated by a dim and grimy gauge lamp, showed full.

We had the right away from the platform staff and with a little slipping, edged our way out of the station. The regulator was put on the second valve and with the lever well down on the rack, we stormed away with 45512,

which seemed to enjoy being flogged, blowing off at the valves.

"None of your Western pampering with these engines." The fireman shouted in my ear.

We roared along to Cheltenham where the bag was put in to top up the tender again. I brought some more coal forward in the tender and once again the fireman gave the engine the hefty 'Derby charge' after filling the tank. My intention had been to sit back quietly to observe how one of the rebuilt 7P's was fired and I was rather taken by surprise when he asked his driver if I could take over the firing.

"All I want is steam," replied Joe. "And I don't care who gets it."

I checked that we had a good fire in the box, a full boiler with the engine close to blowing-off point and decided there was nothing I could do to improve matters except to kill the few minutes left at Cheltenham by giving the footplate a good sweeping. Just because it was an LMS engine wasn't sufficient reason for not taking a pride in the thing. Dreadfully scruffy lot, the Midland.

Leaving Cheltenham, the regulator was once again pushed over after the first couple of hundred yards had been covered with the lever being quickly wound back. Joe evidently had little faith in Great Western techniques since he could hardly stop glowering at the steam and water gauges. I was glad to see that as the journey progressed these glances became fewer as he concluded I could be trusted with his engine. His partner was rather more relaxed and settled back on the seat, occasionally calling out the names of stations and signal boxes and almost as frequently being corrected by Joe. I was relieved to find that 45512 steamed as well in my hands as it had in my counterpart's and happier that it was now reasonably tidy although I would have given a lot to have been able to clean the gauge glass which was almost impossible to read.

The engine steamed quite well and there was no difficulty in firing to Joe's demands although the work was fairly continuous, made up of cycles of ten to a dozen shovelfulls with very little time between the cycles.

We called at Worcester, where Joe grumbled that the Great Western clock and his watch showed different times, and continued north; firing still being on the heavy side. Not wanting to appear possessive I asked the Saltley fireman if he wanted to take over but he shook his head.

"No fear, mate, I'm doing okay where I am…."

I was glad of that because I wanted to see the train right through and to take it up the Lickey. No-one at Saltley was going to be able to claim, as they sometimes did, that Great Western men could fire them on the level but not uphill. From the way Joe was hammering the engine I guessed that most Saltley firemen regarded the Lickey as a blessing since the stand at Bromsgrove gave them a chance to ease up on the firing whilst the hard work on the ascent could always be left to the bankers.

We passed Stoke Works, whistled up for assistance and came to a stand just south of Bromsgrove to let the bankers buffer up at the rear. Whistle codes were exchanged and we started away, Joe opening the regulator and working on a very long cut-off. I was determined not to let the bankers do any more work than necessary and fired continuously on the climb, keeping both steam and water at respectable levels. At Blackwell Joe wound back a little and by Barnt Green we were once again running like the wind.

As a sign that the trip was nearing its end Joe, in a single movement, shut the regulator and put the lever in the 45% drift position, telling me to ease the firing. He added that the water level should be allowed to come down so that the 45512 could be kept quiet whilst it was standing in New Street.

We dropped down the smoky approach to the station and came to a stand in one of the platforms; the number of people waiting for the train being surprisingly large given the time of day. I thanked my hosts for the ride and told them how much I had enjoyed it.

"If you're about tomorrow," Joe said. "Come and look me up."

Reward indeed.

Although there was no shortage of express services on the Midland Bristol – Birmingham main line, the fact I usually ended up at Gloucester around breakfast time meant that I normally had to come back on the 06.52 stopping train, the only Birmingham-bound train at that time of day; the first express of the day not leaving for another two hours.

Although rather a modest entry in the time-table, the five-coach 06.52 was rather an interesting train to ride on. Nominally diagrammed for a Barnwood Compound, usually 41123, it was used to return any unbalanced engines to Birmingham with the result that in five consecutive days, the train might see as many classes of engine.

On one of my trips I had the interesting combination of 41123 and an ex-LNWR driver who had very little good to say of the Midland and would regale me during the journey with tales of his firing days on the Wessie, omitting no opportunity to damn the Midland and its products which he

LOCO	CLASS	IN	OUT	LOCO	CLASS	IN	OUT
			OXLEY ALLOCATION : 1959				
7217	8F : 72xx 2-8-2T (1934)	Ex Banbury 9/59	To Ebbw Jcn 12/59	6907	5MT : HALL 4-6-0 (1928)		
7247	8F : 72xx 2-8-2T (1934)			6925	5MT : HALL 4-6-0 (1928)		
2888	8F : 28xx 2-8-0 (1938)	Ex Llanelly 2/59	To Stourbridge 3/59	6934	5MT : HALL 4-6-0 (1928)		
3802	8F : 28xx 2-8-0 (1938)			6806	5MT : GRANGE 4-6-0 (1936)		
3813	8F : 28xx 2-8-0 (1938)			6817	5MT : GRANGE 4-6-0 (1936)		
3820	8F : 28xx 2-8-0 (1938)	Ex Banbury 3/59		6839	5MT : GRANGE 4-6-0 (1936)		
3829	8F : 28xx 2-8-0 (1938)			6877	5MT : GRANGE 4-6-0 (1936)		
3837	8F : 28xx 2-8-0 (1938)		To Ebbw Jcn 3/59	6610	5MT : 56xx 0-6-2T (1927)		To Wrexham (GC) 2/59#
3842	8F : 28xx 2-8-0 (1938)	Ex Pontypool Rd 9/59		6640	5MT : 56xx 0-6-2T (1927)		
3854	8F : 28xx 2-8-0 (1938)	Ex Pontypool Rd 9/59		6645	5MT : 56xx 0-6-2T (1927)		
3861	8F : 28xx 2-8-0 (1938)			4146	4MT : 51xx 2-6-2T (1928)	Ex Stourbridge 9/59	
3863	8F : 28xx 2-8-0 (1938)			6353	4MT : 43xx 2-6-0 (1911)	Ex Gloucester 3/59	
3865	8F : 28xx 2-8-0 (1938)		To Banbury 6/59	7336	4MT : 43xx 2-6-0 (1911)		To Shrewsbury 1/59
2830	8F : 28xx 2-8-0 (1903)			7339	4MT : 43xx 2-6-0 (1911)		
2841	8F : 28xx 2-8-0 (1903)		To Banbury 8/59	7341	4MT : 43xx 2-6-0 (1911)		To Croes Newydd 11/59
2850	8F : 28xx 2-8-0 (1903)			8417	4F : 94XX 0-6-0T (1949)		W/D 3/59
2857	8F : 28xx 2-8-0 (1903)	Ex Pontypool Rd 2/59	To Pontypool Rd 3/59	8428	4F : 94XX 0-6-0T (1949)		
2859	8F : 28xx 2-8-0 (1903)	Ex Canton 2/59	To Pontypool Rd 12/59	8462	4F : 94XX 0-6-0T (1949)	Ex Wolverhampton 1/59	W/D 8/59
6975	5MT : MOD-HALL 4-6-0 (1944)	Ex Wolverhampton 5/59		8464	4F : 94XX 0-6-0T (1949)	Ex Canton 11/59	
6980	5MT : MOD-HALL 4-6-0 (1944)	Ex Shrewsbury 3/59		9408	4F : 94XX 0-6-0T (1948)		
7915	5MT : MOD-HALL 4-6-0 (1944)			3698	3F : 57xx 0-6-0T (1933)	Ex Llanelly 1/59	
4912	5MT : HALL 4-6-0 (1928)	Ex Shrewsbury 3/59		9739	3F : 57xx 0-6-0T (1933)		
4913	5MT : HALL 4-6-0 (1928)		To Laira 6/59	9752	3F : 57xx 0-6-0T (1933)		
4957	5MT : HALL 4-6-0 (1928)			9768	3F : 57xx 0-6-0T (1933)		
4963	5MT : HALL 4-6-0 (1928)			7759	3F : 57xx 0-6-0T (1929)		
4966	5MT : HALL 4-6-0 (1928)			7797	3F : 57xx 0-6-0T (1929)		W/D 10/59
4984	5MT : HALL 4-6-0 (1928)			13034	0F : 350hp 0-6-0		
4997	5MT : HALL 4-6-0 (1928)			13035	0F : 350hp 0-6-0		
5900	5MT : HALL 4-6-0 (1928)			13036	0F : 350hp 0-6-0		
5916	5MT : HALL 4-6-0 (1928)			13037	0F : 350hp 0-6-0		
5919	5MT : HALL 4-6-0 (1928)	Ex Bristol (BR) 3/59		13038	0F : 350hp 0-6-0		
5944	5MT : HALL 4-6-0 (1928)			13039	0F : 350hp 0-6-0		
5965	5MT : HALL 4-6-0 (1928)	Ex Oxford 3/59		13191	0F : 350hp 0-6-0		
5985	5MT : HALL 4-6-0 (1928)			D3431	0F : 350hp 0-6-0		
5991	5MT : HALL 4-6-0 (1928)			D3752	0F : 350hp 0-6-0	Ex Danygraig 10/59	
5995	5MT : HALL 4-6-0 (1928)						

For most purposes GW engines were not allowed to run coupled to any other engines because of vacuum brake differences and the assisting engine for 45390 of Crewe has had to come from Monument Lane. 45429 and 45390 head through Solihull in May 1957 with fourteen coaches of empty stock for a Stratford - Glasgow special.

claimed had diluted the spirit of a great railway. Almost every sentence was prefaced with the words: "You'll understand that I am a Nor-Western man…".

Although rather grimy and rough riding, there was nothing wrong with 41123's steaming and at times the fireman's hardest task was to keep the engine from blowing off. The driving technique was novel to me and after each stop the regulator would be opened in the normal manner for a short distance and then jerked right across the guide and back to the halfway mark to bring compounding into play. It seemed a fairly straightforward operation from where I was standing although the LNWR driver made heavy weather of it.

I was standing on Eastgate one summer morning wondering what to go home on when a Saturday extra unexpectedly arrived, headed by a Stanier 5MT 4-6-0.

"Are you a GW man?" the driver called across to me and I nodded.

"Would you care do a bit of firing. My mate's had it."

I was on the footplate in a jiffey and found things in a sorry state. The footplate was in the usual Midland mess but what was worse, the fireman was an inexperienced passed cleaner and the engine had been coaled at Bath with soft 'blind' coal which Midland men were unused to. The lad was on his first main line trip and had made the error of la-

dling as much coal as he could into the firebox with the result that the needle was down to 100lb with the water only just showing in the bottom of the glass. It was a surprise that they had got as far as Gloucester.

Whilst the cleaner filled the tender I took a critical look at the sorrowful half-burnt black sticky mess in the firebox, brought the bar down from the tender and ran it along the firebars to give the fire a good root up. The driver looked at the chimney and remarked that it was the first smoke he had seen all day.

It was all that was needed and with the blower and injector on by the time the cleaner had the tender filled, pressure was approaching 200lb with the boiler about three-quarters full.

He took a look at the gauge and announced that he would spend the rest of the journey in the train: a decision that was promptly killed by his driver who told him to watch and learn something.

Leaving Eastgate, I gave the fire another run through with the pricker, and once it had burnt through, I started to rebuild it and by the time we left Cheltenham we were in much better shape. We had a nice steady run and I was able to more or less play with the engine for we encountered numerous signal checks.

Black 5's and 5XP Jubilee 4-6-0's were the regular locomotives for most Bristol – Birmingham trains and when you have seen one, you have seen them all. Thus one hot Saturday afternoon I decided that for once I would ride back in the train and get some sleep, having been up since early morning.

My tiredness vanished the minute the train came into sight for instead of the usual 4-6-0, it ran in behind a Horwich 2-6-0 Crab, a very rare type on an express. The driver was happy to let me come up but declared that I must be mad to want to ride on 'this thing.'

"We've no steam, the injectors won't work and the riding is terrible…"

"How did you get this on an express?"

"Our 5XP failed at Barrow Road and this was all they had."

I had a look round and saw the a Crab was a lot larger than I had thought. The

STOURBRIDGE ALLOCATION : 1950						
LOCO CLASS	IN	OUT	LOCO CLASS		IN	OUT
2885 8F : 28xx 2-8-0 (1938)			2246 3MT : 2251 0-6-0 (1930)			
3821 8F : 28xx 2-8-0 (1938)			2270 3MT : 2251 0-6-0 (1930)			
3827 8F : 28xx 2-8-0 (1938)			2279 3MT : 2251 0-6-0 (1930)			
2852 8F : 28xx 2-8-0 (1903)			3649 3FT : 57xx 0-6-0T (1933)			
2856 8F : 28xx 2-8-0 (1903)			3667 3FT : 57xx 0-6-0T (1933)			
2857 8F : 28xx 2-8-0 (1903)			3710 3FT : 57xx 0-6-0T (1933)	Ex Old Oak Common 9/50		
2874 8F : 28xx 2-8-0 (1903)			3740 3FT : 57xx 0-6-0T (1933)			
6609 5MTT : 56xx 0-6-2T (1927)	Ex Oxley 12/50		4638 3FT : 57xx 0-6-0T (1933)			
6617 5MTT : 56xx 0-6-2T (1927)			4687 3FT : 57xx 0-6-0T (1933)			
6646 5MTT : 56xx 0-6-2T (1927)			4696 3FT : 57xx 0-6-0T (1933)			
6667 5MTT : 56xx 0-6-2T (1927)			8791 3FT : 57xx 0-6-0T (1933)			
6674 5MTT : 56xx 0-6-2T (1927)			8792 3FT : 57xx 0-6-0T (1933)			
6677 5MTT : 56xx 0-6-2T (1927)			8797 3FT : 57xx 0-6-0T (1933)			
6678 5MTT : 56xx 0-6-2T (1927)			9613 3FT : 57xx 0-6-0T (1933)			
5606 5MTT : 56xx 0-6-2T (1924)	Ex Oxley 11/50		9636 3FT : 57xx 0-6-0T (1933)			
5651 5MTT : 56xx 0-6-2T (1924)			9741 3FT : 57xx 0-6-0T (1933)			
5658 5MTT : 56xx 0-6-2T (1924)			9767 3FT : 57xx 0-6-0T (1933)			
6828 5MT : GRANGE 4-6-0 (1936)			5719 3FT : 57xx 0-6-0T (1929)			
6857 5MT : GRANGE 4-6-0 (1936)			5726 3FT : 57xx 0-6-0T (1929)			
4104 4MTT : 51xx 2-6-2T (1928)			5754 3FT : 57xx 0-6-0T (1929)			
4146 4MTT : 51xx 2-6-2T (1928)			5794 3FT : 57xx 0-6-0T (1929)			
4150 4MTT : 51xx 2-6-2T (1928)			5795 3FT : 57xx 0-6-0T (1929)			
4173 4MTT : 51xx 2-6-2T (1928)			7705 3FT : 57xx 0-6-0T (1929)			
5101 4MTT : 51xx 2-6-2T (1928)			8704 3FT : 57xx 0-6-0T (1929)			
5105 4MTT : 51xx 2-6-2T (1928)			8742 3FT : 57xx 0-6-0T (1929)			
5107 4MTT : 51xx 2-6-2T (1928)			7402 2PT : 74xx 0-6-0T (1936)			
5122 4MTT : 51xx 2-6-2T (1928)		W/D 9/50	7428 2PT : 74xx 0-6-0T (1936)			
5134 4MTT : 51xx 2-6-2T (1928)			7429 2PT : 74xx 0-6-0T (1936)			
5136 4MTT : 51xx 2-6-2T (1928)			7430 2PT : 74xx 0-6-0T (1936)			
5147 4MTT : 51xx 2-6-2T (1928)			7432 2PT : 74xx 0-6-0T (1936)			To Wrexham 10/50
5155 4MTT : 51xx 2-6-2T (1928)			7432 2PT : 74xx 0-6-0T (1936)	Ex Wrexham 11/50		
5160 4MTT : 51xx 2-6-2T (1928)			7435 2PT : 74xx 0-6-0T (1936)			To Wrexham 10/50
5165 4MTT : 51xx 2-6-2T (1928)			7448 2PT : 74xx 0-6-0T (1936)			
5167 4MTT : 51xx 2-6-2T (1928)			7449 2PT : 74xx 0-6-0T (1936)			
5170 4MTT : 51xx 2-6-2T (1928)			2090 2FT : 2021 0-6-0T (1897)			
5180 4MTT : 51xx 2-6-2T (1928)			2107 2FT : 2021 0-6-0T (1897)			
5189 4MTT : 51xx 2-6-2T (1928)			1621 2FT : 16xx 0-6-0PT (1949)			
5191 4MTT : 51xx 2-6-2T (1928)			1410 1PT : 14xx 0-4-2T (1932)	Ex Wolverhampton 10/50		
5193 4MTT : 51xx 2-6-2T (1928)			1414 1PT : 14xx 0-4-2T (1932)			
5196 4MTT : 51xx 2-6-2T (1928)			1438 1PT : 14xx 0-4-2T (1932)			
5197 4MTT : 51xx 2-6-2T (1928)			1458 1PT : 14xx 0-4-2T (1932)	Ex Banbury 12/50		
5199 4MTT : 51xx 2-6-2T (1928)			8 1P : RAILCAR			
5300 4MT : 43xx 2-6-0 (1911)		To Oxley 11/50	14 1P : RAILCAR			
6332 4MT : 43xx 2-6-0 (1911)			29 1P : RAILCAR		Ex Leamington 11/50	To Leamington 12/50
6354 4MT : 43xx 2-6-0 (1911)	Ex Banbury 12/50		33 1P : RAILCAR			
6391 4MT : 43xx 2-6-0 (1911)	Ex Wolverhampton 12/50		2185 1FT : 2181 0-6-0T (1899)			
8418 4FT : 94XX 0-6-0T (1949)			2186 1FT : 2181 0-6-0T (1899)			
8419 4FT : 94XX 0-6-0T (1949)			2187 1FT : 2181 0-6-0T (1899)			
			2189 1FT : 2181 0-6-0T (1899)			

footplate was very hot, the firebox was huge and the seats were not unlike coffee bar stools. I brought some coal forward in the tender and lent the fireman a hand with the column after which he gave the firebox a charge and turned the injector off with the aid of a sharp clout from a spanner to seat the clack. The injectors were on the firebox backplate which caused them to overheat and fail very easily; the solution being either to use the spanner or, if you didn't mind getting your feet wet, throwing a bucket of cold water over them.

We pulled away from Gloucester with the Crab blowing off hard and thumped our way past the Great Western shed where a couple of shed men made plain what they thought of our engine. Pressure began to fall very quickly and it was only the fact that we were in a queue of trains with checks at every distant that prevented us from coming to grief. At Churchdown we were overtaken by a Great Western train hauled by a Grange 4-6-0 and I was treated to a commentary on my railway by the Midland men.

"They wouldn't have got away we that if we had our usual engine. Them Great Western 4-6-0's are very sluggish...."

The further we went the worse the steaming and riding got and at one point I was offered a seat, only to surrender it a minute later in favour of standing. Had we had a clear run conditions would have become intolerable very quickly – always assuming we would have had enough steam to keep going – but for once the repeated signal delays were welcome and allowed us to keep ahead, just, of the deteriorating situation.

Our big concern was the Lickey incline and by the time Bromsgrove came into sight we were in a very bad way for both steam and water. Even with assistance in the rear there was a very real possibility that we would stick on the bank and block the main line. Had Bromsgrove been a proper locomotive depot we would probably have called for a fresh engine.

For not the first time that day the congested state of the line came to our rescue when it became clear that Bromsgrove had run out of bankers, a situation that gave us an opportunity to try and get the engine into some sort of shape. I used the delay to bring coal forward in the tender whilst the LM man ladled it into the firebox; the driver tending the injectors which were still as temperamental as ever. However, by the time a pair of 84xx 0-6-0T bankers appeared from the Blackwell direction and buffered up behind us, we had succeeded in getting the Crab into a tolerable condition.

After the usual exchange of whistles, we shuffled through Bromsgrove station and onto the incline in which short distance the Crab was already showing signs of distress. We did our best but the bankers realised very quickly that we were in trouble as they seemed to push rather more fiercely than usual which was as well seeing that not only were we in trouble again for steam but the water level was falling at an alarming rate and straining nerves on the footplate. As we were pushed past Blackwell I was about to remark on the good job the bankers had done but seeing the rather tense expression on the driver's face decided to keep quiet.

After the time we had spent waiting for bankers and getting up the hill, the main line ahead of us ought to have been clear but we continued to receive signal checks which allowed us to keep the Crab going after a fashion. Ironically we ran into New Street with everything in good order, not because the engine had decided to improve but because we were held by signals for twenty minutes at Selly Oak which gave us the opportunity to have a go at the firebox.

The driver asked me if I wished now that I had ridden in the train instead of on the engine. I told him that I had quite enjoyed the experience.

"You must be mad."

If the Crab demonstrated the Midland at its worst, a run I made a little later showed it at its best.

I had worked up to Bristol with Joe Smith and was waiting for a ride home from Temple Meads when a West of England – Sheffield express ran in behind a Grange 4-6-0. Anticipating a 5XP taking over, I took my leave of Joe and walked up to the head of the train to watch the engine change, hardly being able to believe my eyes when rebuilt Royal Scot 4-6-0 46151 'The Royal Horse Guardsman' backed down and coupled up. For years it had been a Crewe North engine but had recently been transferred to Sheffield Millhouses whose workings included occasional forays to the West.

In contrast to what I usually found on the Midland, the footplate was not only clean and tidy but the backplate had even been wiped down. Clearly the advent of large engines on the Midland had had an effect on morale. The engine had recently had an overhaul at Crewe and was in first class condition with a huge fire in the box and everything was at it ought to have been.

"Ah, you've nothing like this on the Western," the fireman told me as he started to charge the fire with a round of thirty shovelfulls in preparation for the stiff climb to Mangotsfield.

After a lot of flag-waving and whistling by the platform staff, the driver gave a blast on the hooter, opened the regulator and after a little slipping we made our way past East box and onto the Midland. We stopped a little farther on for rear end assistance, and once the banker had whistled up, started up the bank, fairly roaring up the gradient with the six beats coming up the chimney as crisp and clear as I have ever heard a three-cylinder engine blast them out. Firing up the bank was almost continuous but the fireman had no trouble at all in maintaining steam and water. Once over the top of the bank, we pounded away until steam was shut off to negotiate the tight curve at Mangotsfield where the safety valves suddenly lifted.

"What a racket." I remarked.

"Well at least we know they work." replied the driver making 46151 almost literally come to life by opening up and pulling the lever up the rack.

"What are your nerves like?" he suddenly asked as he got off his seat and moved to the centre of the footplate, giving a long crow on the whistle. A second later we were in Wickwar tunnel and I understood the implication of his question. On the falling gradient and in complete darkness with smoke shrouding the cab, the rolling that took place on the engine was enough to test the strongest set of nerves and I was glad when we emerged at the far end.

"You would have had to pay for a ride like that on a big dipper." He shouted as he regained his seat.

At Standish Junction the Great Western Swindon – Gloucester line ran in from the east and all eyes were on the competition to see if there was a train to race with. For once we were in luck and were rapidly overhauling a Great Western service. I hoped that I was not going to be shown up, impressive as the Scot was, and although 46151 won the day, I was consoled by the fact that its adver-

LOCO	CLASS	IN	OUT	LOCO	CLASS	IN	OUT
	STOURBRIDGE ALLOCATION : 1951						
2885	8F : 28xx 2-8-0 (1938)			9450	4FT : 94XX 0-6-0T (1949)	New 7/51	
3821	8F : 28xx 2-8-0 (1938)			2232	3MT : 2251 0-6-0 (1930)	Ex Wrexham 6/51	
3827	8F : 28xx 2-8-0 (1938)			2246	3MT : 2251 0-6-0 (1930)		
2852	8F : 28xx 2-8-0 (1903)			2270	3MT : 2251 0-6-0 (1930)		
2856	8F : 28xx 2-8-0 (1903)			2279	3MT : 2251 0-6-0 (1930)		
2857	8F : 28xx 2-8-0 (1903)		To Banbury 10/51	3649	3FT : 57xx 0-6-0T (1933)		
2874	8F : 28xx 2-8-0 (1903)			3658	3FT : 57xx 0-6-0T (1933)	Ex Wolverhampton 6/51	
3028	7F : R.O.D. 2-8-0 (1917)	Ex Wrexham 1/51		3667	3FT : 57xx 0-6-0T (1933)		To Chester 9/51
6609	5MTT : 56xx 0-6-2T (1927)			3710	3FT : 57xx 0-6-0T (1933)		
6617	5MTT : 56xx 0-6-2T (1927)		To Wrexham 6/61	3740	3FT : 57xx 0-6-0T (1933)		
6646	5MTT : 56xx 0-6-2T (1927)			3743	3FT : 57xx 0-6-0T (1933)	Ex Tyseley 6/51	
6667	5MTT : 56xx 0-6-2T (1927)			3751	3FT : 57xx 0-6-0T (1933)	Ex Tyseley 6/51	
6674	5MTT : 56xx 0-6-2T (1927)			4638	3FT : 57xx 0-6-0T (1933)		
6677	5MTT : 56xx 0-6-2T (1927)			4646	3FT : 57xx 0-6-0T (1933)	Ex Banbury 6/51	
6678	5MTT : 56xx 0-6-2T (1927)			4687	3FT : 57xx 0-6-0T (1933)		
5606	5MTT : 56xx 0-6-2T (1924)			4696	3FT : 57xx 0-6-0T (1933)		
5651	5MTT : 56xx 0-6-2T (1924)			8791	3FT : 57xx 0-6-0T (1933)		
5658	5MTT : 56xx 0-6-2T (1924)			8792	3FT : 57xx 0-6-0T (1933)		
6803	5MT : GRANGE 4-6-0 (1936)	Ex Banbury 7/51		8797	3FT : 57xx 0-6-0T (1933)		
6828	5MT : GRANGE 4-6-0 (1936)			9613	3FT : 57xx 0-6-0T (1933)		
6857	5MT : GRANGE 4-6-0 (1936)			9636	3FT : 57xx 0-6-0T (1933)		
4104	4MTT : 51xx 2-6-2T (1928)			9741	3FT : 57xx 0-6-0T (1933)		
4146	4MTT : 51xx 2-6-2T (1928)			9767	3FT : 57xx 0-6-0T (1933)		
4150	4MTT : 51xx 2-6-2T (1928)			9782	3FT : 57xx 0-6-0T (1933)	Ex Banbury 7/51	
4172	4MTT : 51xx 2-6-2T (1928)	Ex Tyseley 12/51		5719	3FT : 57xx 0-6-0T (1929)		
4173	4MTT : 51xx 2-6-2T (1928)			5726	3FT : 57xx 0-6-0T (1929)		
5101	4MTT : 51xx 2-6-2T (1928)			5754	3FT : 57xx 0-6-0T (1929)		
5105	4MTT : 51xx 2-6-2T (1928)			5794	3FT : 57xx 0-6-0T (1929)		
5107	4MTT : 51xx 2-6-2T (1928)			5795	3FT : 57xx 0-6-0T (1929)		
5134	4MTT : 51xx 2-6-2T (1928)		w/d 4/51	7705	3FT : 57xx 0-6-0T (1929)		
5136	4MTT : 51xx 2-6-2T (1928)		w/d 10/51	8704	3FT : 57xx 0-6-0T (1929)		
5147	4MTT : 51xx 2-6-2T (1928)			8742	3FT : 57xx 0-6-0T (1929)		
5155	4MTT : 51xx 2-6-2T (1928)			7402	2PT : 74xx 0-6-0T (1936)		
5160	4MTT : 51xx 2-6-2T (1928)			7428	2PT : 74xx 0-6-0T (1936)		
5165	4MTT : 51xx 2-6-2T (1928)			7429	2PT : 74xx 0-6-0T (1936)		
5167	4MTT : 51xx 2-6-2T (1928)			7430	2PT : 74xx 0-6-0T (1936)		
5170	4MTT : 51xx 2-6-2T (1928)			7432	2PT : 74xx 0-6-0T (1936)	Ex Wrexham 1/51	
5180	4MTT : 51xx 2-6-2T (1928)			7435	2PT : 74xx 0-6-0T (1936)		
5189	4MTT : 51xx 2-6-2T (1928)			7448	2PT : 74xx 0-6-0T (1936)		
5191	4MTT : 51xx 2-6-2T (1928)			7449	2PT : 74xx 0-6-0T (1936)		
5193	4MTT : 51xx 2-6-2T (1928)			1621	2FT : 16xx 0-6-0PT (1949)		
5196	4MTT : 51xx 2-6-2T (1928)			1624	2FT : 16xx 0-6-0PT (1949)	Ex Wrexham 6/51	To Machynlleth 7/51
5197	4MTT : 51xx 2-6-2T (1928)			2090	2FT : 2021 0-6-0T (1897)		To Oswestry 7/51
5199	4MTT : 51xx 2-6-2T (1928)			2107	2FT : 2021 0-6-0T (1897)		
4375	4MT : 43xx 2-6-0 (1911)	Ex Wrexham 1/51		1414	1PT : 14xx 0-4-2T (1932)		
5371	4MT : 43xx 2-6-0 (1911)	Ex Swindon 9/51		1438	1PT : 14xx 0-4-2T (1932)		
6327	4MT : 43xx 2-6-0 (1911)	Ex Wrexham 1/51		1458	1PT : 14xx 0-4-2T (1932)		
6332	4MT : 43xx 2-6-0 (1911)		To Banbury 7/51	8	1P : RAILCAR		
6354	4MT : 43xx 2-6-0 (1911)			14	1P : RAILCAR		
6391	4MT : 43xx 2-6-0 (1911)			33	1P : RAILCAR		
8418	4FT : 94XX 0-6-0T (1949)		To Duffryn 8/51	2185	1FT : 2181 0-6-0T (1899)		To Wrexham 6/61
8419	4FT : 94XX 0-6-0T (1949)			2186	1FT : 2181 0-6-0T (1899)		To Wrexham 6/61
9427	4FT : 94XX 0-6-0T (1949)	New 1/51		2187	1FT : 2181 0-6-0T (1899)		

0-6-0PT 1835 stands at Longbridge with the 17.09 workman's for Old Hill in 1947.

sary was only the Chalford Car and its 14xx 0-4-2T. Its rods flashing round – the 14xx's could get up to 70mph – the auto passed us, backwards, its fireman flogging the engine with an imaginary whip.

Shortly afterwards we shut off and cruised into Gloucester (Eastgate) where I pulled some coal forward. I also indicated I should be happy to take over the shovel but the Midland fireman smiled a refusal: he was as much an enthusiast as I was.

We pounded out of Eastgate, past the G.W. shed and, beautifully cleaned, Castle 5017 'The Gloucestershire Regiment'.

"Looks nice," the driver commented.

"Not bad," added the fireman and I asked him if he had ever had a trip on one. He shook his head.

"You haven't lived." I told him, looking out of the corner of my eye at a Great Western express which was leaving the South Junction and running in our direction. Our driver had also seen it and, ready for another race,

wound the gear forward a couple of turns. Coming via the loop at 35 mph the Great Western had the advantage and by the time we had joined the four track section at Engine Shed Junction we were trailing the rear coach by about a carriage length. The engine on the GW was no 14xx this time and do as he might, the LM driver could do no more than keep his opponent's tail lamp in sight. The honours, I thought, had evened a little.

We halted at Lansdown long enough to pull some coal forward and water the tender, the fireman filling the box up just before we pulled out. The LM driver opened the regulator on second valve and we leapt away, shooting a column of smoke high in the air. Once 46151 had hold of the train, the driver simply left the cut-off and regulator where they were and about all he did between there and Bromsgrove was to polish his seat. Talk about automatic pilots.

Having sampled all the engines regularly used on the Midland line between Bristol and

STOURBRIDGE ALLOCATION : 1952							
LOCO	CLASS	IN	OUT	LOCO	CLASS	IN	OUT
2885	8F : 28xx 2-8-0 (1938)			9450	4FT : 94XX 0-6-0T (1949)		
3821	8F : 28xx 2-8-0 (1938)			9477	4FT : 94XX 0-6-0T (1949)	New 8/52	
3827	8F : 28xx 2-8-0 (1938)			2209	3MT : 2251 0-6-0 (1930)	Ex Wrexham 10/52	
2804	8F : 28xx 2-8-0 (1903)	Ex Severn T. Jcn 11/52		2232	3MT : 2251 0-6-0 (1930)		
2852	8F : 28xx 2-8-0 (1903)			2246	3MT : 2251 0-6-0 (1930)		
2856	8F : 28xx 2-8-0 (1903)		To Tyseley 10/52	2270	3MT : 2251 0-6-0 (1930)		
2865	8F : 28xx 2-8-0 (1903)	Ex Oxley 12/52		2279	3MT : 2251 0-6-0 (1930)		
2868	8F : 28xx 2-8-0 (1903)	Ex Oxley 11/52		3649	3FT : 57xx 0-6-0T (1933)		
2874	8F : 28xx 2-8-0 (1903)			3658	3FT : 57xx 0-6-0T (1933)		
3028	7F : R.O.D. 2-8-0 (1917)			3667	3FT : 57xx 0-6-0T (1933)	Ex Chester 1/52	
6609	5MTT : 56xx 0-6-2T (1927)			3710	3FT : 57xx 0-6-0T (1933)		
6630	5MTT : 56xx 0-6-2T (1927)	Ex Tyseley 10/52		3740	3FT : 57xx 0-6-0T (1933)		To Slough 5/52
6646	5MTT : 56xx 0-6-2T (1927)			3743	3FT : 57xx 0-6-0T (1933)		
6667	5MTT : 56xx 0-6-2T (1927)			3751	3FT : 57xx 0-6-0T (1933)		
6674	5MTT : 56xx 0-6-2T (1927)			4638	3FT : 57xx 0-6-0T (1933)		To Slough 5/52
6677	5MTT : 56xx 0-6-2T (1927)			4646	3FT : 57xx 0-6-0T (1933)		
6678	5MTT : 56xx 0-6-2T (1927)			4687	3FT : 57xx 0-6-0T (1933)		
5606	5MT : 56xx 0-6-2T (1924)			4696	3FT : 57xx 0-6-0T (1933)		
5642	5MT : 56xx 0-6-2T (1924)	Ex Shrewsbury 10/52		8791	3FT : 57xx 0-6-0T (1933)		
5651	5MT : 56xx 0-6-2T (1924)			8792	3FT : 57xx 0-6-0T (1933)		
5658	5MT : 56xx 0-6-2T (1924)			8797	3FT : 57xx 0-6-0T (1933)		
6803	5MT : GRANGE 4-6-0 (1936)			9613	3FT : 57xx 0-6-0T (1933)		
6828	5MT : GRANGE 4-6-0 (1936)			9636	3FT : 57xx 0-6-0T (1933)		
6857	5MT : GRANGE 4-6-0 (1936)			9719	3FT : 57xx 0-6-0T (1933)	Ex Chester 10/52	
4104	4MTT : 51xx 2-6-2T (1928)			9741	3FT : 57xx 0-6-0T (1933)		
4146	4MTT : 51xx 2-6-2T (1928)			9767	3FT : 57xx 0-6-0T (1933)		
4150	4MTT : 51xx 2-6-2T (1928)			9782	3FT : 57xx 0-6-0T (1933)		
4172	4MTT : 51xx 2-6-2T (1928)		To Tyseley 2/52	5719	3FT : 57xx 0-6-0T (1929)		
4173	4MTT : 51xx 2-6-2T (1928)			5726	3FT : 57xx 0-6-0T (1929)		
5101	4MTT : 51xx 2-6-2T (1928)			5754	3FT : 57xx 0-6-0T (1929)		
5105	4MTT : 51xx 2-6-2T (1928)			5794	3FT : 57xx 0-6-0T (1929)		
5107	4MTT : 51xx 2-6-2T (1928)			5795	3FT : 57xx 0-6-0T (1929)		
5147	4MTT : 51xx 2-6-2T (1928)		To Truro 10/52	7705	3FT : 57xx 0-6-0T (1929)		
5155	4MTT : 51xx 2-6-2T (1928)			8726	3FT : 57xx 0-6-0T (1929)		
5160	4MTT : 51xx 2-6-2T (1928)			8742	3FT : 57xx 0-6-0T (1929)		
5165	4MTT : 51xx 2-6-2T (1928)			7402	2PT : 74xx 0-6-0T (1936)		
5167	4MTT : 51xx 2-6-2T (1928)			7428	2PT : 74xx 0-6-0T (1936)		
5170	4MTT : 51xx 2-6-2T (1928)			7429	2PT : 74xx 0-6-0T (1936)		
5180	4MTT : 51xx 2-6-2T (1928)			7430	2PT : 74xx 0-6-0T (1936)		
5189	4MTT : 51xx 2-6-2T (1928)			7432	2PT : 74xx 0-6-0T (1936)		
5191	4MTT : 51xx 2-6-2T (1928)			7435	2PT : 74xx 0-6-0T (1936)		
5193	4MTT : 51xx 2-6-2T (1928)		To Truro 10/52	7441	2PT : 74xx 0-6-0T (1936)	Ex Slough 5/52	
5196	4MTT : 51xx 2-6-2T (1928)		To Truro 10/52	7442	2PT : 74xx 0-6-0T (1936)	Ex Slough 5/52	To Wrexham 7/52
5197	4MTT : 51xx 2-6-2T (1928)			7448	2PT : 74xx 0-6-0T (1936)		
5199	4MTT : 51xx 2-6-2T (1928)			7449	2PT : 74xx 0-6-0T (1936)		
9312	4MT : 43xx 2-6-0 (1932)	Ex Oxley 5/52	To Oxley 6/52	2107	2FT : 2021 0-6-0T (1897)		To Wrexham 12/52
4375	4MT : 43xx 2-6-0 (1911)			1612	2FT : 16xx 0-6-0PT (1949)	Ex Gloucester 3/52	To Gloucester 5/52
5309	4MT : 43xx 2-6-0 (1911)	Ex Oxley 5/52	To Oxley 6/52	1621	2FT : 16xx 0-6-0PT (1949)		
5313	4MT : 43xx 2-6-0 (1911)	Ex Oxley 1/52		1401	1PT : 14xx 0-4-2T (1932)	Ex Banbury 1/52	To Westbury 6/52
5371	4MT : 43xx 2-6-0 (1911)			1414	1PT : 14xx 0-4-2T (1932)		
5379	4MT : 43xx 2-6-0 (1911)	Ex Oxley 1/52		1438	1PT : 14xx 0-4-2T (1932)		
6327	4MT : 43xx 2-6-0 (1911)			1458	1PT : 14xx 0-4-2T (1932)		
6332	4MT : 43xx 2-6-0 (1911)	Ex Banbury 4/52		8	1P : RAILCAR		
6354	4MT : 43xx 2-6-0 (1911)			14	1P : RAILCAR		
6391	4MT : 43xx 2-6-0 (1911)			33	1P : RAILCAR		
8419	4FT : 94XX 0-6-0T (1949)			2187	1FT : 2181 0-6-0T (1899)	w/d 2/52	
9427	4FT : 94XX 0-6-0T (1949)						

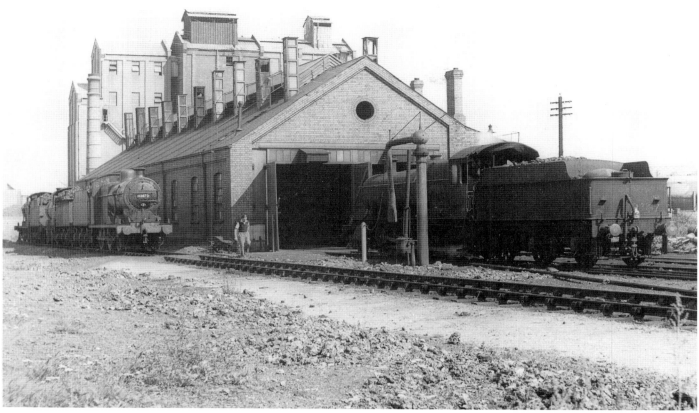

Stratford loco in September 1957 with LMS 4F and GWR 2251 0-6-0's on shed.

Birmingham, there was no doubt in my mind that a Rebuilt Scot was the engine for the line. Looking down along the boiler towards the curiously shaped smoke deflectors and huge double-chimney, even the look of the things suggested power and speed and this was reflected in the way we dashed through Cleeve, Ashurch and Bredon; the Scot simply eating up the miles. Of course, the class had spent most of their time working fifteen and sixteen coach trains out of Euston and a ten vehicle Midland train was child's play. If there was one criticism to be made of the Scots, it lay in the riding and although it had been improved since their earlier days, the engines did seem to transmit track weaknesses through to the footplate in a very efficient manner.

As we braked for Bromsgrove, I wondered if 46151 wouldn't manage on its own and no sooner had this thought passed my mind than we swept by the bankers siding which, unusually, held only one engine, an 84xx 0-6-0T which did not look as though it had much life in it.

It buffered up and we started away, our Driver looking back to see how much work the 0-6-0 was shouldering. Deciding that the 84xx was having its work cut out moving itself, let alone its proportion of the train, we opened up and with the fireman working like a navvy not only did we keep going but the valves actually lifted halfway up the bank. With Blackwell in sight we passed gaggle of bankers on their way downhill, their crews – clearly aware of how much help we were getting – shouting all sorts of encouragement.

46151 ought to have been winded but it wasn't and from the way we picked up speed after Blackwell, it could have been fresh off shed.

"Next time, "said the driver as we came to a halt in New Street. "perhaps my mate will let you have the shovel – then we'll see what you're made of…"

Normally the presence of an LMS engine at Tyseley was as rare a sight as one could expect to see but in April 1963, thanks to a football match involving a team from Southampton, the shed played host to engines from all four companies. No less than thirteen specials were run from Southampton and, uniquely, the engines worked through with GW pilotmen and were serviced at Tyseley. (Nine of the trains came via Reading and Leamington and the balance via Worcester and Stourbridge; the latter being given an LMS

			STOURBRIDGE ALLOCATION : 1953					
LOCO	CLASS	IN	OUT	RETURNED	LOCO	CLASS	IN	OUT
2885	8F : 28xx 2-8-0 (1938)				8437	4FT : 94XX 0-6-0T (1949)	New 6/53	
3821	8F : 28xx 2-8-0 (1938)				8438	4FT : 94XX 0-6-0T (1949)	New 6/53	
3827	8F : 28xx 2-8-0 (1938)				9427	4FT : 94XX 0-6-0T (1949)		To Aberbeeg 12/53
3861	8F : 28xx 2-8-0 (1938)	Ex Shrewsbury 12/53			9450	4FT : 94XX 0-6-0T (1949)		To Aberbeeg 12/53
2804	8F : 28xx 2-8-0 (1903)				9477	4FT : 94XX 0-6-0T (1949)		
2852	8F : 28xx 2-8-0 (1903)				2209	3MT : 2251 0-6-0 (1930)		To Wrexham 5/53
2865	8F : 28xx 2-8-0 (1903)				2232	3MT : 2251 0-6-0 (1930)		To Shrewsbury 5/53
2868	8F : 28xx 2-8-0 (1903)				2246	3MT : 2251 0-6-0 (1930)		To Banbury 5/53
2874	8F : 28xx 2-8-0 (1903)				2270	3MT : 2251 0-6-0 (1930)		To Banbury 5/53
3028	7F : R.O.D. 2-8-0 (1917)				2279	3MT : 2251 0-6-0 (1930)		
6609	5MT : 56xx 0-6-2T (1927)		To Oxley 9/53		3206	3MT : 2251 0-6-0 (1930)	Ex Wrexham 5/53	
6630	5MT : 56xx 0-6-2T (1927)		To Llanelly 3/53		3216	3MT : 2251 0-6-0 (1930)	Ex Banbury 5/53	
6646	5MT : 56xx 0-6-2T (1927)		To Tyseley 10/53	Ex Tyselet 11/53	3217	3MT : 2251 0-6-0 (1930)	Ex Shrewsbury 5/53	
6667	5MT : 56xx 0-6-2T (1927)				3218	3MT : 2251 0-6-0 (1930)	Ex Banbury 5/53	
6674	5MT : 56xx 0-6-2T (1927)		To Neyland 6/53	Ex Neyland 7/53	3649	3FT : 57xx 0-6-0T (1933)		
6677	5MT : 56xx 0-6-2T (1927)				3658	3FT : 57xx 0-6-0T (1933)		
6678	5MT : 56xx 0-6-2T (1927)				3667	3FT : 57xx 0-6-0T (1933)		
6681	5MT : 56xx 0-6-2T (1927)	Ex Hereford 12/53			3710	3FT : 57xx 0-6-0T (1933)		
6683	5MT : 56xx 0-6-2T (1927)	Ex Shrewsbury 5/53			3743	3FT : 57xx 0-6-0T (1933)		
6692	5MT : 56xx 0-6-2T (1927)	Ex Aberdare 12/53			3751	3FT : 57xx 0-6-0T (1933)		
6698	5MT : 56xx 0-6-2T (1927)	Ex Shrewsbury 5/53			4646	3FT : 57xx 0-6-0T (1933)		
5606	5MT : 56xx 0-6-2T (1924)				4687	3FT : 57xx 0-6-0T (1933)		
5642	5MT : 56xx 0-6-2T (1924)				4696	3FT : 57xx 0-6-0T (1933)		
5651	5MT : 56xx 0-6-2T (1924)				8791	3FT : 57xx 0-6-0T (1933)		
5658	5MT : 56xx 0-6-2T (1924)				8792	3FT : 57xx 0-6-0T (1933)		
6803	5MT : GRANGE 4-6-0 (1936)				8797	3FT : 57xx 0-6-0T (1933)		
6823	5MT : GRANGE 4-6-0 (1936)	Ex Swindon 5/53			9613	3FT : 57xx 0-6-0T (1933)		
6828	5MT : GRANGE 4-6-0 (1936)				9636	3FT : 57xx 0-6-0T (1933)		
6857	5MT : GRANGE 4-6-0 (1936)				9719	3FT : 57xx 0-6-0T (1933)		
4104	4MT : 51xx 2-6-2T (1928)				9741	3FT : 57xx 0-6-0T (1933)		To Wellington 2/53
4146	4MT : 51xx 2-6-2T (1928)				9767	3FT : 57xx 0-6-0T (1933)		
4150	4MT : 51xx 2-6-2T (1928)		To Bristol (BR) 5/53		9782	3FT : 57xx 0-6-0T (1933)		
4173	4MT : 51xx 2-6-2T (1928)				5719	3FT : 57xx 0-6-0T (1929)		
5101	4MT : 51xx 2-6-2T (1928)				5726	3FT : 57xx 0-6-0T (1929)		To Oswestry 8/53
5105	4MT : 51xx 2-6-2T (1928)				5754	3FT : 57xx 0-6-0T (1929)		
5107	4MT : 51xx 2-6-2T (1928)				5794	3FT : 57xx 0-6-0T (1929)		
5155	4MT : 51xx 2-6-2T (1928)		To Severn T. Jcn 4/53		5795	3FT : 57xx 0-6-0T (1929)		
5160	4MT : 51xx 2-6-2T (1928)				7705	3FT : 57xx 0-6-0T (1929)		
5165	4MT : 51xx 2-6-2T (1928)				8704	3FT : 57xx 0-6-0T (1929)		
5167	4MT : 51xx 2-6-2T (1928)				8742	3FT : 57xx 0-6-0T (1929)		
5170	4MT : 51xx 2-6-2T (1928)		To Banbury 5/53		7402	2PT : 74xx 0-6-0T (1936)		To Machynlleth 6/53
5180	4MT : 51xx 2-6-2T (1928)				7428	2PT : 74xx 0-6-0T (1936)		
5189	4MT : 51xx 2-6-2T (1928)				7429	2PT : 74xx 0-6-0T (1936)		
5191	4MT : 51xx 2-6-2T (1928)				7430	2PT : 74xx 0-6-0T (1936)		
5197	4MT : 51xx 2-6-2T (1928)		To Bristol (BR) 5/53		7432	2PT : 74xx 0-6-0T (1936)		
5199	4MT : 51xx 2-6-2T (1928)				7435	2PT : 74xx 0-6-0T (1936)		
4326	4MT : 43xx 2-6-0 (1911)	Ex Didcot 4/53			7441	2PT : 74xx 0-6-0T (1936)		
4375	4MT : 43xx 2-6-0 (1911)				7448	2PT : 74xx 0-6-0T (1936)		
5313	4MT : 43xx 2-6-0 (1911)				7449	2PT : 74xx 0-6-0T (1936)		
5371	4MT : 43xx 2-6-0 (1911)				1619	2FT : 16xx 0-6-0PT (1949)	Ex Wellington 2/53	
5379	4MT : 43xx 2-6-0 (1911)				1621	2FT : 16xx 0-6-0PT (1949)		
6324	4MT : 43xx 2-6-0 (1911)	Ex Worcester 3/53	To Worcester 5/53		1414	1PT : 14xx 0-4-2T (1932)		
6327	4MT : 43xx 2-6-0 (1911)				1438	1PT : 14xx 0-4-2T (1932)		
6332	4MT : 43xx 2-6-0 (1911)				1458	1PT : 14xx 0-4-2T (1932)		
6354	4MT : 43xx 2-6-0 (1911)		To Worcester 5/53		8	1P : RAILCAR		
6391	4MT : 43xx 2-6-0 (1911)				14	1P : RAILCAR		
8419	4FT : 94XX 0-6-0T (1949)				33	1P : RAILCAR		To Southall 4/53

8F 2-8-0 to assist them up Old Street bank).

Twelve of the Southern engines were rebuilt West Country Pacifics, which we were able to make sense of, but the thirteenth, 34094, was an unrebuilt type and no-one could make head or tail of it. It was left to Passed Fireman Dennis Herbert to fathom it out and he looked after for the rest of the day.

From somewhere an LNER B1 4-6-0 turned up and this completed the set.

In more normal times, the odd LMS engines seen at Tyseley arrived and left with their own crews and it was unusual for a Tyseley driver to handle anything but a Great Western engine. When strangers did appear they could almost be guaranteed to throw the older boys into a state of confusion.

Jim Rudge and I, together with another set of men, were waiting in the relief cabin at Tysley one Sunday to take over a pair of ballast trains en route from Oswestry to Princes Risborough. The other driver rang control to find out where the first of the trains was.

"It's left Snow Hill, Engine 895."

The driver replaced the phone and turned to me.

"895. What sort of an engine's that, Jacks?"

I had to scratch my head for a minute before remembering it was a Cambrian 0-6-0. The Cambrian was as foreign as the LNER and the driver was not impressed although I would have cheerfully changed places with his fireman.

They went out and shortly afterwards the controller rang Jim to tell him our train was getting close. Like the other driver, he turned to me as he put the phone down.

"46515. What kind of engine's that, Jacks?"

"Well," I told him, picking up my traps. "It's not Cambrian."

We went outside and relieved a set of Wolverhampton men who were full of woe. The thing wouldn't steam, there wasn't enough coal in the tender to see the trip through and what sort of idiot arranged for such a small engine to do such a long trip. Jim told them to tell control that they would have to change engines at Banbury which in the event was just as well since, with only a moderate load, we had to stop at Southam Road and Harbury to blow up. Eventually we reached Banbury where we left the train and dropped the engine on the loco. I had a good look round for 895 but it had evidently worked through: so much for old age.

We actually saw more of the Cambrian 0-6-0's than most people realise since they were maintained at Stafford Road works and run in afterwards on an Oxley – Bordesley goods, being turned and serviced at Tyseley. Occasionally one would become stranded at Tyseley – when, for example, its back working had been cancelled – and we would use them locally for a day or two. A favourite job for such engines was the 'back out' which involved propelling four passenger coaches out of the sidings to Tyseley via Tyseley South to form the 17.44 all-stations to Wolverhampton.

I was on the carriage pilot one afternoon when a Dean Goods 0-6-0 was sent out for the pull-out and although it looked very smart in its ex-works condition, the carriage sidings inspector had his doubts and made us follow the stock out in case the elderly 0-6-0 had trouble on the steep hump outside the sidings. He needn't have worried since the Dean worked them without a cough which is more than an LMS 5XP managed to do some years later when it had to be assisted on the same job by a 350hp shunter.

It goes without saying that there was nothing on the other systems which could hold a candle to a Great Western engine although I always enjoyed the novelty of working on a foreigner and the best way of achieving this was to cover a vacancy at Leamington, as we often did from Tyseley, after it had taken over a number of jobs from the LMS at Warwick, Milverton Street.

In the old days a stint at Leamington usually meant firing a 51xx 2-6-2T on a local to Snow Hill but in later times I found myself on Stanier 8F 2-8-0's working LNW turns to Coventry and Rugby.

The Rugby trip was like a breath of fresh air to someone who had never worked off the Great Western and I enjoyed every mile of the trip, looking forward to witnessing some of the activity that Rugby was famous for. One thing I remember in particular was the urgency with which we had to come off the branch and get into Rugby yard without stopping anything on the main line. Once inside we were told to take the engine to the shed since, for our return working, we would relieve a through Peterborough – Hatton working in the down yard.

Up to the point of arriving it had been a tremendously interesting experience and it was unfortunate that my experience of Rugby loco rather spoilt things. We left our train in the yard and ran light to the shed where I rang the loco foreman for instructions.

"No. 14 road and dispose the engine."

"I'm Great Western on loan," I tried to explain, "and we don't dispose of engines."

"Just do as your bloody told and…"

"We don't," I repeated patiently, "dispose of engines on the Great Western."

The telephone crashed down at his end and I set the road for fourteen and waved my driver forward. We got about three-quarters of the way down the line when the foreman, complete with bowler hat, stopped us. At his grade he should have known that the Great Western had a different set of rules from the LNW and made proper arrangements for the engine's disposal. He didn't seem to be too clear where Tyseley was, let alone what we did (and didn't do) there, but took my name and number saying that I would be put on report. (As it happened, I heard no more of the incident and imagine that the authorities at Rugby were given some advice on the differing conditions of service between regions).

My driver, who was an LNW man and therefore supposed to dispose his engine, was quite happy since he was spared the unpleasant job of throwing the fire out and we walked across to the down yard for our back working.

My interest in wandering must have come to the attention of a sympathetic list clerk who one day sent me to cover a vacancy a far-off Wellington, a pleasant little shed with nine 57xx 0-6-0T's and a couple of 51xx 2-6-2T's. No details as to the job I was to cover were given to me and on the train down I mused upon the possibilities, regretting the demise of the 44xx 2-6-2T's which used to work the Much Wenlock branch.

I reported to the timekeeper and was directed to the Buildwas trip engine which that day was being worked by 'Flying Pig' 2-6-0 43022 of Nuneaton. I found the driver lying on a strip of grass who told me that the job consisted of two return trips to Buildwas power station but that we were waiting for someone to provide a guard. My enthusiasm at the prospect of working over the Buildwas branch and firing an Ivatt 2-6-0 was dampened when I was told that they hadn't had a guard all week. We sat and waited but in the end we didn't so much as turn a wheel and I returned passenger to Tyseley conscious of having had an interesting, if rather unproductive, day out.

LOCO	CLASS	IN	OUT	LOCO	CLASS	IN	OUT
				STOURBRIDGE ALLOCATION : 1954			
2885	8F : 28xx 2-8-0 (1938)			8438	4FT : 94XX 0-6-0T (1949)		
3821	8F : 28xx 2-8-0 (1938)			9477	4FT : 94XX 0-6-0T (1949)		
3827	8F : 28xx 2-8-0 (1938)			2279	3MT : 2251 0-6-0 (1930)		To Tyseley 1/54
3861	8F : 28xx 2-8-0 (1938)		To Oxley 9/54	3206	3MT : 2251 0-6-0 (1930)		To Didcot 1/54
2804	8F : 28xx 2-8-0 (1903)			3216	3MT : 2251 0-6-0 (1930)		To Carmarthen 1/54
2874	8F : 28xx 2-8-0 (1903)			3217	3MT : 2251 0-6-0 (1930)		To Worcester 1/54
6609	5MTT : 56xx 0-6-2T (1927)			3218	3MT : 2251 0-6-0 (1930)		To Worcester 1/54
6646	5MTT : 56xx 0-6-2T (1927)			3649	3FT : 57xx 0-6-0T (1933)		
6667	5MTT : 56xx 0-6-2T (1927)			3658	3FT : 57xx 0-6-0T (1933)		
6674	5MTT : 56xx 0-6-2T (1927)			3667	3FT : 57xx 0-6-0T (1933)		
6677	5MTT : 56xx 0-6-2T (1927)			3710	3FT : 57xx 0-6-0T (1933)		
6678	5MTT : 56xx 0-6-2T (1927)			3729	3FT : 57xx 0-6-0T (1933)	Ex Canton 11/54	
6681	5MTT : 56xx 0-6-2T (1927)			3743	3FT : 57xx 0-6-0T (1933)		
6683	5MTT : 56xx 0-6-2T (1927)			3745	3FT : 57xx 0-6-0T (1933)	Ex Oxley 4/54	
6692	5MTT : 56xx 0-6-2T (1927)			3751	3FT : 57xx 0-6-0T (1933)		
6698	5MTT : 56xx 0-6-2T (1927)			4646	3FT : 57xx 0-6-0T (1933)		
5606	5MTT : 56xx 0-6-2T (1924)			4687	3FT : 57xx 0-6-0T (1933)		
5642	5MTT : 56xx 0-6-2T (1924)		To Cardiff (E. Dck) 1/54	4696	3FT : 57xx 0-6-0T (1933)		
5651	5MTT : 56xx 0-6-2T (1924)			8791	3FT : 57xx 0-6-0T (1933)		
5658	5MTT : 56xx 0-6-2T (1924)			8792	3FT : 57xx 0-6-0T (1933)		
6803	5MT : GRANGE 4-6-0 (1936)			8797	3FT : 57xx 0-6-0T (1933)		
6823	5MT : GRANGE 4-6-0 (1936)			9613	3FT : 57xx 0-6-0T (1933)		
6828	5MT : GRANGE 4-6-0 (1936)			9636	3FT : 57xx 0-6-0T (1933)		
6857	5MT : GRANGE 4-6-0 (1936)			9719	3FT : 57xx 0-6-0T (1933)		
4104	4MTT : 51xx 2-6-2T (1928)			9767	3FT : 57xx 0-6-0T (1933)		
4146	4MTT : 51xx 2-6-2T (1928)			9782	3FT : 57xx 0-6-0T (1933)		
4173	4MTT : 51xx 2-6-2T (1928)			5719	3FT : 57xx 0-6-0T (1929)		
5101	4MTT : 51xx 2-6-2T (1928)			5754	3FT : 57xx 0-6-0T (1929)		
5105	4MTT : 51xx 2-6-2T (1928)			5794	3FT : 57xx 0-6-0T (1929)		To Canton 11/54
5107	4MTT : 51xx 2-6-2T (1928)			5795	3FT : 57xx 0-6-0T (1929)		
5160	4MTT : 51xx 2-6-2T (1928)			7705	3FT : 57xx 0-6-0T (1929)		
5165	4MTT : 51xx 2-6-2T (1928)			8704	3FT : 57xx 0-6-0T (1929)		
5167	4MTT : 51xx 2-6-2T (1928)			8742	3FT : 57xx 0-6-0T (1929)		
5180	4MTT : 51xx 2-6-2T (1928)			7428	2PT : 74xx 0-6-0T (1936)		
5189	4MTT : 51xx 2-6-2T (1928)			7429	2PT : 74xx 0-6-0T (1936)		
5191	4MTT : 51xx 2-6-2T (1928)			7430	2PT : 74xx 0-6-0T (1936)		
5199	4MTT : 51xx 2-6-2T (1928)			7432	2PT : 74xx 0-6-0T (1936)		
9318	4MT : 43xx 2-6-0 (1932)	Ex Oxley 9/54		7435	2PT : 74xx 0-6-0T (1936)		
4326	4MT : 43xx 2-6-0 (1911)			7441	2PT : 74xx 0-6-0T (1936)		
4375	4MT : 43xx 2-6-0 (1911)			7448	2PT : 74xx 0-6-0T (1936)		
5313	4MT : 43xx 2-6-0 (1911)			7449	2PT : 74xx 0-6-0T (1936)		
5371	4MT : 43xx 2-6-0 (1911)			1619	2FT : 16xx 0-6-0PT (1949)		
5379	4MT : 43xx 2-6-0 (1911)			1621	2FT : 16xx 0-6-0PT (1949)		
6327	4MT : 43xx 2-6-0 (1911)		To Tyseley 1/54	1414	1PT : 14xx 0-4-2T (1932)		
6332	4MT : 43xx 2-6-0 (1911)			1438	1PT : 14xx 0-4-2T (1932)		
6391	4MT : 43xx 2-6-0 (1911)			1458	1PT : 14xx 0-4-2T (1932)		
8419	4FT : 94XX 0-6-0T (1949)			8	1P : RAILCAR		
8437	4FT : 94XX 0-6-0T (1949)			14	1P : RAILCAR		

BOTTOM OF THE PILE

Although generally associated with the South Wales districts, the 56xx 0-6-2T's were by no means unknown in other parts of the Great Western and nearly a quarter of the class was allocated to sheds on the Northern main line. The heaviest concentration outside Wales was to be found at Stourbridge which had thirteen of the class in 1955. 6646 arrives in the down yard at Stourbridge Junction with a local trip working on 1st July 1961.

Goods trains have never received much prominence in the railway press which is a curious imbalance since not only did they outnumber passenger trains by a considerable margin but absorbed about ninety percent of the railways resources and activities. The trains fell into broad two groups. There were the fitted and partly fitted trains which ran to much the same disciplines as passenger services and ordinary – usually mineral – workings which had to squeeze their way between other trains.

All trains were timetabled to the half minute but it was very rare for the running of a low priority goods to follow the path laid down for it. Typically you would leave Bordesley on time – punctuality in starting was usually pretty good – only to get a mile up the line to find yourself regulated for a series of special van trains arranged at the drop of a hat by the district controller. Thus you would lurch from loop to loop not only getting to your destination well behind time but seri-

ously delaying the back working. Even on the forty-mile trip to Banbury, you could never be certain what time you would get home when working an unfitted service.

In an effort to avoid congestion on the main line around Banbury, quite a number of through goods trains between London and Birmingham were diverted over the North Warwicks line to run via Shirley, Stratford, Honeybourne and Oxford. Whilst the diversions eased matters on the main line, they added to the operational difficulties elsewhere, especially at Honeybourne where the bankers were required to assist a daily minimum of seventeen trains – almost one an hour - up the bank to Chipping Campden.

There was also a limit on the number of additional workings that could be sent along the North Warwicks to Cheltenham since the number of loops and refuge sidings was minimal and it did not take many extra trains to cause congestion.

A fairly typical example of a West Midlands working was the 04.15 Bordesley – Newton Abbot which had to operate via Oxford because no sensible path was available via any of the more direct routes. We would book on at 02.55 and work to Oxford via Shirley and Stratford, where we would stop to take water. Although the climb to Earlswood was a fair

STOURBRIDGE ALLOCATION : 1955								
LOCO	CLASS	IN	OUT	LOCO	CLASS	IN	OUT
2885	8F : 28xx 2-8-0 (1938)			8419	4FT : 94XX 0-6-0T (1949)		To Treherbert 9/55
3821	8F : 28xx 2-8-0 (1938)			8437	4FT : 94XX 0-6-0T (1949)		To Cardiff (ED) 8/55
3825	8F : 28xx 2-8-0 (1938)	Ex Oxley 1/55		8438	4FT : 94XX 0-6-0T (1949)		To Brecon 9/55
3827	8F : 28xx 2-8-0 (1938)		To Ebbw Jcn 10/55	9477	4FT : 94XX 0-6-0T (1949)		To Cardiff (ED) 8/55
2804	8F : 28xx 2-8-0 (1903)		To Chester 7/55	3649	3FT : 57xx 0-6-0T (1933)		
2804	8F : 28xx 2-8-0 (1903)	Ex Chester 12/54		3658	3FT : 57xx 0-6-0T (1933)		
2834	8F : 28xx 2-8-0 (1903)	Ex Banbury 4/55		3667	3FT : 57xx 0-6-0T (1933)		
2874	8F : 28xx 2-8-0 (1903)		To Ebbw Jcn 10/55	3710	3FT : 57xx 0-6-0T (1933)		
2882	8F : 28xx 2-8-0 (1903)	Ex Oxley 1/55		3729	3FT : 57xx 0-6-0T (1933)		
6609	5MTT : 56xx 0-6-2T (1927)			3743	3FT : 57xx 0-6-0T (1933)		
6646	5MTT : 56xx 0-6-2T (1927)			3745	3FT : 57xx 0-6-0T (1933)		
6667	5MTT : 56xx 0-6-2T (1927)			3751	3FT : 57xx 0-6-0T (1933)		To Didcot 8/55
6674	5MTT : 56xx 0-6-2T (1927)			4646	3FT : 57xx 0-6-0T (1933)		
6677	5MTT : 56xx 0-6-2T (1927)			4687	3FT : 57xx 0-6-0T (1933)		
6678	5MTT : 56xx 0-6-2T (1927)			4696	3FT : 57xx 0-6-0T (1933)		
6681	5MTT : 56xx 0-6-2T (1927)			8791	3FT : 57xx 0-6-0T (1933)		
6683	5MTT : 56xx 0-6-2T (1927)			8792	3FT : 57xx 0-6-0T (1933)		
6692	5MTT : 56xx 0-6-2T (1927)			8797	3FT : 57xx 0-6-0T (1933)		
6698	5MTT : 56xx 0-6-2T (1927)			9613	3FT : 57xx 0-6-0T (1933)		
5606	5MTT : 56xx 0-6-2T (1924)			9624	3FT : 57xx 0-6-0T (1933)	Ex Wellington 11/55	
5651	5MTT : 56xx 0-6-2T (1924)			9636	3FT : 57xx 0-6-0T (1933)		
5658	5MTT : 56xx 0-6-2T (1924)			9719	3FT : 57xx 0-6-0T (1933)		
6803	5MT : GRANGE 4-6-0 (1936)			9767	3FT : 57xx 0-6-0T (1933)		
6823	5MT : GRANGE 4-6-0 (1936)		To Chester 9/55	9782	3FT : 57xx 0-6-0T (1933)		
6828	5MT : GRANGE 4-6-0 (1936)			5719	3FT : 57xx 0-6-0T (1929)		
6857	5MT : GRANGE 4-6-0 (1936)		To Chester 9/55	5754	3FT : 57xx 0-6-0T (1929)		
4104	4MTT : 51xx 2-6-2T (1928)			5795	3FT : 57xx 0-6-0T (1929)		
4133	4MTT : 51xx 2-6-2T (1928)	Ex Westbury 2/55	To Exeter 3/55	7705	3FT : 57xx 0-6-0T (1929)		
4146	4MTT : 51xx 2-6-2T (1928)			8704	3FT : 57xx 0-6-0T (1929)		
4173	4MTT : 51xx 2-6-2T (1928)			8742	3FT : 57xx 0-6-0T (1929)		
5101	4MTT : 51xx 2-6-2T (1928)			7428	2PT : 74xx 0-6-0T (1936)		
5105	4MTT : 51xx 2-6-2T (1928)			7429	2PT : 74xx 0-6-0T (1936)		
5107	4MTT : 51xx 2-6-2T (1928)			7430	2PT : 74xx 0-6-0T (1936)		
5109	4MTT : 51xx 2-6-2T (1928)	Ex Wellington 5/55		7432	2PT : 74xx 0-6-0T (1936)		
5160	4MTT : 51xx 2-6-2T (1928)			7435	2PT : 74xx 0-6-0T (1936)		
5165	4MTT : 51xx 2-6-2T (1928)			7441	2PT : 74xx 0-6-0T (1936)		
5167	4MTT : 51xx 2-6-2T (1928)		To Wellington 6/55	7448	2PT : 74xx 0-6-0T (1936)		
5180	4MTT : 51xx 2-6-2T (1928)			7449	2PT : 74xx 0-6-0T (1936)		
5189	4MTT : 51xx 2-6-2T (1928)			1619	2FT : 16xx 0-6-0PT (1949)		
5191	4MTT : 51xx 2-6-2T (1928)			1621	2FT : 16xx 0-6-0PT (1949)		
5199	4MTT : 51xx 2-6-2T (1928)			1414	1PT : 14xx 0-4-2T (1932)		
9318	4MT : 43xx 2-6-0 (1932)		To Worcester 1/55	1438	1PT : 14xx 0-4-2T (1932)		
4326	4MT : 43xx 2-6-0 (1911)			1458	1PT : 14xx 0-4-2T (1932)		
4375	4MT : 43xx 2-6-0 (1911)			8	1P : RAILCAR		
5313	4MT : 43xx 2-6-0 (1911)		To Oxley 5/55	14	1P : RAILCAR		
5371	4MT : 43xx 2-6-0 (1911)			13111	1F 350hp Diesel	New 4/55	To Shrewsbury 5/55
5379	4MT : 43xx 2-6-0 (1911)		To Worcester 1/55	13112	1F 350hp Diesel	Ex Shrewsbury 7/55	
6332	4MT : 43xx 2-6-0 (1911)			13113	1F 350hp Diesel	Ex Shrewsbury 7/55	
6391	4MT : 43xx 2-6-0 (1911)		To Bristol (SPM) 4/55	13115	1F 350hp Diesel	Ex Shrewsbury 7/55	
6393	4MT : 43xx 2-6-0 (1911)	Ex Pontypool Rd 7/55					

slog it was nothing compared to the stretch beyond Stratford with its climb all the way to Honeybourne; a gradient which sharpened to 1 in 100 between the East and South Junctions and remained at the same level of severity as far as Chipping Campden.

With so many trains requiring assistance from Honeybourne to Campden, it might have been thought that a full time banker would be allocated to the job but in fact the work was done by one of two yard pilots which would be released as and when required.

We would pause at the South Junction to allow the banker to come onto the rear and then both of us would blast away up the four miles to the summit. Once over the top the banker would drift back to Honeybourne whilst we would struggle to hold our train back on the 1 in 150 fall to Blockley. At the same time I have to repair any damage done to the fire and get the engine in shape for the 1 in 110 climb from Blockley to Moreton which, because much of the bank was on a curve, made the train drag considerably. From Moreton, however, the worst was over and the rest of the trip was a cheerful downhill cruise into Oxford where we would be relieved.

On paper we were booked to run non-stop from Honeybourne East to Handborough but as an H class with a fairly low priority, we would usually wait at Honeybourne for the late-running 01.30 Crewe – Moreton (Didcot) class E to precede and then go inside at Kingham for the ˆ6.30 Worcester – Paddington express.

The stop at Kingham suited us rather well as it gave us an opportunity to have breakfast which for me consisted of some rather unappetising sandwiches whilst my driver fried a meal in the firebox. The guard would come forward and make the tea.

"Is that fire all right?"

The question which was invariably thrown at me as we drifted down from Moreton had nothing to do with steam raising but concerned the far wider issue of the driver's breakfast. I had to ensure that the back of the fire had burned well through by the time we came to a stand at Kingham so that the heat was in the right place for frying on the clinker shovel.

Things could go wrong, as they did one morning when Bert Watkins and I were working the train with ROD 2-8-0 3015 (of Carmarthen!) instead of the usual 43xx 2-6-0. There was nothing much wrong with the ROD's provided you were in no hurry and we plodded our way along the route, the fire being charged after passing Blockley so that it would be in good frying condition by the time we got to Kingham.

Matters were going nicely to plan until we spotted the Moreton distant at caution and were told

by the bobby that we didn't have a margin to Kingham and to set back onto the Shipston branch to let the express by.

I looked at the fire as we shunted back and saw a black mass of unburnt coal. With Bert chaffing as though the end of the world was in sight, I dug the firing shovel in the back end and lifted it to get some air in. The idea was that it would make it burn faster so that by the time the smoke cleared Bert would have enough fire to do his frying. It seemed to work and I conscientiously built up a mound of burning coal just inside the hole so that he could rest the clinker shovel on it whilst his eggs and bacon fried.

Licking his lips, he cracked the eggs and lined the bacon on the shovel, put it on the pile of coal which promptly collapsed, taking the food and shovel into the firebox.

"You," he stuttered, looking from me to the firebox and back again, "ought to be f-f-f-photographed…"

"Have a cheese sandwich."

A district controller of my acquaintance used to maintain that there was an inverse relationship between mishaps and the reports that had to be submitted. He once delayed a goods train for two minutes and received a skin a yard long. A week longer he paralysed the main line for several hours and never heard anything about it. I had a similar experience and whilst Bert gave me a rough time for spoiling his breakfast, the episode paled in comparison with what took place one morning when we were working the 02.08 Basingstoke – Oxley.

A class D train with a high priority, it was booked to travel via Oxford, Kingham and Honeybourne but for some reason had been diverted via Banbury and was well out of course by the time we relieved it at Leamington. Next to the engine were some wagons for Knowle & Dorridge and the guard, who had only just been promoted from the ranks of Bordesley shunters, told us that we should be detaching them en route.

We whistled for the road, got the board and were soon climbing away with 6984 'Owsden

Hall' of Hereford. The 4-6-0 was in good shape but we had a heavy load and called for the banker at Warwick to give us a hand up Hatton bank. Lapworth turned us onto the relief road and shortly afterwards we drew at up Knowle, ready to knock off the leading wagons.

The guard came running up with all the zeal associated with someone in the first week of the job, uncoupled the train about three wagons back, waved us forward and signalled us back into the sidings. When he had uncoupled the engine we ran forward and set back to reattach to our train. Something was wrong but for a minute I couldn't quite put my finger on it, my attention being diverted by the guard who was jumping up and down, waving his hands in the air like a navy signaller.

"It's gone.. It's gone."

"What's gone?"

"The bloody train's gone!"

He was right. The space occupied by our train a few minutes ago was now a void and it took a few seconds for the significance to register. Bert and I peered down the bank towards Lapworth but there was nothing to be seen. We raced up the stairs to the signalman who looked up from his register, wondering what all the fuss was about.

"What d'you mean 'gone'?"

We rattled out an explanation and in a flash he was banging out 2-5-5 (train running away wrong line) to Lapworth and conversing on the phone. We all looked at each other, thinking the same thoughts and imagining a down train coming towards Lapworth and being hit head on by an unmanned goods train careering at full tilt down the bank in the wrong direction. None of cared to think how far it might go before either running out of momentum or piling up at some catch points.

The guard was guilty because he hadn't pinned enough brakes down, the signalman was at fault for not noticing anything amiss until we told him and, when the enquiry was held, someone would doubtless find something that Bert and I ought to have done but didn't. If there was any justice in the world all four of us would be slowly crucified. The bobby finished talking on the phone and put the receiver down.

"You are lucky bleedin' crowd, you are."

We blinked at him. "A set of p.way men saw it coming, jumped in the brake and pinned it down."

"No damage done?" I asked quietly.

"Only to my nervous system…."

He made out a wrong line order form and told us to go back, bang road, halfway to Lapworth and pick it up. As we climbed on the engine he leaned out of the box window and waved a finger at us.

"Say nowt!"

How he managed to keep the thing a se-

LOCO	CLASS	IN	OUT	LOCO	CLASS	IN	OUT
\multicolumn{8}{c}{STOURBRIDGE ALLOCATION : 1956}
2885	8F : 28xx 2-8-0 (1938)			3667	3FT : 57xx 0-6-0T (1933)		
3821	8F : 28xx 2-8-0 (1938)			3710	3FT : 57xx 0-6-0T (1933)		
3825	8F : 28xx 2-8-0 (1938)			3729	3FT : 57xx 0-6-0T (1933)		
2804	8F : 28xx 2-8-0 (1903)			3743	3FT : 57xx 0-6-0T (1933)		
2829	8F : 28xx 2-8-0 (1903)	Ex Severn T. Jcn 1/56		3745	3FT : 57xx 0-6-0T (1933)		
2834	8F : 28xx 2-8-0 (1903)			4646	3FT : 57xx 0-6-0T (1933)		
2882	8F : 28xx 2-8-0 (1903)		To Chester 12/56	4687	3FT : 57xx 0-6-0T (1933)		
6609	5MTT : 56xx 0-6-2T (1927)			4696	3FT : 57xx 0-6-0T (1933)		
6646	5MTT : 56xx 0-6-2T (1927)			8791	3FT : 57xx 0-6-0T (1933)		To Croes N. 8/56
6667	5MTT : 56xx 0-6-2T (1927)			8792	3FT : 57xx 0-6-0T (1933)		
6674	5MTT : 56xx 0-6-2T (1927)			8797	3FT : 57xx 0-6-0T (1933)		
6677	5MTT : 56xx 0-6-2T (1927)			9613	3FT : 57xx 0-6-0T (1933)		
6678	5MTT : 56xx 0-6-2T (1927)			9624	3FT : 57xx 0-6-0T (1933)		
6681	5MTT : 56xx 0-6-2T (1927)			9636	3FT : 57xx 0-6-0T (1933)		
6683	5MTT : 56xx 0-6-2T (1927)			9719	3FT : 57xx 0-6-0T (1933)		
6692	5MTT : 56xx 0-6-2T (1927)			9767	3FT : 57xx 0-6-0T (1933)		
6698	5MTT : 56xx 0-6-2T (1927)			9782	3FT : 57xx 0-6-0T (1933)		
5606	5MTT : 56xx 0-6-2T (1924)			5719	3FT : 57xx 0-6-0T (1929)		
5651	5MTT : 56xx 0-6-2T (1924)			5754	3FT : 57xx 0-6-0T (1929)		
5658	5MTT : 56xx 0-6-2T (1924)			5795	3FT : 57xx 0-6-0T (1929)		
6803	5MT : GRANGE 4-6-0 (1936)			7705	3FT : 57xx 0-6-0T (1929)		
6828	5MT : GRANGE 4-6-0 (1936)			8704	3FT : 57xx 0-6-0T (1929)		
4104	4MTT : 51xx 2-6-2T (1928)			8742	3FT : 57xx 0-6-0T (1929)		
4146	4MTT : 51xx 2-6-2T (1928)			7420	2PT : 74xx 0-6-0T (1936)	Ex Hereford 11/56	
4173	4MTT : 51xx 2-6-2T (1928)			7428	2PT : 74xx 0-6-0T (1936)		
5101	4MTT : 51xx 2-6-2T (1928)			7429	2PT : 74xx 0-6-0T (1936)		
5105	4MTT : 51xx 2-6-2T (1928)			7430	2PT : 74xx 0-6-0T (1936)		
5107	4MTT : 51xx 2-6-2T (1928)		To Penzance 6/56	7432	2PT : 74xx 0-6-0T (1936)		
5107	4MTT : 51xx 2-6-2T (1928)	Ex Penzance 7/56		7435	2PT : 74xx 0-6-0T (1936)		
5109	4MTT : 51xx 2-6-2T (1928)			7441	2PT : 74xx 0-6-0T (1936)		
5160	4MTT : 51xx 2-6-2T (1928)		To Chester 8/56	7447	2PT : 74xx 0-6-0T (1936)	Ex Croes N. 8/56	
5165	4MTT : 51xx 2-6-2T (1928)			7448	2PT : 74xx 0-6-0T (1936)		
5180	4MTT : 51xx 2-6-2T (1928)			7449	2PT : 74xx 0-6-0T (1936)		
5186	4MTT : 51xx 2-6-2T (1928)	Ex Chester 6/56		1619	2FT : 16xx 0-6-0PT (1949)		
5189	4MTT : 51xx 2-6-2T (1928)			1621	2FT : 16xx 0-6-0PT (1949)		
5191	4MTT : 51xx 2-6-2T (1928)			1414	1PT : 14xx 0-4-2T (1932)		
5199	4MTT : 51xx 2-6-2T (1928)			1438	1PT : 14xx 0-4-2T (1932)		
4326	4MT : 43xx 2-6-0 (1911)			1458	1PT : 14xx 0-4-2T (1932)		
4375	4MT : 43xx 2-6-0 (1911)			8	1P : RAILCAR		
5371	4MT : 43xx 2-6-0 (1911)			14	1P : RAILCAR		
6332	4MT : 43xx 2-6-0 (1911)			13112	1F 350hp Diesel		
6393	4MT : 43xx 2-6-0 (1911)			13113	1F 350hp Diesel		
3649	3FT : 57xx 0-6-0T (1933)			13115	1F 350hp Diesel		
3658	3FT : 57xx 0-6-0T (1933)						

Castle 4-6-0 7001 'Sir James Milne' of Old Oak Common pulls away from Knowle and Dorridge in May 1955 with a semi-fast for Paddington.

cret I shall never know but from that day to this we never heard a word of it. It was curious how I was nearly skinned alive for spoiling Bert's breakfast but got off scot free when a train ran away. It was a strange world at times.

Not all signalmen were as co-operative and some could be downright pedantic over points of detail, even when they were in the wrong as Bert and I discovered one night when we were working the 19.15 Bordesley – Stoke Gifford (Bristol) which we took as far as Gloucester, returning home on the Midland night mail from Eastgate.

We were not running especially well and being a class H had a number of other trains on the block behind us. The problem was that there were very few loops on the North Warwickshire and generally trains arrived at Cheltenham in the order they had left Stratford. This night, however, we had a class D on our tail and the district controller told Bishops Cleeve to shunt us across the road to give the faster train preference.

We drew up at the box, received the order from the signalman, the dolly came off and we reversed the train onto the up main where I dutifully placed a red lamp on the front of the engine before going up to the box to make sure that we were properly protected by signals.

A few minutes later the 18.30 Worcester – Cardiff class D came tearing through and as soon as it had cleared the section, the crossover reversed and we pulled forward to regain the down line. Suddenly the signalman stopped us with a red light.

"What's up?" asked Bert.

"You've got a red light on the engine."

"Well of course we have."

I stared to recite the small print from the appendix only to be told by the signalman that he didn't expect lectures on signalling regulations from the likes of me.

We stood there looking at each other until eventually Bert made a suggestion.

"Tell you what, Bobby. We'll draw forward onto the down road as we are. When we get to the starter we'll change the lamps but we won't move until you've walked down and taken a look. How's that suit you?"

"That means I've got to walk nearly half a mile."

"That's true but we don't mind waiting."

The signalman cogitated for a minute then told us to carry on and keep going. Bert opened the regulator and we inched towards the crossover.

"Mind you take that red lamp off," came the signalman's voice over the clanging of buffers, "or you'll stop the whole railway....".

As we approached Malvern Road I remarked to

LOCO	CLASS	IN	OUT	LOCO	CLASS	IN	OUT
2885	8F : 28xx 2-8-0 (1938)			3649	3FT : 57xx 0-6-0T (1933)		
3821	8F : 28xx 2-8-0 (1938)			3658	3FT : 57xx 0-6-0T (1933)		
3825	8F : 28xx 2-8-0 (1938)			3667	3FT : 57xx 0-6-0T (1933)		
2804	8F : 28xx 2-8-0 (1903)			3710	3FT : 57xx 0-6-0T (1933)		
2829	8F : 28xx 2-8-0 (1903)			3729	3FT : 57xx 0-6-0T (1933)		
2834	8F : 28xx 2-8-0 (1903)			3743	3FT : 57xx 0-6-0T (1933)		
2841	8F : 28xx 2-8-0 (1903)	Ex Worcester 6/57		3745	3FT : 57xx 0-6-0T (1933)		
6609	5MTT : 56xx 0-6-2T (1927)			4646	3FT : 57xx 0-6-0T (1933)		
6646	5MTT : 56xx 0-6-2T (1927)			4687	3FT : 57xx 0-6-0T (1933)		
6667	5MTT : 56xx 0-6-2T (1927)			4696	3FT : 57xx 0-6-0T (1933)		
6674	5MTT : 56xx 0-6-2T (1927)			8792	3FT : 57xx 0-6-0T (1933)		
6677	5MTT : 56xx 0-6-2T (1927)			8797	3FT : 57xx 0-6-0T (1933)		
6678	5MTT : 56xx 0-6-2T (1927)			9613	3FT : 57xx 0-6-0T (1933)		
6681	5MTT : 56xx 0-6-2T (1927)		To Shrewsbury 3/57	9624	3FT : 57xx 0-6-0T (1933)		
6683	5MTT : 56xx 0-6-2T (1927)			9636	3FT : 57xx 0-6-0T (1933)		
6692	5MTT : 56xx 0-6-2T (1927)			9719	3FT : 57xx 0-6-0T (1933)		
6698	5MTT : 56xx 0-6-2T (1927)			9767	3FT : 57xx 0-6-0T (1933)		
5606	5MTT : 56xx 0-6-2T (1924)			9782	3FT : 57xx 0-6-0T (1933)		
5651	5MTT : 56xx 0-6-2T (1924)		To Tyseley 9/57	5719	3FT : 57xx 0-6-0T (1929)		To Chester 10/57
5658	5MTT : 56xx 0-6-2T (1924)			5754	3FT : 57xx 0-6-0T (1929)		
6803	5MT : GRANGE 4-6-0 (1936)			5795	3FT : 57xx 0-6-0T (1929)		
6828	5MT : GRANGE 4-6-0 (1936)		To Llanelly 6/57	7705	3FT : 57xx 0-6-0T (1929)		To Didcot 10/57
4104	4MTT : 51xx 2-6-2T (1928)			8704	3FT : 57xx 0-6-0T (1929)		
4146	4MTT : 51xx 2-6-2T (1928)		To Tyseley 1/57	8742	3FT : 57xx 0-6-0T (1929)		
4146	4MTT : 51xx 2-6-2T (1928)	Ex Tyseley 4/57		7420	2PT : 74xx 0-6-0T (1936)		
4168	4MTT : 51xx 2-6-2T (1928)	Ex Ebbw Jcn 12/57		7428	2PT : 74xx 0-6-0T (1936)		
4173	4MTT : 51xx 2-6-2T (1928)			7429	2PT : 74xx 0-6-0T (1936)		
5101	4MTT : 51xx 2-6-2T (1928)		To Leamington 6/57	7430	2PT : 74xx 0-6-0T (1936)		
5105	4MTT : 51xx 2-6-2T (1928)		To Gloucester 10/57	7432	2PT : 74xx 0-6-0T (1936)		
5107	4MTT : 51xx 2-6-2T (1928)		w/d 6/57	7435	2PT : 74xx 0-6-0T (1936)		
5109	4MTT : 51xx 2-6-2T (1928)		w/d 6/57	7441	2PT : 74xx 0-6-0T (1936)		
5165	4MTT : 51xx 2-6-2T (1928)		To Gloucester 7/57	7447	2PT : 74xx 0-6-0T (1936)		
5176	4MTT : 51xx 2-6-2T (1928)	Ex Birkenhead 3/57		7448	2PT : 74xx 0-6-0T (1936)		
5180	4MTT : 51xx 2-6-2T (1928)			7449	2PT : 74xx 0-6-0T (1936)		
5186	4MTT : 51xx 2-6-2T (1928)			6403	2PT : 64xx 0-6-0T (1932)	Ex Pontypool Rd 12/57	
5189	4MTT : 51xx 2-6-2T (1928)			6428	2PT : 64xx 0-6-0T (1932)	Ex Ebbw Jcn 12/57	
5191	4MTT : 51xx 2-6-2T (1928)		To Severn T. Jcn 11/57	1619	2FT : 16xx 0-6-0PT (1949)		
5199	4MTT : 51xx 2-6-2T (1928)			1621	2FT : 16xx 0-6-0PT (1949)		
4326	4MT : 43xx 2-6-0 (1911)		w/d 3/57	1414	1PT : 14xx 0-4-2T (1932)		w/d 4/57
4375	4MT : 43xx 2-6-0 (1911)			1438	1PT : 14xx 0-4-2T (1932)		To Southall 11/57
5341	4MT : 43xx 2-6-0 (1911)	Ex Oxley 9/57		1458	1PT : 14xx 0-4-2T (1932)		To Southall 12/57
5371	4MT : 43xx 2-6-0 (1911)			1459	1PT : 14xx 0-4-2T (1932)	Ex Oswestry 4/57	To Weymouth 11/57
5381	4MT : 43xx 2-6-0 (1911)	Ex Oxley 10/57		7	1P : RAILCAR	Ex Worcester 11/57	
6332	4MT : 43xx 2-6-0 (1911)			8	1P : RAILCAR		
6340	4MT : 43xx 2-6-0 (1911)	Ex Kidderminster 6/57		14	1P : RAILCAR		
6342	4MT : 43xx 2-6-0 (1911)	Ex Tyseley 12/57		15	1P : RAILCAR	Ex Carmarthen 11/57	
6349	4MT : 43xx 2-6-0 (1911)	Ex Gloucester 10/57		13112	1F 350hp Diesel		
6357	4MT : 43xx 2-6-0 (1911)	Ex Shrewsbury 12/57		13113	1F 350hp Diesel		
6393	4MT : 43xx 2-6-0 (1911)			13115	1F 350hp Diesel		

STOURBRIDGE ALLOCATION : 1957

A new arrival at Oxley from Exeter, 94xx 0-6-0T 9474 stands with 2-6-2T 4155, the latter displaced by multiple units, at Swan Village Basin in July 1960. 9474 was working No.33 bank trip which started from Cannock Road, Wolverhampton, at 04.00 and served Priestfield, Wednesbury and Swan Village getting back to Oxley Sidings at 22.05. The 2-6-2T arrived with the 06.10 goods from Bordesley and worked as yard pilot until returning with the 19.40 goods. Local trip working often involved some very long hours.

Bert that he'd been very good natured throughout the whole exchange.

"Ah well." He replied. "We got stopped, had to shunt bang road, wasted time arguing with the bobby and then crossed over again."

"Yes." I said, puzzled.

"Well, you calculate all that in terms of overtime. It all adds up."

Having started my career in a signalbox I probably understood signalmen better than most of my contemporaries although there was one character at Snow Hill who surpassed all human comprehension.

I was firing to Bob Hunt on the 04.15 Bordesley – Longbridge, a nice little job that took us over the Halesowen branch but were badly delayed by thick fog and a late connection with the 21.15 Oxford – Bordesley. We eventually got away almost three hours late with 0-6-0 7438 and picked our way north, slackening off on the approach to Snow Hill where we received a single yellow and an indication we were being routed via No. 5 platform.

The fog was as thick as a bag in Birmingham and we had to nose our way very carefully down the platform, straining our eyes to catch the signal which was half way down the platform and tucked away underneath the platform canopy. When it came into view we saw that we had been given the calling-on arm which meant that we should proceed cautiously as there was another train between us and the next signal.

We assumed that a train had just vacated the platform ahead of us and that we were to trickle down behind it and wait until the platform signal cleared yet when we reached the end of the platform, the signal was displaying a full green aspect.

"He's forgotten to put back after that last train," said Bob. "Nip across and tell him."

It was an easy mistake to make in the confusion of fog but if we had accepted the signal, Hockley would have ended up with two trains in the same block section. I jumped off the engine and ran across to the North box.

"What do you want?" asked the signalman unwelcomingly as I entered the box.

"We got the calling-on followed by a main line green."

"Oh…"

He seemed a little disconcerted and looked carefully at his track circuit diagram.

"My driver wants you to put the signal back to danger and then pull off again."

"Does he now."

"It's in the rule book."

"You listen to me, kid. You can stand there all bloody day

STOURBRIDGE ALLOCATION : 1958							
LOCO CLASS	IN	OUT	LOCO CLASS		IN	OUT	
2885 8F : 28xx 2-8-0 (1938)		To Tyseley 6/58	3667 3FT : 57xx 0-6-0T (1933)				
3821 8F : 28xx 2-8-0 (1938)			3710 3FT : 57xx 0-6-0T (1933)				
3825 8F : 28xx 2-8-0 (1938)			3729 3FT : 57xx 0-6-0T (1933)				
2804 8F : 28xx 2-8-0 (1903)			3743 3FT : 57xx 0-6-0T (1933)				
2812 8F : 28xx 2-8-0 (1903)	Ex Tyseley 12/58		3745 3FT : 57xx 0-6-0T (1933)				
2829 8F : 28xx 2-8-0 (1903)		To Gloucester 6/58	4646 3FT : 57xx 0-6-0T (1933)				
2834 8F : 28xx 2-8-0 (1903)		To Chester 1/58	4687 3FT : 57xx 0-6-0T (1933)				
2841 8F : 28xx 2-8-0 (1903)		To Oxley 9/58	4696 3FT : 57xx 0-6-0T (1933)				
6609 5MTT : 56xx 0-6-2T (1927)			8792 3FT : 57xx 0-6-0T (1933)				
6646 5MTT : 56xx 0-6-2T (1927)			8797 3FT : 57xx 0-6-0T (1933)				
6667 5MTT : 56xx 0-6-2T (1927)			9613 3FT : 57xx 0-6-0T (1933)				
6674 5MTT : 56xx 0-6-2T (1927)			9624 3FT : 57xx 0-6-0T (1933)				
6677 5MTT : 56xx 0-6-2T (1927)			9636 3FT : 57xx 0-6-0T (1933)				
6678 5MTT : 56xx 0-6-2T (1927)			9719 3FT : 57xx 0-6-0T (1933)				
6683 5MTT : 56xx 0-6-2T (1927)			9767 3FT : 57xx 0-6-0T (1933)				
6692 5MTT : 56xx 0-6-2T (1927)			9782 3FT : 57xx 0-6-0T (1933)				
6698 5MTT : 56xx 0-6-2T (1927)			5754 3FT : 57xx 0-6-0T (1929)				
5606 5MTT : 56xx 0-6-2T (1924)		To Tyseley 9/58	5795 3FT : 57xx 0-6-0T (1929)				
5658 5MTT : 56xx 0-6-2T (1924)		To Tyseley 9/58	8704 3FT : 57xx 0-6-0T (1929)				
6987 5MT : MOD-HALL 4-6-0 (1944)	Ex Worcester 9/58		8742 3FT : 57xx 0-6-0T (1929)				
6930 5MT : HALL 4-6-0 (1928)	Ex Worcester 9/58		7420 2PT : 74xx 0-6-0T (1936)				
6803 5MT : GRANGE 4-6-0 (1936)			7428 2PT : 74xx 0-6-0T (1936)			To Croes Newydd 12/58	
4104 4MTT : 51xx 2-6-2T (1928)			7429 2PT : 74xx 0-6-0T (1936)				
4140 4MTT : 51xx 2-6-2T (1928)			7430 2PT : 74xx 0-6-0T (1936)				
4146 4MTT : 51xx 2-6-2T (1928)	Ex Wolverhampton 1/58		7432 2PT : 74xx 0-6-0T (1936)				
4168 4MTT : 51xx 2-6-2T (1928)			7435 2PT : 74xx 0-6-0T (1936)				
4173 4MTT : 51xx 2-6-2T (1928)			7441 2PT : 74xx 0-6-0T (1936)				
5176 4MTT : 51xx 2-6-2T (1928)			7447 2PT : 74xx 0-6-0T (1936)				
5180 4MTT : 51xx 2-6-2T (1928)			7448 2PT : 74xx 0-6-0T (1936)				
5186 4MTT : 51xx 2-6-2T (1928)		To Neyland 6/58	7449 2PT : 74xx 0-6-0T (1936)				
5189 4MTT : 51xx 2-6-2T (1928)		To Bristol (BR) 6/58	6401 2PT : 64xx 0-6-0T (1932)		Ex Ebbw Jcn 12/58		
5199 4MTT : 51xx 2-6-2T (1928)			6403 2PT : 64xx 0-6-0T (1932)				
4375 4MT : 43xx 2-6-0 (1911)		w/d 1/58	6428 2PT : 64xx 0-6-0T (1932)				
5371 4MT : 43xx 2-6-0 (1911)		w/d 7/58	1619 2FT : 16xx 0-6-0PT (1949)				
5381 4MT : 43xx 2-6-0 (1911)		To Pontypool Rd 9/58	1621 2FT : 16xx 0-6-0PT (1949)				
6317 4MT : 43xx 2-6-0 (1911)	Ex Shrewsbury 4/58		7 1P : RAILCAR			To Worcester 1/58	
6332 4MT : 43xx 2-6-0 (1911)			8 1P : RAILCAR				
6340 4MT : 43xx 2-6-0 (1911)			13 1P : RAILCAR		Ex Ebbw Jcn 1/58		
6342 4MT : 43xx 2-6-0 (1911)		To Oswestry 10/58	14 1P : RAILCAR				
6349 4MT : 43xx 2-6-0 (1911)			15 1P : RAILCAR				
6357 4MT : 43xx 2-6-0 (1911)		To Shrewsbury 2/58	13112 1F 350hp Diesel				
6393 4MT : 43xx 2-6-0 (1911)		To Carmarthen 10/58	13113 1F 350hp Diesel				
3649 3FT : 57xx 0-6-0T (1933)			13115 1F 350hp Diesel				
3658 3FT : 57xx 0-6-0T (1933)							

before I reverse that signal. You tell your driver that from me."

I stared at him, not knowing what to say next.

"Now get out of my box."

I went back to the engine and passed the message on. If I expected Bob to grab the shovel and beat the signalman up – as I hoped he would – I was disappointed since he just nodded as I talked, whistled up and opened the regulator.

Bristling with indignation I stamped around the footplate until Bob turned to me.

"Everything you did was correct," he said. "But. He's the bobby and if he says we can go, we go. If we run into something ahead, that's his look out but we've done the best we could."

Wise words but I still smarted for the rest of the morning.

Not all drivers accepted awkward signalmen quite so placidly and I was firing to Harold Barnett early one morning, bringing 2-6-2T 5186 light from Banbury to Tyseley for weighing. Banbury had replaced the axleboxes and wheels but, lacking the equipment to balance the wheels, had to send it to Tyseley for the finishing touches. Since there was an imbalance of weight which could result in the engine running hot, a speed limit of 20 mph was imposed which meant it was going to take us more than two hours to complete the trip.

Such slow movements are anathema to most signalmen since they mess up all their margin calculations and I got off to a bad start when I rang the South box to tell him who we were.

"Engine 5186 light to Tyseley loco. Fabric 20."

He didn't sound very pleased.

"Twenty miles an hour? Is that all."

"Afraid so."

He started a rambling speech about how we would stop the job at that speed but I cut him short by telling him we were ready to move. His tone hardened.

"I'll tell you what I think. I think you should be thoroughly ashamed using an excuse like that to fiddle some overtime. I think…"

I put the receiver down and rejoined Harold on the footplate, passing the message on.

"I'll sort him out."

We came out onto the main line, running on the road right next to the South Box. Harold braked the engine until we were barely moving, the signalman eventually poking his head out to see what the trouble was. At the right moment Harold gave the whistle cord a good tug, the bobby getting the fright of his life.

After that it was a slow ride home with Harold having to restrain the engine all the time and the only incident of note happened just after passing Fenny Compton. I was staring out of the cab into the pitch darkness when all of a sudden there was an almighty roar and the whole area was lit up as though someone had pressed a switch. Harold and I almost jumped out of our skins and it was several seconds before we realised that the illumination and racket was caused by one of the new RAF jet bombers as it came in to land at Gaydon aerodrome.

Fortunately V-bombers and irritable signalmen were few and far between and most days contained more interest than curses; some being better than others.

"I've got an engine for Old Oak. How far are you prepared to take it?"

I was at Oxley shed with Dave Jones, having brought in a goods from Bordesley with no return working. Dave looked at me and I nodded.

"Banbury."

"Right then, lads," said the Foreman. "1501. All ready for you, just needs the tank filling."

My eyes lit up since the 15xx 0-6-0's were rarities in the Birmingham area, most of their time being spent on the ups and downers between Old Oak Common and Paddington.

We located the engine, filled the tank and pulled away from the shed with the boiler full to the whistle. I was surprised to find that the engine rode like a coach since I expected, given the short wheelbase, that the 15xx's would waddle quite a bit on the main line. Perhaps the fact that 1501 was ten tons heavier than most 57xx's made it a little more robust.

We purred up the main line and clattered through Snow Hill with the boiler still full, the injector not having been used since leaving Oxley and it was not until we got to Lapworth, twenty-seven miles, that I had to put any water in the boiler. Usually a trip with a tank engine between Birmingham and Banbury meant continuous worries about water consumption yet 1501 looked as though it was going to run all the way from Wolverhampton without looking at a water column.

When we got to Banbury – one of the fastest trips I had made since we got a clear run throughout, apart from having to wait an age to get onto the loco – I checked the tank and was astonished to find that we had covered nearly sixty miles yet had half a tank of water remaining.

In many respects a fireman's life – provided he had a passion for railways - was an idyllic one and had it gone on forever I don't suppose I would have complained. However our lives were governed by the seniority list and by 1959 the batch of firemen just ahead of me were being passed out for driving. My turn was fast approaching and the knowledge brought me – and a few of my colleagues – down to earth with a bang.

Up to now most of what I knew had been learnt by word of mouth and had no formal basis. If I knew that there were sixteen instances when I could pass a signal at danger, I knew because Driver Bloggs had told me. I didn't know where Driver Bloggs had got it from nor did I know where to look it up for myself yet very shortly I was going to find myself in front of an Inspector who was not only going to ask some pretty searching questions but would want reasons for my answers. It was a solemn prospect especially as we had no mutual improvement classes at Tyseley and had to fall back on our own resources.

For weeks afterwards I closeted myself with rule books, appendixes, block regulations and all the other sources of railway wisdom, absorbing them by night and trying to put them into practice by day. If I saw a signalman give a green handsignal, when I got home I would plough through the manuals to find out why and in the meantime I pestered my drivers with questions on subjects they had forgotten all about.

There was also the practical side of things which was made difficult by the fact that few drivers trusted their firemen with the regulator. It occurred to me that there must have been a huge body of drivers who had never handled an engine until they took their test for driving. (In passing the reluctance of drivers to swap places was perhaps not so much a matter of distrust as the fact they would have to do the firing).

On the whole Tyseley drivers did not make the best tutors and I discovered that for purposes of learning, Stourbridge loco was the place to be since their drivers seemed to have a passion for teaching rules and regulations – evidently a very local speciality – whilst there was nothing a Stourbridge man liked better than a keen pupil.

With a bit of wangling I managed to get myself partnered to Derek Bloomer – Bloom – who was an ex Stourbridge driver and he did a great deal for me. Our job was to travel passenger from Snow Hill to Shrewsbury, in the 18.10 ex Paddington, and bring up the Ellesmere Port – Tyseley tanks. Bloom would start the shift by grilling me in rules and regulations all the way from Birmingham to Salop.

On the first night I did rather well in his examination and, full of confidence, accepted his invitation to take over the regu-

LOCO	CLASS	IN	OUT	LOCO	CLASS	IN	OUT
		STOURBRIDGE ALLOCATION : 1959					
2885	8F : 28xx 2-8-0 (1938)	Ex Tyseley 3/59		3649	3FT : 57xx 0-6-0T (1933)		
2888	8F : 28xx 2-8-0 (1938)	Ex Oxley 3/59		3658	3FT : 57xx 0-6-0T (1933)		
2897	8F : 28xx 2-8-0 (1938)	Ex Tyseley 3/59		3667	3FT : 57xx 0-6-0T (1933)		
3821	8F : 28xx 2-8-0 (1938)			3710	3FT : 57xx 0-6-0T (1933)		
3825	8F : 28xx 2-8-0 (1938)			3729	3FT : 57xx 0-6-0T (1933)		
3831	8F : 28xx 2-8-0 (1938)	Ex Tyseley 3/59		3743	3FT : 57xx 0-6-0T (1933)		
3839	8F : 28xx 2-8-0 (1938)	Ex Tyseley 3/59		3745	3FT : 57xx 0-6-0T (1933)		
3846	8F : 28xx 2-8-0 (1938)	Ex Canton 6/59		4646	3FT : 57xx 0-6-0T (1933)		
2804	8F : 28xx 2-8-0 (1903)		To Banbury 6/59	4687	3FT : 57xx 0-6-0T (1933)		
2812	8F : 28xx 2-8-0 (1903)		w/d 1/59	4696	3FT : 57xx 0-6-0T (1933)		
2823	8F : 28xx 2-8-0 (1903)	Ex Ebbw Jcn 1/59	w/d 4/59	8792	3FT : 57xx 0-6-0T (1933)		
2853	8F : 28xx 2-8-0 (1903)	Ex Banbury 1/59	To Reading 9/59	8797	3FT : 57xx 0-6-0T (1933)		
2856	8F : 28xx 2-8-0 (1903)	Ex Tyseley 3/59		9613	3FT : 57xx 0-6-0T (1933)		
6604	5MTT : 56xx 0-6-2T (1927)	Ex Worcester 3/59		9624	3FT : 57xx 0-6-0T (1933)		
6609	5MTT : 56xx 0-6-2T (1927)			9636	3FT : 57xx 0-6-0T (1933)		
6646	5MTT : 56xx 0-6-2T (1927)			9719	3FT : 57xx 0-6-0T (1933)		
6667	5MTT : 56xx 0-6-2T (1927)			9767	3FT : 57xx 0-6-0T (1933)		
6674	5MTT : 56xx 0-6-2T (1927)		To Croes Newydd 6/59	9782	3FT : 57xx 0-6-0T (1933)		
6677	5MTT : 56xx 0-6-2T (1927)			5754	3FT : 57xx 0-6-0T (1929)		
6678	5MTT : 56xx 0-6-2T (1927)			5795	3FT : 57xx 0-6-0T (1929)		
6683	5MTT : 56xx 0-6-2T (1927)			8704	3FT : 57xx 0-6-0T (1929)		
6692	5MTT : 56xx 0-6-2T (1927)			8742	3FT : 57xx 0-6-0T (1929)		
6698	5MTT : 56xx 0-6-2T (1927)		To Shrewsbury 2/59	7420	2PT : 74xx 0-6-0T (1936)		To Tyseley 3/59
6987	5MT : MOD-HALL 4-6-0 (1944)		To Wolverhampton 12/59	7429	2PT : 74xx 0-6-0T (1936)		
4986	5MT : HALL 4-6-0 (1928)	Ex Wolverhampton 6/59	To Wolverhampton 12/59	7430	2PT : 74xx 0-6-0T (1936)		
6930	5MT : HALL 4-6-0 (1928)		To Wolverhampton 12/59	7432	2PT : 74xx 0-6-0T (1936)		
6803	5MT : GRANGE 4-6-0 (1936)			7435	2PT : 74xx 0-6-0T (1936)		
6855	5MT : GRANGE 4-6-0 (1936)	Ex Penzance 11/59		7441	2PT : 74xx 0-6-0T (1936)		
6879	5MT : GRANGE 4-6-0 (1936)	Ex St Blazey 11/59		7447	2PT : 74xx 0-6-0T (1936)		w/d 4/59
4104	4MTT : 51xx 2-6-2T (1928)			7448	2PT : 74xx 0-6-0T (1936)		
4110	4MTT : 51xx 2-6-2T (1928)	Ex Wellington 9/59		7449	2PT : 74xx 0-6-0T (1936)		
4140	4MTT : 51xx 2-6-2T (1928)			6401	2PT : 64xx 0-6-0T (1932)		
4146	4MTT : 51xx 2-6-2T (1928)		To Oxley 9/59	6403	2PT : 64xx 0-6-0T (1932)		
4161	4MTT : 51xx 2-6-2T (1928)	Ex Wolverhampton 3/59		6428	2PT : 64xx 0-6-0T (1932)		w/d 3/59
4168	4MTT : 51xx 2-6-2T (1928)			1619	2FT : 16xx 0-6-0PT (1949)		
4173	4MTT : 51xx 2-6-2T (1928)			1621	2FT : 16xx 0-6-0PT (1949)		
5176	4MTT : 51xx 2-6-2T (1928)			13	1P : RAILCAR		
5189	4MTT : 51xx 2-6-2T (1928)		w/d 8/59	14	1P : RAILCAR		
5199	4MTT : 51xx 2-6-2T (1928)			15	1P : RAILCAR		w/d 1/59
6317	4MT : 43xx 2-6-0 (1911)			13112	1F 350hp Diesel		
6332	4MT : 43xx 2-6-0 (1911)			13113	1F 350hp Diesel		
6340	4MT : 43xx 2-6-0 (1911)			13115	1F 350hp Diesel		
6349	4MT : 43xx 2-6-0 (1911)			13116	1F 350hp Diesel	Ex Shrewsbury 6/59	
6367	4MT : 43xx 2-6-0 (1911)	Ex Worcester 1/59					

lator of the LMS 8F which we relieved in Coton Hill Yard.

I made myself comfortable, cleaned the front window, and waited for the road. The loop signal came off and I gently eased the 8F out of the yard and over the complex trackwork of Shrewsbury station. Clear of the restrictions I started to relax and, keen to impress Bloom with my expertise, cracked the regulator a little. Bloom charged the fire and gave me a very superior look as the engine blew off.

We trundled on to Wellington after which I though I would extend the 8F a little further and, with the hilly nature of the line in mind, opened the regulator to second valve, dropping the lever down a little. Bloom gave me a pretty hard look as we rasped our way up Hollinswood bank but said nothing. He did, however, manage to get the engine to blow off again which was no mean feat.

No comments had been made about my driving so I took it that I was doing well and carried on flogging the engine until approaching Shifnal when, with a clear road, I shut off and allowed the 22 loaded tanks to push us down the 1 in 100 through the station. Speed picked up very rapidly and soon the 2-8-0 was rolling with such vigour that it was impossible to remain seated. Hanging onto the side of the cab I spotted the Cosford distant at green and continued to let the train roll, opening up just before Cosford station to maintain our rate up the bank to Albrighton. For a finale I left it until the very last minute before shutting off, bringing the 8F to a beautiful stop at the Oxley home signal which was against us.

I opened the cylinder cocks, entered the time in Bloom's log book and sat back, feeling pretty pleased with myself. After handling a train like that, the formality of having to go for a promotional examination seemed a waste of time.

"Why," called Bloom crossing the footplate, "did you run down from Shifnal like that?"

"Well," I replied, "we had the road so I let it run. What's wrong with that?"

Bloom's lip curled and his voice took on a dangerous tone.

"Could you have stopped in the protection distance of a train that had fouled the line we were running on?"

I thought for a minute in silence but could not give the answer.

"Well. Could you?"

Bloom exploded as he answered his own question.

"No, you bloody fool! You couldn't have stopped in three miles let alone three hundred yards."

I hung my head in genuine shame.

"You," Bloom pushed the shovel towards me, "are a danger to me, yourself and everyone one else. Get over here where you can do no harm."

We continued to Tyseley in silence and

even though Bloom explained that having torn a strip of me, the matter was forgotten, I burnt with an embarrassment that glowed.

A couple of nights later we were on the same job, Bloom giving me a thorough rules and regulations interrogation in the train and telling me that I was driving on the way back.

"No thanks," I told him, "I had enough the night before last."

Blooms laugh restored my vanished confidence.

"The only way you'll do any firing is to take the blade off me…"

There was no following that up since Bloom was not only double red but out of gauge from his boots to hat. I took the regulator and drove in copybook style through to Tyseley; far more grateful for being given a second chance than I was at being allowed to drive.

Good old Bloom! Had it not been for his critical teaching, God knows what sort of a hash I might have made of my practical test where I had to drive the 07.06 passenger ex Henley between Snow Hill and Wolverhampton with Inspector Weston breathing down my neck. As it was it went very smoothly with no records broken and no passengers killed even though it was the first time I had legally driven an engine.

Convincing an Inspector that you could drive a 51xx for a dozen miles was relatively easy and the difficult part was being grilled by a head office Inspector on rules and regulations, a proceeding that raised images of a Rabbi having an interview with the late Herr Himmler. The worrying feature was that you only got three bites at the cherry and if you could not pass the examination by the third attempt, you were removed from the line of promotion to spend the rest of your life as a shed labourer.

On the 28th of November 1960 I was summoned to Swindon and, biting my nails all the way, found myself in front of Regional Chief Locomotive Inspector J. Hancock who was ready to make or break me. I didn't mention the fact – neither did he – but I recalled a time when

I had seen him from the window of Small Heath signalbox as a junior driver at Tyseley.

After a few preliminary questions the battle commenced with not a single subject being omitted. Strangely I started to enjoy the questioning which did no more than allow me the opportunity to air what I had learnt to someone who mattered. After all, it wasn't an inquisition but an exchange between two railwaymen who shared the same passion.

There were one or two hiccups, especially when we touched on four cylinder engines, but nothing disastrous. He threw questions on link motion, brake systems and every rule in the book and then, quietly, he started to refer to me as Driver Jacks rather than just plain 'Jacks'. The day was mine and, congratulating me, he passed me a piece of paper confirming the fact.

My success did not mean that I could start driving engines and making firemen's lives hell for them. It meant that I was a Captain without a ship and would continue as a fireman until a driving vacancy occurred; something that was governed by the seniority system.

Back at Tyseley I rather relished the somewhat delicious prospect of being paired with a driver I didn't much care for so that I could have the pleasure, being newly clued up on the theoretical side of things, of pulling him to pieces every time he bent the most minor of rules but as luck would have it I found myself teamed with John Millman who, like me, was a passed fireman, also waiting for a driving vacancy. Our job was the 18.50 Washwood Heath – West Drayton which we worked from Bordesley to Banbury, returning with the 22.25 Eastleigh – Water Orton.

These through jobs from the Midland were worked by LM engines at that time and Milly and I took over a filthily decrepit 8F 2-8-0 from a set of Saltley men who, like most Midland men, never had much to say to us. Shouting the details of the load, they were out of the cab and away, leaving us with an engine that made our Great Western hearts grieve.

With a few minutes in hand before we were booked to leave, we gave the cab a thorough clean and after ten minutes were actually able to see the level of water in the gauge glasses. I got rid of a weeks accumulation of smokebox ash from the front footplating and by the time we received the right away the engine was beginning to look presentable.

Unfortunately the internal state of the engine was worse than the external and there was nothing we could do about it. Milly was driving and although we kept moving on the falling gradients as far as Leamington, the slighest rise almost brought the engine to a stand. Eventually we were tucked inside

LOCO	CLASS	IN	OUT	LOCO	CLASS	IN	OUT
	STOURBRIDGE ALLOCATION : 1960						
2885	8F : 28xx 2-8-0 (1938)			4602	3FT : 57xx 0-6-0T (1933)	Ex Chester 5/60	
2888	8F : 28xx 2-8-0 (1938)			4646	3FT : 57xx 0-6-0T (1933)		
2897	8F : 28xx 2-8-0 (1938)			4687	3FT : 57xx 0-6-0T (1933)		
3816	8F : 28xx 2-8-0 (1938)	Ex Banbury 4/60		4696	3FT : 57xx 0-6-0T (1933)		
3821	8F : 28xx 2-8-0 (1938)			8792	3FT : 57xx 0-6-0T (1933)		
3825	8F : 28xx 2-8-0 (1938)			8797	3FT : 57xx 0-6-0T (1933)		
3831	8F : 28xx 2-8-0 (1938)			9613	3FT : 57xx 0-6-0T (1933)		
3839	8F : 28xx 2-8-0 (1938)			9624	3FT : 57xx 0-6-0T (1933)		
3846	8F : 28xx 2-8-0 (1938)		To Banbury 6/60	9636	3FT : 57xx 0-6-0T (1933)		To Wellington 8/60
2856	8F : 28xx 2-8-0 (1903)			9719	3FT : 57xx 0-6-0T (1933)		
6604	5MTT : 56xx 0-6-2T (1927)			9767	3FT : 57xx 0-6-0T (1933)		
6609	5MTT : 56xx 0-6-2T (1927)			9782	3FT : 57xx 0-6-0T (1933)		
6646	5MTT : 56xx 0-6-2T (1927)			5754	3FT : 57xx 0-6-0T (1929)		w/d 6/60
6667	5MTT : 56xx 0-6-2T (1927)			5795	3FT : 57xx 0-6-0T (1929)		w/d 4/60
6677	5MTT : 56xx 0-6-2T (1927)			7722	3FT : 57xx 0-6-0T (1929)	Ex Old Oak C. 3/60	w/d 9/60
6678	5MTT : 56xx 0-6-2T (1927)			7762	3FT : 57xx 0-6-0T (1929)	Ex Chester 5/60	
6683	5MTT : 56xx 0-6-2T (1927)			8704	3FT : 57xx 0-6-0T (1929)		w/d 2/60
6692	5MTT : 56xx 0-6-2T (1927)			8742	3FT : 57xx 0-6-0T (1929)		
4974	5MT : HALL 4-6-0 (1928)	Ex Tyseley 4/60		7429	2PT : 74xx 0-6-0T (1936)		
5912	5MT : HALL 4-6-0 (1928)	Ex Tyseley 4/60		7430	2PT : 74xx 0-6-0T (1936)		
5930	5MT : HALL 4-6-0 (1928)	Ex Tyseley 4/60		7432	2PT : 74xx 0-6-0T (1936)		
6904	5MT : HALL 4-6-0 (1928)	Ex Shrewsbury 9/60		7435	2PT : 74xx 0-6-0T (1936)		
6803	5MT : GRANGE 4-6-0 (1936)			7441	2PT : 74xx 0-6-0T (1936)		
6855	5MT : GRANGE 4-6-0 (1936)		To Tyseley 4/60	7448	2PT : 74xx 0-6-0T (1936)		To Carmarthen 8/60
6858	5MT : GRANGE 4-6-0 (1936)	Ex Shrewsbury 7/60		7449	2PT : 74xx 0-6-0T (1936)		
6879	5MT : GRANGE 4-6-0 (1936)		To Tyseley 4/60	6401	2PT : 64xx 0-6-0T (1932)		To Ebbw Jcn 5/60
4104	4MTT : 51xx 2-6-2T (1928)			6403	2PT : 64xx 0-6-0T (1932)		To Banbury 1/60
4110	4MTT : 51xx 2-6-2T (1928)			1619	2FT : 16xx 0-6-0PT (1949)		
4140	4MTT : 51xx 2-6-2T (1928)			1621	2FT : 16xx 0-6-0PT (1949)		To Swindon 8/60
4161	4MTT : 51xx 2-6-2T (1928)			1663	2FT : 16xx 0-6-0PT (1949)		
4168	4MTT : 51xx 2-6-2T (1928)			1663	2FT : 16xx 0-6-0PT (1949)	Ex Wrexham (GC) 1/60	
4173	4MTT : 51xx 2-6-2T (1928)			13	1P : RAILCAR		
5176	4MTT : 51xx 2-6-2T (1928)			14	1P : RAILCAR		
5199	4MTT : 51xx 2-6-2T (1928)			13004	1F 350hp Diesel	Ex Tyseley 8/60	
6317	4MT : 43xx 2-6-0 (1911)			13025	1F 350hp Diesel	Ex Tyseley 7/60	
6332	4MT : 43xx 2-6-0 (1911)		w/d 8/60	13029	1F 350hp Diesel	Ex Tyseley 7/60	
6340	4MT : 43xx 2-6-0 (1911)			13112	1F 350hp Diesel		
6349	4MT : 43xx 2-6-0 (1911)			13113	1F 350hp Diesel		
6367	4MT : 43xx 2-6-0 (1911)			13115	1F 350hp Diesel		
3649	3FT : 57xx 0-6-0T (1933)			13116	1F 350hp Diesel		
3658	3FT : 57xx 0-6-0T (1933)			13192	1F 350hp Diesel	Ex Tyseley 8/60	
3667	3FT : 57xx 0-6-0T (1933)			D3980	1F 350hp Diesel	Ex Ebbw Jcn 8/60	
3710	3FT : 57xx 0-6-0T (1933)		To Barry 8/60	D3981	1F 350hp Diesel	Ex Tyseley 8/60	
3729	3FT : 57xx 0-6-0T (1933)		To Hereford 9/60	D3982	1F 350hp Diesel	Ex Tyseley 8/60	
3743	3FT : 57xx 0-6-0T (1933)			D3989	1F 350hp Diesel	Ex Tyseley 9/60	
3745	3FT : 57xx 0-6-0T (1933)			D3991	1F 350hp Diesel	Ex Tyseley 9/60	

Engine crews waiting to relieve through workings at Tyseley would wait in the relief cabin which was situated by the down goods line and known as 'Pneumonia'. It was an elderly clerestory coach with its bogies removed and a few basic amenities added together with a direct telephone line to the district controller who would advise crews when trains were approaching. Rat infested - thanks to the quantity of food that had been discarded over the years - it was replaced in the early 1960's for a few years by a redundant auto coach then, just before the cessation of GW goods traffic, by a purpose-built brick building. 2-6-2T 8108 draws up to 'Old Pneumonia' whilst shunting in Tyseley yard.

at Fenny Compton where Milly wired Banbury to say that we should need a fresh engine.

After an age we struggled onto the up loop at Banbury, uncoupled from the train and went light to Banbury loco, passing our replacement engine on the way. Its driver, a very senior man known as 'The Captain', because of his military background, stopped to have a word with us.

"I'm very pleased," he said with authority in his voice but a smile on his face, "that you didn't just leave that engine for the relief crew to try and work forward."

"No, Captain." Milly and I chorused.

"Don't you stand for having bad engines on the job….."

The next night we had the same job but with a rather better engine and were sitting in the mess room at Banbury when the Captain strode in and sat down with us.

"Now lads," he said with a rather concerned expression on his face. "I'm acting running foreman for the rest of the week."

"Yes, Captain." We said obediently.

"Now," he went on. "You two are both young and very keen as I saw last night. But whatever you do, don't fail any engines at Banbury this week. Doesn't matter how rough they are, let 'em go through."

We blinked at him as he got up to leave.

"Remember lads. I haven't got an engine to scratch my back side with…."

After a fairly happy week with Milly I was paired with an old adversary, Joe Hiccox, working an unfitted up to Banbury and returning home as required. We worked up in silence with a 28xx 2-8-0 and although the temptation to pull Joe to pieces with my newly acquired knowledge and status was overwhelming, I

avoided it. He was such an unpleasant character, it would probably backfire.

The only consistent thing about Joe was that he always wanted to finish work early and this morning was no exception. We reached Banbury, dropped our engine on the shed and, as there was no work for us, made our way to the station for a ride home.

It was a cold morning and Joe decided that we would shelter in a train of stock that was standing in the down bay. He was going to have forty winks whilst I was to keep an eye out for our train even though, from where we were sitting, it was rather difficult to see much of the down platform.

I had forgotten that a number of trains were being worked by two and three car multiple units and sat gazing out of the window, looking for a 4-6-0 and seven or eight vehicles. Suddenly I was brought up to date by the sight of a dmu running slowly down the platform.

I shook Joe and we tumbled out of the stock to board the diesel which sped past us, quickly gathering speed. I then realised that it had stopped at the south end of the station, well out of my line of sight, and the first I had seen of it had been when it was starting away. Joe was furious and his face was a picture. He turned the full heat of his temper on me.

"Well," I said blandly when he had run out of steam. "At least I'll get a couple of hours overtime for this."

"No you won't." He replied. "We have to book off at the normal time."

"Ah." I countered. "You have to book off at the normal time but I book off at the time I shall arrive back at Tyseley. You're the senior man and it's your responsibility to see that your

fireman gets back at the proper time. I'm late because you went to sleep."

That did him and for once in his life he shut up. I didn't, of course, claim the overtime – it would have been skating on very thin ice – but I had had the satisfaction of hanging one of the most unpleasant characters at the shed on his own petard.

"I don't think," he whined when we eventually got a northbound train, "that it would be a good idea to mention this. We might be laughed at…."

More palatable was the task of turning a poor engine into a good one and I had the opportunity when working the 21.15, class D, Oxley – Bristol between Tyseley and Gloucester South. It was something of a panic job since our back working was the 19.20 'D' Landore (Swansea) to Bordesley which was usually waiting for us at Gloucester Central so there was no time to hang about between trains.

Both trains being of importance with a tight turn-round at Gloucester, a good engine was a prerequisite and we always kept a careful look out for the 21.15 Bristol – Oxley, which we usually passed in the vicinity of Honeybourne, since the engine alternated with our train. Forewarned was forearmed.

On the first night out, Les Cresswell and I had a very good trip down to Gloucester with a 59xx Hall 4-6-0 but failed to see any sign of our opposite number until we were approaching Bishops Cleeve. I had just mentioned its absence to Les and as I spoke, the lights of a class D came into view on the up road. As it got closer it was evident they were having a hard time of it, the blower was hard on and the engine, a double-chimney County 4-6-0, coughing as though it was in pain.

51xx 2-6-2T 4165 waits at Henley in Arden with a Stratford - Birmingham stopping train in April 1952. The instructions on BR numbering seems to have confused Stafford Road works who have painted the engine number on the bunker. 4165 left the Birmingham district in the autumn of 1952 to spend six years working from Chester on the joint line to Birkenhead Woodside. In 1958 it was transferred to Gloucester, moving to Newton Abbot in July 1960.

As per diagram, it was our engine the following night and what a tale of woe I had from the Oxley men when we took over from them.

"Won't steam. Poor tools…." They moaned as they left the cab even though they'd only had the engine for a handful of miles.

I made a quick check but couldn't see any obvious signs of trouble. The needle stood at 250lb, the water was well up in the glass and there was a huge fire in the box, quite enough to get our fifty wagons up the bank to Earlswood. What was missing was the smokeplate which I found in the corner of the cab.

The smokeplate was a device designed to fit into the firehole to divert a secondary flow of air underneath the brick arch and thereby create more heat. If it was removed, the air simply flowed straight from the firehole to the tubes, cooling them down. It was an ingenious device but unfortunately it made firing rather an awkward job and therefore most firemen disconnected it and stowed it in the corner of the cab. My practice, strictly forbidden, was to keep it in place but to wedge it back with a spanner so that it deflected the air properly whilst allowing me to fire properly.

I fitted the smokeplate, wedging it in, and Les pulled the train out onto the main line, giving it second valve. As I expected, 1023 stormed its way up the bank and in fact ran so freely that we were pulled up at Earlswood with a wagon running hot.

I walked back, released its brakes and was approached by the guard who assumed we'd stopped because the engine was short of steam. Apparently he'd come down behind 1023 the night before and had had a pretty poor trip.

Getting away from Earlswood twenty-five minutes late, Les set about regaining the delay

and the engine gave him everything he wanted. It was hard work for me, the Counties needed a lot of firing, but there was no shortage of steam and I wouldn't have complained if I'd been given 1023 for every job I ever had.

A set of Bristol men were waiting for us at Gloucester South and when they saw 1023 coming towards them, their faces fell.

"We had this camel a couple of night ago. Fit for the scrap heap."

"Rubbish." I told them, "we've rewritten the timetable with it."

As I climbed off the engine I saw the Bristol man removing the smokeplate and banging it in the corner of the cab…..

Fully fitted goods trains – class C's – were few in number but the handful that did run rated a greater importance than most passenger trains and in 1958 their ranks were increased by the introduction of a new train between Morris Cowley, Oxford, and Longbridge. The interesting thing about the working was that the last few miles of its journey was over the Midland, the train leaving the Great Western at Bordesley and running via New Street and Camp Hill line to reach Longbridge from the South, thus avoiding the difficult gradients at Halesowen. To save time waiting for Midland crews to change engines at Bordesley, Tyseley men were taught the road and for probably the first time in history a goods train worked by Great Western engines and men could be seen passing through New Street.

Initially the diagrammed engines for the train were 43xx 2-6-0's but these gave way to the evil BR Standard 4MT 75000's until the starting point was altered to Swindon when 5MT 73000's took over.

For all my years in Birmingham, it was the first time I had worked over the Midland – apart from my vicarious jaunts between Bristol and New Street – and several points of detail confirmed that it was a very different railway from the one I was used to.

To begin with before the 43xx's could restart the train from Bordesley, a fitter had to be present to clip the ATC gear into the inoperative position whilst the signal telephones on the Midland almost called for a degree in telecommunications.

I worked my first trip on the Panic, as the train was known, with Stan Selway, both of us reminding each other, whilst the fitter did his stuff, not to forget that the ATC would be just an ornament for the rest of the shift. We groped our way onto the Midland, blasted up the bank to Bordesley LMS box and drifted down by St Andrews and Proof House to be pulled up by signals at the tunnel on the southern approach to New Street.

I jumped off the engine and went to the telephone to remind the signalman that we were standing on the main line but was baffled by the telephone controls which were quite different from anything I was used to. I experimented for a while by pressing and pushing buttons but eventually Stan joined me and together we worked out that you pressed a switch up to call the signalman and then pressed it down to speak to him. Simple once you knew.

Eventually we got the road and started away, Stan telling me that we would take a run through New Street because of the steep gradient at the far end of the station. I gave the fire a dozen rounds and then stood by to help him with the dimly lit Midland signals which were not at all easy to see.

The Snow Hill suburban service was one of the earliest to use multiple units and vast sums were expended to knock a paltry four minutes off the running times between Birmingham and Stratford. Noisy with an unpleasant smell, the diesels were a poor substitute for the 51xx 2-6-2 tanks. The 13.10 Moor Street to Henley passes Small Heath North signalbox and Bordesley Up Sidings in July 1962.

We blasted out of the tunnel and along the gloomy night time platforms, Stan peering over the cab side for signals which seemed to be all over the place. Having only just learnt the road, he was by no means as familiar with it as he would have like to have been.

"There's a signal up there somewhere for this road. Keep an eye out for it."

I strained my eyes as we went along and eventually caught sight of a very faint green aspect, well hidden under a bridge. What a miserable railway the Midland was to find signals on.

Clear of the complexities of New Street, Stan found himself on ground that was easier to follow and gave the 2-6-0 second valve as we navigated the series of short tunnels on the murky climb to Church Street. Our engine didn't flinch though and actually blew off, obliging me to put the injector on.

We ran through Selly Oak, Bournville and Kings Norton, diverging onto the Longbridge branch and finishing the journey in the sidings at Northfield.

We shunted our train, turned on the Lifford triangle and set back onto our return load, a train of empties for Cowley. Running downhill for the most part and having become a little more acclimatised to the Midland, I was able to take a greater interest in the proceeding and spent most of the trip looking out of the cab at the unfamiliar surroundings. We stopped at Halesowen Junction for an express to go by and then followed it into New Street, where we had a clear run until Stan stopped the engine at Grand Junction Box. This was a three way facing junction with lines going off to Euston, Derby and Bristol and although we had a clear signal, Stan had a worried look on his face.

"I reckon he's pulled off the wrong route. Go and have a word with him."

I walked to the box thinking how close we were to Moor Street yet how far away the friendly and familiar Great Western seemed. I also spared a thought for the days when I used to wander this neck of the woods collecting engine numbers.

"Morning, bobby. Longbridge to Cowley, Class C. Have we got the right road?"

The signalbox was a typically dark and depressing LNWR box, lit by a solitary gas light and I half expected a frosty reception from the occupant.

"Bless my soul, yes. Look I'll show you."

The signalman turned on another gas light and went to great trouble in pointing out the detail of our route on his track circuit diagram. For all his unsavoury surroundings, he was the most helpful person I'd ever come across on the LM and I thanked him for his kindness.

A little later we were back at Bordesley (GW) Junction where we handed over to a relief crew, finishing our spell of duty with a two mile walk back to the shed.

Fate, liking perhaps to keep things in pairs, followed my week on a strange line with a week with a strange driver.

Joe Smith was a likeable enough character provided one was used to his idiosyncrasies, and he could have given John Knox lessons in bigotry. All his fireman were given a questioning on their religious beliefs and union credentials and any who happened to be NUR Catholic would probably have ended up in the firebox. He also disliked early starts and to keep him sweet I would come on earlier than usual and do as much of his work as I could before he arrived.

"I shall be bloody minded for the next hour," he would announce when he turned up. "But take no notice."

Firing to him was like working on a diesel – and just as frustrating – since he would run with the lever as close to mid gear as possible. This was bad enough on any engine but when we had a BR standard it was all but impossible to get the exhaust injector to operate.

"Use a little more steam, Joe, and I might get some water in the boiler…"

He did, however, save my life once and for that I could forgive him anything.

We were working the 17.20 Snow Hill to Oxford with Castle 4-6-0 5012 'Berry Pomeroy Castle', which was getting rough in its riding. Approaching Fritwell at about 60mph, I was just about to start a round of firing when we hit the crossover at the country end of the station, 5012 giving such a lurch that I was knocked clean off balance. We then took the right hand curve through the station which propelled me

The Northern section was well stocked with 7P Castle 4-6-0's, having sixteen at Stafford Road and four each at Chester and Shrewsbury. One of the early Castle's, 4083 'Abbotsbury Castle', eases a Chester - Weymouth relief round the curves between Dunstall Park and Wolverhampton where the train will be strengthened with additional stock whilst engines are changed. 4083 came to the district from Cardiff Canton in September 1950 and after three months at Shrewsbury, settled at Stafford Road until being moved to Newton Abbot in April 1958. The view was taken in 1955 and shows the train passing under the LNW main line from Wolverhampton (High Level) to Stafford and Crewe.

towards the opening between the engine and tender on Joe's side.

I could see the sleepers flashing underneath me and the next thing I knew was that Joe had somehow grabbed my overall jacket and plucked me back onto the footplate. We were both pretty shaken by the experience but Joe just looked at me, saying "Hold tight, butterfingers."

At quieter times Joe would tell me about his days as a fireman on the City 4-4-0's and coincidentally the preserved 'City of Truro' paid a visit to the shed to work a special from Birmingham to Swindon. Joe and I were led to believe that we would work the train and Joe's fury, when we were upstaged by a pair from another link, was pretty incandescent.

We watched the 4-4-0 pass Tyseley with its train, the sight doing nothing to improve Joe's temper. Referring to the driver, he grumbled that he'd never done any time on Cities and therefore had no right to work 'City of Truro'.

"….and I'd have been doing twenty miles per hour faster at this point."

Joe's opinions on engines did not always hold water. We relieved a Bilston Iron Ore train with an Austerity 2-8-0 one night and as we pulled away down the goods from Tyseley, Joe discovered that his seat had been repositioned in order to make room for the BR AWS equipment. This gave him more room to stretch his legs and rather pleased him.

"You know," he said, "these aren't bad engines. In fact I rather like them."

Five minutes later we were stuck fast in Snow Hill tunnel with the wheels spinning round at express passenger speed. The station pilot pulled us out, only for us to stall a few minutes later on Handsworth bank where the local shunter had to lend a hand to get us moving again. All this, of course, meant a great deal of delay and

running about but the straw that broke the camel's back came between Wednesfield and Bilston when we stalled on the 1 in 104 incline and had to be assisted for the third time in ten miles. We threw in the towel and, defeated, ran light to Oxley shed.

"Never," thundered Joe to the Oxley foreman, banging a report as long as his arm down on the desk, "ever give anyone a bloody engine like that….."

The foreman muttered something to the effect that drivers got whatever engine happened to be in the diagram but Joe had no ears for the views of others.

"… the idiot who designed that rubbish was paid by the bloody Germans!"

Joe's temperament was not improved by rumours in 1962 that the LMS were going to take us over. "Our people won't allow it," he pronounced but we were stabbed in the back and the Birmingham district became part of the LMR on the following New Years day. Nothing changed overnight but gradually one found lower quadrant signals being replaced by LMS types whilst 5MT 4-6-0's and 8F 2-8-0's started to arrive in large numbers at Tyseley.

We were given the choice of retaining GW overalls or being issued with the LMS bib and brace but Joe told the storeman that if he ever offered him bib and brace, there would be a vacancy in the stores.

To people brought up under a certain system and tradition, the imposition of foreign ways was an irritant that effected us all whilst Joe became positively partisan.

We were working the 00.05 Eastleigh – Water Orton one morning, standing at the Landor Street home waiting for the road. Our engine was 43xx 5369 which had just come out of Swin-

don and looked a picture in its gleaming lined green livery. With us was an LM pilotman and Joe had spent a considerable part of the trip showing him various details of the engine and comparing them favourably with anything Crewe, Derby or Horwich could produce.

"You won't ride on an engine like this, my old mate." Joe said for the dozenth time to his rather bored audience when a battered Midland 58xxx 2F 0-6-0 came wheezing by, steam leaking from every joint and a pall of smoke pumping from its chimney. The driver and fireman looked at Joe and 5369 and, in unison, chanted the most provocative thing they could come out with.

"Old Iron."

Joe shot off his seat, screeched some obscenities at them and was halfway off the engine to do some grievous bodily harm before the pilotman and I could restrain him.

For all his mercurial ways Joe was a good engineman with a cool head in an emergency, as I found out one morning when we were on an Oxley – Banbury coal train with (another) Austerity 2-8-0.

We relieved the Oxley men and set off along the up main, Joe showing no signs of remembering his previous problems with Austerities. All the class were as rough as a bag and this was no exception, the big ends sounding as though they were going to come through the framing every time they came round.

The first inkling of trouble came at Lapworth where we received a slight distant check. Joe applied the brake but it had very little effect on our rate.

"The brakes on these things are usually pretty good." I observed but Joe just grunted.

"We'll have to watch this damn thing going down Hatton."

We took things fairly carefully through Rowington and as soon as we passed under the three arch bridge at Hatton I screwed the tender handbrake hard on whilst Joe applied the steam brake. Apart from the fact we gained speed as the gradient steepened, nothing happened and the rather frightening truth that we were beginning to run away was too evident to ignore.

Jumping off the engine to apply wagon brakes was out of the question since we were travelling far too fast and there was nothing we could do except to hang on and hope that the signalmen could give us a clear road until we reached a rising gradient and ran out of momentum. This was hoping for a great deal and being a heavily used line there was a much greater possibility of running into the back of another train with probably fatal results. It was the situation every locoman dreads.

The Austerity banged and bounced down the bank and at Budbrook Joe managed, by whistle and hand signals, to indicate to the signalman what was happening. We kept our fingers crossed that Warwick would be able to keep us main line and not put us into the up loop where we would simply end up as a heap on the up platform.

Warwick's distant came into sight and it was off. I mentally retracted everything I had ever thought or said about signalmen in the past and started to breath again since there was a good chance that the stiff rise between Warwick station and Southam Road would allow us to come to a stand. I noticed that all our signals were off which suggested that the line had been cleared of trains for some distance ahead. We might, I called to Joe, live to tell the tale.

Still clinging onto the sides of our wild Austerity, we bucked through the station where a diesel railcar was standing in the down platform, its driver shouting something incomprehensible to us as we shot by. Ignoring him, I risked a look over the side of our engine, which was not easy given the way it was rolling, and noticed that the brake blocks were not only red hot but sparkling like a firework display.

Eventually the gradient and what was left of the blocks began to have an effect and Joe eventually got control of the train by Avon Bridge, bringing us to a stand in Leamington platform where we sat silently for a minute, savouring the pleasure of standing still.

I got off the engine, filled the tank and went for a walk with Joe round the engine. The driving wheel blocks were red and giving off a lot of blue smoke whilst the tender brakes were stone cold and a closer examination revealed that the steam cock to the tender brake had been shut off and could not be opened. Some heads, I reflected, were likely to be rolling in the maintenance department.

The south signalman walked up to us and pointed out that we had two red lights on the engine. I didn't know what he meant until I had a look at them and realised that they were of the LNER pattern and that the shaking of the engine had caused the red shades to jump over and obscure the white light.

"What," said Joe later in the day, "do you think that diesel driver was trying to say at Warwick?"

"Probably pointing out we had two red lamps on the front of the engine."

"He could have picked a better time and place to tell us."

The runaway Austerity was not the only perilous situation that Joe and I found ourselves in. We were running back bunker-first from Wolverhampton to Tyseley with 51xx 2-6-2T 4111 one Monday morning after working the 07.06 local passenger from Henley and on leaving Snow Hill tunnel we noticed that we were signalled main to up relief at Moor Street.

Both of us were leaning against the cab lockers and we both saw the danger at the same time: there was something indefinably wrong about the look of the points. "Hold tight" yelled Joe his arms moving like an octopus over the engine's controls as 4111 banged across the pointwork, lurching one way and then the other. We came to a stop and got down to see what had happened just as the Moor Street signalman, alarmed by the noise, ran over.

At first he was mystified, he had set the road for us and all the detection worked but when we told him that something hadn't looked right as we approached, we had a closer look at the crossover. There were no fishplates and it was a wonder that 4111 had stayed on the road.

The permanent way people turned up and we discovered that they had been working on the track the day before and had, presumably, not checked the work. Joe and I left them to the consequences of the post-mortem and returned to 4111 which had not so much as broken a spring.

What befell the permanent way Inspector I have no idea – leaving fishplates out was not something likely to be viewed lightly – but a few weeks later Joe received a letter of thanks and an award of £2.

"The General Manager," Joe said expansively, waving the page under my nose, "wishes to thank me for being alert whilst in charge of a locomotive....."

"If I'd have been driving we'd have stopped before we got to the crossover."

"Cheeky bugger!"

He laughed and passed over a pound note. Good old Joe.

Times however were changing and we were being dragged, unwillingly, into a hostile world with the LM take-over of the Birmingham district being followed by an increase in main line diesel engines.

For a time it was believed that the tin boxes were going to be the answer to every one of the railway's problems and there were times when they could make an impressive showing.

The arrival of diesels coincided with a block oil train which ran from Southampton, Fawley, to Bromford Bridge via Basingstoke, Didcot, Bordesley and the LM Camp Hill line. It consisted of fifty four-wheeled tank wagons containing something like 400,000 gallons of fuel and was worked by a pair of Southern Region 65xx Type 3 diesels.

The publicity department made a great deal of the service and naturally we hoped that Tyseley men would have a share in the new world glory. In this respect we were disappointed since Didcot men were given the job through to Bromford in both directions.

On the day of the inaugural trip I was paired with Jim Eames – later to become Lord Mayor of Birmingham – and we were sitting spare in the mess room when the shift foreman called us into his office. I hoped he was going to give us an interesting job.

"The district controller is none too confident about this Fawley – Bromford," he told us, "and wants a stand-by engine at Warwick in case the diesels fall to pieces on Hatton bank."

He gave us 4-6-0 5927 'Guild Hall' and instructed us to run light, tender-first, to Warwick and stand by for any eventuality.

We ran the twenty-odd miles to our destination, with me willing the diesels to pack up just as they came into sight: we should be both hero's and preservers of the reputation of steam engines.

At the booked time the down road signals cleared and the signalman indicated that the Fawley was approaching. I kept my fingers crossed and prayed for the worst. A Helicopter suddenly appeared overhead to film the passage of the train and Jim and I thought how splendid it would be if we had to go to the rescue.

The growl of the two Cromptons came into earshot and with a blast on the horn they opened up as they swept their fifty wagons through the station and up towards Hatton. As the leading engine went by, the cab full of bodies, I banged my right fist into the palm of my left hand and received for my pains a few derogatory handsignals from the occupants who evidently did not understand the Great Western indication that we were there to assist if required.

The tanks clattered by at full speed and eventually there was only the smell of petrol as a reminder that the train has passed. The signals went to danger, cleared again and we set off light, unwanted, back to Tyseley. We had seen the new world and I wasn't too sure that I liked it.

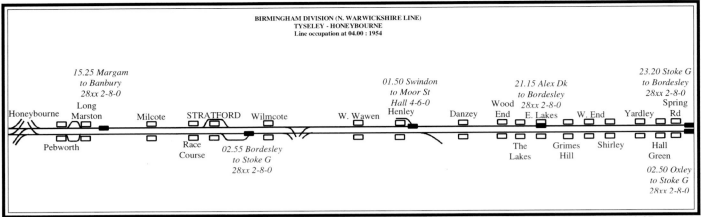

BIRMINGHAM DIVISION (N. WARWICKSHIRE LINE)
TYSELEY - HONEYBOURNE
Line occupation at 04.00 : 1954

Since the North Warwickshire main line never received the attention given to the Wolverhampton – Paddington route, a page devoted to it makes as good a conclusion as any to a book on the West Midlands' lines.

The North Warwicks was a railwayman's line. It was characterised by very steep gradients, a heavy service of passenger and goods trains and a near-dearth of running loops. Once a westbound goods train got onto the line at Tyseley, it was a matter of going hammer and

The busiest part of the line was the four mile section between Stratford and Bearley West Junction, where the Leamington and Banbury trains branched off and which also provided an alternative route to Birmingham. On a normal weekday the volume of traffic amounted to seventy-two passenger trains and fifty-five goods workings, giving a movement every eleven minutes of the day on average.

One of the reasons why the line rarely attracted much attention was because very few

Central to Snow Hill and the 12.27 return to Cheltenham.

The line diagrams give some indication of the traffic volume and mix of trains; the 10.30 chart showing the deluge of trains that ran in the wake of the down Cornishman, seen leaving Stratford. A Moor Street local follows the express whilst two goods trains run the gauntlet of the 10.20 passenger from Birmingham. The first of these is the 09.25 Bordesley – Swindon

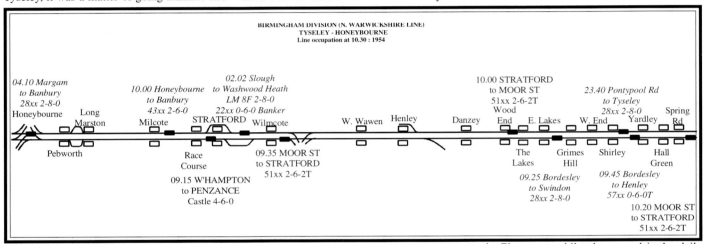

BIRMINGHAM DIVISION (N. WARWICKSHIRE LINE)
TYSELEY - HONEYBOURNE
Line occupation at 10.30 : 1954

tongs all the way for fear of delaying anything that might have been following. Margins were very tight and delays tended to be investigated with embarrassing thoroughness.

Eastbound workings were equally difficult to work although one had the benefit of assistance from Stratford to either Wilmcote or Earlswood Lakes, depending on the weight of the train and what sort of shape the engine was in. (In the majority of cases, if a train had to be assisted as far as Earlswood, both engines would continue through to Birmingham, saving the Stratford 22xx 0-6-0 from having to return sixteen miles tender-first).

express services were seen, the exception being the daily Wolverhampton – Penzance 'Cornishman' which was also one of the few workings to be diverted away from the Bearley – Tyseley section in favour of the Leamington branch and Hatton West Curve. The remainder of the passenger service was made up of locals from Stratford to Birmingham and Leamington, the latter in the hands of GW Railcars, and occasional semi-fast trains to Worcester and Evesham. One particular novelty was an express railcar working which operated the 09.56 Gloucester

via Gloucester whilst the second is the daily pick-up which shunts for the 10.20 in the yard at Shirley and then follows it to Earlswood and Henley. In the up direction an overnight mineral from South Wales is given a run ahead of the 10.00 Stratford – Moor Street whilst an LMS visitor is banked out of Stratford, the Stanier 8F having taken the train over at Honeybourne after exchanging loads at with the 06.17 Washwood Heath – Didcot. The working was one of the few co-operative arrangements between the LM and WR, introduced to save a change of engines and crews at Bordesley.

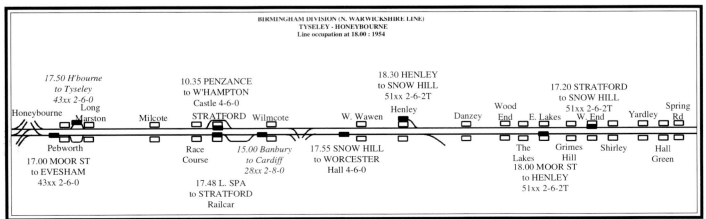

BIRMINGHAM DIVISION (N. WARWICKSHIRE LINE)
TYSELEY - HONEYBOURNE
Line occupation at 18.00 : 1954